The Eversley Edition

THE
LIFE OF RICHARD COBDEN

MACMILLAN AND CO., Limited
LONDON · BOMBAY · CALCUTTA
MELBOURNE

THE MACMILLAN COMPANY
NEW YORK · BOSTON · CHICAGO
ATLANTA · SAN FRANCISCO

THE MACMILLAN CO. OF CANADA, Ltd
TORONTO

THE LIFE
OF
RICHARD COBDEN

BY

JOHN MORLEY

IN TWO VOLUMES

VOL. I

MACMILLAN AND CO., LIMITED
ST. MARTIN'S STREET, LONDON
1908

First published in The Eversley Series, 1908

TO

THE RIGHT HONOURABLE

JOHN BRIGHT

THIS MEMOIR

OF HIS CLOSE COMRADE

IN THE

CAUSE OF WISE JUST AND SEDATE GOVERNMENT

IS INSCRIBED

WITH THE WRITER'S SINCERE RESPECT

PREFACE

Owing to various circumstances, with which I have no right to trouble the reader, the publication of these volumes has been delayed considerably beyond the date at which I hoped to bring them to an end. As things have turned out, the delay has done no harm. My memoir of Mr. Cobden appears at a moment when there is a certain disposition in men's minds to subject his work and his principles to a more hostile criticism than they have hitherto encountered. So far perhaps it is permitted to me to hope that the book will prove opportune. It is possible, however, that it may disappoint those who expect to find in it a completely furnished armoury for the champions of Free Trade. I did not conceive it to be my task to compile a polemical handbook for that controversy. For this the reader must always go to the parliamentary debates between 1840 and 1846, and to the manuals of Political Economy.

It will perhaps be thought that I should have done better to say nothing of Mr. Cobden's private affairs. In the ordinary case of a public man, reserve on these matters is possibly a good rule. In the present instance, so much publicity was given to Mr. Cobden's affairs—some of it of a very malicious kind—that it seemed best, not only to the writer, but to those whose feelings he was bound first and exclusively to consider, to let these take their place along with the other facts of his life.

The material for the biography has been supplied in great abundance by Mr. Cobden's many friends and correspondents. His family with generous confidence entrusted it to my uncontrolled discretion, and for any lack of skill or judgment that may appear in the way in which the materials have been handled, the responsibility is not theirs but mine. Much of the correspondence had been already sifted and arranged by Mr. Henry Richard, the respected Member for Merthyr, who handed over to me the result of his labour with a courtesy and good-will for which I am particularly indebted to him. Lord Cardwell was obliging enough to procure for me Mr. Cobden's letter to Sir Robert Peel (vol. i. ch. 17), and, along with Lord Hardinge, to give me permission to print Sir Robert Peel's reply. Mr. Bright, with an unwearied kindness for which I can never be too grateful, has allowed me to consult him constantly, and has abounded in helpful corrections and suggestions while the sheets were passing through the press. Nor can I forget to express the many obligations that I owe to my friend, Sir Louis Mallet. It was he who first induced me to undertake a piece of work which he had much at heart, and he has followed it with an attention, an interest, and a readiness in counsel and information, of which I cannot but fear that the final product gives a very inadequate idea.

J. M.

September 29th, 1881.

CONTENTS

CHAPTER I

Early Life

CHAPTER II

Commercial and Mental Progress

CHAPTER III

Travels in West and East

CHAPTER IV

The Two Pamphlets

CHAPTER V

Life in Manchester, 1837-9

CHAPTER VI

The Foundation of the League

CHAPTER VII

The Corn Laws

CHAPTER VIII

Cobden enters Parliament—First Session

CHAPTER IX

Cobden as an Agitator

CHAPTER X

The New Corn Law

CHAPTER XI

Sir Robert Peel's New Policy

CHAPTER XII

Renewed Activity of the League—Cobden and Sir Robert Peel—Rural Campaign

CHAPTER XIII

The Session of 1844—Factory Legislation—The Constituencies

CHAPTER XIV

Bastiat—New Tactics—Activity in Parliament—Maynooth Grant—Private Affairs

CHAPTER XV

The Autumn of 1845

CHAPTER XVI

Repeal of the Corn Laws and Fall of the Government

CHAPTER XVII

Correspondence with Sir Robert Peel—Cessation of the League

CHAPTER XVIII

Tour over Europe

CHAPTER XIX

Election for the West Riding—Purchase of Dunford—Correspondence

APPENDIX

CHAPTER I

EARLY LIFE

HEYSHOTT is a hamlet in a sequestered corner of West Sussex, not many miles from the Hampshire border. It is one of the crests that, like wooded islands, dot the great Valley of the Weald. Near at hand the red housetops of Midhurst sleep among the trees, while Chichester lies in the flats a dozen miles away, beyond the steep escarpments of the South Downs, that here are nearing their western edge. Heyshott has a high rolling upland of its own, part of the majestic wall that runs from Beachy Head almost to Portsmouth. As the traveller ascends the little neighbouring height of West Lavington, he discerns far off to the left, at the end of a dim line, the dark clump of sentinel trees at Chanctonbury, whence one may look forth over the glistening flood of the Channel, or hear the waters beat upon the shore. The country around Midhurst is sprinkled thinly with farms and modest homesteads. Patches of dark forest mingle with green spaces of common, with wide reaches of heath, with ponds flashing in the sunlight, and with the white or yellow clearing of the fallows. The swelling turf of the headland, looking northward across the Weald to the loved companion downs of

1804. Surrey, is broken by soft wooded hollows, where the shepherd finds a shelter from the noontide sun, or from the showers that are borne along in the driving flight of the south-west wind.

Here, in an old farm-house, known as Dunford, Richard Cobden was born on June 3, 1804. He was the fourth of a family of eleven children. His ancestors were yeomen of the soil, and it is said, with every appearance of truth, that the name can be traced in the annals of the district as far back as the fourteenth century. The antiquarians of the county have found out that one Adam de Coppdene was sent to Parliament by the borough of Chichester in 1314. There is talk of a manor of Cobden in the ninth of Edward IV. (1470). In 1562 there is a record of William Cobden devising lands on the downs in Westdean. Thomas Cobden of Midhurst was a contributor of twenty-five pounds to the fund raised for resisting the Spanish Armada. When hearth-money was levied in 1670, Richard Cobden, junior, is entered as paying for seven out of the seventy-six hearths of the district. In the Sussex election poll-book for 1734 a later Richard Cobden is put down as a voter for the parish of Midhurst, and four or five others are entered as freeholders in other parts of West Sussex. The best opinion seems to be that the settlement of the Cobdens at Midhurst took place sometime in the seventeenth century, and that they were lineal descendants of Sir Adam and Sir Ralph of former ages.

However all this may be, the five hundred years that intervened had nursed no great prosperity. Cobden's grandfather and namesake was a maltster and farmer, and filled for several years the principal office of bailiff for the borough of Midhurst. When he died in 1809, he left a very modest property

1809-13.

behind him. Dunford was sold, and William Cobden, the only son of Richard the elder, and the father of the Richard Cobden with whom we are concerned, removed to a small farm on the outskirts of Midhurst. He was a man of soft and affectionate disposition, but wholly without the energy of affairs. He was the gentlest and kindest of men. Honest and upright himself, he was incapable of doubting the honesty and uprightness of others. He was cheated without suspecting it, and he had not force of character enough to redeem a fortune which gradually slipped away from him. Poverty oozed in with gentle swiftness, and lay about him like a dull cloak for the rest of his life. His wife, the mother of Richard Cobden, had borne the gracious maiden-name of Millicent Amber. Unlike her kindly helpless husband, she was endowed with native sense, shrewdness, and force of mind, but the bravery of women in such cases can seldom avail against the shiftlessness of men. The economic currents of the time might seem to have been all in their favour. The war and the scarcity which filled all the rest of the country with distress, rained gold upon farmers and landlords. In the five years during which William Cobden was at Guillard's Oak (1809-13), the average price of wheat was just short of five pounds a quarter. In spite of tithes, of war-taxes, and of tremendous poor-rates, the landowners extracted royal rents, and the farmers drove a roaring trade. To what use William Cobden put these good times, we do not know. After the harvest of 1813, the prospect of peace came, and with it a collapse of the artificial inflation of the grain markets. Insolvency and distraint became familiar words in the farm-houses that a few months before had been revelling in plenty.

1814-19.
Æt. 10-15.

William Cobden was not the man to contrive an escape from financial disaster. In 1814 the farm was sold, and they moved from home to home until at length they made a settlement at Westmeon, near Alton in Hampshire. His neighbours were as unfortunate as himself, for Cobden was able to say in later years that when he returned to his native place, he found that many of those who were once his playfellows had sunk down to the rank of labourers, and some of them were even working on the roads.

It is one of the privileges of strength to add to its own the burdens of the weak, and helpful kinsfolk are constantly found for those whom character or outer circumstance has submerged. Relatives of his own, or his wife's, charged themselves with the maintenance of William Cobden's dozen children. Richard, less happy than the others, was taken away from a dame's school at Midhurst, and cheerful tending of the sheep on his father's farm, and was sent by his mother's brother-in-law, a merchant in London, to a school in Yorkshire. Here he remained for five years, a grim and desolate time, of which he could never afterwards endure to speak. This was twenty years before the vivid genius and racy style of Dickens had made the ferocious brutalities of Squeers and the horrors of Dotheboys Hall as universally familiar as the best-known scenes of Shakespeare. The unfortunate boy from his tenth to his fifteenth year was ill fed, ill taught, ill used; he never saw parent or friend; and once in each quarter he was allowed such singular relief to his feelings as finds official expression in the following letter (March 25, 1817):—

"HONOURED PARENTS,

"You cannot tell what rapture I feel at my once more having the pleasure of addressing my Parents, and though the distance is so great, yet I have an opportunity of conveying it to you free of expense. It is now turned three years since our separation took place, and I assure you I look back with more pleasure to that period than to any other part of my life which was spent to no effectual purpose, and I beg to return you my most sincere thanks as being the means of my gaining such a sense of learning as will enable me to gain a genteel livelihood whenever I am called into the world to do for myself."

It was not until 1819 that this cruel and disgusting mockery of an education came to an end. Cobden was received as a clerk in his uncle's warehouse in Old Change. It was some time before things here ran easily. Nothing is harder to manage, on either side, than the sense of an obligation conferred or received. Cobden's uncle and aunt expected servility in the place of gratitude, and in his own phrase, "inflicted rather than bestowed their bounties." They especially disapproved of his learning French lessons in the early hours of the morning in his bedroom, and his fondness for book-knowledge was thought of evil omen for his future as a man of business. The position became so unpleasant, that in 1822 Cobden accepted the offer of a situation in a house of business at Ghent. It promised considerable advantages, but his father would not give his approval, and Cobden after some demur fell in with his father's wish. He remained where he was, and did not quarrel with such opportunity as he had, simply because he had missed a better. It is one of the familiar puzzles of life, that those whose want of energy has sunk their lives in failure, are often so eager to check and disparage the energy of stronger natures than their own.

William Cobden's letters all breathe a soft domesticity which is more French than English, and the only real discomfort of his poverty to him seems to have been a weak regret that he could not have his family constantly around his hearth. Frederick, his eldest son, was in the United States for several years; his father was always gently importunate for his return. In 1824 he came home, having done nothing by his travels towards bettering fortunes that remained stubbornly unprosperous to the end of his life. Between Frederick Cobden and Richard there always existed the warmest friendship, and when the former found a situation in London, their intercourse was constant and intimate. There were three younger brothers, Charles, Miles, and Henry; and Richard Cobden was no sooner in receipt of a salary, than he at once took the place of a father to them, besides doing all that he could to brighten the shabby poverty of the home at Westmeon. Whenever he had a holiday, he spent it there; a hamper of such good cheer as his purse could afford was never missing at Christmas; and on the long Sundays in summer he knew no happier diversion than to walk out to meet his father at some roadside inn on the wide Surrey heaths, midway between Alton and the great city. His little parchment-bound diary of expenses at this time shows him to us as learning to dance and to box, playing cards with alternating loss and gain, going now and again to Vauxhall Gardens, visiting the theatre to see Charles Mathews, buying Brougham on Popular Education, Franklin's Essays, and *Childe Harold*. The sums are puny enough, but a gentle spirit seems still to breathe in the poor faded lines and quaint French in which he made his entries, as we read of the little gifts to his father and brothers, and how he is debtor by *charité*, 1s.—*donné un pauvre garçon*, 1d.—*un pauvre garçon*, 2d. By and by the sombre Shadow fell upon them all. In 1825 the good mother of the house helped to nurse a neighbour's sick child, in the midst of an epidemic of typhoid; she caught the fever, and died at the age of eight and forty. "Our sorrow would be torment," Frederick Cobden wrote to his father, "if we could not reflect on our conduct towards that dear soul, without calling to mind one instance in which we had wilfully given her pain." And with this gentle solace they seem to have had good right to soothe their affliction.

The same year which struck Cobden this distressing blow, brought him promotion in his business. The early differences between himself and his uncle had been smoothed away by his industry, cheerfulness, and skill, and he had won the approval and good-will of his employers. From the drudgery of the warehouse, he was now advanced to the glories of the road. We may smile at the keen elation with which he looked to this preferment from the position of clerk to that of traveller; but human dignities are only relative, and a rise in the hierarchy of trade is doubtless as good matter for exultation, as a rise in hierarchies more elaborately robed. Cobden's new position was peculiarly suited to the turn of his character. Collecting accounts and soliciting orders for muslins and calicoes gave room in their humble sphere for those high inborn qualities of energy, and sociability, which in later years produced the most active and the most persuasive of popular statesmen. But what made the life of a traveller so specially welcome to Cobden, was the gratification that it offered to the master-passion of his life, an insatiable desire to know the affairs of the world. Famous men, who became his friends in the years to come, agree in the admission that they have never known a man in whom this trait of a sound and rational desire to know and to learn was so strong and so inexhaustible. It was not the curiosity of the infantile dabbler in all subjects, random and superficial; and yet it was as far removed from the dry parade of the mere tabulist and statistician. It was not bookish, for Cobden always felt that much of what is best worth knowing is never written in books. Nor was it the curiosity of a speculative understanding; yet, as we shall see presently, there soon grew up in his mind a body of theoretic principles, and a philosophic conception of modern society, round which the knowledge so strenuously sought was habitually grouped, and by which the desire to learn was gradually directed and configured.

The information to be gathered in coaches and in the commercial rooms of provincial hotels was narrow enough in some senses, but it was varied, fresh, and in real matter. To a man of Cobden's active and independent intelligence this contact with such a diversity of interest and character was a congenial process of education. Harsh circumstance had left no other education open to him. There is something pathetic in an exclamation of one of his letters of this period, not merely because it concerns a man of Cobden's eminence and public service, but because it is the case of thousands of less conspicuous figures. In his first journey (August–October 1825) he was compelled to wait for half a day at Shrewsbury, for a coach to Manchester. He went to the abbey, and was greatly impressed by its venerable walls and painted glass. "Oh that I had money," he says to his brother, in plain uncultured speech, "to be deep skilled in the mysteries of mullions and architraves, in lieu of black and purple and pin grounds! How happy I should be." He felt as keenly as Byron himself how

1825.

ÆT. 21.

> The lore
> Of mighty minds doth hallow in the core
> Of human hearts the ruin of a wall,
> Where dwelt the wise and wondrous.

1826.

In his second journey he visited the birthplace of Robert Burns, and he wrote to his brother from Aberdeen (Feb. 5, 1826):—"It is a sort of gratification that I am sure you can imagine, but which I cannot describe, to feel conscious of treading upon the same spot of earth, of viewing the same surrounding objects, and of being sheltered by the same roof, as one who equally astonished and delighted the world." He describes himself as boiling over with enthusiasm upon approaching "Alloway's auld haunted kirk," the brig o' Doon, and the scene of Tam o' Shanter's headlong ride. With a pang of disillusion he found the church so small that Cuttie-Sark and her hellish legion can have had scanty space for their capering, while the distance to the middle of the old bridge, and the length of the furious immortal chase, can have been no more than one hundred yards. The party on this occasion were accompanied by a small manufacturer from Paisley, who cared little for the genius of the place, and found Cobden's spirit of hero-worship tiresome. "Our worthy Paisley friend remarked to us, as we leaned over the Bridge of Doon, and as its impetuous stream rushed beneath us, 'How shamefully,' said he, 'is the water-power of this country suffered to

1826. — ÆT. 22.

run to waste: here is the force of twenty horses running completely idle.' He did not relish groping among ruins and tombstones at midnight, and was particularly solicitous that we should leave matters of discussion until we reached Burns's birthplace, where he understood that they kept the best whisky in that vicinity." To Burns's birthplace at length they came, where at first their reception was not cordial. "But my worthy friend from Paisley had not forgotten the whisky; and so, tapping the chin of the old dame with his forefinger, he bade her bring a half-mutchkin of the best, 'to set the wheels going,' as he termed it, and, having poured out a glass for the hostess, which she swallowed, I was pleased to find that it did set the wheels of her tongue going. 'Ye would maybe like to gang and see the verra spot where poor Robbie was borned,' she said, and we instantly begged her to show it to us. She took us along a very short passage, and into a decent-looking kitchen with a good fire. There was a curtain hung from the ceiling to the floor, which appeared to cover one part of the wall. She drew aside the curtain, and it disclosed a bed in a recess of the wall, and a man who had been hidden in the clothes first put his head out and looked round in stupid amazement, and then rose up in the bed and exclaimed, 'What the deil hae ye got here, Lizzie?' 'Whisht, whisht, gudeman!' said the old dame, out of whose head the whisky had driven all thoughts of her husband, 'the gentlemen will be verra pleased to hear ye tell them a' about poor Robbie.' Our Paisley friend had again poured out a glass of whisky and presented it to our host, who drank it off, and, bringing his elbow round with a knowing flourish, he returned the glass upside down, to show he drank clean. 'I knew Robbie weel,' said he, wiping his mouth with his shirt-sleeve. 'I was the last man that drank wi' him afore he left this country for Dumfries. Oh, he was a bonnie bairn, but owre muckle gien to braw company.' 'And this is the spot, gentlemen,' said the impatient gudewife, catching the narrative from her husband, 'where Robbie was borned, and sic a night that was, as I have heard Nancy Miller, the coachman's mither, say; it blew, and rained, and thundered, just like as if heaven and earth were dinged thegither, and ae corner of the house was blawn away afore the morning, and so they removed the mither and the bairn into the next room the day after.' Now I believe if these two bodies were put upon their oath to all they told us, that they would not be guilty of falsehood or perjury, for I am quite sure they are both persuaded that their tale is true, and from no other cause than that they have told it so often. And yet I would venture to bet all I possess, and what is more, *all I owe*, that they never saw Burns in all their lives."[1]

The genial eye for character and the good-humoured tolerance of foibles, which so singularly distinguished Cobden in the days when he came to act with men for public objects, are conspicuous in these early letters. His hospitable observation, even in this rudimentary stage, seemed to embrace all smaller matters as well as great. Though he was little more than one and twenty, he had already a sense for those great facts of society which are so much more important than landscape and the picturesque, whether in books or travels, yet for which the eye and thought of adolescence are usually trained to be so dull. On his first journey in Ireland (September 1825), he notices how

[1] *To F. Cobden*, Feb. 5, 1826.

1825.
—
ÆT. 21.

immediately after the traveller leaves Dublin "you are reminded by the miserable tenements in the road-side that you are in the land of poverty, ignorance, and misrule. Although my route afforded a favourable specimen of the Irish peasantry, it was a sight truly heartrending. There appears to be no middle class in Ireland: there are the rich, and those who are objects of wretchedness and almost starvation. We passed through some collections of huts called towns, where I observed the pig taking his food in the same room with the family, and where I am told he is always allowed to sleep. Shoes and stockings are luxuries that neither men nor women often aspire to. Their cabins are made of mud or sometimes stone. I observed many without any glass, and they rarely contain more than one room, which answers the purpose of sitting-room and sleeping-room for themselves and their pig."

Even in Dublin itself he saw what made an impression upon him, which ten years later he tried to convey to the readers of his first pamphlet. "The river Liffey intersects the city, and ships of 200 tons may anchor nearly in the heart of Dublin; but it is here the stranger is alone disappointed; the small number of shipping betrays their limited commerce. It is melancholy to see their spacious streets (into some of which the whole tide of Cheapside might with ease move to and fro), with scarcely a vehicle through their whole extent. Whilst there is so little circulation in the heart, can it be wondered at that the extremities are poor and destitute?"[1]

If one side of Cobden's active and flexible mind was interested by these miserable scenes, another side, as we have said, was touched by the strange whimsicalities of man. In February 1826, he crossed

[1] *To F. Cobden*, Sept. 20, 1825.

from Donaghadee, on the north-east coast of Ireland, to Portpatrick.

"Our captain was named Paschal—he was a short figure, but made the most of a little matter by strutting as upright as a dart, and throwing back his head, and putting forward his little chest in an attitude of defiance. It appeared to be the ambition of our little commander to make matters on board his little dirty steam-boat wear the same air of magnitude as on board a seventy-four. I afterwards learned he had once been captain on board of a king's ship. His orders were all given through a ponderous trumpet, although his three men could not be more than ten yards distant from him. Still he bore the air of a gentleman, and was accustomed to have the fullest deference paid him by his three seamen. On approaching near the Harbour of Portpatrick, our captain put his huge trumpet down the hole that led below, and roared out, at the risk of stunning us all, 'Steward-boy, bring up a gun cartridge, and have a care you don't take a candle into the *Magazine*!' The order was obeyed, the powder was carried up, and after a huge deal of preparation and bustling to and fro on the deck, the trumpet was again poked down to a level with our ears, and the steward was again summoned to bring up a match. Soon after which we heard the report of something upon deck like the sound of a duck-gun. After that, the order was given, 'All hands to the larboard—clear the gangway and lower the larboard steps,' or in other words, 'Help the passengers to step on to the pier.'"[1]

In the same letter he congratulates himself on having been fortunate enough, when he strolled into the Court of Session, to see Jeffrey, Cockburn, and

[1] *To F. Cobden.*

1826. — ÆT. 22.

Sir Walter Scott. One cannot pass the mention of the last and greatest of the three—the bravest, soundest-hearted, and most lovable of men,—without noting that this day, when Cobden saw him, was only removed by three weeks from "that awful seventeenth of January," when Scott received the staggering blow of desperate and irretrievable ruin. It was only ten days before that he had gone to the Court for the first time, "and like the man with the large nose, thought that everybody was thinking of him and his mishaps."

This, in fact, was the hour of one of the most widely disastrous of those financial crashes which sweep over the country from time to time like great periodic storms. The ruin of 1825 and 1826 was never forgotten by those who had intelligence enough to be alive to what was going on before their eyes. The whirlwind that shook the fabric of Scott's prosperity to the ground, involved Cobden's humbler fortunes in a less imposing catastrophe. His employers failed (February 1826), as did so many thousands of others, and he was obliged to spend some time in unwelcome holiday at Westmeon.

Affairs were as straitened under his father's roof as they had always been. The sun was not likely to be shining in that little particular spot, if the general sky were dull. The perturbations of the great ocean were felt even in that small circle, and while retail customers at their modest shop were reluctant to buy or unable to pay, the wholesale provider in London was forced to narrow his credit and call in his debts. The family stood closely to one another in the midst of a swarm of shabby embarrassments, and their neighbours looked on in friendly sympathy, impotent to help. Strangely enough, as some may think, they do not seem to have been very unhappy. They were all blessed by nature with a kind of blissful mercurial simplicity, that hindered their anxieties from eating into character. Their healthy buoyancy would not allow carking care to put the sun out in the heavens. When things were dreariest, Richard Cobden rowed himself across the Solent and back, and with one of his sisters enjoyed cheery days in the Isle of Wight, and among his kinsfolk at Chichester and elsewhere. Perhaps it was fortunate that his energetic spirit was free for the service of his family, at a moment when they seemed to be sinking below the surface. It was clear that means for the support of the household could only be found in some more considerable place than Westmeon. Presently it was resolved to migrate to Farnham, renowned for the excellence of its hop-gardens, for the stateliest of episcopal castles, and for its associations with two of the finest writers of English prose, William Cobbett who was the son of a Farnham cottager, and Jonathan Swift who had been Sir William Temple's secretary at Moor Park a mile or two away. Thinking less of any of these things, than of the hard eternal puzzle how to make sure of food and a roof-tree in the world, William Cobden migrated hither in the beginning of 1827. "The thought of leaving this dear village," one of his daughters had written (July 1826), "endeared to us by a thousand tender recollections, makes me completely miserable." This dejection was shared in a supreme degree by the head of the household. He found some consolation in the good-will that he left behind him; and his old neighbours, when they were busy with turnip-sowing, hay-making, and sheep-shearing, were wont to invite him, partly for help and work, and partly for kindly fellowship's sake, to pay them long visits, never failing to send a horse up the road to meet him for his convenience and the furtherance of his journey.

Richard Cobden, meanwhile, had found a situation in London, in the warehouse of Partridge and Price. Mr. Partridge had for seven years been one of Cobden's employers in the house which had failed, and he now resumed business with a new partner. He had learned, in his own words, Cobden's capacity of rendering himself pre-eminently useful, and he re-engaged him after a certain effort to drive a hard bargain as to salary. In September 1826, Cobden again set out on the road with his samples of muslin and calico prints. He continued steadily at work for two years, travelling on an average, while on his circuit, at what was then thought, when the Manchester and Liverpool railway was only in course of construction, the brisk rate of forty miles a day.

1828. Two years afterwards, in 1828, Cobden took an important step. He and two friends who were in the same trade determined to begin business on their own account. The scheme of the three friends was to go to Manchester, and there to make an arrangement with some large firm of calico-printers for selling goods on commission. More than half of the little capital was borrowed. When the scheme first occurred to Cobden, he is said to have gone to Mr. Lewis of the well-known firm in Regent Street, to have laid the plan before him, and asked for a loan. The borrower's sanguine eloquence, advising a project that in itself was not irrational, proved successful, and Mr. Lewis's advance was supplemented by a further sum from a private friend.

Cobden wrote many years afterwards: "I began business in partnership with two other young men, and we only mustered a thousand pounds amongst

1828.

Æt. 24.

us, and more than half of it was borrowed. We all got on the "Peveril of the Peak" coach, and went from London to Manchester in the, at that day [September 1828], marvellously short space of twenty hours. We were literally so ignorant of Manchester houses that we called for a directory at the hotel, and turned to the list of calico-printers, theirs being the business with which we were acquainted, and they being the people from whom we felt confident we could obtain credit. And why? Because we knew we should be able to satisfy them that we had advantages from our large connexions, our knowledge of the best branch of the business in London, and our superior taste in design, which would ensure success. We introduced ourselves to Fort Brothers and Co., a rich house, and we told our tale, honestly concealing nothing. In less than two years from 1830 we owed them forty thousand pounds for goods which they had sent to us in Watling Street, upon no other security than our characters and knowledge of our business. I frequently talked with them in later times upon the great confidence they showed in men who avowed that they were not possessed of £200 each. Their answer was that they would always prefer to trust young men with connexions and with a knowledge of their trade, if they knew them to possess character and ability, to those who started with capital without these advantages, and that they had acted on this principle successfully in all parts of the world."[1]

This is from a letter written to express Cobden's firm belief in the general circumstance, "that it is the character, experience, and connexions of the man wanting credit, his knowledge of his business, and opportunities of making it available in the

[1] *Letter to Mr. W. S. Lindsay,* March 24, 1856.

1828. — ÆT. 24.

struggle of life, that weigh with the shrewd capitalist far more than the actual command of a few thousands more or less of money in hand." We may find reason to think that Cobden's temperament perhaps inclined him to push this excellent truth somewhat too far. Meanwhile, the sun of kindly hope shone. The situation is familiar to all who have had their own way to make from obscurity to success, whether waiting for good fortune in Temple chambers, or a publisher's anteroom, or the commercial parlour of some provincial Crown or Unicorn. "During the time we have been here," Cobden wrote from Manchester, while affairs were still unsettled, "we have been in a state of suspense, and you would be amused to see us but for one day. Oh, such a change of moods! This moment we are all jocularity and laughter, and the next we are mute as fishes and grave as owls. To do ourselves justice, I must say that our croakings do not generally last more than five minutes."

Intense anxiety for the success of the undertaking was brightened by modest hopes of profits, of which a share of one-third should amount to eight hundred pounds a year. And in Cobden's case these hopes received a suffusion of generous colour from the prospect which they opened to his affectionate solicitude for his family. "I knew your heart well enough," he wrote to his brother Frederick, "to feel that there is a large portion of it ever warmly devoted to my interests, and I should be doing injustice to mine if I did not tell you that I have not one ambitious view or hope from which you stand separated. I feel that Fortune, with her usual caprice, has in dealing with us turned her face to the least deserving, but we will correct her mistake for once, and I must insist that you from henceforth consider yourself as by right my associate in all her favours" (Sept. 21, 1828).

The important thing is that all this is no mere coinage of fair words, but the expression of a deep and genuine intention which was amply and most diligently fulfilled to the very last hour of Cobden's life.

CHAPTER II

COMMERCIAL AND MENTAL PROGRESS

1829.

ÆT. 25.

COBDEN had not been many months in his new partnership before his energetic mind teemed with fresh projects. The arrangement with the Forts had turned out excellently. The Lancashire printers, as we have seen, sent up their goods to the warehouse of Cobden and his two partners in Watling Street, in London. On the commission on the sale of these goods the little firm lived and throve from the spring of 1829 to 1831. In 1831 they determined to enlarge their borders, and to print their own goods. The conditions of the trade had just undergone a remarkable change. It had hitherto been burdened by a heavy duty, which ranged from as much as fifty or sixty, to even one hundred, per cent of the value of the goods. In addition to excess in amount, there was a vexatious eccentricity of incidence; for woollens and silks were exempt, while calicoes were loaded with a duty that, as has been said, sometimes actually made up one-half of the total cost of the cloth to the purchasers. As is invariably the case in fiscal history, excessive and ill-adjusted imposts led to systematic fraud. Amid these forces of disorder, it is no wonder that from 1825 to 1830 the trade was stationary. The Lancashire calico-printers kept up a steady agitation, and at one time it was proposed to raise four thousand pounds for the purchase of a seat in Parliament for a representative of their grievances. The agitation was successful. The duty was taken off in the spring of 1831, and between 1831 and 1841 the trade doubled itself.

This great change fully warranted the new enterprise of Cobden and his partners. They took over from the Forts an old calico-printing factory at Sabden,—a remote village on the banks of a tributary of the Calder, near the ruined gateways and chapel of the Cistercian abbey at Whalley in Lancashire, and a few miles from where are now the fine mills and flourishing streets of Blackburn. The higher part of the Sabden valley runs up into the famous haunted Forest of Pendle; and notwithstanding the tall chimneys that may be seen dimly in the distance of the plain, the visitor to this sequestered spot may well feel as if the old world of white monks and forest witches still lingered on the bleak hillsides. Cobden was all with the new world. His imagination had evidently been struck by the busy life of the county with which his name was destined to be so closely bound up. Manchester, he writes with enthusiasm, is the place for all men of bargain and business. His pen acquires a curiously exulting animation, as he describes the bustle of its streets, the quaintness of its dialect, the abundance of its capital, and the sturdy veterans with a hundred thousand pounds in each pocket, who might be seen in the evening smoking clay pipes and calling for brandy-and-water in the bar-parlours of homely taverns. He declared his conviction, from what he had seen, that if he were stripped naked and turned into Lancashire with only his experience for a capital, he would still make a large fortune. He would not give anybody sixpence to guarantee him wealth, if he only lived.[1] And so forth, in a vein of self-confidence which he himself well described as Napoleonic. "I am ever solicitous," he wrote to his brother (Jan. 30, 1832), "for your future prosperity, and I wish that I could convince you, as I feel convinced, that it all depends upon your bringing out with spirit the talents you possess. I wish that I could impart to you a little of that *Bonapartian* feeling with which I am imbued—a feeling that spurs me on with the conviction that all the obstacles to fortune with which I am impeded, will (nay, *shall*) yield if assailed with energy. All is lost to you, if you succumb to those desponding views which you mentioned when we last spoke. Dame Fortune, like other fair ones, loves a brisk and confident wooer. I want to see you able to pitch your voice in a higher key, especially when you are espousing your own interests, and above all, never to see you yield or become passive and indifferent when your cause is just, and only wants to be spiritedly supported to be sure of a triumph. But all this must proceed from within, and can be only the fruits of a larger growth of *spirit*, to the cultivation of which without further lecture I most earnestly commend you."

A more curious picture still is to be found in another letter, also to his brother, written a few months later (April 12, 1832). He describes his commercial plans as full of solidity, "sure for the present, and what is still better, opening a vista to my view of ambitious hopes and schemes almost boundless. Sometimes I confess I allow this sort of feeling to gain a painful and harassing ascendancy over me. It disquiets me in the night as well as day. It gnaws my very entrails (a positive truth), and yet if

[1] *Letters to Frederick Cobden*, Aug. 11, 1831, Jan. 6, 1832, etc.

I ask, What is all this yearning after? I can scarcely give myself a satisfying answer. Surely not for money; I feel a disregard for it, and even a slovenly inattention to its possession, that is quite dangerous. I have scarcely ever, as usual, a sovereign in my pocket, and have been twice to Whalley, to find myself without the means of paying my expenses. I do not think that the possession of millions would greatly alter my habits of expense."

1832. — ÆT. 28.

As we might have expected in so buoyant and overflowing a temperament, moments of reaction were not absent, though the shadow was probably as swiftly transient with him as with any man that ever lived. In one of the letters of this period he writes to his brother:—"I know I must rise rapidly if not too heavily weighted. Another doleful letter from poor M. [one of his sisters] came yesterday. Oh, this is the only portion of the trials of my life that I could not go through again—the ordeal would send me to Bedlam! Well, I drown the past in still hoping for the future, but God knows whether futurity will be as great a cheat as ever. I sometimes think it will. I tell you candidly, I am sometimes out of spirits, and have need of *co-operation*, or Heaven knows yet what will become of my fine castles in the air. So you must bring *spirits—spirits—spirits*."

Few men indeed have been more heavily weighted at the start than Cobden was. His family were still dogged and tracked from place to place by the evil genius of slipshod fortune. In 1829 Frederick Cobden began the business of a timber merchant at Barnet, but unhappily the undertaking was as little successful as other things to which he ever put his hand. The little business at Farnham had failed, and had been abandoned. William Cobden went to

1832. — ÆT. 28.

live with his son at Barnet, and amused a favourite passion by watching the hundred and twenty coaches which each day whirled up and down the great north road. Nothing prospered. Death carried off a son and a daughter in the same year (1830). Frederick lost health, and he lost his brother's money, and spirits followed. He and his father make a strong instance of the deep saying of Shakespeare's Enobarbus, how men's judgments are a parcel of their fortunes, and things outward draw the inward quality after them to suffer all alike. Stubborn and besetting failure generally warps good sense, and this is the hard warrant for the man of the world's anxiety to steer clear of unlucky people.

Richard Cobden, however, had energy enough and to spare for the rest of his family. He pressed his brother to join him at Manchester where he had bought a house in what was then the genteel private quarter of Mosley Street.[1] Gillett and Sheriff carried on the business at the London warehouse, and Mr. George Foster who had been manager under the Forts, was now in charge as a partner at the works at Sabden.

[1] To those who care for a measure of the immense growth in the great capital of the cotton trade, the following extract will have some interest :—

"I have given such a start to Mosley Street, that all the world will be at my heels soon. My next door neighbour, Brooks, of the firm of Cunliffe and Brooks, bankers, has sold his house to be converted into a warehouse. The owner of the house on the other side has given his tenant notice for the same purpose. The house immediately opposite to me has been announced for sale, and my architect is commissioned by George Hole, the calico-printer, to bid 6000 guineas for it; but they want 8000 for what they paid 4500 only five years ago. The architect assures me if I were to put up my house to-morrow, I might have 6000 guineas for it. So as I gave but 3000, and all the world is talking of the bargain here, and there being but one opinion or criterion of a man's ability—*the making of money*—I am already thought a clever fellow."—*Letter to Frederick Cobden*, Sept. 1832.

It is at Sabden that we first hear of Cobden's interest in the affairs of others than himself and his kinsfolk. There, in a little stone school-house, we see the earliest monument of his eager and beneficent public spirit, which was destined to shed such prosperity over his country, and to contribute so helpfully to the civilization of the globe. In no part of England have the last forty years wrought so astonishing a change as among the once lonely valleys and wild moors of east Lancashire. At Sabden, in 1832, though the print-works alone maintained some six hundred wage-receivers, there was no school, and there was no church. A diminutive Baptist chapel, irregularly served, was the only agency for bringing, so far as it did bring, the great religious tradition of the western world within reach of this isolated flock. The workers practised a singular independence towards their employers. They took it as matter of course that they were free, whenever it was their good pleasure, and without leave asked or given, to quit their work for a whole week at once, and to set out on a drinking expedition to some neighbouring town, whence they would have been ashamed to return until their pockets were drained to the last penny. Yet if there was little religion, there was great political spirit. There is a legend still surviving, how Mr. Foster, a Liberal of the finest and most enlightened type, with a clear head and a strong intelligence, and the good old-fashioned faith in freedom, justice, and progress, led the Sabden contingent of zealous voters to Clitheroe for the first election after the Reform Act, and how like a careful patriarch, he led them quickly back again after their civil duty was done; leaving the taverns of Clitheroe behind, and refreshing themselves at the springs on the hillside. The politics of

1832.

ÆT. 28.

Sabden were not always so judicious, for it appears that no baptismal name for the children born in the valley between 1830 and 1840 was so universally popular as that of Feargus O'Connor.

It was in this far-off corner of the world that Cobden began his career as an agitator, and for a cause in which all England has long since come round to his mind. His earliest speeches were made at Clitheroe on behalf of the education of the young, and one of his earliest letters on what may fairly be called a public question is a note making arrangements for the exhibition at Sabden of twenty children from an infant school at Manchester, by way of an example and incentive to more backward regions. It was characteristic of him, that he threw as much eager enthusiasm into the direction of this exhibition of school-children, as ever he did afterwards into great affairs of State. His partner was a worthy colleague.

"You have ground," Cobden wrote to him, "for very great and just self-gratulation in the movement which you announce to have begun in behalf of infant schools at Sabden. There is never the possibility of knowing the extent to which a philanthropic action may operate usefully—because the good works again multiply in like manner, and may continue thus to produce valuable fruits long after you cease to tend the growth of them. I have always been of opinion that good examples are more influential than bad ones, and I like to take this view of the case, because it strengthens my good hopes for general and permanent ameliorations. Look how perishable is the practice, and therefore how little is to be dreaded the eternity of evil; whilst goodness or virtue by the very force of example, and by its own indestructible nature, must go on increasing and multiplying for ever! I really think you may achieve the vast honour of making Sabden a light to lighten the surrounding country, and carrying civilization into towns that ought to have shed rays of knowledge upon your village; when you have furnished a volunteer corps of your infant troops to teach the tactics of the system to the people of Clitheroe, you should make an offer of a similar service gratis to the good people of Padiham. Let it be done in a formal and open manner to the leading people of the place and neighbourhood, who will thus be openly called upon to exert themselves, and be at the same time instructed how to go about the business. *There are many well-meaning people in the world who are not so useful as they might be, from not knowing how to go to work.*"[1]

His perception of the truth of the last sentence, coupled as it was with untiring energy in coping with it, and showing people how they could go to work best, was the secret of one of the most important sides of Cobden's public service. It was this which, along with his acute political intelligence, made him so singularly effective. "You tell me," he wrote on one occasion to his partner, "to take time and be comfortable, but I fear quiet will not be my lot this trip. I sometimes dream of quiet, but then I recollect Byron's line,—

> Quiet to quick bosoms is a hell,

and I am afraid he is nearly right in my case."[2] Yet this disquiet never in him degenerated into the sterile bustle which so many restless spirits have mistaken for practical energy. Behind all his san-

[1] *To Mr. George Foster*, April 14, 1836.
[2] *Ibid.* May 14, 1836.

guine enthusiasm as to public ends, lay the wisest patience as to means.

What surprises one in reading the letters which Cobden wrote between 1833 and 1836, is the quickness with which his character widened and ripened. We pass at a single step from the natural and wholesome egotism of the young man who has his bread to win, to the wide interests and generous public spirit of the good citizen. His first motion was towards his own intellectual improvement. Even at a moment when he might readily have been excused for thinking only of money and muslins, he felt and obeyed the necessity for knowledge: but of knowledge as an instrument, not as a luxury. When he was immersed in the first pressing anxieties of his new business at Manchester, he wrote to his brother in London (September 1832):—

"Might we not in the winter instruct ourselves a little in Mathematics? If you will call at Longmans and look over their catalogue, I daresay you might find some popular elementary publication that would assist us. I have a great disposition, too, to know a little Latin, and six months would suffice if I had a few books. Can you trust your perseverance to stick to them? I think I can. Let me hear from you. I wished Henry to take lessons in Spanish this winter; it is most useful as a commercial language; the two Americas will be our best and largest customers in spite of tariffs."

He had early in life felt the impulse of composition. His first writing was a play, entitled *The Phrenologist*, and Cobden offered it to the manager of Covent Garden Theatre. He rejected it — "luckily for me," Cobden added, "for if he had accepted it, I should probably have been a vagabond all the rest of my life." Another comedy still survives in manuscript; it is entirely without quality, and if the writer ever looked at it in riper years, he probably had no difficulty in understanding why the manager would have nothing to do with it. His earliest political work consisted of letters addressed anonymously to one of the Manchester newspapers (1835) on the subject of the incorporation of the borough. But it was the pamphlet of 1835, *England, Ireland, and America*, which first showed the writer's power. Of the political teaching of this performance we shall say something in another chapter. Here we mention it as illustrating the direction in which Cobden's thoughts were busy, and the kind of nourishment with which he was strengthening his understanding during the years previous to his final launch forth upon the sea of great affairs.

This pamphlet and that which followed it in the next year, show by their references and illustrations that the writer, after his settlement in Manchester in the autumn of 1832, had made himself acquainted with the greatness of Cervantes, the geniality of Le Sage, the sweetness of Spenser, the splendid majesty of Burke, no less than with the general course of European history in the past, and the wide forces that were then actually at work in the present. One who had intimate relations with Cobden in these earlier years of his career, described him to me as always writing and speaking "*to the top of his knowledge.*" The real meaning of this, I believe, was that Cobden had a peculiar gift for turning everything that he read to useful purpose in strengthening or adorning his arguments. He only read or listened where he expected to find help, and his quickness in assimilating was due to a combination of strong concentration of interest on his own subject, with keen dexterity in turning light upon it from other subjects. Or, in saying that Cobden always spoke and wrote to the top of his knowledge, our informant was perhaps expressing what any one may well feel in reading his pamphlets and speeches, namely, that he had a mind so intensely alive, so penetrative, so real, as to be able by means of moderate knowledge rapidly acquired, to get nearer to the root of the matter, than others who had laboured after a far more extensive preparation.

Very early in life Cobden perceived, and he never ceased to perceive, that for his purposes no preparation could be so effective as that of travel. He first went abroad in the summer of 1833 (July), when he visited Paris in search of designs for his business. He did not on this occasion stay long enough to derive any ideas about France that are worth recording now. He hardly got beyond the common English impression that the French are a nation of grown-up children, though he described the habit of Parisian life in a happy phrase, as "*pleasure without pomp.*" [1]

1834.

In the following year he again went to France, and continued his journey to Switzerland. The forests and mountains inspired him with the admiration and awe that no modern can avoid. Once in after years, a friend who was about to visit the United States, asked him whether it would be worth while to go far out of his way for the sake of seeing the Falls of Niagara. "Yes, most assuredly," was Cobden's reply. "Nature has the sublimity of rest, and the sublimity of motion. The sublimity of rest is in the great snow mountains; the sublimity of motion is in Niagara."

Although he had to its fullest extent this sentiment for the imposing glories of the inanimate

[1] *To F. Cobden*, July 27, 1833.

universe, yet it is characteristic of his right sense of the true measure of things, that after speaking of Swiss scenery, he marks to his brother, as "*better still*," that he has made acquaintance with people who could tell him about the life and institutions of the land. "The people of this country are I believe the best governed and therefore the most prosperous and happy in the world. It is the only Government which has not one *douanier* in its pay, and yet, thanks to free trade, there is scarcely any branch of manufacturing industry which does not in one part or other of the country find a healthy occupation. The farmers are substantial. Here is a far more elevated character of husbandry life than I expected to see. Enormous farm-houses and barns; plenty of out-houses of every kind; and the horses and cows are superior to those of the English farmers. The sheep and pigs are very, very bad. They have not adopted the Chinese breed of the latter, and the former they do not pay much attention to. I did not see a field of turnips in all the country. Cows are the staple of the farming trade."[1]

1834. — ÆT. 30.

It was to the United States, rather even than to Switzerland, that Cobden's social faith and enthusiasm turned; and after his pamphlet was published in the spring of 1835, he resolved to see with his own eyes the great land of uncounted promise. Business was prosperous, and though his partners thought in their hearts that he might do better by attending to affairs at home, they allowed some freedom to the enterprising genius of their ally, and made no objection to his absence.

1833.

Meanwhile his father had died (June 15, 1833). When Frederick Cobden had joined his brother in

[1] *To F. Cobden.* From Geneva, June 6, 1834.

1833. — ÆT. 29.

Manchester, the old man had gone to live with his daughters in London. But he could not bear the process of transplanting. He pined for his old life in the beloved country, and his health failed rapidly. They removed him shortly before he died to Droxford, but it was too late, and he did not long survive the change. The last few months of a life that would have been very dreary but for the undying glow of family affection, were gilded by the reflection of his son's prosperity.

It is the bitterest element in the vast irony of human life that the time-worn eyes to which a son's success would have brought the purest gladness, are so often closed for ever before success has come.

CHAPTER III

TRAVELS IN WEST AND EAST

1835.

ÆT. 31.

ON May 1, 1835, Cobden left Manchester, took his passage in the *Britannia*, and after a boisterous and tiresome voyage of more than five weeks in the face of strong west winds, arrived in the port of New York on June 7. His brother, Henry, who had gone to America some time previously, met him on the wharf. In his short diary of the tour, Cobden almost begins the record by exclaiming, "What beauty will this inner bay of New York present centuries hence, when wealth and commerce shall have done their utmost to embellish the scene!" And writing to his brother, he expresses his joy at finding himself in a country, "on the soil of which I fondly hope will be realized some of those dreams of human exaltation, if not of perfection, with which I love to console myself."[1]

It is not necessary to follow the itinerary of the thirty-seven days which Cobden now passed in the United States. He visited the chief cities of the Eastern shore, but found his way no farther west than Buffalo and Pittsburg. Cobden was all his life long remarkable for possessing the traveller's most priceless resource, patience and good-humour under discomfort. He was a match for the Americans

[1] *To F. C.*, June 7, 1835.

1835.
Æт. 31.

themselves, whose powers of endurance under the small tribulations of railways and hotels excite the envy of Europeans. "Poland [in Ohio]," Cobden notes in his journal, "where we changed coaches, is a pretty thriving little town, chiefly of wood, with two or three brick houses, quite in the English style. We proceeded to Young's Town, six miles, and there again changed coaches, but had to wait three hours of the night until the branch stage arrived, and I lost my temper for the first time in America, in consequence."

He remarked that politics were rarely discussed in public conveyances. "Here [in Ohio] I found, as in every other company, the slavery blot viewed as an indelible stain upon, and a curse to, the country. An intelligent old gentleman said he would prefer the debt of Great Britain to the coloured population of the United States. All agreed in the hopelessness of any remedy that had been proposed."

Cobden's curiosity and observation were as alert and as varied as usual, from wages, hours of labour, quality of land, down to swift trotters, and a fellow-traveller "who wore gold spectacles, talked of 'taste,' and questioned me about Bulwer, Lady Blessington, and the Duke of Devonshire, but chewed tobacco and spat incessantly, clearing the lady, out of the window." He felt the emotions of Moses on Pisgah, as he looked down from one of the northern spurs of the Alleghanies:—

"Passing over the last summit of the Alleghanies, called Laurel Hill, we looked down upon a plain country, the beginning of that vast extent of territory known as the Great Mississippi Valley, which extends almost without variation of surface to the base of the Rocky Mountains, and increases in fertility and beauty the further it extends westward. Here will one day be the head-quarters of agricultural and manufacturing industry; here will one day centre the civilization, the wealth, the power of the entire world. The country is well cleared, it has been occupied by Europeans only eighty years, and it is the best soil I have seen on this side of the Atlantic. Any number of able-bodied labourers may, the moment they tread the grass west of the Alleghanies, have employment at two shillings a day and be 'found.' We arrived at Brownsville at four o'clock, the only place I have yet seen that uses coals for fuel. We are now in the State of Pennsylvania. Thank God I am no longer in the country of slaves."[1]

On coaches and steamboats he was constantly struck, as all travellers in America have been, by the vehement and sometimes unreasonable national self-esteem of the people. At the theatre at Pittsburg he remarked the enthusiasm with which any republican sentiment was caught up, and he records the rapturous cheers that greeted the magniloquent speech of one of the characters,—"No crowned head in Christendom can boast that he ever commanded for one hour the services of this right arm." The Americans were at that time suffering one of their too common fits of smart and irritation under English criticism. They never saw an Englishman without breaking out against Mrs. Trollope, Captain Basil Hall, and, above all, Fanny Kemble. "Nothing but praise unqualified and unadulterated will satisfy people of such a disposition. We passed by the scene of Braddock's defeat by the French and Indians on Turtle Creek. Our American friends talked of New Orleans."[2] Their self-glorification sometimes roused Cobden to protest, though he thought he

[1] *To F. Cobden*, June 15, 1835.
[2] *Ibid.* June 16, 1835. See below, p. 38, *n.*

1835.
—
ÆT. 31.

saw signs that it was likely to diminish, as has indeed been the case:—

"It strikes me that the organ of self-esteem is destined to be the national feature in the craniums of this people. They are the most insatiable gourmands of flattery and praise that ever existed. I mean praise of their country, its institutions, great men, etcetera. I was, for instance, riding out with a Judge Boardman and a lady, when the Judge, speaking of Daniel Webster, said, quite coolly, and without a smile, for I looked for one very closely, thinking he joked, 'I do not know if the great Lord Chatham might not have been his equal, but certainly no British statesman has since his day deserved to be compared with him.' And the lady, in the same serious tone, asked me if I did not find the private carriages handsomer in New York than ours were in England! I have heard all sorts of absurdities spoken in reference to the glorious incidents of this nation's history, and very often have been astonished to find my attention called (with a view to solicit my concurrence with the enthusiastic praises of the speaker) to battles and other events which I had never heard of before, and which yet the Americans consider to be as familiarly known to all the world as to themselves. I consider this failing—perhaps, as a good phrenologist, I might almost term it a *disease*—to be an unfortunate peculiarity. There is no cure for it, however. On the contrary, it will go on increasing with the increase of the wealth, power, and population of the United States, so long as they are *United*, but no longer. I have generally made it a rule to parry the inquiries and comparisons which the Americans are so apt to thrust at an Englishman. On one or two occasions, when the party has been numerous and worth powder and shot, I have, however, on being hard pressed, and finding my British blood up, found the only mode of allaying their inordinate vanity to be by resorting to this mode of argument:—'I admit all that you or any other person can, could, may, or might advance in praise of the past career of the people of America. Nay, more, I will myself assert that no nation ever did, and in my opinion none ever will, achieve such a title to respect, wonder, and gratitude in so short a period; and further still, I venture to allege that the imagination of statesmen never dreamed of a country that should in half a century make such prodigious advances in civilization and real greatness as yours has done. And now I must add, and I am sure you, as intelligent, reasonable men, will go with me, that fifty years are too short a period in the existence of nations to entitle them to the palm of history. No, wait the ordeal of wars, distresses, and prosperity (the most dangerous of all), which centuries of duration are sure to bring to your country. These are the test, and if, many ages hence, your descendants shall be able only to say of their country as much as I am entitled to say of mine *now*, that for seven hundred years we have existed as a nation constantly advancing in liberty, wealth, and refinement; holding out the lights of philosophy and true religion to all the world; presenting mankind with the greatest of human institutions in the trial by jury; and that we are the only modern people that for so long a time withstood the attacks of enemies so heroically that a foreign foe never put foot in our capital except as a prisoner (*this last is a poser* [1]);—if many centuries hence your

[1] The reader will remember, as Cobden's listeners did, that Washington was occupied by British forces in 1814.

descendants will be entitled to say something equivalent to this, then, and not till then, will you be entitled to that crown of fame which the historian of centuries is entitled to award.' There is no way of conveying a rebuke so efficiently as upon the back of a compliment. So in like manner, if I have been bored about New Orleans, I have replied, 'I join in all that can be said in favour of General Jackson. As a commander he has probably achieved more than any other man by destroying two thousand of his enemies with only the loss of twenty men. But the merit rests solely with the General, for you, as intelligent men, will agree that there could be no honour reaped by troops who never were even *seen* by their enemies.'"[1]

Of the great glory of the American continent, Cobden thought as rapturously as any boaster in the land. We have previously quoted his expression about Niagara being the sublimity of motion, and here is the account of his first visit to the incomparable Falls. "From Chippewa village, the smoke (as it appears to be) rising from the cataract is visible. There was not such a volume of mist as I had expected, and the noise was not great. I reached the Pavilion Hotel near the falls at one o'clock. I immediately went to see this greatest of natural wonders alone. I jealously guarded my eyes from

[1] *To F. Cobden*, from Boston, July 5, 1835. Cobden's reference is to the engagement of the 8th of January 1815, when Andrew Jackson at New Orleans repulsed the British forces under Sir Edward Pakenham. The Americans mowed the enemy down from behind high works. The British loss was 700 killed, 1400 wounded, and 500 prisoners; Jackson's loss, eight killed, and thirteen wounded. As it happened, the two countries were no longer at war at the moment, for peace had been signed at Ghent a fortnight before (Dec. 24, 1814). General Pakenham, who was Wellington's brother-in-law, fell while bravely rallying his columns under a murderous fire.

wandering until I found myself on the Table Rock. Thank God that has bestowed on me health, time, and means for reaching this spot, and the spirit to kindle at the spectacle before me! The Horseshoe is the all-absorbing portion of the scene from this point; the feathery graceful effect of the water as it tumbles in broken and irregular channels over the edge of the rock has not been properly described. Nor has the effect of the rapids above the shoot, seen from this point, as they come surging, lashing, and hissing in apparent agony at the terrific destiny before them. This rapid above the falls might be called a rush of the waters preparatory to their taking their awful leap. The water is thrown over an irregular ledge, but in falling it completely hides the face of the perpendicular rock down which it falls. Instead of an even sheet of glassy water, it falls in light and graceful festoons of foaming, nay almost vapoury fluid, possessing just enough consistency to descend in various-sized and hardly distinguishable streams, whilst here and there one of these foaming volumes encounters a projecting rock in its descent, which forces it back in heavy spray into the still descending torrent above; thus giving indescribable beauty and variety to the scene. In the afternoon I crossed the river below the falls, and visited Goat's Island. At the foot of the staircase there is a view of the American fall at a point of rock near the bottom of the cascade, terrific beyond conception, and totally opposite to the effect of the Horseshoe Fall as seen from Table Rock. I ascended the stairs and passed over the bridge to Goat's Island. The view from the platform overhanging the Horseshoe Fall, when you look right down into the abyss, and are standing immediately over the descending water, is horrible. I do not think people would take

1835. — ÆT. 31.

any pleasure in being placed in this fearful position, unless others were looking on, or unless for the vain gratification of talking about it. In the evening I again looked at the Horseshoe Fall from Table Rock until dark—oh for an English twilight! The effect of this fall is improved by the water which flows over the ledge being of very different depths, from two to twenty feet, which of course causes the water to flow more or less in a mass, so that in one part it descends nearly half-way in a blue, unbroken sheet, whilst not far off it is scattered into the whitest foam almost as soon as it has passed the edge of the rock. The water for several hundred yards below the fall is as white as drift snow—not a mere white froth, but wherever it is disturbed it shows nothing but a white milk-like effect unlike any water I ever saw."[1]

. . . . . .

"In the morning I went in a coach with Messrs. Cunningham and Church, and Henry, to see the whirlpool three miles down the stream. I was disappointed; I don't know if it was that the all-absorbing influence of the falls prevented my taking any interest in other scenes. After dinner I descended to view the Horseshoe Fall from behind the curtain of water; the stunning noise and the heavy beating of the water render this a severe adventure, but there is no danger. The effect of the sound is that of the most terrific thunder. There is very little effect for the eye. We went to view the burning well, which would certainly light a town with gas. Putting a tub over the well produces a complete gasometer. A tree was thrown into the rapid, but the effect is not great; it dropped immediately it passed the ledge more perpendicularly than the cascade, and so dis-

[1] *To F. C.*, June 21, 1835.

appeared. In the balcony looking over the falls there was a stupid-looking man, telling a stupid story, about a stupid *lord*. It assured me that I was amongst my own countrymen again. The negro barber here is a runaway black from Virginia.

"From Table Rock we saw a rainbow which formed nearly a complete circle. We crossed again to the American side with Mr. Cunningham, and took a bath, for there is not one on the Canada side. The ferryman told us of a gentleman who swam over three times. I felt less disposed than ever to quit this spot, so full of ever-increasing attraction. Were I an American, I would here strive to build me a summer residence. In the evening there were drunken people about. I have seen more intoxicated persons at this first Canada town than in any place in the States. The view from Table Rock was rather obscured by the mist. At dinner a crowded table was wholly vacated in twenty minutes! Think of sixty persons at an English watering-place dining and leaving the table in twenty minutes! I took a last and reluctant leave of this greatest of all nature's works."[1]

Cobden summed up his impressions in a long letter to his brother at Manchester:—

"I am thus far on my way back again to New York, which city I expect to reach on the 8th inst., after completing a tour through Philadelphia, Baltimore, Washington, Pittsburg, Lake Erie to Buffalo, Niagara Falls, Albany (*viâ* Auburn, Utica, Schenectady) and the Connecticut valley to Boston, and Lowell, etc., to-morrow. On my return to New York, I purpose giving two days to the Hudson river, going up to Albany one day, and returning the next; after which I shall have two or three days for the purpose

[1] June 22, 1835.

1835. — ÆT. 31.

of taking leave of my good friends in New York, previously to going on board the *Britannia* on the 16th. My journey may be called a real *pleasure* trip, for without an exception or interruption of any kind, I have enjoyed every minute of the too, too short time allowed me for seeing this truly magnificent country. No one has yet done justice to the splendid scenery of America. Her lakes, rivers, forests, and above all her cataracts are peculiarly her own, and when I think of their superiority to all that we own in the Old World, and, still more, when I recollect that by a mysterious ordinance of their Creator, these were hid from 'learned ken' till modern times, I fall into the fanciful belief that the Western continent was brought forth at a second birth, and intended by nature as a more perfect specimen of her handiwork. But how in the name of breeding must we account for the degeneracy of the human form in this otherwise mammoth-producing soil? The men are but sorry descendants from the noble race that begot their ancestors; and as for the women! My eyes have not found one resting-place that deserves to be called a wholesome, blooming, pretty woman since I have been here. One-fourth part of the women look as if they had just recovered from a fit of the jaundice, another quarter would in England be termed in a state of decided consumption, and the remainder are fitly likened to our fashionable women when haggard and jaded with the dissipation of a London season. There, haven't I *out-trolloped* Mrs. Trollope, and overhauled even Basil Hall?

"But leaving the physique for the morale. My estimate of American character has improved, contrary to my expectations, by this visit. Great as was my previous esteem for the qualities of this people, I find myself in love with their intelligence, their sincerity, and the decorous self-respect that actuates all classes. The very genius of activity seems to have found its fit abode in the souls of this restless and energetic race. They have not, 'tis true, the force of Englishmen in personal weight or strength, but they have compensated for this deficiency by quickening the momentum of their enterprises. All is in favour of celerity of action and the saving of time. Speed, speed, speed, is the motto that is stamped in the form of their ships and steamboats, in the breed of their horses, and the light construction of their waggons and carts: and in the ten thousand contrivances that are met with here, whether for the abridging of the labour of months or minutes, whether a high-pressure engine or a patent boot-jack. All is done in pursuit of one common object, the economy of time. We like to speculate upon the future, and I have sometimes tried to conjecture what the industry and ingenuity and activity of that future people of New Holland, or of some other at present unknown continent, will amount to, which shall surpass and supersede the Yankees in the career of improvements, as effectually as these have done the natives of the Old World. They must be a race that will be able to dispense with food and sleep altogether, for the Americans have certainly discovered the minimum of time that is required for the services of their beds and boards. Their mechanical engines must work miracles 'till panting time toils after them in vain.' In fact I regard it as *almost* as improbable for another community to rival the population of these states in prosperity, as for an *individual* to surpass our indefatigable friend and self-sacrificed free-born slave, K——, in the race of hard-earned fortune. You know I predicted when leaving England for this

1835.

ÆT. 31.

continent, that I should not find it sufficiently to my taste to relish a sojourn here for life. My feelings in this respect are quite altered. I know of no reasonable ground for an aversion to this country, and none but unreasonable minds could fail to be as happy here as in England, provided friendly attachments did not draw them to the Old Country. My own predilection is rather in favour of Washington as a residence. Baltimore is also, I should imagine, a pleasant town. These two are now by means of the railroad almost identical. By the bye, when running through those towns on my way to the west, and in the design of extending my journey as far as Montreal, which I have since found to be impracticable, unfortunately I resisted all kind invitations to remain even for the purpose of being introduced to old Hickory, which would have delayed me only a day. I have since regretted this very much."[1]

Cobden arrived in England in the middle of August, after an uneventful voyage, in which he found no better way of amusing himself than by analyzing the character of his fellow-passengers, and reducing them to types. Early in life his eager curiosity had been attracted by the doctrines of phrenology, and however crude the pretensions of phrenology may now appear, it will always deserve a certain measure of historic respect as being the first attempt to popularize the study of character by system, and the arrangement of men's faculty and disposition in classes. To accept phrenology today would stamp a man as unscientific, but to accept it in 1835 was a good sign of mental activity. Cobden's portraits of his shipmates, if they are not so deep-reaching as La Bruyère, serve to illustrate his

[1] *To F. C.*, July 5, 1835, from Boston.

habit of watching the ways of men, of studying the differences among them, and of judging them with the kindly neutrality of the humorist or the naturalist. How useful this habit became to the leader of a political agitation, in which patient and versatile handling of different characters is so important a gift, we shall soon see.

After his return from America, Cobden remained at home for fifteen months, from the summer of 1835 to the autumn of 1836. He began by making up all arrears of business, and discussing new projects with his partners. But public affairs drew him with irresistible attraction. It was probably in this interval that he made his first public speech. The object of the meeting, which was small and unimportant, was to further the demand of a corporation for Manchester. Cobden was diffident, and unwilling to speak. He was at length induced to rise, but his speech is described as a signal failure. "He was nervous," says the chronicler, "confused, and in fact practically broke down, and the chairman had to apologize for him." The first occasion on which his name appears in the newspapers is the announcement that he was chosen to be on the committee of the newly established Athenæum at Manchester, and he modestly seconded a resolution at the meeting.[1] The important piece of work of this date was the pamphlet on *Russia*, which was published in the summer of 1836.[2] The earlier

[1] Oct. 1, 1835.

[2] The original advertisement is as follows:—"On Monday, July 25, will be published, price 8*d.*, *Russia*, by a Manchester Manufacturer, author of *England, Ireland, and America*. Contents —1. Russia, Turkey, and England. 2. Poland, Russia, and England. 3. The Balance of Power. 4. Protection of Commerce. . . . This is not a party pamphlet, nor will Russia be found, as the title might seem to imply, to be exclusively the subject of inquiry in the following pages."

1835. ÆT. 31.

pamphlet, *England*, *Ireland*, *and America*, had been published, as I have already mentioned, in the spring of 1835, and within twelve months had gone through three editions, at what we should now consider the high price of three shillings and sixpence; it had in April 1836 reached a fifth edition at sixpence. The newspapers had been liberal in its praise, and its author had been described in the sonorous style of the conventional leading article as a man of a liberal and comprehensive mind, an acute and original thinker, a clear and interesting writer, "and in the best because not an exclusive sense of the term—a true patriot."[1] Mr. Ridgway, the publisher, informed Cobden that nobody ought to print a pamphlet unless he had some other object in view, besides publication. "I have another object," Cobden adds, "in distant and dim perspective."[2] We may assume that, when he said this, he was thinking, with natural ambition, of the pedestal from which a place in Parliament enables a man to address his audience. These two pieces are important enough in Cobden's history to deserve a chapter of their own, but it will be convenient before dealing with them to complete the travels which followed the publication of the

1836.

second of them. Shortly afterwards the strain of so many interests affected Cobden's health. He had

[1] *Manchester Guardian*, May 23, 1835. The London *Times*, May 5, 1836, describes the pamphlet as having "some sound views of the true foreign policy of England, and some just and forcible reflections on the causes which keep us in the rear of improvement," etc.

The *Manchester Guardian*—we may notice as a point in that important matter, the history of the periodical press—was from Jan. 1, 1830, to Sept. 15, 1836, published once a week, and sold for sevenpence. After the duty on paper was reduced (Sept. 15, 1836), it was published twice a week, and its price brought down to fourpence.

[2] *To F. Cobden*, March 31, 1835.

suffered severely from an illness at the end of the previous year, and the doctors counselled a winter abroad. As the business was in good order, and the mainspring, to use Cobden's own figure in the matter, was not necessary until the following spring, he resolved to set forth eastward. On the 22nd of October he sailed from Plymouth. He arrived in Falmouth harbour, on his return, on the 21st of April 1837.

The ship touched at Lisbon and Cadiz, and Cobden wrote lively accounts to his friends at home of all that he saw. His description of Cadiz was stopped short by recollecting Byron's famous account, and the only subject on which he permitted himself to expatiate repeatedly and at length was the beauty of the ladies and their dress. "At Cadiz too," he writes to his partner at Sabden, "you may see the loveliest female costume in the world—the Spanish mantilla! All the head-dresses in Christendom must yield the palm to this. It is, as you may see in the little clay figures of Spanish ladies which are sold in England, a veil and mantle combined, which falls from a high comb at the back of the top of the head, down to the elbow in front, and just below the shoulders behind. A fan, which is universally carried, is twirled and brandished about, with an air quite murderous to the hearts of sensitive bachelors. Black silk is the national costume, and thus these sable beauties are always seen in the streets or at the promenade. Judge of the climate, judge of the streets, and of the atmosphere of their cities, where all the ladies appear in public in full dress! Sorry, however, am I to tell you that the demon innovation is making war upon the mantilla, in the shape of foreign fashions—French bonnets are beginning to usurp the throne of the black mantilla. Reformer as I am, I would fain be a conservative of that ancient and venerable institution, *the mantilla.* The French will have much to answer for, if they supersede with their frippery and finery this beautiful mode."[1]

Now, as in the busiest days of his life, Cobden was a voluminous and untiring letter-writer. In the hottest time of the agitation against the Corn Laws, he no sooner flung off his overcoat on reaching the inn after a long journey or a boisterous meeting, than he called for pen and ink, and sat down to write letters of argument, remonstrance, persuasion, direction. And when, as now, he was travelling for relaxation, the same impulse was irresistibly strong upon him, the same expansive desire to communicate to others his impressions, ideas, and experiences. "I am writing this," he says on one occasion, "whilst sailing down the Nile on my return to Alexandria, and it is penned upon no better desk than my knees, while sitting cross-legged upon my mattress, in the cabin of a boat not high enough in the roof to allow me even to stand."[2] No physical inconvenience and no need of repose ever dulled his willingness either to hear or to speak. The biographer's only embarrassment is difficulty of selection from superabundant material. Journals and letters alike show the same man, of quick observation, gay spirits, and a disposition that, on its serious side, was energetically reflective rather than contemplative. I wish that I could reproduce his journals, but they are too copious for the limits of my space; and the statements of commercial fact which they contain are no longer true, while the currents of trade which Cobden took such pains to trace out, have long since shifted their direction. He was an eager and incessant

[1] *To Mr. Foster,* from Alexandria, Nov. 28, 1836.
[2] *To Charles Cobden,* Jan. 8, 1837.

questioner, and yet his journals show a man who is acquiring knowledge, not with the elaborate conscientiousness of a set purpose, but with the ease of natural and spontaneous interest. There is no overdone earnestness; life is not crushed out of us by the sledge-hammer of the statistical bore; there is the charm of disengagement, and the faculty of disengagement is one of the secrets of the most effective kind of character. Elaborate inquiries as to imports and exports do not prevent him from being well pleased to go ashore at Tenos, "to amuse ourselves for a day with leaping, throwing, and jumping." As the serious interests of his journey—the commercial and political circumstances of Egypt, Greece, and Turkey—are no longer in the same case, it can hardly be worth while to transcribe his account of them.

The following extracts from his letters to his sisters will serve to show his route:—

Gibraltar, 11 *Nov.* 1836.—"Before us arose the towering and impregnable fortress; on every side land was distinctly visible; my first inquiry was, Where is the coast of Africa? It was a natural curiosity. A quarter of the globe where white men's feet have but partially trod, whose sandy plains and mountains are unknown, and where imagination may revel in unreal creations of the terrible, was for the first time presented to my view. Can you doubt that the thought which arose in my mind for a time absorbed all other reflections? Yet all I could see was the dark sable outline of the coast of Barbary, a congenial shroud for the gloomy scene of pagan woes and Christian crimes that have been enacted in the regions beyond!

"The two particulars," he continued, "which strike most strongly the eye of the visitor who has

1836. — ÆT. 32.

passed from Spain and Portugal to this place, are the bustling activity of Gibraltar, as contrasted with the deserted condition of Lisbon and Cadiz, and the variety of the costumes and characters which suddenly offer themselves to his notice. To see both to advantage, it is necessary to visit the open square opposite to the Exchange, where the auctions and other business draw a concourse of all the inhabitants and sojourners in this rocky Babel.

"Fortunately our hotel opens immediately upon this lively scene, and I have spent hours in surveying from above the variegated lines of the motley multitude below. By far the most dignified and interesting figure is the Moor, who, with his turban, rich yellow slippers, ample flowing robes, and bare legs, presents a picturesque figure which is admirably contrasted with that of a Catalonian, who—with a red cap, which depends from a black band that encircles his head, like a long bag down nearly to his waist, pantaloons which are braced up to his armpits, and short round jacket,—may be seen jostling with the idle smuggler, with his leather embroidered leggings, his breeches of velvet adorned with side rows of bright basket buttons, his sash, embroidered jacket, and grotesque conical hat; whose life is a romance and probably a tragedy, and every one of whose gestures is viewed with interest as the by-play of one who by turns acts the part of a contrabandista, a bandit, or an assassin. Next is the Jew, who is here beheld in the most abject guise of his despised class: a rude mantle of the coarsest blanketing covers his crouching figure, bent by the severe toil with which he here earns a miserable subsistence; he is waiting with a patient and leaning aspect the call of some purchaser. His bare legs and uncovered head and the ropes indicative of his laborious calling, which are probably fastened loosely about his waist, altogether give him the appearance of one who has been condemned to a life of penance for the expiation of some heinous crimes:—alas, he is only the personification of the fate of his tribe! But I could not find space to portray the minor features of the scene before me. Here are English, French, Spanish, Italian, Mahometans, Christians, and Jews, all bawling and jostling each other, some buying, others selling or bartering, whilst the fierce competition for profit is maintained by a mingled din of the Spanish, Arabic, Lingua Franca, and English tongues. This is a scene only to be viewed in Gibraltar, and it is worthy of the pains of a pilgrimage from afar to behold it."

Gibraltar, 11 *Nov.* 1836.—"A trip was made by a party of five of us on horseback to a convent fifteen miles off. The road lies through a cork wood, and it is a favourite excursion from the garrison. It was delightful, after seeing nothing but barren rocks, and being confined to the limits of this fortress—which is seven miles in circumference—to find ourselves galloping through woods where hundreds of pathways allowed one unlimited range, and where thousands of beautiful trees and plants peculiar to this part arrested our attention. The doctor[1] was in a botanical mood at once, and we all gathered about to learn from him the names and properties of such plants as were to us new acquaintances. After filling our pockets with seeds and specimens, we pursued our journey to the convent, which is a dilapidated building, in which we found only one solitary monk. A large courtyard, in which were two or three gaunt-looking dogs, who from their manners appeared unused to receive visitors; exten-

[1] Dr. Wilson, his travelling companion, whose acquaintance he had first made in his voyage home from the United States.

sive stables, in which we found only the foals of an ass, in place of a score of horses; a belfry without ropes; vast kitchens, but no fire; and spacious corridors, dormitories, and refectories, in which I could not discover a vestige of furniture, revealed a picture of desolation and loneliness. We walked into the gardens and found oranges ripening, and the fig tree, pomegranate, sago palm, olives, and grape-vines flourishing amidst weeds that were almost impervious to our feet. The country around was wild, and harmonized with the ruined and abandoned fortunes of the convent. After partaking of some brown bread, eggs, and chestnuts, from the hands of the monk, and after enlivening his solitary cloisters with the unwonted echoes of our merriment, in which we found our poor old host willing to indulge, we left him, and returned through the cork wood to our quarters here."

Alexandria, 30 *Nov.* 1836.—"In consequence of the arrival of the governor, we were greeted with much noise and rejoicing by the good folks of Malta. The town was illuminated, bands of singers paraded the streets, the opera was thrown open, and all was given up to fun and revelry. We saw all that we could of the proceedings, and heard during the night more than we could have wished, considering that we wanted a quiet sleep. However, it was necessary for us to be up betimes in the morning, to make some preparations for our journey in Egypt. The good doctor was in a great bustle, purchasing the biscuits, brandy, and other little commodities; it was necessary also that we should engage a trusty servant at Malta, to accompany us through the voyage. Our friends recommended a man named Rosario Villa, who had made the excursion up the Nile several times with English tourists—spoke Arabic, English, and Italian, and knew the whole of Egypt and Syria thoroughly. Rosario was introduced to us. Now, I ask you, does not the name at once tell you that he was a smart elegant young fellow, with a handsome face, good figure, and an insinuating address? Such is the idea which you will naturally have formed of a Maltese named Rosario Villa. Stop a moment till I have described him. He is a little elderly man with a body as dried and shrivelled as a reindeer's tongue, only not so fresh-coloured—for his face is of the hue of the inside of tanned shoe-leather, but wrinkled over like a New Zealand mummy; a low forehead, a mouth made of two narrow strips of skin drawn back nearly to the ear over white teeth, and with his hair cut close, but leaving a little fringe of stragglers round the front—such is the picture of Rosario! We had no time to be fastidious, and his character being unquestionable, we engaged him at once, and in two hours he had made all his worldly arrangements and was on the way at our side to the steamboat. Here he was met by his friends and acquaintances, who took leave of him with many embraces, and I could not doubt that the soul was good which drew the kisses at his parting to such a body!

1836.

Æt. 32.

"It was five o'clock in the evening and the sun was beginning to prepare to leave this latitude for your western lands, when we slipped out of the boat upon the quay of Alexandria. A scene followed which I must endeavour to describe. Our luggage and that of an Irish friend was brought from the boat and deposited on a kind of platform immediately in front of a shed, which is ennobled by the name of Custom-House. Upon a bench, a little raised, sat a fat little Turk with a broad square face, whose fat cheeks hung down in pendulous masses on each side of his mouth, after the fashion of the English mastiff dog shown as a specimen in the Zoological Gardens. Our servant Rosario has endeavoured to hire a camel to put our luggage upon, but there is none at hand. A crowd of Arab porters has gathered about, offering their services, and each is talking at the top of his voice; after due bargaining, or rather jostling, haggling, and gesticulating, the agreement is concluded, and a dozen of the shortest of the *hammals* or porters have proceeded to adjust their several portions of the luggage, when whack, crack, thwack, a terrible rout is here!

"The little fat Turk whom I verily believe to have been dreaming as he sat so tranquilly smoking his long pipe, whose glowing ashes had the moment before attracted my eye by its glare in the advancing twilight, has caused this panic. Throwing aside his chibouque, and grasping a short cane, without troubling himself to speak a word, he has rushed with the suddenness of inspiration into the midst of the screaming and litigious gang, and plying his baton right and left over the shoulders, head, and arms, dealing out an extra share of chastisement upon those who, from having been loaded with our chattels, could not so easily escape his fury, until he has cleared the ground of every turbaned rogue of them, and left us standing amidst our scattered and disordered trunks, bags, and portmanteaus, not knowing what was to follow. I am soon able, however, to guess what is at the bottom the meaning of this unexpected apparition of the little dignitary, and the sudden Hegira of our porters; for after calmly resuming his pipe, and giving it two or three inspirations to reanimate the decaying embers, he takes Rosario on one side and whispers a few words in his ear, the import of which you may suppose is that the luggage must all go to the custom-house, but to save us that trouble he will allow us in consideration of some backshish (or a present of money) to take them with us.

"This little difficulty being got over, our luggage and ourselves are under weigh through the dark streets of Alexandria, whose houses appear to have rudely turned their back premises to the front, for you can see nothing but blank walls without windows or doors. The English hotel lay at some distance, and we had occasion to pass through one of the gates of the town, where we were met by a guard, a fellow in a white turban, who laid violent hands upon the leader of our party, who happened to be the good doctor himself, and arrested our further progress under some pretence which I could not comprehend, but I distinctly again caught the sound of the word *backshish.* We hesitated whether we should give the rascal a shilling or a good beating; —the doctor had raised his heavy umbrella in favour of the latter alternative, when my vote, which you know is always in favour of peace, decided it in behalf of a fee, to the extent of five piastres, and with this subsidy to the Pacha's representative we departed amicably. On the way through the narrow streets of Alexandria we met many Turks, whose attendants bore small lamps of paper or gauze, with which they always politely showed us our road. I begin to think that these are well-bred barbarians, after all my abuse of them and their religion.

"Mrs. Hume's hotel is a large detached building situated a long distance from the Turkish quarter, and surrounded by date trees of luxuriant growth. I ran out and wandered here by moonlight the very night of my arrival. The scene was indeed delicious

1836. — ÆT. 32.

after a tedious and unpleasant voyage. I thought of you all, and only wished for one of you at least to share my exciting enjoyment. Well has it been said that '*happiness was born a twin*,' and you, my dear M., somehow or other seem naturally associated with me in my ideal pleasures. I fancied that you were with me, and that we were equally happy.

"When I arose in the morning, I found that it was the season for gathering the dates. The Arabs were swinging about in the branches of this elegant tree by means of ropes, and gathering in large baskets the ripe fruit, which hung in luxuriant bunches. I am an admirer of the useful, you know, but how much more do I love the combination of utility and elegance! On the date tree you find both in perfection. There is the handsomest tree in the world, bearing the sole fruit which afforded nourishment to the wandering children of the desert, and a charming fruit is the date. I have subscribed a trifle to the Turk who rents this plantation, for the privilege of walking through it whenever I please, and helping myself freely to its produce. There are very few curiosities to detain the traveller in Alexandria. Pompey's Pillar, and Cleopatra's Needle, and the catacombs, and a few other half-buried ruins are all that now remains to attest the ancient splendour of a city which once contained 4000 baths, and counted a population of 600,000 souls. These curious fragments of departed grandeur have been often described, and are so little *intrinsically* interesting, that I shall say nothing about them.

"The monuments called Cleopatra's Needles are enormous masses of granite. One only stands, the other was thrown down and half-buried in the sand in an attempt to remove it to England. Mark the folly and injustice of carrying these remains from the site where they were originally placed, and from amidst the associations which gave them all their interest, to London or Paris, where they become merely objects of vulgar wonderment, and besides are subjected to the destroying effects of our humid climate. It is to be hoped that good taste, or at least the feelings of economy which now pervade our rulers' minds, will prevent this vestige of the days of the Pharaohs from being removed.[1]

"I dined with Mr. Muir at twelve o'clock. His Greek servant, a man of remarkable elegance and gracefulness, quiet, grave, and full of dignity at every gesture. What a power such grace has over my mind!"[2]

Cairo, *Dec.* 20, 1836.—"I slept tolerably well after having been for the first time made acquainted with my old torment, the fleas. You will wonder when I tell you that use has since made me almost indifferent to such trifles. The Arab sailors who formed our crew were miserable wretches, half clothed in dirty rags, and two of them were suffering from ophthalmia. I had heard much of the character of the degraded population of Egypt, and was told by

[1] Théophile Gautier makes the Paris obelisk muse in Cobden's sense :—

Sur cette place je m'ennuie,
Obélisque dépareillé ;
Neige, givre, bruine, et pluie
Glacent mon flanc déjà rouillé ;

Et ma vieille aiguille, rougie
Aux fournaises d'un ciel de feu,
Prend des pâleurs de nostalgie
Dans cet air qui n'est jamais bleu.

La sentinelle granitique,
Gardienne des énormités,
Se dresse entre un faux temple antique
Et la chambre des députés.

And so forth.

[2] *Journal.*

1836. — ÆT. 32.

those who knew no better, that severity and harshness were the only methods of making them work. My idea is, you know, that rewards and not punishments are the most effectual means of stimulating men, and so it proved. The *backshish* kept the boat going, when stripes would have only made it stand. At Atfeh we paid the *reis* or captain his five dollars, and gave his men a few piastres, and I parted with my usual good opinion of human nature.

"Scarcely had we reached the shore, when we were followed by the *reis*, bringing three bad pieces of money which he accused the good doctor, the cashier, of having paid him. It was clearly an imposition, and Rosario told us we should encounter similar conduct at every stage. We changed the money, resolving to be on our guard in future. *My ideas of human nature were less exalted for a minute and a half than usual.*

"To proceed from Atfeh to Cairo, a distance of 150 miles by the Nile, it was necessary to embark on board a larger boat, but here we found that the ladies, who had just preceded us, had taken all the good boats. We learnt, however, that a new and commodious boat was lying at the town of Fooah on the opposite side of the river, rather higher up the stream, and we took a ferry, and carried our luggage over, accompanied by the Vice-Consul, a little Italian, who, politely as we thought, agreed to bargain for us. The boat with twelve men was hired for 500 piastres, or £5, and it was agreed that we should start as soon as our luggage was on board. In the meantime I went into a cotton-mill in the neighbourhood, which presented a miserable appearance. Upon leaving, I gave *backshish* to one of the managers, who followed me immediately with a bad piece of money, which he accused me of having paid him. I threatened to shoot him, or something equally improbable, and thus escaped this attempt. Our Vice-Consul now left us, and we proposed to start, but the owner of the boat very coolly ordered a cargo of wood to be laid alongside, which he was determined to take along with its owner to Cairo. As this would have left no room for Rosario or Hussein for sleeping, we resisted, and all began to grow out of humour. We threw the wood out of the boat, and drove the porters, who were attempting to load, ashore. A fresh difficulty now arose. The owner of the boat refused to let her start until the next day, and very soon all the crew, *reis* and all, disappeared. *My opinion of humanity sank several degrees.* It now grew towards evening. We were moored alongside of the town of Fooah, and just opposite to a khan or coffee-house, in the balcony of which sat the owner of the boat, smoking his long pipe and surrounded by a party of lazy rascals like himself, who were all singing and laughing, probably amused at our dilemma. Much as it is against my principles, I now resorted to brute force. I took the pistols out of the portmanteau where Fred had placed them loaded and primed, but not without secret resolves that I would not injure any one. The doctor also arrived, and we went ashore to find the governor of the town, intending to make a complaint. It was dark, and we had a difficulty in finding out that the principal officer of Fooah was from home, but on inquiry for his deputy, we were told that the owner of the boat against whom we complained, was the man himself! Thus the judge and criminal were one person, which was certainly against our cause. However, we proceeded straight to the khan, and by means of Rosario for an interpreter, we made the vice-governor understand that he was a rascal, and threatened to have him punished by our friend the Pacha. He protested that he only acted for the safety of ourselves; that the Vice-Consul had entrusted us to his charge as travellers of the first consideration; that the sky predicted a storm; and that he could not, out of regard for such valuable lives, suffer us to go out that night. So finding there was no help for our difficulties but in patience and submission, we went on board, laughed at ourselves, supped, and slept.

"In the morning (Sunday, December 4th) we started with a favourable wind up the Nile. On looking round, however, we found that we had only six sailors instead of twelve, and we now learnt that this was the reason why the boat could not venture out at night. We found also from our man Hussein, that the Vice-Consul had received a handsome backshish out of the £5 we were to pay for the boat. Altogether my opinion of the Egyptians received a smart shock—they were *for an hour or so* down at zero. The aspect of the scenery of the Nile at and above Fooah, though flat, was very interesting to us at first. The minarets in the distance, the palms on the banks, the brilliant foliage, all gave it a pleasant effect to a stranger to such scenes. The river, which is of a yellow-red complexion, is here of the width of the Thames at London.

"This day (December 16th) is an era in my travels. I went with Captain E. and Mr. Hill to see the Pyramids. They disappoint the visitor until he gets close to them. My first feelings, along with a due sense of astonishment, were those of vexation at the enormous sum of ingenious labour which here was wasted. Six millions of tons of stone, all shaped and fitted with skill, are here piled in a useless form. The third of this weight of material and less than a tenth part of the labour sufficed to construct the most useful public work in England—the Plymouth Breakwater."[1]

Cairo, December 20th, 1836.—"Last evening was the interesting time appointed for an interview with no less a personage than Mehemet Ali, the Pacha of Egypt. Our Consul, Colonel C.,[2] had the day before waited upon this celebrated person, to say that he wished to present some British travellers to his Highness, and he appointed the following evening at six o'clock, which is his usual hour of receiving visitors during the fast of Ramadan. At the appointed hour we assembled, to the number of six individuals, at the house of Colonel C., and from thence we immediately proceeded to the palace, which is in the citadel, and about half an hour's ride from the Consul's.

"Our way lay through the most crowded part of the town. It was quite dark, but being at the season of the Ramadan (the Mahommedan Lent), when Turks fast and abstain from business during the day, but feast and illuminate their bazaars and public buildings during the night, we found the streets lighted up, and all the population apparently just beginning the day's occupations. . . . Away we went through streets and bazaars, some of which were less than eight feet wide, and all of them being crowded with Turks, Arabs, camels, horses, and donkeys. All, however, made way at the approach of the janissary and the uplifted grate of fire, both of which are signs of the rank of the persons who followed. Besides, to do justice even to Turks, I must add that I never

[1] *Journal.*

[2] "A martinet taken from the regimental mess, to watch and regulate the commercial intercourse of a trading people with a merchant pacha."—*Journal.*

1836. ÆT. 32.

saw a people less disposed to quarrel with you about trifles than the population of Cairo. You may run over them, or pummel them with your feet, as you squeeze them almost to death against the wall, and they only seem astonished that you give yourself any concern afterwards, to know if they be still in the land of the living. As for the foot of an ass or dromedary, if it be placed gently on their toes, and only withdrawn in time for them to light their pipe or say their prayers, which are the only avocations they follow, why, they say nothing about such trifles.

"As we proceeded along the streets, or rather alleys, of this singular city, it was curious to observe the doings of the good Mussulmans, who had just an hour before been released from the observance of the severe ordinance of the prophet. Some were busy cooking their savoury stews over little charcoal fires; here you might see a party seated round a dish, into which every individual was actively thrusting his fist; and occasionally we passed a public fountain, around the doors and windows of which crowds of half-famished true believers were pressing, eager to quench their thirst, probably for the first time since sunrise. Some, who no doubt had already satisfied the more pressing calls of nature, were seated round a company of musicians, and listening with becoming gravity to strains of barbarous music, whilst in another place a crowd of turbans had gathered about a juggler, who was exercising the credulity of the faithful by his magical deceptions. By far the greater portion, however, of those we passed were sitting cross-legged, enjoying the everlasting pipe, and so intent were they upon the occupation that they scarcely deigned to cast a glance at us as we passed.

"As we approached nearer to the citadel, the

scene changed. We now met numbers of military of all ranks who were issuing from the head-quarters, some accoutred for the night-watch, others dressed in splendid suits and mounted upon spirited horses. I saw some officers in the Mameluke costume, which you may see pictured in old books of travel in this country. Contrasted with these was the dress of the private troops who led the way, and whose white cotton garments, close jacket, and musket with bayonet, gave them a half European aspect. Here too we found ourselves surrounded by numerous horsemen, who like ourselves were proceeding at this, his customary hour of levée, to pay their respects to the Pacha. At length we entered the gates of the citadel, and immediately the road assumed a steep winding character admirably adapted for the purposes of defence. On each side, as we advanced, we found ourselves enclosed by lofty walls, and, by the light of the burning grate of pine-wood which was raised aloft in our van, I could distinguish the embrasures and loop-holes for musketry. I shuddered as I thought of the massacre of the Mamelukes, which was perpetrated near this very spot, a deed unparalleled in the annals of the world for perfidious and cold-blooded atrocity.

"The circumstances of the massacre are briefly these. Mehemet Ali having by a series of daring attacks, and aided by much cunning artifice, deposed the Mameluke rulers who had governed Egypt for more than seven centuries, and placed himself upon the throne of the country, made a kind of capitulation with the fallen chiefs, by which he agreed to give them support and protection. In consequence they came to reside in great numbers in Cairo, where they conducted themselves peaceably. On the occasion of a fête in honour of his son, the Pacha invited the Mamelukes to attend and assist at the festivities.[1] They entered the palace of the citadel, to the number of 470, dressed in their gorgeous and picturesque costume, but without arms. Mehemet Ali received them with smiles, and it was remarked that he was more than usually courteous. They departed, their hearts lighted up with a glow by his affability, and proceeded in a gay procession down to the gate which we had just passed; it was closed; as the first victim reached the gate, a hundred discharges of musketry from the walls on each side opened upon them. They turned to retreat, but the gate behind was also closed, and they were fast in the toils of their betrayer and destroyer. Only one man is said to have escaped, who rode his horse up a steep bank, and forced him over the battlement and into a gulf seventy feet deep below. The horse was killed, but the rider escaped, and made his way to Europe. Such is the substance of a deed of blood which had no provocation, no State necessity, nor a semblance even of justice, to palliate its unmitigated character of treachery, and yet here am I—I recollected with emotions of shame—passing over the scene of such a bloody tragedy, to do obeisance to the principal actor!

"The citadel is in extent and appearance something like a considerable town. As we proceeded through the steep and winding avenue, we came upon a thoroughfare lighted up like a bazaar with shops or stalls on each side, before which the soldiers were loitering and buying fruit or other articles from the lazy dealers, who sat cross-legged upon their mats, enveloped in tobacco smoke. Having passed under another gateway, and along a winding arched passage of massive masonry, an abrupt turning or

[1] The massacre of the Mamelukes took place on March 1, 1811.

two brought us to a large open square, the opposite sides of which were lighted up. Here, as we approached the centre of power from whence all rank, wealth, and authority are derived in this region of despotism, the throng of military of all ranks became more dense, just as the rays of light or the circles of water are closest where the heat or motion which gives them existence has its origin. We dismounted at the principal entrance and found ourselves in a hall, which, with the stairs that we immediately ascended, was almost impassable for the crowds of military who lounged and loitered in no very orderly manner by the way. At the head of the stairs we entered a very large hall, which presented a curious spectacle. Along its whole length and breadth, with only just sufficient interval towards one of the sides to afford room for passing to a door at the farther extremity, were seen cross-legged upon the floor, on little mats, an immense number of Turkish and Arab soldiers, whose arms and slippers were lying beside them. We passed along the entire length of the large room, too quickly to allow of more than a moment's surprise at the scene before us, when entering another apartment we found ourselves in a great, lofty chamber, from the centre of which hung a chandelier holding probably twenty yellowish-white wax candles, and in the centre of the floor stood a row of four gigantic silver candlesticks like those used in Catholic chapels, and each holding a huge candle of four feet in length, and a proportionate diameter. By their united light we could very indistinctly see to the extremities of the room, from whose farthest corner one or two persons hastily retired as we entered, leaving us, as I thought, alone in this huge apartment.

"Colonel C., who preceded our party a few steps,

now bowed towards the farthest corner of the room —a movement which we all imitated as we followed. A dozen steps brought my feet close to the bowl of a long, superbly enriched pipe which rested in a little pan on the floor, the other extremity of which was held by a short and rather fat personage, who was seated alone just to the right of the corner of the room upon a broad and soft divan, which ran round the apartment like a continual sofa. He laid aside his pipe, uttered several times a sentence, which we guessed was an expression of welcome, from its being delivered in a good-natured and affable tone, and accompanied at each repetition by the motion of his hands, as he pointed with more of hurry than dignity to the divan on each side of him, as signs for us to be seated. The colonel took his place to the right, and the rest of the party sat down upon the divan in the order in which they were standing. It chanced that I was placed immediately to his left, and thus I found myself quite close, or at least as near as I desire ever to be, to Mehemet Ali! It happened that at the moment of our arrival the dragoman or interpreter was not in attendance, and therefore as soon as we were seated a slight embarrassment ensued. The Pacha did not appear in the least ruffled by the neglect of his officer; he looked towards the door, called for somebody, but not impatiently; then turned to the colonel, uttered a few words, but immediately laughed as if at the recollection of his not being understood. Again he turned his eye towards the door, called in a louder but still not angry tone for some person, but nobody appearing, he then turned to Colonel C. and to us, smiled, fidgeted on his seat, rubbed his knee, and twisted the fingers of a remarkably white and handsome little hand in the handle of his sword. All this was but the affair of a minute or two, when an attendant of apparent rank entered, and walked quickly up to the Pacha, who appeared to explain good-humouredly the nature of our predicament, and he instantly began the duty of interpreting. The Pacha commenced the conversation by offering us a welcome; upon this the colonel made an observation about the weather, which however excusable it might have been in a country where Englishmen have adopted it as the habit of introducing themselves, is little suited to this latitude, where uninterrupted sunshine prevails for seven years together. Let me leave the speakers to settle the preliminaries of their interview, whilst in the meantime I describe a little more minutely the principal character before me.

"Mehemet Ali is, I am told, about five feet six or seven inches high, but as he now sat beside me, sunk deeply in a soft divan, he did not appear even so tall; he was plainly dressed in a dark and simple suit, and wore the red fez or tarboosh cap, which is now generally substituted for the turban by men of rank. His features are regular and good, and his face might be called handsome, but being somewhat rounded by fatness, I shall use the term comely as more expressive of its character. His beard is quite white, but I have seen many amongst his subjects with richer-looking tufts upon their chins. I glanced at the form of his head, which is, as far as I could discern through its cover, confirmatory of the science of phrenology—its huge size according with the extraordinary force of character displayed by this successful soldier, whilst a broad and massive forehead harmonizes with the powerful intellect he has displayed in his schemes of personal aggrandizement. Yet upon the whole there is nothing extraordinary or striking in the countenance of Mehemet Ali. He

1836.

Æt. 32.

appeared to me like a good-humoured man, and had I been called upon at a cursory glance to give an opinion upon such a person in a private station, I might have pronounced him an amiable and jocular fellow! However, as I was seated beside an extraordinary person, it was natural that I should scrutinize the expression of his features with the hope, nay the determination, of finding something more than common in his physiognomy. In doing so I encountered his dark eye several times, and thought it did not improve upon closer acquaintance. His mouth, too, which is almost concealed beneath his white moustachio, seemed only to pretend to smile; and once or twice I observed that whilst the lips were putting on the semblance of laughter, his eye was busily glancing round from under its heavy brows, with anything but an expression of unguarded mirth. If the eye do not reveal the human character, it will be vain to look for it in the more ignoble features of the countenance, and the constant workings of this 'mirror of the soul' alone revealed the restless spirit of Mehemet Ali. I never beheld a more unquiet eye than his, as it glided from one to another of the persons around him; it was incessantly in motion. Its glance, however, had none of that overpowering character which beams only from the soul of real genius;—there was neither moral nor intellectual grandeur in the look of the person before me, and I could not help thinking, as he stole furtive glances first at us and next at the door, that that eye might have been employed in watching the store of his *quondam* tobacco shop from the pilfering hands of his Albanian countrymen, with greater appropriateness than in now looking down upon us from the divan of a pacha.[1]

[1] Mehemet Ali, the founder of the present system of govern-

"Altogether there was as little dignity as possibly can be conceived in the personal appearance of Mehemet. Were I to confess what were the feelings which predominated in my mind as I regarded him whilst he sat, or rather perched, upright on the middle of the divan, without resting or reclining upon its pillows, and with his legs tucked beneath him, so as to leave only his slippers peeping out from each side of his copious nether garments, they certainly partook largely of the ridiculous.

"Coffee was brought to us in little cups enclosed in covers of filagree-work made of silver, and which I was afterwards told by one of the party (I did not myself notice them) was richly set with diamonds.

"When the first civilities had passed, the Pacha, as if impatient of unmeaning puerilities, took up the conversation with an harangue of considerable length, which he delivered with great animation. I felt curious to know what was the subject which seemed to possess so much interest with the practical mind of the Pacha. Judge then of my astonishment when I found that the burden of his discourse was *cotton*! The speaker was boasting of the richness and fertility of his territory, and to illustrate the productiveness of Egypt, he gave us an account of the harvest of a particular village in his favourite article of cotton: he entered into a minute calculation of the population, number of acres, the weight of the produce, the cost of raising, and the value in the market, and then gave a glowing picture of the wealth and prosperity of this village, which bore no resemblance to any place ever seen by myself

ment in Egypt, was born in 1768 at a small town on the Albanian coast, of an obscure family. For some years he dealt in tobacco, and he was thirty years old or more before he effectively began his military career.

or any other traveller in his miserable country. It was certainly the most audacious puff ever practised upon the credulity of an audience, when Mehemet Ali vaunted the happiness and wealth of some 'sweet Auburn' in his wretched and oppressed Pachalick. In reply to his statement, which savoured so little of truth that I thought it harmonized completely with the false expression of the lips which uttered it, the Consul directed the Pacha's attention to the gentleman immediately to his left, who was from Manchester in England, and whom he described to be better acquainted than any person present with the subject he was speaking upon. At this remark, he turned sharply round, and directed a look towards me, in which, as in every glance of his eye, suspicion and cunning predominated. He paused for a moment, and the colonel, not knowing whether his hesitation arose from having imperfectly understood him, repeated in substance his observation, and explained that Manchester was the chief seat of the British manufacture, and that Liverpool was the port by which the materials reached that place. Mehemet Ali had not apparently ever heard of either of these cities. There was another pause of half a minute, and a slight embarrassment in his manner (I was told by one of the party afterwards that it appeared as though a slight flush came over his face at the same instant), when he abruptly changed the topic of conversation, and began to talk of his navy. I was puzzled at the moment to divine the cause why the Pacha shunned a discussion about his favourite cotton; it afterward occurred to me, and the idea was confirmed by the opinions of others of the party, that he avoided talking on a subject on which he was conscious that he had greatly exaggerated, with one whom he believed, from the too favourable account of the Consul, to be better informed than himself.

"The Pacha now proceeded to maintain stoutly that the quality of his Syrian pines was equal to that of British oak for the purposes of shipbuilding. There was nothing remarkable in the conversation that followed, excepting the practical shrewdness which characterized the choice and handling of his subjects on the part of Mehemet Ali. After an interview of about half an hour, in which, from the defective tact and address of Colonel C., no person of the party but himself took any share, we made our parting salutations, and retired from the audience-chamber, which, as I again traversed it, I thought was on a par with a ball-room in a second-rate English country town. On proceeding through the large anteroom, we found the company listening to the address of their spiritual guide. On our way down the declivity from the citadel we passed the menagerie, and I heard the lion growling in his den. I thought of Mehemet Ali."

Cobden had another interview with Mehemet Ali on December 26, in which they had an hour's conversation on the Pacha's way of managing his cotton factories. He confesses himself to have been particularly struck with the Pacha's readiness in replying and reasoning, with his easy handling of his 2½ per cents and 20 per cents, and with his "love of facts and quickness of calculation." "It is this calculating talent, aided by higher powers of combination and reflection, that has contributed so greatly towards elevating him to his present position; for whatever daring or courage he may have shown upon emergencies, it is notorious that he has always preferred the use of diplomacy to the more open tactics of the sword."

1836.
ÆT. 32.

Cairo, Dec. 22nd, 1836.—"Mehemet Ali is pursuing a course of avaricious misrule, which would have torn the vitals from a country less prolific than this, long since. As it is, everything is decaying beneath his system of monopolies. It is difficult to understand the condition of things in Egypt without visiting it. The Pacha has, by dint of force and fraud, possessed himself of the whole of the property of the country. I do not mean that he has obtained merely the rule or government, but he *owns* the whole of the soil, the houses, the boats, the camels, etc. There is something quite unique in finding only one landowner and one merchant in a country, in the person of its pacha! He has been puffed by his creatures in Europe as a regenerator and a reformer —*I can trace in him only a rapacious tyrant.* It is true he has, to gratify an insatiate ambition, attempted to give himself a European fame, by importing some of the arts of civilized countries into Egypt; but this has been done, not to benefit his people, but to exalt himself. His cotton factories are a striking instance of this. I have devoted some time to the inspection of these places, of which I am surprised to find there are twenty-eight in the country, altogether presenting a waste of capital and industry unparalleled in any other part of the world. Magnificent buildings have been erected, costly machinery brought from England and France, and the whole after a few years presents such an appearance of dilapidation and mismanagement that to persevere in carrying them forwards must be to incur fresh ruin every year. At first, steam-engines were put down at the principal mills; but these were soon stopped, and bullock-wheels were substituted, which are now in use at all the establishments! I saw them carding with engines almost toothless; the spinning, which is of low numbers, running from 12 to 40, is of the worst possible kind; and, in weaving, the lumps and knots keep the poor weaver in constant activity cutting and patching his web. There is one mill, built at the side of the river, which presents a splendid appearance as you approach from Alexandria; it contains the finest roomful of Sharp and Roberts's looms that I ever saw. The engine of this does not work, and they have therefore turned these power-looms into hand-looms, and are making cloth that could not be sold at any price in Manchester. All this waste is going on with the best raw cotton, which ought to be sold with us, and double its weight of Surats bought for the manufacturer of such low fabrics. This is not all the mischief, for the very hands that are driven into these manufactures are torn from the cultivation of the soil, which is turned into desert for want of cultivation, whilst it might be the most fertile in the world. But the most splendid of all his buildings is the print-works. Think of a couple of block shops, each nearly a hundred yards long and fifteen feet high; imagine a croft enclosed with solid walls, containing nearly fifty acres, and conceive this to be intersected with streams of water in all directions, and with taps for letting on the water at any particular place; think of such a place, compared with which ours or the best of the Lancashire works are but as barns, and then what do you say when I tell you that one of these block shops contained about fifteen tables at work, whilst in the other the tables were all piled up in one corner, and the only occupants of it were a couple of carpet-weavers trying to produce a hearth-rug! All this is not the work of Mehemet Ali. The miserable adventurers from Europe, who have come here to act the parasites of such a blood-stained despot—they are partly the cause of the evil. But they know his selfish nature, and his lust of fame, and this is only their mode of deluding the one and pandering to the other."[1]

1837. On the 19th of January Cobden left Alexandria, and arrived at Constantinople on the 1st of February:—

On board the Sardinian Brig, La Virtu, in the Sea of Marmora, Jan. 29th, 1837.—"On the 24th we found ourselves becalmed under the island of Scio, the most fertile and the largest of the Archipelago. In the evening the moon rose, and diffused over the atmosphere, not merely a light, but a blaze, which illuminated the hills and vales of Scio, and shed a rosy tint over every object in the island. The sea was as tranquil as the land, and everything seemed to whisper security and repose. How different was the scene on this very island twelve years ago, when the Turks burst in upon a cultivated, wealthy, and contented population, and spread death and destruction through the land, changing in one short day this paradise of domestic happiness into a theatre of the most appalling crimes. I must recall to your minds the particulars of this dreadful tragedy. Scio had taken no part in the revolution of the Greeks, and its inhabitants, who were industrious and rich, voluntarily placed hostages of their chief men in the hands of the Turkish Government, as a proof that they were not disposed to rebel against their rulers. It happened, however, that some young men of the neighbouring islands of Samos and Ipsara landed at one extremity of the island, and there planted the standard of revolt, which, however, was not followed by the Sciotes. On the contrary, they protested against it; and, as they had delivered

1 *To Mr. George Foster*, from Cairo, December 22, 1836.

up their arms as a proof of their peaceful intentions, they could do no more. The pretence, however, was seized upon by the Government of Constantinople, and the island was doomed to a visit from the Turkish Admiral, and a body of ruffianly troops who were promised a free licence of blood and plunder.

1837.
—
ÆT. 33.

"The riches of the island, the beauty and accomplishments of the females, were held out as inducements to draw all the ruffians of the capital to join in the expedition of rapine and murder. The situation of the island, too, afforded the opportunity of passing from the mainland across a narrow strait of about seven miles, and thousands of the miscreants from all the towns of the coast of Asia Minor, including Smyrna, flocked to the scene of woe. Now only picture to yourselves such a scene as the Isle of Wight, supposing it to be one-third more populous and larger in circumference, and then imagine that its inhabitants in the midst of unsuspecting security were suddenly burst upon by 20,000 of the butchers, porters, thieves, and desperadoes of London, Portsmouth, etcetera. Imagine these for three days in unbridled possession of the persons and property of every soul in that happy island; conceive all the churches filled with mangled corpses, the rich proprietors hanging dead at their own house doors, the ministers of religion cruelly tortured—imagine all that could happen from the knives, swords, and pistols of men who were inured to blood, and suppose the captivity and sufferings of every young female or male, who were without exception torn away and sold into captivity; —and you will not then picture a quarter part of the horrors which happened at the massacre of Scio. Of nearly 100,000 persons on the island in the month of May, not more than 700 were left alive there at the end of two months after. Upwards of 40,000 young persons of both sexes were sold into infamous slavery throughout all the Mahometan cities of Europe and Asia, and not one house was left standing except those of the European Consuls!"

Constantinople, February 14th, 1837.—"Do not expect a long or rhapsodical letter from me, for I am at the moment of writing both cold and cross. A copper pan of charcoal is beside me, to which I cannot apply for warmth, because it gives me the headache. There is a hole in the roof, which lets down a current of melted snow, which trickles over my bed and spatters one corner of the table on which I am writing. To complete the agreeable position of the writer, he is lodging in a house where the good man (albeit a tailor!) has a child of every age, from the most disagreeable and annoying of all ages—eighteen months—upwards to ten. My landlady is a bustling little Greek, with a shrill voice which is never tired; but I seldom hear it, because, as her children are generally in full chorus during the whole day, it is only when they are in bed and she takes advantage of the calm to scold her husband, that her *solo* notes are distinguishable. But you will say that I have very little occasion to spend my time indoors, surrounded as I am by the beauties of Constantinople. Alas! if I sally out, the streets are choked with snow and water; the thoroughfares, which are never clean, are now a thousand times worse than Hanging Ditch or Deansgate in the middle of December. If one walks close to the houses, then there are projecting windows from the fronts which just serve to pour an incessant stream of water down on your head and neck; if, to escape drowning, he goes into the middle of the street, then the passenger is up to his knees every step, and sometimes by chance he plunges into a hole of mud and water from which he must emerge by the charity of some good Turk or Christian. Then, to complete the picture of misery, every man or woman you meet dodges you in order to escape contagion, and it would be as difficult almost in Pera, the Frank quarter, to touch a person, as if the whole population were playing a game of prisoner's base. With this multitude of miseries to encounter without and within doors, I have seen little here to amuse or gratify me; and if it were not for the extreme kindness of all the merchants here, with almost all of whom I have dined or visited; and if I had not had other objects in view than merely to see this city and neighbourhood, I should scarcely have stayed a week at Constantinople. The plague has been more than commonly destructive; various accounts give from 50 to 100,000 deaths, and I have little doubt that more than one-eighth of the population has been swept away. I must, however, tell you for your satisfaction that it has now almost disappeared, and that it has quite lost its virulence. Fortunately, the very day of my arrival a north wind set in, and brought with it the snows and frosts of the Black Sea, against which the pestilence could not exist. Had I arrived a week earlier, the weather was as mild as summer. That would have given me a better opportunity of seeing the country, but not with the same security from the plague as at present. As I entered the harbour of Constantinople, the country was free from snow, and therefore I saw the view to pretty good advantage considering that it was the winter-time. It is too fine, too magical, for description, and all the accounts that you read of it do not do justice to it."

1837. — ÆT. 33.

Smyrna, *Feb.* 24*th*, 1837.—"After I wrote to you from Constantinople, I made an excursion up the Bosphorus to see the scenery which all concur in praising as the most beautiful in Europe. I wish I had seen it before I landed in Turkey;—the misery, the dirt, the plague, and all the other disagreeables of Constantinople, haunted me even in the quiet and solitude of natural beauties which, apart from such associations, are certainly enough to excite the romantic fervour of the most chilly-hearted. From these causes I am afraid I have not done justice to the scene of the Bosphorus. I could not look upon the palaces, the kiosks, and wooden houses which crowded the banks of the beautiful channel with the interest which they might have imparted, if I had not known the poverty, vice, and tyranny of their possessors. Must I confess it? I think the Hudson river a much more beautiful scene than the Bosphorus. But let the scenes be reversed—if the Bosphorus were in the United States, and the Hudson in Turkey—and I should consider probably the former incomparably the most beautiful; so much are we the creatures of association."[1]

[1] In the pamphlet on *England, Ireland, and America*, Cobden had already indulged a joyous vision of what Constantinople might become under the genius of a free government:—"Constantinople, outrivalling New York, may be painted, with a million of free citizens, as the focus of all the trade of Eastern Europe. Let us conjure up the thousands of miles of railroads, carrying to the very extremities of this empire—not the sanguinary satrap, but the merchandise and the busy traders of a free state; conveying—not the firman of a ferocious Sultan, armed with death to the trembling slave, but the millions of newspapers and letters, which stimulate the enterprise and excite the patriotism of an enlightened people. Let us imagine the Bosphorus and the Sea of Marmora swarming with steamboats, connecting the European and Asiatic continents by hourly departures and arrivals; or issuing from the Dardanelles, to reanimate once more with life and fertility the hundred islands of the Archipelago; or conceive the rich shores of the Black Sea in the power of the New Englander, and the Danube pouring

Smyrna, Feb. 24*th*, 1837.—"In the steamer which brought me from Constantinople to this place, we had a great number of passengers, chiefly Turks: there were a few Persians. They all rested on deck during the whole time. For their convenience little raised platforms were placed along each side of the steamer, to prevent the wet, if any rain fell, reaching their beds. Hereon they spread their mats and arranged their cloaks, and it was amusing to watch each drawing forth his long pipe, and preparing with the aid of a bag of tobacco to sustain the fatigues and sufferings of two nights' exposure in such a position. These Turks are the most quiet and orderly people in the world when their religious fanaticism is untouched, in which case they are at once changed into the most sanguinary savages imaginable. Some of our passengers were people of good quality, with servants accompanying them, and they slept in the cabin; but the whole of the day was spent in reposing upon their mats, their legs tucked under, and their long pipes in their mouths. A few words sometimes were exchanged, but the conversation seemed always to be a secondary affair to the enjoyment of the pipe.

1837. —— ÆT. 33.

"I found great amusement in walking up and down the deck between these rows of quiet, grave Mussulmans, whose picturesque dresses and arms of various kinds afforded me constant interest; whilst the honest Turks felt equal amusement in ruminating over their pipes upon the motives which could cause

down its produce on the plains of Moldavia and Wallachia, now subject to the plough of the hardy Kentuckian. Let us picture the Carolinians, the Virginians, and the Georgians transplanted to the coasts of Asia Minor, and behold its hundreds of cities again bursting from the tomb of ages, to recall religion and civilization to the spot from whence they first issued forth upon the world. Alas! that this should only be an illusion of the fancy!"

a Giaour like me to set myself the task of walking to and fro on the deck for nothing that they could understand, unless for some religious penance. There were two old men with green turbans, who five times during the day put aside their pipes, turning to the east, and, bowing their foreheads to their feet, uttered with great fervour their prayers. All this passed unnoticed by their very next neighbours—for the Turks are not (what nurses say of children) arrived at the age for *taking notice.* I have seen all sorts of strange scenes happen without disturbing the dreaming attention of the Turk. Once in Cairo I was looking out of a window, beneath which three smokers were sitting upon their mats: a boy was driving an ass loaded with gravel and sand, which tripped just as it was passing full trot by the place, and fell close to the smokers, upsetting the contents of the panniers upon their mats. The boy immediately set to work shovelling up the sand with his hands, and scraping it as well as he could from amongst their legs, and having loaded his donkey, he cantered away. Not a word or look passed between him and the smokers, who never moved from their seats; and two hours afterwards I passed by them when their posture was precisely the same, and their legs were still surrounded by the remains of the load of sand!"

Smyrna, Feb. 24th, 1837.—"The house in which I am staying is a large, elegantly-furnished one, and the management is of the solid kind which Mr. Rhoades' establishment used to be characterized by.[1] Old, queer-looking servants trot about large corridors; there are rooms for Monsieur, snuggeries for Madame, little retreats for visitors, in one of which I am sitting, writing; and all have good substantial fires. In the evening after a six o'clock dinner, parties of ladies

[1] Mr. Rhoades was the husband of one of his aunts.

walk in without ceremony; they and the young gentlemen of the house, with Madame W—— (who does not speak English), sit down to the faro-table, around which you soon hear a babel of tongues, English, French, Greek, and Italian, whilst Mr. W—— and I *cause* over Russian politics or political economy. One by one the company disappears, after taking a cup of coffee the size of a pigeon's egg; and so noiseless and little ceremonious are their appearances and disappearances, that a spectator would imagine the visitors to be members of the family, who joined each other from different parts of this great house to an evening's amusement, and then retired again for the night to their several apartments. This *is visiting as it should be done.*"

The following extracts from his journal may serve to show the chief topics of conversation in these very useful visits:—

Smyrna, *Feb.* 3*rd.*—"At Mr. Crespin's, in a conversation upon the trade of Turkey, I heard that £350,000 of British goods are now lying here for the Persian markets, full one-half of the goods that came here last year were for Persia. The Persian trade was formerly carried on principally from Bombay, or through the German fairs. At present these currents are changed. Mr. W—— says that he has been at Constantinople from seventeen to eighteen years, and he recollects when the first vessel cleared out hence for England. At present an attempt is being made to impose transit duty upon the Persian silk coming through Constantinople. The trade of France is very much diminished; query is the whole demand for Turkey greater now than forty years ago? Smyrna has declined. Wool which formerly went to France now goes to London, linseed is now exported from Turkey."

1837. — Æt. 33.

Feb. 4th.—"Again heavy snows; confined to the house during the day. In the evening I accompanied Mr. Longworth to visit Mr. Simmonds, a fine old gentleman who has spent thirty-five years in Turkey. Like almost all the residents, he is favourable to the Turks, and anxious to support them against the Russians; his experiments in farming the high lands for the first time, tolerably successful. In the course of conversation he said that last year the Government sent a firman to Salonica, and intercepted the grain crops which were ready for exportation, ordering them to be delivered to its stores at ten piastres and thirty paras the kilo (about a bushel); he went to the Seraskier and complained, and advised him of the impolicy of such a step, upon which he promised to inquire into it. The Government then sent its agents to purchase the grain at eleven or twelve piastres from the farmers, who, as the firman had not been withdrawn, sold it eagerly. A remonstrance, however, had been sent to the Government by the farmers of the vicinity of the capital, declaring that they could not produce their grain at less than fifteen piastres the kilo. . . . It snowed all day. I remained at home, and read, and made extracts from pamphlets, etc."

Feb. 5th.—"In the morning received a call from Mr. Perkins. He spoke of the steamer which goes in about three days to Trebizond. She sails every fifteen days, and is usually full of freight and passengers; the deck passengers pay 200 piastres, or about two pounds, cabin passengers ten pounds. She carries a great number of porters, who come to Constantinople for work, remain perhaps for six months, and then return. The goods sent to Trebizond are forwarded chiefly to Erzeroum, from whence they are distributed throughout Persia and the surrounding countries. Long-cloths and prints are the principal articles. I received a visit from Dr. Millingen.[1] Says Mr. Urquhart is Scotch, was educated at college, went out to the aid of the Greeks at their revolution, was severely wounded on two occasions, afterwards travelled for some years in Turkey, discovered 'the municipalities, direct taxation, and freedom of trade,' which were the secret preservers of Turkey. Afterwards he went to England, agitated the press, the ministers, and the king in favour of Turkey. He succeeded in making every newspaper editor and reviewer adopt his views, excepting Tait. He afterwards wrote his *Resources of Turkey*, and then his pamphlet. He was patronized by Lord Ponsonby, until he received his appointment of Secretary of Legation, when his active and personal exertions in promoting his own peculiar policy produced a coolness between them. He was sent out by the English Government to arrange the commercial treaty. He, the ambassador, and the consul are all at daggers drawn.

"There are no associations at all amongst the Turks, such as are alluded to by Urquhart, under the name of Municipalities. Those amongst the rayahs have reference to the regulation of their own affairs in the manner of the English Quakers or Methodists, excepting that in their own disputes they are allowed to arbitrate without appealing to Turkish tribunals. The term, *Municipalities*, is misapplied, and only calculated to deceive. In taxing the *rayahs*, the amounts levied are arbitrary, and the only privilege the various sects possess is to raise the money in the best way they can, as a body amongst themselves, instead of the Turkish authorities coming in contact with individuals. The system was no doubt originated

[1] The well-known physician who attended Byron in his last illness, and who died at Constantinople last year (1878).

for the purpose of enabling the Turks to levy their imposts with greater facility. The Greeks, Armenians, Jews, etc., have no protection from these imaginary municipalities."

Feb. 7th.—"In the morning I called on Mr. Perkins, who is opposed to the belief in the regeneration of the Turks. The municipalities are aptly ridiculed in the novel of *Anastasius* (by Hope), where the Turk sits upon the ground smoking under a tree, and leaves the people of the village, where he had been sent to levy contributions, to raise the money in the best way they can. Mr. Ralli attributes the evils of Turkey to the radical vices of the institutions, to the monopolies, and above all to the depreciation of the standard of value in the money. The trade to Persia through Constantinople has increased very much, but fluctuates greatly. One year it has been probably 7 to £800,000; at another, owing to a glut, not half of that amount. But he is certain that the trade to Persia, etc., is double that of Constantinople for Turkey. In the evening I dined with Mr. Thomasset, and met Mr. Boudrey, a French gentleman of intelligence. He says the trade direct with France has nearly fallen away entirely with Turkey. Belgian, Swiss, and German fabrics have superseded those from France. No regular impost is levied by Government all through its dominions; every pacha is to raise a certain sum, and he does it in his own way. Mustapha Pacha, of Adrianople, when ordered to send a certain quantity of corn to Government at a certain price, fixed 12 piastres as the value, because the Europeans would give it, and he would not let his people supply it for less. *He is an exception*, and popular."

Feb. 8th.—"In the evening I dined with Mr. Perkins and met Mr. Webster, etc. I was told that no fortunes have been made by British merchants at Constantinople; that the business is so insecure, and that they are beginning to wish for the Russians, more money being made by the residents at Odessa."

Feb. 9th.—"Mr. Cartwright, the consul, called. In speaking of trade to Persia, he said that, previous to 1790, the commerce went by way of Aleppo, where there were twenty-eight English houses. The shipments were made at two seasons of the year, in six large vessels to Scanderoon, or Ladikiyeh, where there were large warehouses for depôts. After that epoch the stream of commerce went in the direction of Bombay for the lower division of Persia, and by way of Russia for the other quarters of it. The modern route by Constantinople is not more than fifteen years old. After our treaty of 1820, Turkey began its system of imposts upon internal commerce. He thinks that Mehemet Ali gave the impulse to Mahmoud in many of his reforms. The change is only in the dress and whitewashing of the houses, nothing fundamental being altered. After the destruction of the Janissaries, it seems that he has been quite at sea. Ruined, worn-out country."

Feb. 11th.—"Mr. Hanson thinks that matters are worse since the time of the Janissaries, who were the opposition and check of the Government. Then the people were only plundered and oppressed by the Sultan and his Grand Vizier, but now every one of the pachas about the person of the Sultan can, by obtaining firmans, oppress the poor agriculturalist. Mr. Perkins thinks the trade for Turkey does not, in Constantinople, exceed £400,000; he was told that Persia took in one year £1,200,000. The trade to Persia is new for the last few years by this route; he thinks it both a creation and a transition;

some of it is merely removed from Bombay. A ship or two in the year comes from Trieste, bringing goods from the German fairs to the Black Sea. In the evening I dined with Mr. Cartwright, and met a party of merchants. After dinner we discussed the trading prospects of Turkey. All agreed that the money amount of the consumption of British goods is diminishing, and that the trade to Persia forms two-thirds of the imports into Constantinople. Mr. Cartwright spoke of a person who, in Turkey, told him he had bought cloth for his coat which cost him only half as much as he would have paid for it in England. The company are obliged by their charter to take so much woollen cloth, which they sold at a loss. Russia, Mr. Cartwright thinks, will again let the trade go through Georgia, by which route it formerly reached Persia; he says that, after exhausting the fortunes of the Armenians and others, he, the Sultan, has since been preying upon agriculture. The Exchange operations of the Government are merely depreciating his currency, and robbing the people by purchasing the non-interference of the foreign merchant. Russia is continually increasing the number of her subjects by naturalization. The rayahs, who form the most industrious and best, besides the most numerous part of the community, would certainly benefit by a Christian Government. Mr. Cartwright and all present agreed that the Turks have not themselves the power of regeneration, and that, unless foreign aid prevent it, they must fall to pieces in less than twenty years. But absolute occupation and authority must be possessed by the power that would regenerate Turkey. Every public servant, from the highest to the lowest, must be dismissed, as they are all corrupt. A Turk, the moment he enters the public service, is necessarily a rascal. *England must, if she interposes at all, take the part of a principal, not an auxiliary.*"

From Smyrna, after a fortnight's cruise among the islands, Cobden arrived at Athens, March 19th, where the political and economic circumstances of the new Hellenic kingdom interested him more keenly than the renowned monuments, though he did not fail in attention to them also. His inquiries filled him, as is usually the case with travellers, with admiration for the gifts of the Greek people, and confidence in their future. The perverse diplomacy which settled the limits and constitution of the kingdom, he viewed with a contempt which the course of Eastern events in the forty years since his visit has fully justified. His hopes for the future of the Greeks were not coloured by the conventional acceptance of the glories of their past. He was amazed to find the mighty states of Attica and Sparta within an area something smaller than the two counties of Yorkshire and Lancashire. "What famous puffers those old Greeks were! Half the educated world in Europe is now devoting more thought to the ancient affairs of these Lilliputian states, the squabbles of their tribes, the wars of their villages, the geography of their rivulets and hillocks, than they bestow upon the modern history of the South and North Americas, the politics of the United States, and the charts of the mighty rivers and mountains of the new world."[1]

"The antiquities of Athens may be cursorily viewed in half a day. I was not so highly impressed with the merits of these masterpieces from reading and plates, as I found myself to be on looking at the actual remains of those monuments and temples, whose ruins crown the rocky platform of the

[1] *To F. Cobden*, from Smyrna, March 3rd, 1837.

1837. — ÆT. 33.

Acropolis. I am satisfied that there is nothing now in existence which for beauty of design, masterly workmanship, and choice of situation, can compare with that spectacle of grandeur and sublimity which the public temples of ancient Athens presented two thousand years ago. What a genius and what a taste had those people! *And, mind, the genius is there still.* All the best deeds of ancient times will be again rivalled by the Greeks of a future age. Do not believe the lying and slandering accounts which the dulness of some travellers, the envy of Levant merchants, and the Franks of Constantinople, utter against the Greek character. The raw material of all that is noble, brilliant, refined, and glorious, is still latent in the character of this people: overlaid, as is natural, with the cunning, falsehood, meanness, and other vices inherent in the spirits of slaves.

"Do not, however, fancy that I am predicting the revival of Greek greatness, through the means of the present little trumpery monarchy of that name, which will pass away like other bubbles blown by our shallow statesmen. All the East will be Greek, and Constantinople, no matter under what nominal sovereignty it may fall, will by the force of the indomitable genius of the Greeks become in fact the capital of that people."[1]

Athens, March 22.—"In the evening at Sir E. Lyons' I met Captain Fisher, who spoke of the haste with which he was ordered to sea for the Levant. He left his own son behind him, whom I met in Egypt, going to India, and for whom he had not dared to wait twenty-four hours. He also left behind two guns. He remarked that if the lives and fortunes of a nation were at stake, he could not have used more pressing expedition—yet all for no

[1] *To F. Cobden*, April 18, 1837.

purpose that can be discovered! The *Portland* is carrying home Count Armansperg, the dismissed Minister of Greece, after bringing the King and Queen of Greece.[1] I saw this ship at Malta on my way out to Egypt in November. She was fitted up superbly for this young lady and gentleman, and their maids of honour and attendants. She went to Venice, and was in waiting for the royal holiday folks for two months. The *Madagascar*, Capt. Lyons, brought out the Regency and the young king. The wives of the members of the Regency quarrelled even on the passage. Some time ago the *Medea* steamer was carrying the old King of Bavaria and his son to the islands of the Archipelago and the coast of Asia Minor. We are general carriers for erratic royalty all over the world; witness, Donna Maria Miguel, old Ferdinand of Naples, the King of Portugal and their precious minions, were the choice freights of our ships of war. When will this folly have an end?"

1837.
ÆT. 33.

March 24.—"At twelve o'clock at night [in the Piræus harbour] I went on board a little boat, which set sail immediately for Kalamaki [in the Isthmus of

[1] The new kingdom was entrusted to a Regency until the completion of King Otho's twentieth year (June 1, 1835). Count Armansperg was President, and Von Maurer was his principal colleague. The pair showed that Germans are capable of rivalling the Greeks themselves in hatred and intrigue. "Count Armansperg, as a noble, looked down on Maurer as a pedant and law professor. Maurer sneered at the count as an idler, fit only to be a diplomatist or a master of the ceremonies" (*Finlay*, vii. 12). When King Otho returned to his kingdom in the *Portland* (Feb. 1837), he brought with him his young bride, Queen Amelia, and Rudhart to be his prime minister. Armansperg was recalled to Bavaria, after disastrous failure in his administration. Cobden might have found an excellent text for a sermon, in the childish perversity which marked Lord Palmerston's dealings with Greece in these years, from his stubborn defence of Count Armansperg down to his disputes about Court etiquette, and his employment of the fleet to enforce the payment of a trifling debt.

1837.
Æt. 33.

Corinth]. It was a clear, fresh, moonlight night, and a favourable breeze soon carried us from among the ships in the harbour."

March 25.—"In the morning we were halfway across the gulf [the Saronic Gulf] by nine o'clock. . . . At eight o'clock in the evening we arrived at Kalamaki. On the beach were two persons fishing with a blazing torch and spear. We entered the khan. A few phials were on a little bar, behind which sat the master. At the other ends of the room were raised platforms of two stages, reaching to the ceiling, or rather roof (for there was no interior covering), on which the travellers had spread mats, and on some of which their snoring occupants were reposing for the night, whilst others were sitting smoking their pipes. An officer in the new uniform, and another in the Albanian dress, were sitting at a little table taking their supper with their fingers from the same dish. A little wood fire was blazing at one side of the room, upon which was some hot water, and by the side hung coffee-pots of every size, from the bigness of a thimble upwards. A large mortar of marble stood by the side of the fire, into which the coffee-grains were thrown by the servant, and pounded with a pestle, previous to being boiled for his customers. This custom of pounding instead of grinding the coffee, is, I believe, universal in the East.

"We found a proprietor of a boat from the other side of the isthmus, and engaged with him to take us to Patras for twelve dollars. We hired horses and set off across the isthmus, a distance of about six miles to Loutraki. The night was clear and cool, and the moon at nearly its full; the scenery of the mountainous and rugged neck of land which we traversed, and of the gulfs on each side, was romantic.

At Loutraki we saw the caves and hollows in the sides of the mountains, into which the women and children were thrust for concealment during the war.

"We got on board at midnight, and set sail down the gulf of Corinth or Lepanto for Patras. Parnassus on our right, covered with snow—a cold bed for the muses! On each side the hills are crowned with snow. At night the wind was foul and contrary, and our boat took shelter in a port on the Roumeliot side of the gulf, and, on the morning of the 27th of March, finding that there was no chance of getting forward, I turned to the opposite coast, and ran for a little village, where I determined to hire horses, and push forward for Patras by land. We came to anchor near a shop, where the proprietor sold every variety of petty merchandise, such as wine, paper, candles, nails, etc., and we took some coffee, whilst a person went in search of horses. The owner of the cattle arrived soon afterwards, to make a bargain of a dollar each horse for Vostizza. He had left his animals concealed behind a bridge, and, as soon as we had agreed to his terms, they were produced. This cunning is the result of a long experience of Turkish violence. We set off with some companions for Vostizza, along a road bordering close upon the gulf, at the foot of lofty banks or hills that bound either side of the water. We passed some rich little valleys, finely cultivated and all planted with the little currant trees. Stopped at a hut in the middle of the day, and ate some black bread and olives, and drank some wine and water. Again set forward and reached Vostizza, a little sea-port situated in a rich and well-cultivated valley, all planted with currants. The people appeared industriously at work. On walking out into the town of Vostizza, I found a few stone houses, apparently lately erected, and of public utility. Saw a concourse of people around one of these, in which there was to be an auction of public lands.

"In the khan or lodgings where I put up, there was nothing to be had to eat but eggs and caviare. I went to bed early, intending to be called at three o'clock, but could not sleep from the noise of Greeks, who were laughing and dancing in the next room. When I had by dint of threats and vociferations quieted these fellows, I was beset by such multitudes of fleas that I could not obtain a moment's repose. I therefore arose at two o'clock, and, as the horses soon afterwards appeared, we set off for Patras. The moon was bright and the air cool, and we proceeded along a path close to the gulf; passed some shepherds' huts in which the lights were burning, and the dogs gave note of watchfulness. As daylight appeared, I looked anxiously to the coast for the spectacle of a sunrise behind the mountains of Roumelia. The first rays lighted up the summits of Parnassus and the other lofty mountains, whose snowy peaks were tinged with rosy hues. By degrees the sky assumed a dark dull red aspect, above the eastern range of hills; this shade gradually grew more lurid, until little by little the horizon, from a sombre red, assumed a dazzling appearance of fiery brightness, and shortly afterwards the sun flamed above the mountainous outline over the gulf, hills, and valleys around us. The path all the way lay through a thicket of shrubs of a thousand kinds, some evergreen, others aromatic, and the whole wearing the appearance of a pleasure-ground in England. The flowers, too, were fragrant, and the whole scene was full of luxuriant richness and beauty.

"We stopped at a hut at nine o'clock to breakfast, where we found a poor mud cottage, containing a few coarse articles of use for sale, as well as some bread and cheese of a very uninviting quality. I saw Lepanto on the opposite side of the gulf, and soon afterwards the Castles of Patras and Roumelia, which guard the entrance of the Gulf of Lepanto. At half-past twelve o'clock we entered Patras and went straightway to the Consul's house, to learn the time when the steamer would sail. I washed, dressed, and dined, and immediately afterwards went on board the *Hermes* steamer, Captain Blount, which arrived from Corfu. We set sail at four o'clock. In the evening, at ten, we called off Zante for letters, and then proceeded with favourable breezes for Malta."

At Malta Cobden formed some very decided opinions as to the policy of naval administration, as illustrated at that station.

"The Malta station is the hot-bed for naval patronage, and the increase of our ships of war. They are sent to the Mediterranean for five years, the large ships are for six or eight months of each year anchored in Malta harbour, or else in Vourla or Tenedos. In the summer, for the space of four or five months, they make excursions round Sicily, or in the Archipelago as far as Smyrna or Athens, and then they return again to their anchorage to spend the winter in inactivity; the officers visiting in the city, or perhaps enjoying a long leave of absence, whilst the men, to the number of six, seven, or eight hundred, are put to such exercise or employment as the ingenuity of the first lieutenant can devise on board ship, or else are suffered to wander on shore upon occasional leaves of absence. This is not the way either to make good sailors, or to add

1837. — Æt. 33.

to the power of the British empire. The expenses are borne by the industry of the productive classes at home. The wages of these idlers are paid out of the taxes levied upon the soap, beer, tobacco, etc., consumed by the people of England. But what a prospect of future expense does this state of things hold out to the nation. Every large ship contains at least forty or fifty quarter-deck officers, each one of whom, from the junior supernumerary midshipman up to the first lieutenant, has entered the service, hoping and relying that he will in due course of time, either by means of personal merit or aided by the influence of powerful friends, attain to the command of a ship of war, and all these will press their claims upon the Admiralty for future employment, and will be entitled to hope, as they grow older, that their emoluments, rank, and prospects will improve every year with their increased necessities. What then is the prospect which such a state of things holds out to the two parties concerned, the nation on the one hand, and its servants, its meritorious servants, on the other? Unwise to encourage this increase of the navy, parents might find a much better field in unsettled regions abroad."[1]

Leaving Malta on April 4, and touching at Gibraltar, he there in the course of his indefatigable questioning found new confirmation of his opinions from competent and disinterested informants.

April 15, 1837.—"In conversation Waghorn said that the admirals are all too old, and that this accounts for the service being less efficient now than heretofore; that the ships are put up for six months in the winter months at Malta, during which there is of course no exercise in seamanship for the men. Mr. Andrews told me that there are sometimes

[1] *Journal*, March 31, 1837.

twenty ships of war lying at one time in Malta. The mode of promotion is as bad or worse now than under the Tories; there are captains now in the command of ships who five years ago had not passed as midshipmen, and there are hundreds of mates pining for lieutenancies, who have passed ten years. The Treasury presses upon the Admiralty for the promotion of friends and dependants of the ministers of the day, and thus leaves no room for the exercise of justice towards the old and deserving officers. This was more excusable at the time of the rotten boroughs than now, when no such interest can be necessary. There are thirty or forty midshipmen in one of the first-raters; how much incipient disappointment, poverty, and neglect! The Admiral states that it is enough to depress his spirits to see so many young men, some of them twenty-five, and capable of commanding the best ships, filling the situation of boys only. Young Baily in conversation spoke of the way in which the *Portland* was fitted up for the Queen of Greece and her maids of honour, twenty guns removed and the space converted into elegant rooms draped and furnished for the king, queen, and suite. The queen, on arriving at Athens, was so pleased with her lodging on board, that she sent an artist to take a drawing of her rooms. The vessel waited a couple of months at Trieste and Venice for the royal pair. After bringing them and their ministers, the *Portland* carried back Count Armansperg to Malta."[1]

On the 21st of April Cobden arrived at Falmouth, after an absence of six months. I must repeat here what I said at the beginning of these extracts, that the portions of his letters and journals which record the most energetic of his interests and his inquiries,

[1] *Journal*, April 15.

1837. — ÆT. 33.

are precisely those which are no longer worth reproducing, because the facts of commerce and of politics, which formed the most serious object of his investigation, have undergone such a change as to be hardly more to our purpose than the year's almanac. When we come to the journals of ten years later, the reader will be able to judge the spirit and method with which Cobden travelled, and perhaps to learn a lesson from him in the objects of travel. Meanwhile, Cobden could hardly have spent a more profitable holiday, for he had laid up a great stock of political information, and acquired a certain living familiarity with the circumstances of the eastern basin of the Mediterranean and the Turkish Government — then as now the centre of our active diplomacy — and with the real working of those principles of national policy which he had already condemned by the light of native common sense and reflection.

CHAPTER IV

THE TWO PAMPHLETS

1835-6.

ÆT. 31-2.

It is not at the first glance very easy to associate a large and theorizing doctrine of human civilization with the name of one who was at this time a busy dealer in printed calicoes, and who almost immediately afterwards became the most active of political agitators. There may seem to be a certain incongruity in discussing a couple of pamphlets by a Manchester manufacturer, as if they were the speculations of an abstract philosopher. Yet it is no strained pretension to say that at this time Cobden was fully possessed by the philosophic gift of feeling about society as a whole, and thinking about the problems of society in an ordered connexion with one another. He had definite and systematic ideas of the way in which men ought now to travel in search of improvement; and he attached new meaning and more comprehensive purpose to national life.

The agitations of the great Reform Act of 1832 had stirred up social aspirations, which the Liberal Government of the next ten years after the passing of the Act were utterly unable to satisfy. This inability arose partly from their own political ineptitude and want alike of conviction and courage; and partly from the fact that many of these aspirations lay wholly outside of the sphere of any government.

To give a vote to all ten-pound householders, and to abolish a few rotten boroughs, was seen to carry the nation a very little way on the journey for which it had girded itself up. The party which had carried the change seemed to have sunk to the rank of a distracted faction, blind to the demands of the new time, with no strong and common doctrine, with no national aims, and hardly even with any vigorous personal ambitions. People suddenly felt that the interesting thing was not mechanism but policy, and unfortunately the men who had amended the mechanism were in policy found empty and without resource. The result of the disappointment was such a degree of fresh and independent activity among all the better minds of the time, that the succeeding generation, say from 1840 to 1870, practically lived upon the thought and sentiment of the seven or eight years immediately preceding the close of the Liberal reign in 1841. It was during those years that the schools were formed and the principles shaped, which have attracted to themselves all who were serious enough to feel the need of a school or the use of a principle.

If the change in institutions which had taken place in 1832 had brought forth hardly any of the fruit, either bitter or sweet, which friends had hoped and enemies had threatened, it was no wonder that those who were capable of a large earnestness about public things, whether civil or ecclesiastical, turned henceforth from the letter of institutions to their spirit; from their form and outer framework to the operative force within; and from stereotyped catchwords about the social union to its real destination. It was now the day of ideals in every camp. The general restlessness was as intense among reflecting Conservatives as among reflecting Liberals; and those who looked to the past agreed with those who looked to the future, in energetic dissatisfaction with a sterile present. We need only look around to recognize the unity of the original impulse which animated men who dreaded or hated one another; and inspired books that were as far apart as a humoristic novel and a treatise on the Sacraments. A great wave of humanity, of benevolence, of desire for improvement—a great wave of social sentiment, in short,—poured itself among all who had the faculty of large and disinterested thinking. The political spirit was abroad in its most comprehensive sense, the desire of strengthening society by adapting it to better intellectual ideals, and enriching it from new resources of moral power. A feeling for social regeneration, under what its apostles conceived to be a purer spiritual guidance, penetrated ecclesiastical common-rooms no less than it penetrated the manufacturing districts. It was in 1835 that Dr. Pusey threw himself with new heartiness into the movement at Oxford, that Dr. Newman projected Catenas of Anglican divines, and began to meditate Tract Ninety. In the opposite quarter of the horizon Mr. Mill was still endeavouring, in the *Westminster Review*, to put a new life into Radical politics by giving a more free and genial character to Radical speculations, and—a far more important task—was composing the treatise which gave a decisive tone to English ways of thinking for thirty years afterwards. Men like Arnold and like Maurice were almost intoxicated with their passion for making citizenship into something loftier and more generous than the old strife of Blues and Yellows: unfortunately they were so beset with prejudices against what they confusedly denounced as materialism and utilitarianism, that they turned aside from the open ways of common sense and truth to fact, to nourish themselves on vague dreams of a Church which, though it rested on the great mysteries of the faith, yet for purposes of action could only after all become an instrument for the secular teaching of Adam Smith and Bentham. To the fermentation of those years Carlyle contributed the vehement apostrophes of *Chartism* and *Past and Present*, glowing with eloquent contempt for the aristocratic philosophy of treadmills, gibbets, and thirty-nine Acts of Parliament "for the shooting of partridges alone," but showing no more definite way for national redemption than lay through the too vague words of Education and Emigration. Finally, in the same decade, the early novels of Charles Dickens brought into vivid prominence among the objects of popular interest such types of social outlawry as the parish apprentice, the debtor in prison, the pauper in the workhouse, the criminal by profession, and all the rest of that pitiful gallery. Dickens had hardly any solution beyond a mere Christmas philanthropy, but he stirred the sense of humanity in his readers, and from great imaginative writers we have no right to insist upon more.

Notwithstanding their wide diversity of language and of method, still to all of these rival schools and men of genius the ultimate problem was the same. With all of them the aim to be attained was social renovation. Even the mystics of Anglo-Catholicism, as I have said, had in the inmost recesses of their minds a clear belief that the revival of sacramental doctrine and the assertion of apostolic succession would quicken the moral life of the nation, and meet social needs no less than it would meet spiritual needs. Far apart as Cobden stood from these and all the other sections of opinion that I have named, yet his early pamphlets show that he discerned as keenly as any of them that the hour had come for developing new elements in public life, and setting up a new standard of public action. To Cobden, as to Arnold or to Mill, the real meaning of his activity was, in a more or less formal and conscious way, the hope of supplying a systematic foundation for higher social order, and the wider diffusion of a better kind of well-being.

He had none of the pedantry of the doctrinaire, but he was full of the intellectual spirit. Though he was shortly to become the leader of a commercial movement, he never ceased to be the preacher of a philosophy of civilization; and his views on trade were only another side of views on education and morality. Realist as he was, yet his opinions were inspired and enriched by the genius of social imagination.

Some readers will smile when I say that no teacher of that day was found so acceptable or so inspiring by Cobden as George Combe. He had read Combe's volume before he wrote his pamphlets, and he said that "it seemed like a transcript of his own familiar thoughts."[1] Few emphatically second-rate men have done better work than the author of the *Constitution of Man*. That memorable book, whose principles have now in some shape or other become the accepted commonplaces of all rational persons, was a startling revelation when it was first published (1828), showing men that their bodily systems are related to the rest of the universe, and are subject to general and inexorable conditions; that health of mind and character are connected with states of body; that the old ignorant or ascetical disregard of the body is hostile both to happiness and mental power; and that health is a true department of

[1] *Life of George Combe*, ii. 11.

morality. We cannot wonder that zealous men were found to bequeath fortunes for the dissemination of that wholesome gospel, that it was circulated by scores of thousands of copies, and that it was seen on shelves where there was nothing else save the Bible and *Pilgrim's Progress*.

It is easy to discern the attraction which teaching so fresh and inspiriting as this would have for a mind like Cobden's, constitutionally eager to break from the old grooves of things, alert for every sign of new light and hope in the sombre sky of prejudice, and confident in the large possibility of human destiny. To show, as Combe showed, that the character and motives of men are connected with physical predispositions, was to bring character and motive within the sphere of action, because we may in that case modify them by attending to the requirements of the bodily organization. A boundless field is thus opened for the influence of social institutions, and the opportunities of beneficence are without limit. There is another side on which Cobden found Combe's teaching in harmony with the impulses of his own temperament: it rests upon the natural soundness of the human heart, and its methods are those of mildness and lenity. In his intrepid faith in the perfectibility of man and society, Cobden is the only eminent practical statesman that this country has ever possessed, who constantly breathes the fine spirit of that French school in which the name of Turgot is the most illustrious.

The doctrine of the pamphlets has its avowed source in the very same spirit which has gradually banished violence, harshness, and the darker shapes of repression from the education of the young, from the treatment of the insane, from the punishment of criminals, and has substituted for those time-honoured but most ineffective processes, a rational moderation and enlightened humanity, the force of lenient and considerate example and calm self-possession. Non-intervention was an extension of the principle which, renouncing appeals through brute violence, rests on the nobler and more powerful qualities of the understanding and the moral nature. Cobden's distinction as a statesman was not that he accepted and applied this principle in a general way. Charlatans and marauders accept such principles in that way. His merit is that he discerned that England, at any rate, whatever might be true of Germany, France, or Russia, was in the position where the present adoption of this new spirit of policy would exactly coincide with all her best and largest interests. Now and at all times Cobden was far too shrewd and practical in his temper to suppose that unfamiliar truths will shine into the mind of a nation by their own light. It was of England that he thought, and for England that he wrote; and what he did was not to declaim the platitudes of rose-coloured morality, but by reference to the hardest facts of our national existence and international relations, to show that not only the moral dignity, but the material strength, the solid interests, the real power of the country, alike for improvements within and self-defence without, demanded the abandonment of the diplomatic principles of a time which was as unenlightened and mischievous on many sides of its foreign policy, as everybody knows and admits it to have been in the schoolroom, in the hospital, and in the offices of the national revenue.

The pamphlets do not deal with the universe, but with this country. Their writer has been labelled a cosmopolitan,—usually by those who in the same breath, by a violent contradiction, reproached him for preaching a gospel of national selfishness and isolation. In truth Cobden was only cosmopolitan in the sense in which no other statesman would choose to deny himself to be cosmopolitan also; namely, in the sense of aiming at a policy which, in benefiting his own country, should benefit all the rest of the world at the same time. "I am an English citizen," he would have said, "and what I am contending for is that England is to-day so situated in every particular of her domestic and foreign circumstances, that by leaving other governments to settle their own business and fight out their own quarrels, and by attending to the vast and difficult affairs of her own enormous realm and the condition of her people, she will not only be setting the world an example of noble morality which no other nation is so happily free to set, but she will be following the very course which the maintenance of her own greatness most imperatively commands. It is precisely because Great Britain is so strong in resources, in courage, in institutions, in geographical position, that she can, before all other European powers, afford to be moral, and to set the example of a mighty nation walking in the paths of justice and peace."

Cobden's political genius perceived this great mark of the time, that, in his own words, "at certain periods in the history of a nation, it becomes necessary to review its principles of domestic policy, for the purpose of adapting the government to the changing and improving condition of its people." Next, "it must be equally the part of a wise community to alter the maxims by which its foreign relations have in times past been regulated, in conformity with the changes that have taken place over the entire globe."[1] Such a period he conceived

[1] Advertisement to *Russia* (1836).

to have come for England in that generation, and it had come to her both from her internal conditions, and from the nature of her connexions with the other nations of the globe. The thought was brought to him not by deliberate philosophizing, but by observation and the process of native good sense, offering a fresh and open access to things. The cardinal fact that struck his eye was the great population that was gathering in the new centres of industry in the north of England, in the factories, and mines, and furnaces, and cyclopean foundries, which the magic of steam had called into such sudden and marvellous being.

1835-6.

Æt. 31-2.

It was with no enthusiasm that he reflected on this transformation that had overtaken the Western world, and in his first pamphlet he anticipated the cry, of which he heard more than enough all through his life, that his dream was to convert England into a vast manufactory, and that his political vision was directed by the interests of his order. "Far from nourishing any such *esprit-de-corps*," he says in the first pamphlet, "our predilections lean altogether in an opposite direction. We were born and bred up amid the pastoral charms of the south of England, and we confess to so much attachment for the pursuits of our forefathers, that, had we the casting of the parts of all the actors in this world's stage, we do not think we should suffer a cotton-mill or a manufactory to have a place in it. . . . But the factory system, which sprang from the discoveries in machinery, has been adopted by all the civilized nations in the world, and it is in vain for us to think of discountenancing its application to the necessities of this country; it only remains for us to mitigate, as far as possible, the evils that are perhaps not inseparably connected with this novel social element."

To this conception of the new problem Cobden always kept very close. This was always to him the foundation of the new order of things, which demanded a new kind of statesmanship and new ideas upon national policy. It is true that Cobden sometimes slips into the phrases of an older school, about the rights of man and natural law, but such lapses into the dialect of a revolutionary philosophy were very rare, and they were accidents. His whole scheme rested, if ever any scheme did so rest, upon the wide positive base of a great social expediency. To political exclusion, to commercial monopoly and restriction, to the preponderance of a territorial aristocracy in the legislature, he steadfastly opposed the contention that they were all fatally incompatible with an industrial system, which it was beyond the power of any statesman or any order in the country to choose between accepting and casting out.

Fifty years before this, the younger Pitt, when he said that any man with twenty thousand pounds a year ought to be made a peer if he wished, had recognized the necessity of admitting bankers and merchants to a share of the political dignity which had hitherto been confined to the great families. It had now ceased to be a question of a few peerages more or less for Lombard Street or Cornhill. Commercial interests no less than territorial interests were now overshadowed by industrial interests; the new difficulties, the new problems, the new perils, all sprang from what had taken place since William Pitt's time, the portentous expansion of our industrial system. Between the date of Waterloo and the date of the Reform Act, the power-looms in Manchester had increased from two thousand to eighty thousand, and the population of Birmingham had grown from ninety to one hundred and fifty thousand. The same wonders had come to pass in enormous districts over the land.

1835-6.

ÆT. 31-2.

Cobden was naturally led to begin his survey of society, as such a survey is always begun by the only kind of historian that is worth reading. He looked to wealth and its distribution, to material well-being, to economic resources, to their administration, to the varying direction and relative force of their currents. It was here that he found the key to the stability and happiness of a nation, in the sense in which stability and happiness are the objects of its statesmen. He declined to make any excuse for so frequently resolving questions of State policy into matters of pecuniary calculation, and he delighted in such business-like statements as that the cost of the Mediterranean squadron in proportion to the amount of the trade which it was professedly employed to protect, was as though a merchant should find that his traveller's expenses for escort alone were to amount to 6s. 8d. in the pound on his sales. He pointed to the examples in history, where some of the greatest and most revolutionary changes in the modern world had a fiscal or economic origin. And if Cobden had on his visit to Athens seen Finlay, he might have learnt from that admirable historian the same lesson on a still more imposing scale in the ancient world. He would have been told that even so momentous an event in the annals of human civilization as the disappearance of rural slavery in Europe, was less due to moral or political causes than to such a decline in the value of the products of slave-labour as left no profit to the slave-owner. From the fall of the Roman Empire to the mortal decay of Spain, and the ruin of the ancient monarchy of France, history shows that Cobden was amply justified in laying down the principle that the affairs

1835-6. — Æt. 31-2.

of a nation come under the same laws of common sense and homely wisdom which govern the prosperity of a private concern.

In material well-being he maintained, and rightly maintained, that you not only have the surest foundation for a solid fabric of morality and enlightenment among your people, but in the case of one of our vast and populous modern societies of free men, the only sure bulwark against ceaseless disorder and violent convulsion. It was not, therefore, from the side of emotional sympathy that Cobden started, but from that positive and scientific feeling for good order and right government which is the statesman's true motive and deepest passion. The sentimental benevolence to which Victor Hugo and Dickens have appealed with such power, could give little help in dealing with the surging uncontrollable tides of industrial and economic forces. Charity, it is true, had been an accepted auxiliary in the thinly peopled societies of the Middle Ages; but for the great populations and complex interests of the Western world in modern times, it is seen that prosperity must depend on policy and institutions, and not on the compassion of individuals.

It is not necessary that we should analyse the contents of pamphlets which any one may read through for himself in a few hours, and which well deserve to be read through even by those who expect their conclusions to be most repugnant. The pamphlet on *England, Ireland, and America* is a development of the following thought:—A nation is growing up on the other side of the Atlantic which by the operation of various causes, duly enumerated by the writer, must inevitably at no distant date enter into serious competition with our own manufactures. Apart from the natural advantages possessed by this new competitor, there are two momentous disadvantages imposed upon the English manufacturer, which tend to disable him in the struggle with his formidable rival. These two disadvantages are first, protection and the restriction of commerce; second, the policy of intervention in European feuds. The one loads us with a heavy burden of taxation and debt; the other aggravates the burden by limiting our use of our own resources. The place of Ireland in the argument, after a vivid and too true picture of the deplorable condition of that country, is to illustrate from the most striking example within the writer's own knowledge, "the impolicy and injustice of the statesmen who have averted their faces from this diseased member of the body politic; and at the same time have led us, thus maimed, into the midst of every conflict that has occurred on the continent of Europe." In fine, the policy of intervention ought to be abandoned, because it has created and continues to augment the debt, which shackles us in our industrial competition; because it has in every case been either mischievous or futile, and constantly so even in reference to its own professed ends; and because it has absorbed energy and resource that were imperiously demanded by every consideration of national duty for the improvement of the backward and neglected portions of our own realms.

In the second pamphlet the same principles are applied to the special case which the prejudice of the time made urgent. David Urquhart, a remarkable man, of prodigious activity, and with a singular genius for impressing his opinions upon all sorts of men from aristocratic dandies down to the grinders of Sheffield and the cobblers of Stafford, had recently published an appeal to England in favour of Turkey.

He had furnished the ministers with arguments for a policy to which they leaned by the instinct of old prejudice, and he had secured all the editors of the newspapers. Mr. Urquhart's book was the immediate provocation for Cobden's pamphlets. In the second of them the author dealt with Russia. With Russia we were then, as twenty years later and forty years later, and, as perhaps some reader of the next generation may write on the margin of this page, possibly sixty years later, urged with passionate imprecations to go to war in defence of European law, the balance of power, and the security of British interests.

Disclaiming a spirit of partiality for any principle of the foreign or the domestic policy of the Government of St. Petersburg, Cobden proceeded to examine each of the arguments by which it was then, as now, the fashion to defend an armed interference by England between Russia and Turkey. A free and pointed description, first of Turkey, and next of Russia, and a contrast between the creation of St. Petersburg and the decline of Constantinople, lead up to the propositions:—first, that the advance of Russia to the countries which the Turk once wasted by fire and sword, and still wastes by the more deadly processes of misgovernment, would be a great step in the progress of improvement; second, that no step in the progress of improvement and the advance of civilization can be inimical to the interests or the welfare of Great Britain. What advantage can it be to us, a commercial and manufacturing people, that countries placed in the healthiest latitudes and blessed with the finest climate in the world, should be retained in a condition which hinders their inhabitants from increasing and multiplying; from extracting a wealth from the soil which would enable them to purchase the products of Western lands; and so from changing their present poverty-stricken and plague-stricken squalor, for the manifold enjoyment of their share of all the products of natural resource and human ingenuity. As for Russia, her treatment of Poland was cruel and unjust, but let us at least put aside the cant of the sentimental declaimers who, amid a cloud of phrases about ancient freedom, national independence, and glorious republic, obscure the fact that the Polish nation meant only a body of nobles. About nineteen out of every twenty of the inhabitants were serfs without a single civil or political right; one in twenty was a noble; and the Polish nobles were the vainest, most selfish, most cruelly intolerant, most violently lawless aristocracy of ancient or modern times. Let us join by all means in the verdict of murder, robbery, treason, and perjury which every free and honest nation must declare against Russia, Prussia, and Austria for their undissembled wickedness in the partition. Let us go further, and admit that the infamy with which Burke, Sheridan, and Fox laboured to overwhelm the emissaries of British violence in India, was justly earned at the very same period by the minions of Russian despotism in Poland. But no honest man who takes the trouble to compare the condition of the true people of Poland under Russia, with their condition under their own tyrannical nobles a century ago—and here Cobden gives ample means of comparison—will deny that in material prosperity and in moral order of life the advance has been at least as great as in any other portion of the habitable globe. Apart from these historic changes, the Russo-maniac ideas of Russian power are demonstrably absurd. With certain slight modifications, Cobden's demonstration

1835-6.
ÆT. 31-2.

of their absurdity remains as valid now as it was forty years ago.

The keen and vigorous arguments by which Cobden attacked the figment of the balance of power are now tacitly accepted by politicians of all schools. Even the most eager partisans of English intervention in the affairs of other nations now feel themselves bound to show as plausibly as they can, that intervention is demanded by some peril to the interests of our own country. It is in vain that authors of another school struggle against Cobden's position, that the balance of power is not a fallacy nor an imposture, but a chimera, a something incomprehensible, undescribed, and indescribable. The attempted definitions of it fall to pieces at the touch of historic analysis. If we find the smaller states still preserving an independent existence, it is owing, Cobden said, not to the watchful guardianship of the balancing system, but to limits set by the nature of things to unduly extended dominion; not only to physical boundaries, but to the more formidable moral impediments to the invader,—"unity of language, law, custom and traditions; the instinct of patriotism and freedom; the hereditary rights of rulers; and, though last, not least, that homage to the restraints of justice, which nations and public bodies have in all ages avowed, however they may have found excuses for evading it."

That brilliant writer, the historian of the Crimean War, has described in a well-known passage what he calls the great Usage which forms the safeguard of Europe. This great Usage is the accepted obligation of each of the six Powers to protect the weak against the strong. But in the same page a limitation is added, which takes the very pith and marrow out of this moral and chivalrous Usage, and reduces

1835-6.
ÆT. 31-2

it to the very commonplace principle that nations are bound to take care of themselves. For, says the writer, no Power is practically under this obligation, unless its perception of the wrong that has been done is reinforced by a sense of its own interests.[1] Then it is the self-interest of each nation which is the decisive element in every case of intervention, and not a general doctrine about the balance of power, or an alleged common usage of protecting the weak against the strong? But that is exactly what Cobden started from. His premise was that "no government has the right to plunge its people into hostilities, except in defence of their own honour and interests." There would seem then to be no difference of principle between the military and the commercial schools of foreign policy. The trader from Manchester and the soldier from Aldershot or Woolwich, without touching the insoluble, because only half intelligible, problem of the balance of power, may agree to discuss the propriety of a given war on the solid ground of national self-interest. Each will be affected by professional bias, so that one of them will be apt to believe that our self-interest is touched at a point which the other will consider too remote to concern us; but neither can claim any advantage over the other as the disinterested champion of public law and the rights of Europe. If there is a difference deeper than this, it must be that the soldier or the diplomatist of the old school has really in his mind a set of opinions as to the ends for which a nation exists, and as to the relations of class-interests to one another, of such a colour that no serious politician in modern times would venture openly to avow them.

If the two theories of the duty of a nation in

[1] Kinglake, vol. i. ch. ii.

regard to war are examined in this way, we see how unreasonable it is that Cobden's theory of non-intervention should be called selfish by those who would be ashamed to base an opposite policy on anything else than selfishness. "Our desire," Cobden said, "is to see Poland happy, Turkey civilized, and Russia conscientious and free: it is still more our wish that these ameliorations should be bestowed by the hands of Britain upon her less instructed neighbours: so far the great majority of our opponents and ourselves are agreed. *How* to accomplish this beneficent purpose, is the question whereon we differ." They would resort, as Washington Irving said in a pleasant satire on us, to the cudgel, to promote the good of their neighbours and the peace and happiness of the world. There is one unanswerable objection to this, Cobden answered: experience is against it; it has been tried for hundreds of years, and has failed. He proposed to arrive at the same end by means of our national example, by remaining at peace, vigorously pursuing reforms and improvements, and so presenting that spectacle of wealth, prosperity, power, and invincible stability, which reward an era of peace wisely and diligently used. Your method, he said, cannot be right, because it assumes that you are at all times able to judge what will be good for others and the world—which you are not. And even if your judgment were infallible, the method would be equally wrong, for you have no jurisdiction over other states which authorizes you to do them good by force of arms.

The source of these arguments lay in three convictions. First, the Government of England must always have its hands full in attending to its domestic business. Second, it can seldom be sure which party is in the right in a foreign quarrel, and very seldom indeed be sure that the constituencies, ignorant and excitable as they are, will discern the true answer to that perplexing question. Finally, the government which keeps most close to morality in its political dealings, will find itself in the long-run to have kept most close to the nature of things, and to that success which rewards conformity to the nature of things. It followed from such reasoning as this that the author of the pamphlets denounced by anticipation the policy of compelling the Chinese by ships of war to open more ports to our vessels. Why, he asked in just scorn, should not the ships of war on their way out compel the French to transfer the trade of Marseilles to Havre, and thus save us the carriage of their wines through the Straits of Gibraltar? Where is the moral difference? And as to Gibraltar itself, he contended, that though the retention of conquered colonies may be regarded with some complacency, because they are reprisals for previous depredations by their parent states, yet England for fifty years at Gibraltar is a spectacle of brute violence, unmitigated by any such excuses. "Upon no principle of morality," he went on, "can this unique outrage upon the integrity of an ancient, powerful, and renowned nation be justified; the example, if imitated, instead of being shunned universally, would throw all the nations of the earth into barbarous anarchy." Here as everywhere else we see how wrong is the begetter of wrong, for if England had not possessed Gibraltar, she would not have been tempted to pursue that turbulent policy in the Mediterranean, which is still likely one day to cost her dear.[1]

[1] It is perhaps not out of place to mention that, several years ago, the present writer once asked Mr. Mill's opinion on the ques-

1835-6. — ÆT. 31-2.

Again, the immoral method has failed. Why not try now whether commerce will not succeed better than war, in regenerating and uniting the nations whom you would fain improve? Let governments have as little to do with one another as possible, and let people begin to have as much to do with one another as possible. Of how many cases of intervention by England does every Englishman now not admit that they were monstrous and inexcusable blunders, and that if we had pursued the alternative method of doing the work of government well at home and among our dependencies, improving our people, lightening the burdens of commerce and manufactures, husbanding wealth, we should have augmented our own material power, for which great national wealth is only another word; and we should have taught to the governments that had been exhausting and impoverishing themselves in war, the great lesson that the way to give content, enlightenment, and civil virtues, to your people, and a solid strength to their government, is to give them peace. It is thus, Cobden urged, that the virtues of nations operate both by example and precept; and such is the power and rank they confer, that in the end "states will all turn moralists in self-defence."

These most admirable pages were no mere rhetoric. They represented no abstract preference, but a concrete necessity. The writer was able to point to a nation whose example of pacific industry, wise care of the education of her young, and abstinence from such infatuated intervention as ours in the

tion of the possession of Gibraltar. His answer was that the really desirable thing in the case of strong places commanding the entrance to close seas is that they should be in the hands of a European League. Meanwhile, as the state of international morality is not ripe for such a League, England is perhaps of all nations least likely to abuse the possession of a strong place of that kind.

affairs of others, would, as he warned us, one day turn us into moralists in self-defence, as one day it assuredly will. It is from the peaceful nation in the West, and not from the military nations of the East, that danger to our strength will come. "In that portentous truth, *The Americas are free*, teeming as it does with future change, there is nothing that more nearly affects our destiny than the total revolution which it dictates to the statesmen of Great Britain in the commercial, colonial, and foreign policy of our Government. America is once more the theatre upon which nations are contending for mastery; it is not, however, a struggle for conquest, in which the victor will acquire territorial domain—the fight is for commercial supremacy, and will be won by the cheapest."[1] Yet in the very year in which Cobden thus predicted the competition of America, and warned the English Government to

[1] "Looking to the natural endowments of the North American continent—as superior to Europe as the latter is to Africa—with an almost immeasurable extent of river navigation—its boundless expanse of the most fertile soil in the world, and its inexhaustible mines of coal, iron, lead, etc.:—looking at these, and remembering the quality and position of a people universally instructed and perfectly free, and possessing, as a consequence of these, a new-born energy and vitality very far surpassing the character of any nation of the Old World—the writer reiterates the moral of his former work, by declaring his conviction that it is from the West, rather than from the East, that danger to the supremacy of Great Britain is to be apprehended;—that it is from the silent and peaceful rivalry of American commerce, the growth of its manufactures, its rapid progress in internal improvements, the superior education of its people, and their economical and pacific government—that it is from these, and not from the barbarous policy or the impoverishing armaments of Russia, that the grandeur of our commercial and national prosperity is endangered. *And the writer stakes his reputation upon the prediction, that, in less than twenty years, this will be the sentiment of the people of England generally; and that the same conviction will be forced upon the Government of the country.*" If Cobden had allowed fifty years, instead of twenty, for the fulfilment of his prediction, he would perhaps have been safe.

prepare for it by husbanding the wealth of the country and educating its people, the same assembly which was with the utmost difficulty persuaded to grant ten thousand pounds for the establishment of normal schools, spent actually fifty times as much in interfering in the private quarrels of two equally brutal dynastic factions in Spain. Our great case of intervention, between the rupture of the peace of Amiens and the battle of Waterloo, had left a deep and lasting excitability in the minds of Englishmen. They felt that if anything were going wrong in any part of the world, it must be owing to a default of duty in the British Government. One writer, for instance, drew up a serious indictment against the Whigs in 1834, on the ground that they had only passed a Reform Bill and a Poor Law Bill at home, while abroad the Dutch question was undecided; the French were still at Ancona; Don Carlos was fighting in Spain; Don Miguel was preparing for a new conflict in Portugal; Turkey and Egypt were at daggers drawn; Switzerland was quarrelling about Italian refugees; Frankfort was occupied by Prussian troops in violation of the treaty of Vienna; Algiers was being made a French colony, in violation of French promises made in 1829; ten thousand Polish nobles were still proscribed and wandering all over Europe; French gaols were full of political offenders. This pretty list of wrongs it was taken for granted that an English Ministry and English armies should make it their first business to set right. As Cobden said, if such ideas prevailed, the Whig Government would leave Providence nothing to attend to. Yet this was only the *reductio ad absurdum* of that excitability about foreign affairs which the long war had left behind. The vulgar kind of patriotic sentiment leads its professors to exult in military interventions even so indescribably foolish as this. What Cobden sought was to nourish that nobler and more substantial kind of patriotism, which takes a pride in the virtue and enlightenment of our own citizens, in the wisdom and success of our institutions, in the beneficence of our dealings with less advanced possessions, and in the lofty justice and independence of our attitude to other nations.

No one claims for Cobden that he was the first statesman who had dreamed the dream and seen the vision of a great pacification. Everybody has heard of the Grand Design of Henry the Fourth of France, with its final adjustment of European alliances, and its august Senate of the Christian Republic. In the eighteenth century, so rich as it was in great humane ideas, we are not surprised to find more than one thinker and more than one statesman enamoured of the policy of peaceful industry, from the Abbé de Saint Pierre, who denounced Lewis XIV. for seeking aggrandizement abroad while destroying prosperity at home, down to Kant, who wrote an essay on perpetual peace; and to the French Encyclopædists, who were a standing peace party down to the outbreak of the Revolution. Apart from these Utopias of a too hopeful philosophy, there is one practical statesman whom the historian of political opinion in England may justly treat as a precursor of Cobden's school. This is Lord Shelburne, the political instructor of the younger Pitt. He was the first powerful actor in our national affairs, in whom the great school of the Economists found a sincere disciple. It was to Morellet, the writer in the Encyclopædia and the friend of Turgot, rather even than to Adam Smith and Tucker, that Shelburne professed to owe those views on peace and international relations which appeared in the negotiations of his government with

France after the war with the American colonies, and which, alas, after a deplorable interval of half a century, the next person to enforce as the foundation of our political system, was the author of the two Manchester pamphlets. In the speech which closed his career as a Minister (1783), Shelburne had denounced monopoly as always unwise, but for no nation under heaven so unwise as for England. With more industry, he cried, with more enterprise, with more capital than any trading nation in the world, all that we ought to covet upon earth is free trade and open markets. His defence of the pacific policy as most proper for this country was as energetic as his enthusiasm for free trade, and he never displayed more vigour and conviction than when he attacked Pitt for allowing himself,—and this was before the war with the French Republic,—to be drawn again into the fatal policy of European intervention in defence of the integrity of the Turkish empire.

The reason why Shelburne's words were no more than a passing and an unheeded voice, while the teaching of Cobden's pamphlets stamped a deep impression on men's minds,—which time, in spite of inevitable phases of reaction and the temporary recrudescence of bad opinions, has only made more definite,—is the decisive circumstance which has already been sufficiently dwelt upon, that the huge expansion of the manufacturing interests had, when Cobden appeared, created a powerful public naturally favourable to the new principles, and raised what would otherwise have been only the tenets of a school into the programme of a national party.

As we shall see when we come to the Crimean War, the new principles did not at once crush out the old; it was not to be expected by any one who reflects on the strength of prejudice, especially prejudice supported by the consciousness of an honourable motive, that so sudden a change should take place. But the pamphlets are a great landmark in the history of politics in England, and they are still as well worth reading as they ever were. Some of the statements are antiquated; the historical criticism is sometimes open to doubt; there are one or two mistakes. But they are mostly like the poet's, who spoke of "*i miei non falsi errori.*" If time has weakened their literal force, it has confirmed their real significance.

1835-6.

ÆT. 31-2.

In a personal biography, it is perhaps not out of place to dwell in conclusion on a point in the two pamphlets, which is of very secondary importance compared with their political teaching, and yet which has an interest of its own; I mean the literary excellence of these performances. They have a ringing clearness, a genial vivacity, a free and confident mastery of expression, which can hardly be surpassed. Cobden is a striking instance against a favourite plea of the fanatics of Latin and Greek. They love to insist that a collegian's scholarship is the great source and fountain of a fine style. It would be nearer the truth to say that our classical training is more aptly calculated to destroy the qualities of good writing and fine speaking, than any other system that could have been contrived. Those qualities depend principally, in men of ordinary endowment, upon a certain large freedom and spontaneousness, and next upon a strong habit of observing things before words. These are exactly the habits of mind which our way of teaching, or rather of not teaching, Latin and Greek inevitably chills and represses in any one in whom literary faculty is not absolutely irrepressible.

What is striking in Cobden is that after a lost and wasted childhood, a youth of drudgery in a warehouse, and an early manhood passed amid the rather vulgar associations of the commercial traveller, he should at the age of one and thirty have stepped forth the master of a written style, which in boldness, freedom, correctness, and persuasive moderation, was not surpassed by any man then living. He had taken pains with his mind, and had been a diligent and extensive reader, but he had never studied language for its own sake.

It was fortunate for him that, instead of blunting the spontaneous faculty of expression by minute study of the verbal peculiarities of a Lysias or an Isocrates, he should have gone to the same school of active public interests and real things in which those fine orators had in their different degrees acquired so happy a union of homeliness with purity, and of amplitude with measure. These are the very qualities that we notice in Cobden's earliest pages; they evidently sprang from the writer's singular directness of eye, and eager and disinterested sincerity of social feeling, undisturbed as both these gifts fortunately were by the vices of literary self-consciousness.

CHAPTER V

LIFE IN MANCHESTER, 1837-9

A FEW weeks after Cobden's return home from the East, William the Fourth died (June 20), and the accession of Queen Victoria to the throne was followed by a general election. For some months Cobden's name had been before the politicians of Stockport, and while he was abroad, he had kept his brother constantly instructed how to proceed in the various contingencies of electioneering. Frederick Cobden seems even at this early stage to have expressed some not unnatural anxiety, lest public life should withdraw the indispensable services of his brother from their business. He had even remonstrated against any further pamphlets. "Do not fear," replied Richard Cobden, "I am not author-mad. But I have written a letter to the editor of the *Globe*, in which,"—and so forth.[1] He was in no sense author-mad, but still he was overflowing with thoughts and arguments and a zeal for the commonwealth, which made publication in one shape or another as much a necessity to him, as it is a necessity to a poet or an apostle. In the same letter, in answer to a friend's warning that he should not spoil his holiday by anxiety as to affairs at home, he said:—"I am not, I assure him, giving one

1837.

ÆT. 33.

[1] *To F. Cobden*, Nov. 11, 1836.

1837.

ÆT. 33.

moment's thought to the Stockport electors. The worthy folks may do as they please. They can make me M.P. by their favour, but they cannot mar my happiness if they reject me. It is 'the cause' with which I am in some degree identified, that makes me anxious about the result. Personally, as you well know, I would rather have my freedom for two years more." . . . "Let me say once for all, in reference to the Stockport affair, that I shall be quite happy, whichever way the die falls. You know me better than any other person, and I am sure you will believe that my peace or happiness does not depend upon external circumstances of this or any similar nature."[1]

Yet even in this free mood, Cobden knew his own mind, as he never failed to do, and he intended to be elected if possible. He belonged to the practical type, with whom to have once decided upon a course becomes in itself a strong independent reason for continuing in it. "One word as to your own private feelings," he writes to his brother, "which may from many causes be rather inclined to lead you to wish that my entrance into public life were delayed a little. I shall only say that on this head it is now too late to parley; it is now useless to waver, or to shrink from the realization of that which we had resolved upon and entered upon, not as children, but as men knowing that action must follow such resolves. Your temperament and mine are unequal, but in this matter I shall only remind you that *my* feelings are more deeply implicated than your own, and that whilst I can meet with an adequate share of fortitude any failure which comes from insuperable causes, whatever may be the object I have in view, yet if in this case my defeat should

[1] *To F. C.*, Jan. 4, 1837.

spring from your timidity or sensitiveness (shall I say *disinclination*?), it would afflict me severely, and I fear lastingly."[1]

As the election drew nearer, Cobden was overtaken by that eager desire to succeed, which gradually seizes even the most philosophical candidate as the passion of battle waxes hotter around him. He threw himself into the struggle with all his energy. It is historically interesting to know what Liberal electors were thinking about in those days. We find that they asked their candidate his opinion as to the property qualification for Members of Parliament, Primogeniture, the Poor Law Amendment Act, and the Factory Question. The last of the list was probably the most important, for Cobden had taken the trouble many months before to set out his opinions on that subject in a letter to the chairman of his committee. The matter remains of vital importance in our industrial system to the present time, and is still, in the face of the competition of other nations, the object of a controversy which is none the less alive in the region of theory, because the legislature has decided it in one way in the region of practice. As that is so, it is interesting still to know Cobden's earliest opinions on the matter; and I have therefore printed at the end of the volume the letter that Cobden wrote, in the autumn of 1836, on the restriction by Parliament of the hours of labour in factories.[2]

What he said comes to this, that for plain physical reasons no child ought to be put to work in a cotton mill so early as the age of thirteen, but whatever restrictions on the hours of labour might be desirable, it was not for the legislature to impose them: it was for the workmen to insist upon them, relying

[1] *To F. C.*, Jan. 28, 1837. [2] See Appendix, Note A.

1837.
—
ÆT. 33.

not on Parliament, but on their own action. A workman by saving the twenty pounds that would carry him across the Atlantic, could make himself as independent of his employer, as the employer is independent of him; and in this independence he would be free, without the emasculating interference of Parliament, to drive his own bargain as to how many hours he would work. In meeting his committee at Stockport, Cobden repeated his conviction that the factory operatives had it in their power to shorten the hours of labour without the aid of Parliament, but to infant labour, as he had said before, he would afford the utmost possible protection. He laughed at the mock philanthropy of the Tory landowners, who took so lively an interest in the welfare of the factory population, and yet declined to suffer the slightest relaxation of the Corn Laws, though these did more to degrade and pauperize the labouring classes, by doubling the price of food and limiting employment, than any other evil of which they had to complain.

Whether these views alienated any of those who would otherwise have supported him, we do not know. Probably the most effective argument against Cobden's candidature was the fact that he was a stranger to the borough. On the day of election he was found to be at the bottom of the poll.[1] He wrote to his uncle, Mr. Cole, explaining his defeat:—

"The cause of failure was that there was *too much confidence* on the part of the Reformers. We were too satisfied, and neglected those means of ensuring the election which the Tories used, and by their activity at Stockport as elsewhere they gained

[1] Henry Marsland (Reformer) 480; Major Marsland (Tory) 471; Richard Cobden (Reformer) 418.

the victory. If the battle had to be fought again to-morrow, I could win. To revenge themselves for the loss of their man, the Radicals have since the election adopted a system of exclusive dealing (*not countenanced by me*), and those publicans and shop-keepers who voted for the Major now find their counters deserted. The consequence is that the Reformers place printed placards over their shops, *Voted for Cobden*, inscribed in large characters, and the butchers and greengrocers in the market-place cry out from their stalls, Cobden beef, Cobden potatoes, etc. So you see I have not lost ground, by my failure at the poll, with the unwashed. But the truth is I am quite reconciled to the result. There are many considerations which make me conclude it is all for the best."[1]

His friends made arrangements for presenting him with a piece of plate, and seventeen thousand subscribers of one penny each raised the necessary fund. For some reason, Daniel O'Connell was invited to be present. He and Cobden drove together in an open carriage to Stockport (November 13, 1837), where they addressed an immense meeting in the open air, and afterwards spoke at a public dinner. To the great Liberator the reporter of the day generously accords three columns, while Cobden's words were condensed into that scanty space which is the common lot of orators who have won no spurs. His chief topic seems to have been the ballot; he declared that without that protection, household suffrage, the repeal of the Corn Laws, the shortening of parliaments, would all be insecure benefits. There is in this a certain inversion of his usual order of thinking about the proper objects of political solicitude, for he commonly paid much less heed to

[1] *To Mr. Cole*, Sept. 6, 1837.

1838.

ÆT. 34.

the machinery, than to the material objects of government.

It was quite as well for Cobden's personal interests that he was left free for a little time longer to attend to his business. The rather apprehensive character of his brother made him little able to carry on the trade in an intrepid and enterprising spirit, and at every step the judgment, skill, and energy of a stronger head were wanted. At this time the scale of the business which had started from such small beginnings had become so extensive that Cobden estimated the capital in it as no less than £80,000, with a credit in acceptances of at least £25,000: he represented the turn-over as £150,000.[1] In 1836 the books show that the nett profits of the firm had exceeded £23,000 for the year; and though the trade was so fluctuating that the first half of the following year only showed a profit of £4000, Cobden's sanguine temperament led him to speak as if their capital were being regularly augmented at the rate ot £2000 a month. We can easily understand Frederick Cobden's unwillingness to be left to his own resources in the administration of a business of this size, and his brother promised repeatedly not to throw so heavy a responsibility upon him. From the time of Cobden's return from the East they had both nourished the idea of separating from the London firm, as well as from the Sabden factory, and the idea remained in their minds for a couple of years. Then, as we shall presently see, it was carried into execution.

Cobden, however, had made up his mind after the Stockport election that to push his material fortunes was not to be the great aim of his life. "I am willing to give a few years of entire exertion," he

[1] *Letter to F. Cobden*, Feb. 24, 1837.

wrote in 1838, "towards making the separation successful to ourselves. But at the same time all my exertions will be with an eye to make myself independent of all business claims on my time and anxieties. Towards this, Henry and Charles [their two younger brothers] will for their own sakes, I expect, contribute. And I hope and expect in five years they will be in a situation to *force* me out of the concern, a *willing exile.* At all events I am sure there will not want talent of some kind about us, to take advantage of my determination to be at ease, and have some time for leisure to take care of my health, and indulge tastes which are in some degree essential to my happiness. With reference to health, both you and I must not omit reasonable precautions; we are not made for rivalling Methuselah, and if we can by care stave off the grim enemy for twenty years longer, we shall do more than nature intended for us. At all events let us remember that to live usefully is far better than living long. And do not let us deprive ourselves of the gratification at last, a gratification which the selfish never have, that we have not embittered our whole lives with heaping up money, but that we have given a part of our time to more rational and worthy exertions."[1]

Even now, when the indispensable work of laying a base of material prosperity was still incomplete, and when his own business might well have occupied his whole attention, he was always thinking much more earnestly about the interests of others than his own. The world of contemporaries and neighbours seldom values or loves this generous and unfamiliar spirit, and the tone of Manchester was in this respect not much higher than that of the rest of the world. It cannot surprise us to learn that for some time

[1] *To F. C.*, Oct. 26, 1838.

1838.
ÆT. 34.

Cobden made no great progress in Manchester society. He was extremely self-possessed and self-confident, and as a consequence he was often thought to be wanting in the respect that is due from a young man to his elders, and from a man who has a fortune to make, towards those who have made it. His dash, his freedom of speech, his ardour for new ideas, were taken for signs of levity; and a certain airy carelessness about dress marked a rebel against the minor conventions of the world. The patient endurance of mere ceremonial was at this time impossible to him. He could not be brought to attend the official dinners given by the Lord of the Manor. When he was selected to serve as assessor at the Court-leet for manorial purposes, though the occasion brought him into contact with men who might have been useful to him in his business, he treated the honour very easily. He sat restlessly on his bench, and then strolled away after an hour or two had shown him that the proceedings were without real significance. He could not even understand the urgency of more prudent friends that he should return. It was not conceit nor conscious defiance, but the incapacity inborn in so active and serious an intelligence, of contentedly muffling itself even for half a day under idle forms. He was born a political man; his most real interests in the world were wholly in affairs of government and institution, and his dominant passion was a passion for improvement. His whole mind was possessed by the high needs and great opportunities of society, as the minds of some other men have been possessed by the aspirations of religion, and he had as little humour for the small things of worldly punctilio as Calvin or as Knox may have had.

I have already described the relation of some of

Cobden's ideas to those of George Combe. It was, above all other things, for the sake of the prospect which it held out of supplying a sure basis and a trustworthy guide in the intricate and encumbered path of national education, that he was drawn for a time to Combe's system of phrenology. His letters during the years of which we are now speaking abound pretty freely in the terms of that crude catalogue, but with him they are less like the jargon of the phrenological fanatic of those days, than the good-humoured language of a man who believes in a general way that there is something in it. In 1835 he had been instrumental in forming a phrenological society in Manchester, and the first of a series of letters to Combe is one in 1836, pressing him to deliver a course of lectures in that town. It is interesting as an illustration of the amazing growth both in rational tolerance and scientific opinion, when we compare the very moderate heterodoxy of phrenology with the doctrines that in our own day are publicly discussed without alarm. "The Society which we profess to have here," Cobden writes, "is not well supported, and for nearly a twelvemonth it can hardly be said to have manifested many signs of existence.

"The causes are various why phrenology languishes, but probably the primary one may be sought in that feeling of fashionable timidity among the leading medical men and others who, although professing to support it privately, have not yet openly avowed themselves disciples of the science of Spurzheim and Gall. But phrenology is rapidly disenthralling itself from that 'cold obstruction' of ridicule and obloquy, which it has, in common with every other reform and improvement, had to contend against, and probably the mind of the community of Manchester presents at this moment as fine a field, in which to sow the seeds of instruction by means of a course of lectures by the author of *The Constitution of Man*, as could be found anywhere in the world. . . . The difficulty of religious prejudice exists here, and it requires delicate handling. Thanks, however, to the pursuits of the neighbourhood, to the enlightening chemical and mechanical studies with which our industry is allied, and to the mind-invigorating effect of an energetic devotion to commerce, we are not, as at Liverpool, in a condition to tolerate rampant exhibitions of intolerance here. . . . The High Church party stands sullenly aloof from all useful projects, and the severer sectarians restrict themselves here, as elsewhere, to their own narrow sphere of exertion, but the tone of public opinion in Manchester is superior to the influence of either of these extremes. How I pity you in Scotland, the only country in the world in which a wealthy and intelligent middling class submits to the domination of a spiritual tyranny."[1]

Though he was intolerant of the small politics of the Borough-reeve and the Constables, Cobden did not count it as small politics to agitate with might and main on behalf of the incorporation of the great city to which he belonged. His large comprehension of the greater needs of civilization and his country never at any time in his life dulled his interest in the need that lay close to his hand. The newspapers of the time show him to have been the moving spirit in the proceedings for incorporation, from the first requisition to the Borough-reeve and Constable to call a meeting of the rate-payers (February 3, 1838), down to the final triumph.

The Municipal Reform Act had been passed by

[1] *To George Combe*, Aug. 23, 1836.

Lord Melbourne's Government in 1835, on the return of the Whigs to power after the short Ministry of Sir Robert Peel. It was the proper complement to the greater Reform of 1832. By extending the principle of self-government from national to local affairs, it purified and enlarged the organs of administrative power, and furnished new fields of discipline in the habits of the good citizen. In 1833 Brougham had introduced a measure for immediately incorporating such towns as Manchester and Birmingham, and directly conferring local representative government upon them by Act of Parliament. But between 1833 and 1835 things had happened which quenched these spirited methods. A process which had been imperative in 1833, had by 1835 dwindled down to the permissive. Places were allowed to have charters, on condition that a majority of the rate-payers, being inhabitant householders, expressed their desire for incorporation by petition to the Crown in Council. A muddy sea of corruption and chicane was stirred up. All the vested interests of obstruction were on the alert. The close and self-chosen members of the Court Leet, and the Streets Commission, and the Town Hall Commission, could not endure the prospect of a system in which the public business would no longer be done in the dark, and the public money no longer expended without responsibility to those who paid it. The battle between privilege and popular representation which had been fought on the great scene at Westminster in 1832, was now resumed and fought out on the pettier stage of the new boroughs. The classes who had lost the power of bad government on a large national scale, tried hard to retain it on a small local scale. The low-minded and corrupt rabble of freemen and potwallopers united with those who were on principle the embittered enemies of all improvement, the noisy, inglorious Eldons of the provincial towns, and did their best to thwart the petitions. The Tories and the Residuum, to use the phrase of a later day, made that alliance which Cobden calls unholy, but which rests on the natural affinities of bigotry and ignorance. The Whig, as usual, was timid and uncomfortable; he went about murmuring that a charter was unnecessary, and muttered something about expense.

"When your former kind and friendly letter reached me," Cobden writes to Tait, the Edinburgh publisher, "I was engaged before the Commissioners, employed in exposing the trickery of the Tories in getting up their petition against the incorporation of our borough. For three weeks I was incessantly occupied at the Town Hall. By dint of hard work and some expense, we got at the filth in their Augean stable, and laid their dirty doings before the public eye. I believe now there is little doubt of our being chartered before the next November election, and it will be a new era for Manchester when it shakes off the feudal livery of Sir Oswald Mosley, to put on the democratic garb of the Municipal Reform Act.

"So important do I consider the step for incorporating the borough, that I have been incessantly engaged at the task for the last six months. I began by writing a letter of which I circulated five thousand copies, with a view of gaining the Radicals by showing the popular provisions of the Act. Will you credit it—the low, blackguard leaders of the Radicals joined with the Tories and opposed us. The Poor-law lunatics raised their demented yell, and we were menaced with nothing but defeat and annihilation at the public meeting. However, we sent a circular to every one of the £10 parliamentary electors who support liberal men, calling upon them to aid us at the public meeting, and they came forward to our rescue. The *shopocracy* carried the day. Two or three of the Tory-Radical leaders now entered the service of the Tories, with a view to obtain the signature of their fellows to a petition against incorporation. They pretended to get upwards of thirty thousand names, for which they were well paid. But the voting has shown that four-fifths were forgeries. So much for the unholy alliance of Tory and Radical!

"I mention all this as my best excuse for not having written to you, or for you, for so many months. What with going twice to London on deputations, and fighting the battle with two extreme political parties in Manchester, I have been so constantly engaged in action, that I have not had time for theorizing upon any topic. Still I have not abandoned the design of using my pen for your magazine. I have half collected materials for an article on convulsions in trade and banking, which when published will probably attract some notice from people engaged in such pursuits."[1]

"Not having received a word of news, good or bad, from you since I came here," he wrote to his brother, "I conclude that nothing particularly important can have occurred. You will have heard, I dare say, the result of our interview with the Lords of the Council. There is, I think, not a shadow of doubt of the ultimate result of the application, but I am not pleased with the Whig Ministry's mode of proceeding in these Corporation affairs. It is quite certain that they are willing we should be put to quite as much trouble by the Tories, as that party is

[1] *To Mr. W. Tait, of Edinburgh*, July 3, 1838.

able to impose on us. In the case of the Sheffield petition, I do not think the Charter will be granted at all, merely because the Tories have contrived to get a greater number of ragamuffins to sign against it, than have subscribed for the Charter. I saw one of the deputation to-day, who is quite disgusted with the whole set; and Scholefield of Birmingham told me that if he and Attwood had not bullied the Whigs, and threatened to vote against them, the Birmingham petition would not have been acceded to. They are a bad lot, and the sooner they go out, the better for the real reformers."[1]

"That truckling subserviency," he writes later in this year, "of the Ministry to the menaces of the Tories, is just in character with the conduct of the Whigs, on all questions great or little. Without principle or political honesty, they are likewise destitute of any atom of the courage or independence which honesty can inspire, and the party which bullies them most will be sure to command their obedience. In the matter of municipal institutions their hearts are against us. C. P. Thomson[2] told us plainly that he did not like local self-government, and are his Whig colleagues more liberal than he? I am sorry I am not at home to give a helping hand to my old colleagues. I will never desert, and if the matter be still in abeyance when I get back, I shall be ready and willing to give my assistance."

[1] *To F. W. Cobden*, London, May 4, 1838.

[2] Charles Poulett Thomson, afterwards Lord Sydenham, was one of the representatives of Manchester from 1832 to 1839. On the reconstruction of the Whig Government under Lord Melbourne, he was appointed to be President of the Board of Trade—a post which he afterwards gave up, in order to go out as Governor-General of Canada. As we shall see in a later chapter, he has a place in the apostolic succession of the Board of Trade, after Huskisson and Deacon Hume.

In the autumn of 1838, Lancashire was disturbed by torchlight meetings, destruction of property, and other formidable proceedings, under the lead of the Chartists,—Stephens, Oastler, and others. This superficial outbreak had no alarms for Cobden. In a vein which is thoroughly characteristic of the writer, he proceeds in the letter from which I have been quoting:—

"As respects general politics, I see nothing in the present radical outbreak to cause alarm, or make one dread the fate of liberalism. On the contrary, it is preferable to the apathy of the three years when prosperity (or seemingly so) made Tories of all. Nor do I feel at all inclined to give up politics in disgust, as you seem to do, because of the blunders of the Radicals. They are rash and presumptuous, or ignorant if you will, but are not the governing factions something worse? Is not selfishness, or systematic plunder, or political knavery as odious as the blunders of democracy? We must choose between the party which governs upon an exclusive or monopoly principle, and the people who seek, though blindly perhaps, the good of the vast majority. If they be in error we must try to put them right, if rash to moderate; but *never*, *never* talk of giving up the ship. . . . *I think the scattered elements may yet be rallied round the question of the Corn Laws. It appears to me that a moral and even a religious spirit may be infused into that topic, and if agitated in the same manner that the question of slavery has been, it will be irresistible.* I can give this question a great lift when I return, by publishing the result of my inquiries into the state of things on the Continent, and particularly with reference to the Prussian Union."[1]

Yet Cobden had in his heart no illusions on the

[1] *To F. C.*, Oct. 5, 1838.

1838.
Æt. 34.

subject of his countrymen, or their special susceptibility to either light or enthusiasm. He was well aware of the strong vault of bronzed prejudice which man mistakes for the luminous firmament of truth, and with him as with the philosophic reformers in France on the eve of the Revolution, the foundation of his hope lay in a *peuple éclairé*, the enlightenment of the population.

"Do not let your zeal for the cause of democracy," Cobden wrote to Tait, the Edinburgh bookseller, "deceive you as to the fact of the *opaque ignorance* in which the great bulk of the people of England are wrapt. If you write for the masses politically, and write soundly and honestly, they will not be able at present to appreciate you, and consequently will not support you. You cannot pander to the new Poor-law delusion, or mix up the Corn Laws with the Currency quackeries of Attwood. Nothing but these cries will go down with the herd at present. There is an obvious motive about certain agitators' movements. They hold up *impracticabilities*; their stock in trade will not fall short. Secondly, these prevent intelligent people from joining said agitators, who would be likely to supersede them in the eyes of their followers. There is no remedy for all this but improved education. Such as the tail and the body are, such will be the character of the head. Nature does not produce such monsters as an ignorant or vicious community, and virtuous and wise leaders. In Scotland you are better off because you are better educated. The great body of the English peasants are not a jot advanced in intellect since the days of their Saxon ancestors.

"I hope you will join us in a cry for schoolmasters as a first step to Radicalism. . . . Whilst I would caution you against too much political stuff in your magazine, let me pray you to strike a blow for us for education. I have unbounded faith in the people, and would risk universal suffrage to-morrow in preference to the present franchise. But we shall never obtain even an approach towards such a change, except by one of two paths — Revolution or the Schoolhouse. By the latter means we shall make permanent reform; by the former we shall only effect convulsive and transient changes, to fall back again like Italy, or Spain, into despotism or anarchy."[1]

In August 1838, Cobden again started for a month's tour in Germany, partly perhaps to appease that spirit of restlessness which made monotony the worst kind of fatigue, and partly to increase his knowledge of the economic condition of other countries. "What nonsense," he once exclaimed, "is uttered even by the cleverest men when they get upon that least of all understood, and yet most important of all topics, the Trade of this country! And yet every dunce or aristocratic blockhead fancies himself qualified by nature to preach upon this complicated and difficult question."[2] He was careful not to lay himself open to the same reproach of trusting to the light of nature for wide and accurate knowledge, and he turned his holiday in the countries of the Elbe and the Rhine to good account by getting together, as he said, some ammunition about the Corn Laws. This subject was now beginning definitely to take the chief place in his interests.

There remains among his correspondence with his brother during this trip, one rather remarkable letter, the doctrine of which many of my readers will certainly resent, and it is indeed open to serious criticism. The doctrine, however, is too char-

[1] *To W. Tait*, Aug. 17, 1838.
[2] *Ibid*. May 5, 1837.

1838. — Æt. 34.

acteristic of a peculiarity in Cobden's social theory, for me to omit this strong illustration of it; characteristic, I mean, of his ruling willingness, shown particularly in his dealings with the Emperor of the French in 1860, and on some other occasions, to treat political considerations as secondary to those of social and economic well-being.

"Although," he says, "a very rapid one, my journey has given me a better insight into German character and the prospects of Central Europe than I could have ever gained from the eyes of others. Prussia must be looked upon as a rising state, whose greatness will be based upon the Commercial League [the Zollverein].[1] . . . The effect of the League must inevitably be to throw the preponderating influence over thirty millions of people into the hands of the Cabinet of Berlin. By the terms of the Union, the money is to be collected and paid by Prussia; a very little financial skill will thus very easily make the smaller states the pensioners of the paymaster. Already, I am told, Prussia has been playing this game; she is said to be two millions of dollars a year out of pocket by her office, owing to her having guaranteed the smaller partners certain amounts of revenue. Besides the power that such a post of treasurer will confer upon Prussia, other causes must tend to weaken the influence of the lesser states' governments. A common standard of weights and measures, as well as of money, is preparing, and

[1] The Zollverein or Customs Union had been planned as far back as 1818, but it was not until 1833 that the treaty was signed which bound most of the German states, except Austria, to a policy of free trade among themselves, while protective duties were maintained against foreign nations. Poulett Thomson and other English officials of the same liberal stamp, rightly regarded the new system without apprehension, for it recognized the expediency of abolishing commercial restrictions over a great area, though the area was not quite great enough.

these being assimilated, and the revenue received from Prussia, whose literature and modes will become the standard for the other portions of Germany, what shall prevent this entire family of one common language, and possessing perfect freedom of intercourse, from merging into one nation? In fact they are substantially one nation now, and their remaining subdivisions will become by and by only imaginary; and some Radicals will hereafter propose, as we have done in Manchester, to get rid of the antiquated boundaries of the *townships* of Hesse, Oldenburg, etc., and place the whole under one Common Council at Berlin. There are heads in Berlin which have well reflected upon this, and their measures will not disappoint their country.

"I very much suspect that at present, for the great mass of the people, Prussia possesses the best Government in Europe. I would gladly give up my taste for talking politics to secure such a state of things in England. Had our people such a simple and economical Government, so deeply imbued with justice to all, and aiming so constantly to elevate mentally and morally its population, how much better would it be for the twelve or fifteen millions in the British Empire, who, while they possess no electoral rights, are yet persuaded they are freemen, and who are mystified into the notion that they are not political bondmen, by that great juggle of the '*English Constitution*'—a thing of monopolies, and Church-craft, and sinecures, armorial hocus-pocus, primogeniture, and pageantry! The Government of Prussia is the mildest phase in which absolutism ever presented itself. The king, a good and just man, has, by pursuing a systematic course of popular education, shattered the sceptre of despotism even in his own hand, and has for ever prevented his suc-

1838.
—
ÆT. 34.

cessors from gathering up the fragments. . . . You have sometimes wondered what becomes of the thousands of learned men who continually pass from the German universities, whilst so few enter upon mercantile pursuits. Such men hold all the official and Government appointments; and they do not require £1000 a year to be respectable or respected in Prussia. Habits of ostentatious expenditure are not respectable there. The king dines at two, rides in a plain carriage, without soldiers or attendants, and dresses in a kind of soldier's relief cap. The plays begin at six and close at nine, and all the world goes to bed at ten or eleven."[1]

It is to be remembered in reading this, that it was written forty years ago. Not a few considerate observers even now hold that the prospect of German progress which Cobden sketches, would have been happily realized, if Prussian statesmen of a bad school had not interrupted the working of orderly forces by a policy of military violence which precipitated unity, it is true, but at a cost to the best causes in Germany and Europe, for which unity, artificial and unstable as it now is, can be no worthy recompense. As for the contempt which the passage breathes for the English constitution, it is easy to understand the disgust which a statesman with the fervour of his prime upon him, and with an understanding at once too sincere and too strong to be satisfied with conventional shibboleths, might well feel alike for the hypocrisy and the shiftlessness of a system, that behind the artfully painted mask of popular representation concealed the clumsy machinery of a rather dull plutocracy. It is not right to press the phrases of the hasty letter of a traveller too closely. If, as it is reasonable to think, Cobden only meant that the

[1] *To F. Cobden*, Sept. 11, 1838.

energetic initiative of central authorities in promoting the moralization of a country is indispensable in the thick populations and divided interests of modern times, and that the great want of England is not a political equality which she has got, nor a natural equality, which neither England nor any other country is ever likely to get, but a real equality in access to justice and in chances of mental and moral elevation,—then he was feeling his way to the very truths which, of all others, it is most wholesome for us to understand and to accept. Whatever we may think of the good word which Cobden seems to have for beneficent absolutism, it is at least a mark of true sagacity to have discerned that manners may have as much to do with the happiness of a people, as has the form of their government.

In a letter to his sister, he shows that his journey has supplied him with material for an instructive contrast:—"Let me give you an idea of society here by telling you how I spent yesterday, being *Sunday*. In the first place I went to the cathedral church at nine o'clock in the morning, a very large building, pretty well filled (the ladies were as five to one in the congregation, against the number of male attendants).

"The singing would have been a treat; but unhappily I was placed beside a little old man whose devotion was so great, that he sang louder than all the congregation, in a screaming tone that pierced my tympanum. I heard nothing but the deep notes of the organ, and the little man's notes still ring in my ears, and his ugly little persevering face will haunt me till I reach the Rhine. The sermon lasted forty minutes; the service was all over in one hour and a half, and at eleven o'clock I went in a coach to the country palace of the king at Charlottenburg, where is a splendid mausoleum and a statue of his late wife to be seen. The statue is a masterpiece of the first Prussian sculptor, and as I always criticise masterpieces, I thought it stiff. Passing through a wood laid out in pleasant walks, interspersed with sheets of water and provided with seats, I saw numbers of the cockneys strolling about, and again I might have fancied myself in Kensington Gardens. But the variety of head-dress, the frequent absence of the odious bonnet which seems a part of the Englishwoman's nature, and the substitution of the lace or gauze covering, which aids rather than hides the prettiest accessory of a woman's face, her well-managed hair, reminded me that I was from home. It was a quarter to two as I returned, and I met the king's sons going to dine with their father, who takes that meal exactly at two. So you see we are not so unfashionable in Quay Street as we imagined. After taking a hasty dinner myself, I hired a horse and rode again into the country by another road, and visited the Tivoli Gardens. On the way I passed some good houses, the families of which were all outside, either in balconies or in the gardens before the door, with tables laid out with refreshments, at which the gentlemen were smoking, the ladies knitting or sewing, and perhaps the children playing around with frolicsome glee. All this close to the great thoroughfare to Tivoli, along which crowds of pedestrians of all ranks, and great numbers of carriages and horsemen, were proceeding. Yet nobody turned his head to sneer, or to insult others; there was no intrusion or curiosity. I thought of Old England, and as I knew it would be impossible there to witness such a scene, I hope I did right in condemning the good people of Berlin for their *irreligious* conduct. At the Tivoli Gardens, which are about two miles from the town, they have a good view of the city. Here are Montagnes Russes and other amusements. The day was splendid, and such a scene! Hundreds of well-dressed and still better behaved people were lounging or sitting in the large gardens, or several buildings of this gay retreat; in the midst were many little tables at which groups were sitting. The ladies had their work-bags, and were knitting, or sewing, or chatting, or sipping coffee or lemonade; the gentlemen often smoking, or perhaps flirting with their party. Then the scene at the Montagnes Russes! The little carriages were rattling down one after another along this undulating railroad with parties of every kind and age, from the old officer to the kitten-like child, who clung with all its claws to the nurse, or sister, or mamma who gave it the treat. Then there was music, and afterwards fireworks, and so went off the day at Tivoli, without clamour, rudeness, or drunkenness. After Tivoli I looked in at the two principal theatres, which were crammed; and so ended the day which to me was not a day of rest. If you think this is an improper picture of a Protestant Sunday, on the other hand, the sober and orderly German thinks the drunkenness, the filthy public-houses, the miserable and moping mechanic that pines in his dark alley in our English cities on the Sabbath Day, are infinitely worse features of a Protestant community, than his Tivoli Gardens. Are both wrong?"[1]

With one other and final contrast, we may leave the memorials of the foreign tour of 1838:—

"I do hope the leather-headed bipeds who soak themselves upon prosperous market-days in brandy and water at the White Bear, will be brought to the temperature of rational beings by the last twelve

[1] *To Miss Cobden*, Sept. 3, 1838.

months' regimen of low prices. And then let us hope that we may see them trying at least to bestow a little thought upon their own interests, in matters beyond the range of their factory walls. It humiliates me to think of the class of people at home, who belong to the order of intelligent and educated men that I see on the Continent, following the business of manufacturing, spinning, etc. Our countrymen, if they were possessed of a little of the *mind* of the merchants and manufacturers of Frankfort, Chemnitz, Elberfeld, etc., would become the De Medicis, and Fuggers, and De Witts of England, instead of glorying in being the toadies of a clodpole aristocracy, only less enlightened than themselves!"[1]

In other words they would become the powerful and independent statesmen of the country, the creators and champions of a new policy adapted to the ends of a great trading community. Thrusting aside the nobles by force of vigorous intellectual and moral ascendency, the wealthy middle class would place themselves at the head of a national life with new types and wiser ideals. Any one who reflects on the gain for good causes in England, if only the foremost men of this class would dare to be themselves, and show by grave and self-respecting example that a great citizen is beyond the rivalry of the great noble, will cherish the vision that passed for an instant before Cobden's social imagination. As for his contrast between the educated traders of the Continent, and the haunters of the White Bear with their leathern heads, we may be sure that all this was the result of true observation, and was due to no childish propensity to think everything abroad better than anything at home. Cobden had far too much integrity of understanding to yield either to

[1] *To F. C.*, Oct. 6, 1838.

the patriotic bias, or the anti-patriotic bias; and he knew able men when he saw them, as well in his own country as elsewhere.

In the summer of the previous year he had, in one of his visits to London, sought the acquaintance of some of the prominent journalists and politicians, and he wrote down his impressions of them.

"Yesterday,"—this was in June 1837—"we went along with Cole to see the print-works of Surrey, and dined with Makepeace. The day before, being Sunday, I went in the morning to hear Benson (in the Temple Church) abuse the Dissenters and the Catholics, and compare the persecuted Church of England to the ark of the Israelites, when encompassed by the Amalekites. . . . Then I went to the Zoological Gardens, and after staying there till the last minute, I accompanied Cole home to his house, and dined and slept. . . . On Saturday in the morning I was at the Clubs; was introduced to Fonblanque (*Examiner*), Rintoul (*Spectator*), Bowring, Howard Elphinstone, etc. In the evening of the same day I dined with Hindley, and met ——, ——, ——, etc. etc. [a party of north-country members of Parliament and candidates]. They are a sad lot of soulless louts, and I was, as compared with the intellectual atmosphere of the morning, precipitated from the temperature of blood heat down to zero. . . . I have not seen C. P. Thomson. I have left my card and address, but he has not noticed it, and if he does not send, I'll not call again.

"I hear queer accounts of our Right Hon. Member; they tell me he is not the man of business we take him for. We shall see. *The more I see of our representatives from Lancashire, the more ashamed I feel at being so served*, and like Falstaff I begin to dread the idea of going through Coventry (for at Coventry they are generally to be found) with such a crew. I suppose you will have more failures by and by amongst the people at Manchester and Liverpool. I begin now to fear that our distress will be greater and more permanent than I had expected at first. It will be felt here, too, for some time, in failures amongst those old merchant princes who are princes only at spending, but whose gettings have been and will be small enough. The result of all will be that Liverpool and Manchester will more and more assume their proper rank as commercial capitals. London must content itself with a gambling trade in the bills drawn by those places.

"I have had invitations without end, and shall if I stay a year still be in request; but too much talking and running about will not suit me, and I am resolved to turn churlish and morose. I have seen, through S——'s friend T——, some of the Urquhart party: they are as mad as ever. I have called upon Roebuck, but have not been able to see him."[1]

"I was yesterday introduced to Mrs. and Mr. Grote at their house. I use the words Mrs. and Mr. because she is the greater politician of the two. He is a mild and philosophical man, possessing the highest order of moral and intellectual endowments; but wanting something which for need of a better phrase I shall call *devil.* He is too abstract in his tone of reasoning, and does not aim to influence others by any proof excepting that of ratiocination; *tusy musy*, as Braham calls it, he is destitute of. Had she been a man, she would have been the leader of a party; he is not calculated for it.

[1] *To F. Cobden*, June 6, 1837.

"I met at their house (which by the way is the great resort of all that is clever in the Opposition ranks) Sir W. Molesworth, a youthful, florid-looking man of foppish and conceited air, with a pile of head at the back (firmness) like a sugar-loaf. I should say that a cast of his head would furnish one of the most singular illustrations of phrenology. For the rest he is not a man of superior talents, and let him *say* what he pleases, there is nothing about him that is democratic in principle. . . .

"I have been visiting, and visited by, all sorts of people, the Greek Ambassador, Wm. Allen, of Plough Court, the chemist and Quaker philanthropist, Roebuck, and Joseph Parkes, of Birmingham, amongst the number. I spent a couple of hours with Roebuck at his house. He *is* a clever fellow, but I find that his mind is more active than powerful. He is apt to take lawyer-like views of questions, and, as you may see by his speeches, is given to cavilling and special pleading. . . .

"Easthope of the *Chronicle* is very anxious that I should see Lord Palmerston, but I told him I had made up my mind that his lordship is incurable. He says that he is open to conviction, and a cleverer man than most of his colleagues. What a beautiful *ensemble* they must be! I have seen nothing of C. P. Thomson; I would have called again, but I think it better to reserve myself till he calls on me. I hear from all sides that he is not the man of business we take him for in Manchester. Although I have been so much taken up with new acquaintances, I have not failed to make calls upon all our old friends and relations."[1]

"One of the very cleverest men I have ever met with is Joseph Parkes, late of Birmingham, the eminent

[1] *To F. Cobden*, June 12, 1837.

1837. — ÆT. 33.

constitutional lawyer and writer. He was employed to prepare the Municipal Bill and other measures. He is not only profound in his profession, but skilled in political economy, and quite up to the spirit of the age in practical and popular acquirements. He has been very civil to me. He received a letter from his friend Lord Durham, requesting him to find out who the author of *Russia*, etc., was, as those pamphlets contained more statesmanlike views than all the heads of the whole British Cabinet. His lordship goes thoroughly and entirely with me in my principles upon Turkey. Perhaps the truth is he went to St. Petersburg with opposite views, but having been wheedled by the Czar and his wife, he is glad to find in my arguments some useful pleas for justifying his change."[1]

One general impression of great significance Cobden acquired from this and some later visits to London. Combe had in one of his letters been complaining of the bigotry with which he had to contend in Scotland. "What you say of the intolerance of Scotland," said Cobden to him in reply, "applies a good deal to Manchester also. There is but one place in the kingdom in which a man can live with perfect freedom of thought and action, and that is London."[2] However, he acted on the old and worthy principle, *Spartam nactus es, hanc exorna*, and did not quarrel with the society in which his lot was cast, because it preferred the echoes of its own prejudices to any unfamiliar note.

Manchester did not receive its charter of incor-

[1] The Czar said to Sir Robert Peel :—"Years ago Lord Durham was sent to me, a man full of prejudices against me. By merely coming to close quarters with me, all his prejudices were driven clean out of him."—Stockmar, quoted in Mr. Martin's *Life of the Prince Consort*, i. 216.

[2] *To G. Combe*, March 9, 1841.

poration until the autumn of 1838. Cobden's share in promoting this important reform was recognized by the inhabitants of the new borough, and he was chosen for alderman at the first election. The commercial capital of Lancashire was now to show its fitness to be the source and centre of a great national cause.

1838.

ÆT. 34.

CHAPTER VI

THE FOUNDATION OF THE LEAGUE

1838.
Æt. 34.

THE French economist who recounted to his countrymen the history of the great agitation in which Cobden now gradually rose to a foremost place, justly pointed out that the name and title of the Anti-Corn-Law League gave to foreigners a narrow and inadequate idea of its scope, its depth, and its animating spirit. What Bastiat thus said with regard to foreigners, is just as true with regard to ourselves of a later generation. We too are as apt as Frenchmen or Germans to think narrowly and inadequately of the scope and animating spirit of this celebrated confederation. Yet the interest of that astonishing record of zeal, tact, devotion, and courage, into some portions of which the biographer of Cobden has now to enter, lies principally for us in the circumstance that the abolition of the protective duties on food and the shattering of the protective system was, on one side, the beginning of our great modern struggle against class preponderance at home, and on another side, the dawn of higher ideals of civilization all over the world.

It was not of himself assuredly that Cobden was speaking, when at the moment of the agitation reaching its height, he confessed that when it first began they had not all possessed the same comprehensive view of the interests and objects involved, that came to them later. "I am afraid," he said, "that most of us entered upon this struggle with the belief that we had some distinct class-interest in the question, and that we should carry it by a manifestation of our will in this district, against the will and consent of other portions of the community."[1] There was in this nothing that is either astonishing or discreditable. The important fact was that the class-interest of the manufacturers and merchants happened to fall in with the good of the rest of the community; while the class-interest against which they were going up to do battle, was an uncompensated burden on the whole commonwealth. Besides this, it has been observed on a hundred occasions in history, that a good cause takes on in its progress larger and unforeseen elements, and these in their turn bring out the nobler feelings of the best among its soldiers. So it was here. The class-interest widened into the consciousness of a commanding national interest. In raising the question of the bread-tax, and its pestilent effects on their own trade and on the homes of their workmen, the Lancashire men were involuntarily opening the whole question of the condition of England.

The backbone of the discussion in its strictly local aspect was in the question which Cobden and his friends at this time kept incessantly asking. With a population increasing at the rate of a thousand souls a day, how can wages be kept up, unless there be constantly increasing markets found for the employment of labour; and how can foreign countries buy our manufactures, unless we take in return their corn, timber, or whatever else they are able to produce? Apart, moreover, from increase

[1] Speech at Manchester, Oct. 19, 1843.

of population, is it not clear that if capitalists were free to exchange their productions for the corn of other countries, the workmen would have abundant employment at enhanced wages? A still more formidable argument even than these lay in the mouths of the petitioners. They boldly charged Parliament with fostering the rivalry of foreign competitors; and the charge could not be answered. By denying to America and to Germany the liberty of exchanging their surplus food for our manufactures, the English Legislature had actually forced America and Germany to divert their resources from the production of food, in order to satisfy their natural demand for manufactures. It was the Corn Laws which nursed foreign competition into full vitality.

But this strictly commercial aspect could not suffice. Moral ideas of the relations of class to class in this country, and of the relations of country to country in the civilized world, lay behind the contention of the hour, and in the course of that contention came into new light. The promptings of a commercial shrewdness were gradually enlarged into enthusiasm for a far-reaching principle, and the hard-headed man of business gradually felt himself touched with the generous glow of the patriot and the deliverer.

Cobden's speculative mind had speedily placed the conflict in its true relation to other causes. We have already seen how ample a conception he possessed of the transformation for which English society was ripe, and how thoroughly he had accustomed himself to think of the Corn Laws as merely part of a great whole of abuse and obstruction. But he was now, as at all times, far too wise a man to fall into the characteristic weakness of the system-monger, by passing over the work that lay to his hand, and insisting that people should swallow his system whole. Nobody knew better how great a part of wisdom it is for a man who seeks to improve society, to be right in discerning at a given moment what is the next thing to be done, or whether there is anything to be done at all. His interest in remoter issues did not prevent him from throwing himself with all the energy of apostolic spirit upon the particular point at which the campaign of a century first opened. As he said to his brother in a letter that has already been quoted, he had convinced himself that a moral, and even a religious, spirit might be infused into the question of the Corn Laws, and that if it were agitated in the same manner as the old question of slavery, the effect would be irresistible.[1]

Cobden was in no sense the original projector of an organized body for throwing off the burden of the corn duties. In 1836 an Anti-Corn-Law Association had been formed in London; its principal members were the parliamentary Radicals, Grote, Molesworth, Joseph Hume, and Mr. Roebuck. But this group, notwithstanding their acuteness, their logical penetration, and the soundness of their ideas, were in that, as in so many other matters, stricken with impotence. Their gifts of reasoning were admirable, but they had no gifts for popular organization, and neither their personality nor their logic offered anything to excite the imagination or interest the sentiment of the public. "The Free Traders," Lord Sydenham said, with a pang, in 1841, "have never been orators since Mr. Pitt's early days. We hammered away with facts and figures and some arguments; but we could not elevate the subject and excite the feelings of the people." An economic demonstration went

[1] Above, p. 137.

for nothing, until it was made alive by the passion of suffering interests and the reverberations of the popular voice. Lord Melbourne, in 1838, sharply informed all petitioners for the repeal of the Corn Laws, that they must look for no decided action on the part of the Government, until they had made it quite clear that the majority of the nation were strongly in favour of a new policy. London, from causes that have often been explained and are well understood, is no centre for the kind of agitation which the Prime Minister, not without some secret mockery, invited the repealers to undertake. In London there is no effective unity; interests are too varied and dispersive; zeal loses its directness and edge amid the distracting play of so many miscellaneous social and intellectual elements. It was not until a body of men in Manchester were moved to take the matter in hand, that any serious attempt was made to inform and arouse the country.

The price of wheat had risen to seventy-seven shillings in the August of 1838; there was every prospect of a wet harvesting; the revenue was declining; deficit was becoming a familiar word; pauperism was increasing; and the manufacturing population of Lancashire were finding it impossible to support themselves, because the landlords, and the legislation of a generation of landlords before them, insisted on keeping the first necessity of life at an artificially high rate. Yet easy as it is now to write the explanation contained in the last few words, comparatively few men had at that time seized the truth of it. That explanation was in the stage of a vague general suspicion, rather than the definite perception of a precise cause. Men are so engaged by the homely pressure of each day as it comes, and the natural solicitudes of common life are so instant, that a bad institution or a monstrous piece of misgovernment is always endured in patience for many years after the remedy has been urged on public attention. No cure is considered with an accurate mind, until the evil has become too sharp to be borne, or its whole force and weight brought irresistibly before the world by its more ardent, penetrative, and indomitable spirits.

In October 1838, a band of seven men met at a hotel in Manchester, and formed a new Anti-Corn-Law Association. They were speedily joined by others, including Cobden, who from this moment began to take a prominent part in all counsel and action.

That critical moment had arrived, which comes in the history of every successful movement, when a section arises within the party, which refuses from that day forward either to postpone or to compromise. The feeling among the older men was to stop short in their demands at some modification of the existing duty. This was the mind of the President and most of the directors of the Manchester Chamber of Commerce. A meeting of this important body was held in December (1838). The officers of the Chamber had, only for the second time in ten years, prepared a petition to the House of Commons, but the petition spoke only of modifications, and total repeal was not whispered. The more energetic members protested against these faltering voices. Cobden struck into the debate with that finely tempered weapon of argumentative speech, which was his most singular endowment. The turbid sediment of miscellaneous discussion sank away, as he brought out a lucid proof that the Corn Law was the only obstacle to a vast increase of their trade, and that every shilling of the protection on corn which thus obstructed their prosperity, passed into the pockets of the land-owners, without conferring an atom of advantage on either the farmer or the labourer.

The meeting was adjourned, to the great chagrin of the President, and when the members assembled a week later, Cobden drew from his pocket a draft petition which he and his allies had prepared in the interval, and which after a discussion of many hours was adopted by an almost unanimous vote. The preamble laid all the stress on the alleged facts of foreign competition, in words which never fail to be heard in times of bad trade. It recited how the existing laws prevented the British manufacturer from exchanging the produce of his labour for the corn of other countries, and so enabled his foreign rivals to purchase their food at one half of the price at which it was sold in the English market; and finally the prayer of the petition called for the repeal of all laws relating to the importation of foreign corn and other foreign articles of subsistence, and implored the House to carry out to the fullest extent, both as affects manufactures and agriculture, the true and peaceful principles of Free Trade.

In the following month, January 1839, the Anti-Corn-Law Association showed that it was in earnest in the intention to agitate, by proceeding to raise a subscription of an effective sum of money. Cobden threw out one of those expressions which catch men's minds in moments when they are already ripe for action. "Let us," he said, "invest part of our property, in order to save the rest from confiscation." Within a month six thousand pounds had been raised, the first instalment of many scores of thousands still to come. A great banquet was given to some of the parliamentary supporters of Free

Trade; more money was subscribed, convictions became clearer, and purpose waxed more resolute. On the day after the banquet, at a meeting of delegates from other towns, Cobden brought forward a scheme for united action among the various associations throughout the country. This was the germ of what ultimately became the League. It is worth noticing that more than four years before this, he had in his first pamphlet sketched in a general form the outlines of the course eventually followed by the League,—so fertile was his mind in practical methods of enlightening opinion, even without the stimulation of a company of sympathetic agitators. There he had asked how it was that so little progress had been made in the study of which Adam Smith was the great luminary, and why, while there were Banksian, Linnæan, Hunterian societies, there was no Smithian society, for the purpose of disseminating a more just knowledge of the principles of trade. Such a society might enter into correspondence with similar bodies abroad, and so help to amend the restrictive policy of foreign governments, while at home prizes might be offered for the best essays on the Corn question, and lecturers might be sent to enlighten the agriculturalists, and to invite discussion upon a subject which, while so difficult, was yet of such paramount interest to them and to the rest of the country.[1] The hour for the partial application of these very ideas had now come. Before the month of January, the Manchester Anti-Corn-Law Association was completely organized, and its programme laid before the public. The object was declared to be to obtain by all legal and constitutional means, such as the formation of local associations, the delivery of lectures, the distribution of tracts, and

[1] Cobden's *Political Writings*, i. 32.

the presentation of petitions to Parliament, the total and immediate repeal of the Corn and Provision Laws. Cobden was appointed to be a member of the executive committee, and he continued in that office until the close of the agitation.

In the February of 1839, as Cobden gaily reminded a great audience on the eve of victory six years later, three of them in a small room at Brown's hotel in Palace Yard were visited by a nobleman who had taken an active part in advocating a modification of the Corn Laws, but who could not bring himself to the point of total repeal. He asked what had brought them to town, and what it was that they wanted. They had come, they said, to seek the total and immediate repeal of the Corn Laws. With an emphatic shake of the head, he answered, "You will overturn the monarchy as soon as you will accomplish that."[1] For the moment it appeared as if this were really true. Mr. Villiers moved in the House of Commons (Feb. 18), that a number of petitions against the Corn Laws should be referred to a Committee of the whole House. The motion was negatived without a division. The next day he moved that certain members of the Manchester Association should be heard at the bar, in support of the allegations of a petition which they had presented three days before. Though this was a Whig Parliament, or because it was a Whig Parliament, the motion was thrown out by a majority of more than two to one in a House of more than five hundred members.

We cease to be amazed at this deliberate rejection of information from some of the weightiest men in the kingdom, at one of the most critical moments in the history of the kingdom, when we recall the fact

[1] Cobden's *Speeches*, i. 345.

that notwithstanding the pretended reform of Parliament in 1832, four-fifths of the members of the House of Commons belonged to the old landed interests. The bewilderment of the Government was shown by the fact that Lord John Russell and Lord Palmerston went into the lobby with the Protectionists, while the President of the Board of Trade followed Mr. Villiers. Yet Lord John had declared a short time before, that he admitted the duties on corn as then levied to be untenable. The whole incident is one of the most striking illustrations on record of one of the worst characteristics of parliamentary government, its sluggishness in facing questions on their merits. In this instance, the majority found before long that behind the industrial facts which they were too selfish and indolent to desire to hear, were political forces which they and their leader together were powerless to resist.

A few days later (March 12) Mr. Villiers brought forward his annual motion, that the House should resolve itself into committee to take into consideration the act regulating the importation of foreign corn. Across Palace Yard were assembled delegates from the thirty-six principal towns in the kingdom, to enforce a prayer that had been urged by half a million of petitioners. But the motion, after a debate which extended over five nights, received only one hundred and ninety-seven votes out of a House of five hundred and forty-one. The delegates returned to their homes with the conviction that they had still a prolonged struggle before them. In the picturesque phrase of a contemporary writer, their departure was like the break-up of a Mahratta camp; it did not mean that the war was over, but only that attack would be renewed from another quarter. Some of them were inclined to despond, but the greater part almost

1839.

ÆT. 35.

instantly came round to the energetic mind of Cobden. He recalled the delegates to the fact that in spite of the House over the way, they represented three millions of the people. He compared the alliance of the great towns of England to the League of the Hanse Towns of Germany. That League had turned the castles which crowned the rocks along the Rhine, the Danube, and the Elbe into dismantled memorials of the past, and the new league would not fail in dismantling the legislative stronghold of the new feudal oppressors in England. No time was lost in strengthening their organization by drawing isolated societies to an effective centre. Measures were speedily taken (March) for the formation of a permanent union, to be called the Anti-Corn-Law League, to be composed of all the towns and districts that were represented in the delegation, and of as many others as might be induced to form local associations and federate them with the League. The executive committee of the old Manchester Anti-Corn-Law Association was transformed into the council of the new Anti-Corn-Law League. With the same view of securing unity of action, the central offices were established in Manchester, whence from this time forward the national movement was directed.

The impatience of the Free Traders had been irritated, rather than soothed, by a speech of two hours in length from the great leader of the Conservative Opposition, in which he carefully abstained from committing himself to any opinion on the principle at issue. He devised elaborate trains of hypothetical reasoning; he demolished imaginary cases; he dwelt on the irreconcilable contradictions among the best economists. But there was not a single sentence in the whole of Sir Robert Peel's speech,

1839.

ÆT. 35.

that could be taken to tie his hands in dealing with the Corn Laws, while on the contrary there was one sentence which to any one who should have accustomed himself to study the workings of that strong but furtive intellect, might have revealed that the great organ and chief of the landowners was not far removed from the Manchester manufacturer. He had at least placed himself in the mental attitude which made him accessible to their arguments. "I have no hesitation in saying,"—so Sir Robert Peel told the House—"that unless the existence of the Corn Law can be shown to be consistent, not only with the prosperity of agriculture and the maintenance of the landlord's interest, but also with the protection and the maintenance of the general interests of the country, and especially with the improvement of the condition of the labouring class, the Corn Law is practically at an end."[1]

Although such a position was rational and political, as compared with the talk of those who could not get beyond the argument that the proprietors of the soil had a right to do as they pleased with their own, still there remained a long road to travel before Peel could be regarded as a probable auxiliary. The repealers felt that they must depend upon their own efforts, without reference either to Sir Robert or Lord John. They had started a little organ of their own in the press in April; and the *Anti-Corn-Law Circular* used language which was not at all too strong for the taste of most of them, when it cried out that all political factions were equally dishonest and profligate; that the repealers at any rate would not suffer their great question to be made a mere official hobby-horse; that they would pursue an undeviating course of strenuous protest to the nation at large,

[1] March 18, 1839.

knowing well that repeal would never be granted by either the one or the other faction of political pettifoggers by which the kingdom was alternately cursed. If they could only get the honest, simple-hearted, and intelligent portion of the people to see the justice and the necessity of their cause, then they would not be long before they dragged both sections of the State quacks at their chariot wheels, each striving to outbid the other in tenders of service and offers of concession.[1]

In less violent tones, Cobden kept insisting on the same point, after the rebuffs of the year had shown them that the battle would be long, and that its issues went too deep into the social system to suit the aims of traditional parties, for the traditional parties in England were of their very essence superficial and personal. Towards the end of 1839, Dr. Bowring came to Manchester to report on what he had found on the subject of trade with England during a recent official visit to the countries of the German Customs Union. His points were that in consequence of the English obstruction to the import of grain and timber, capital in Germany was being diverted to manufactures; that the German agriculturists were naturally eager for the removal of the protective duties on manufactures, which they could purchase more cheaply from England; but that they were met by the argument that England would never reciprocate by opening a free market for return purchases of grain, as her landlords and agriculturists were far too mighty to be overthrown or even shaken. Cobden, with his usual high confidence of spirit, replied to this by asking how every social change and every religious change had been accomplished otherwise than by an appeal to public opinion. How, he exclaimed, had

[1] December 10, 1839.

they secured the penny postage, which happened to have come into force on the very day of the meeting? Not by sitting still and quietly wishing for it, but by a number of men stepping out, spending their money, giving their time, agitating the community. And in the same way, how could they think that the Corn Laws would be repealed by sitting still at home, and lamenting over their evils? He appealed to them, not as Whigs, Tories, or Radicals, but as men with a sense not more of commercial interest, than of unmistakable national duty.

We have to remember that at this date the admission of Catholics to Parliament was not so remote, that men had forgotten the means by which that triumph of justice and tolerance had been achieved. Catholic emancipation was only ten years old, and it was present to the mind of every politician who wanted to have anything done, that this great measure had been carried by the incessant activity of O'Connell and the Catholic Association. That was a memorable example that the prejudice of the governing classes was to be most effectually overcome by the agitation of a powerful outside confederacy. No two men were ever much more unlike than Cobden and O'Connell, but Cobden had been a subscriber to the great agitator's Rent, and we may be sure that the Irish example was not lost on the leaders of the association against the Corn Laws. In truth here was the vital change that had been finally effected in our system by the Reform Act. Schemes of political improvement were henceforth to spring up outside of Parliament, instead of in the creative mind of the parliamentary leader; and official statesmanship has ever since consisted less in working out principles, than in measuring the force and direction of the popular gale. It is thus the non-official statesman who, by concentrating the currents of common sentiment or opinion, really shapes the policy which the official chiefs accept from his hands.

The first year's campaign convinced the repealers that agitation is not always such smooth work as it had been in Ireland. They learnt how hardly an old class-interest dies. They had begun the work of propagandism by sending out a small band, which afterwards became a large one, of economic missionaries. In Scotland the new gospel found a temperate hearing and much acceptance, but in England the lecturers were not many days in discovering at what peril they had undertaken to assault the prejudice and selfishness of a territorial aristocracy, and the brutality or cowardice of their hangers-on. Though there were many districts where nobody interfered with them, there were many others where neither law nor equity gave them protection. At Arundel the mayor refused the use of the town hall, on the ground that the lecture would make the labourers discontented; and the landlord refused the use of his large room, on the ground that if he granted it, he should lose his customers. A land-owning farmer went further, and offered a bushel of wheat to anybody who would throw the lecturer into the river. At Petersfield, a paltry little borough in Hampshire, almost in sight of Cobden's birthplace, either spite or the timidity of political bondage went so far, that when the lecturer returned, after his harangue in the market-place, to the Dolphin, Boar, or Lion, where he had taken his tea and ordered his bed, the landlord and landlady peremptorily desired him to leave their house. In the eastern counties, again, they were usually well received by the common people, but vexed and harassed by the authorities.

At Louth they were allowed to deliver their address in the town hall one night, but as the lecturer had the fortune to discomfit a local magnate in the discussion which followed, the permission which had been given to use the hall on the next night was arbitrarily withdrawn, and the lecturers were driven to say what they had come to say from a gig in the market-place. Nor was this the end of the adventure. As they were about to leave the town, they were served with a warrant for causing an obstruction in a thoroughfare; they were brought before the very magnate over whom they had won so fatal a victory, and by him punished with a fine. At Stamford they were warned that the mob would tear them to pieces; but they protected themselves with a bodyguard, and the mob was discovered to be less hostile than a small band of people who ought to have deserved the name of respectable. At Huntingdon the town clerk was the leader in provoking an outrageous disturbance, which forced the lecturer to give up the ground. In the Duke of Newcastle's country, at Newark and at Retford, there was not an innkeeper who dared to let the lecturer a room; and at Worksop, not only could the lecturer not find a room, nor a printer who should dare to print a placard, but he was assaulted by hired bullies in the street. It was reserved for a seat of learning to show that no brutality can equal that which is engendered of the union of the violent inherited prejudice of the educated classes with the high spirits of youth. No creature is a more unbridled ruffian than the ruffian undergraduate can be, and at Cambridge the peaceful arguments of the lecturer were interrupted by a destructive and sanguinary riot. The local newspaper afterwards piously congratulated the furious gownsmen on having done their duty as "the friends

1839.
—
ÆT. 35.

1839. — ÆT. 35.

of good government, and the upholders of the religious institutions of the country."[1]

It is only when people want to get something done that all the odd perversities of the human mind spread themselves out in panoramic fulness. A long campaign of reckless and virulent calumny was at once opened in the party organs. One London newspaper described the worst members of the Association as unprincipled schemers, and the best as self-conceited socialists. Another declared with authority that it was composed in equal parts of commercial swindlers and political swindlers. A third with edifying unction denounced their sentiments as subversive of all moral right and order, their organization as a disloyal faction, and their speakers as revolutionary emissaries, whom all peaceable and well-disposed persons ought to assist the authorities in peremptorily putting down. The *Morning Post*, the journal of London idleness, hailed the Manchester workers in a style that would have been grotesque enough, if only it had not represented the serious thought of many of the most important people in the dominant class. "The manufacturing people exclaim, 'Why should we not be permitted to exchange the produce of our industry for the greatest quantity of food which that industry will anywhere command?' To which we answer, Why not, indeed? Who hinders you? Take your manufactures away with you by all means, and exchange them anywhere you will from Tobolsk to Timbuctoo. If nothing will serve you but to eat foreign corn, away with you, you and your goods, and let us never see you more!" This was a quarter from which the language of simpletons was to be expected, but as the repealers had a thousand opportunities of discovering within

[1] May 14, 1839.

the next seven years, the language of simpletons has many dialects. One of the lowest perversions of the right sense of place and proportion in things, was reached by those who cried out angrily that the great and decisive test for candidates at the next general election would not be Corn Laws or Anti-Corn Laws, but "How are your views on the Sabbath question?" The Chartists, of whom we shall say something in another chapter, began a long course of violent hostility by trying at the very outset of the agitation to break up a meeting at Leeds, insisting that the movement was a cheat put on the work-people of the country by cunning and rapacious employers. Even in places where so much strong political intelligence existed as at Birmingham, members of the town council of the borough were found to talk about "the interested movements of the Whig Corn Law intriguers," and to urge that the discussion of the Corn Laws was merely a Whig device to embarrass the patriotic champions of parliamentary reform.[1] Of all this the Leaguers heard much more, and from more troublesome people, in the years to come.

Meanwhile the information which their lecturers brought back to headquarters at Manchester, as to the state of some of the rural districts, inspired the leaders of the agitation with new zeal, and a stronger conviction of the importance of their cause. In Devonshire they found that the wages of the labourers were from seven to nine shillings a week; that they seldom saw meat or tasted milk; and that their chief food was a compost of ground barley and potatoes. It was little wonder that in a county where such was the condition of labour, the lecturer was privately asked by poor men at the roadside if he could tell

[1] Bunce's *History of the Corporation of Birmingham*, i. 166-7.

them where the fighting was to be. Nor need we doubt that he was speaking the simple truth when he reported that, though ignorant of Chartism as a political question, the great mass of the population of Devon were just as ready for pikes and pistols as the most excitable people of the factory towns. In Somersetshire the budget of a labourer, his wife, and five children under ten years of age, was as follows. Half a bushel of wheat cost four shillings; for grinding, baking, and barm, sixpence; firing, sixpence; rent, eighteenpence; leaving, out of the total earnings of seven shillings, a balance of sixpence, out of which to provide the family with clothing, potatoes, and all the other necessaries and luxuries of human existence.

With facts like these before them, the Leaguers read with mockery the idyllic fustian in which even the ablest men of the landlord party complacently indulged their feeling for the picturesque. Sir James Graham, in resisting Mr. Villiers's motion this year, spoke of the breezy call of incense-breathing morn, the neat thatched cottage, the blooming garden, the cheerful village green. The repeal of the Corn Laws would lead to a great migration from all this loveliness to the noisy alley, and the "sad sound of the factory bell." "Tell not to me any more," the orator called out in a foolish ecstasy, "of the cruelties of the conveyance of the Poles to the wintry wastes of Siberia; talk not to me of the transportation of the Hill Coolies from Coromandel to the Mauritius; a change is contemplating by some members of this House, far more cruel, far more heart-rending in the bosom of our native land."[1] If this nonsense was the vein of so able a man as Graham, we may infer the depths of prejudice and fallacy down into which Cobden and his allies had to follow less sensible

[1] March 15, 1839.

people. And the struggle had hardly begun. The landlords were not yet awakened into consciousness that this time the Manchester men were in earnest, and resolutely intended to raise the country upon them. They still believed that the Corn Laws were as safe as the monarchy; and many months passed before they realized that the little group who now met several times in each week in a dingy room on an upper floor at Newall's Buildings in Market Street in Manchester, were not to be daunted either by bad divisions in Parliament, or bad language in the newspapers, because they had become fired by the conviction that what they were fighting against was not merely a fiscal blunder, but a national iniquity.

Cobden lived at this time, along with his brothers and sisters, in a large house in Quay Street, which he had bought very shortly after settling in Manchester, and which was known to the next generation as Owens College. His business was in a flourishing condition, and it would have saved him from many a day of misery if he could have been content to leave it as it was. It was from no selfish or personal motive that he now proceeded to make a change in the arrangements. The reader has already seen how at the beginning of his career Cobden affectionately insisted with his brother, "that you will henceforth consider yourself as by right my associate in all the favours of fortune." And it was in the interest of Frederick Cobden and his two younger brothers that he now broke up the existing partnership. The firm had previously consisted of five members, carrying on business under three titles, one at the warehouse in Watling Street in London; the second at the print-works at Sabden; the third, specifically

1839. — ÆT. 35.

known as Richard Cobden and Company, at Manchester and Crosse Hall, near Chorley in Lancashire. Frederick Cobden was not a member of any of these allied firms, and there seems to have been no willingness to make room for him. At the end of July 1839, Cobden withdrew from his old partners. He left them to carry on the London warehouse and the Sabden print-works on their own account. He then proceeded himself to form a new partnership with Frederick Cobden, to carry on the Manchester warehouse and the print-works at Crosse Hall. This was the arrangement of Cobden's business during the six years of agitation against the Corn Laws.

Though his motive in making the change was the desire to raise the position of his elder brother at once, and to pave the way for his younger brother in the future, yet Cobden had no doubt convinced himself that the change was sound and prudent in itself. A less sanguine man would have found the altered conditions formidable. In the business which he left, though he did not find himself in entire sympathy with one of the London partners, all had been managed with the greatest exactitude, and there had been abundance of capital in proportion to the extent of the business. At Crosse Hall he found himself much less favourably placed. He was thrown entirely on his own unaided resources, for his letters show that Frederick Cobden, with all his excellent qualities, yet was one of the men who mistake feverish anxiety for business-like caution, and then suppose that they repair the errors of timidity by moments of hurried action. Instead of coming into a factory, like the works at Sabden, perfectly organized and superintended by an experienced eye, Cobden had now to find a new staff, and what was perhaps at least as arduous, he had to find new capital, and to earn interest as well as profit from its working.

1839. — ÆT. 35.

He had, moreover, so early as 1835, made speculative purchases of land in various quarters of Manchester, where his too cheerful vision discovered a measureless demand for houses, shops, and factories, as soon as ever the corn duty should be repealed, and the springs of industrial enterprise set free. For five and twenty years waste spaces between Victoria Park and Rusholme, in Quay Street, and Oxford Street, bore melancholy testimony to a miscalculation; and for five and twenty years Cobden paid a thousand pounds a year, in the shape of chief rent, for a property which thus brought him not a shilling of return. In spite of the grave drawbacks which I have named, it is not doubted by those who have the best means of knowing, that the new firm was for some time reasonably successful, and was even visited by gleams of genuine prosperity. But the undertaking was hardly launched, before its chief was drawn away from effective interest in it by a strong vocation which he could not resist, to be the leader of the great national cause of the time.

Meanwhile within a few months of the resettlement of his business, he took another momentous step in marrying (May 1840). His wife was Miss Catherine Anne Williams, a young Welsh lady, whose acquaintance he had made as a school-friend of one of his sisters. She is said by all who knew her to have been endowed with singular personal beauty, and with manners of perfect dignity and charm. Whether in Cobden's case this union was preceded by much deliberation, we do not know; perhaps experience shows that the profoundest deliberation in choosing a wife is little better than the cleverness of people who boast of a scientific secret of winning in a lottery. Although marriage is usually so much the most important element in deciding whether a life shall be heaven or hell, it is that on which in any given instance it is least proper for a stranger to speak.

It would seem that to be the wife of a prominent public man is not always an easy lot. As Goethe's Leonora says of men and women:—

> Ihr strebt nach fernen Gütern,
> Und euer Streben muss gewaltsam seyn.
> Ihr wagt es, für die Ewigkeit zu handeln,
> Wenn wir ein einzig nah beschränktes Gut
> Auf dieser Erde nur besitzen möchten,
> Und wünschen dass es uns beständig bliebe.[1]

If the champion of great causes has to endure the loss of domestic companionship, he is at least compensated by patriotic satisfaction in the result; but unless the woman be of more than common strength of public zeal, the thousand lonely days and nights and all the swarm of undivided household cares may well put temper and spirits to a sharp strain. In the last year of Cobden's life, as he and Mrs. Cobden were coming up to London from their home in the country, Mrs. Cobden said to him: "I sometimes think that, after all the good work that you have done, and in spite of fame and great position, it would have been better for us both if, after you and I married, we had gone to settle in the backwoods of Canada." And Cobden could only say, after looking for a moment or two with a gaze of mournful preoccupation through the window of the carriage, that he was not sure that what she said was not too true.

[1] "Ye strive for far-off goals, and strenuous your battle. For immortality to toil, do you aspire. But we one single narrow good, and that nigh to us, would fain possess upon this earth, and only ask that it should steadfast dwell."

But in 1840 evil days had not yet come, and as they took their summer wedding trip through France, Savoy, Switzerland, and Germany, Cobden had as good right as any mortal can ever have, to look forward to a future of material prosperity, domestic happiness, and honest service to his country.

1840.

Æt. 36.

CHAPTER VII

THE CORN LAWS

1825.

ÆT. 21.

It will perhaps not be inconvenient if I here pause in my narrative, to introduce a short parenthesis setting forth what actually were the nature and working of the Corn Laws at this time. Their destruction was the one finished triumph with which Cobden's name is associated. The wider doctrines which he tried to impress upon men still await the seal of general acceptance; but it is a tolerably safe prophecy that no English statesman will ever revive a tax upon bread.

Cobden was much too careful a student of the facts of his question to fall into the error of the declaimers on his own side, who assumed that none but the owners of the soil had ever claimed protection by law for their industry. In the first number of the little organ which was issued by the Association,[1] he wrote a paper on the modern history of the Corn Laws, which began by plainly admitting, what it would have been childish to deny, that down to 1820 manufacturers probably enjoyed as ample a share of legislative protection as the growers of corn. Huskisson's legislation from 1823 to 1825 reduced the tariff of duties upon almost every article of foreign manufacture. This stamped that date, in Cobden's words, as the era of a commercial revolution, more

[1] April 16, 1839.

important in its effects upon society, and pregnant with weightier consequences in the future, than many of those political revolutions which have commanded infinitely greater attention from historians. The duty on cotton goods was lowered from a figure ranging from between seventy-five and fifty per cent down to ten per cent. Imported linens sometimes paid as much as one hundred and eighty per cent; they were henceforth to be admitted at twenty-five. Paper had been prohibited; it was now allowed to come in on paying twice the amount levied as excise from the home manufacturer. The duty on a foreign manufacture in no case exceeded thirty per cent. The principle of this immense reform was that, if the article were not made either much better or at a much lower price abroad than at home, then such a duty would be ample for purposes of protection. If, on the contrary, the foreign article were either so much better or so much cheaper as to render thirty per cent insufficient for purposes of protection, then, in the first place, a heavier duty would only put a premium on smuggling; and secondly, said Huskisson, there is no wisdom in bolstering up a competition which this degree of protection will not sustain.

These enlightened opinions, and the measures which followed from them, were the first rays of dawn after the long night of confusion and mediocrity in which the Castlereaghs, Sidmouths, Bathursts, Vansittarts, had governed their unfortunate country. Even now political power was so distributed that, though the new school thus saw the better course, they dared not to venture too rapidly upon it. There was one mighty and imperious interest which, as the parliamentary system was then disposed, even Canning's courage shrank from offending. The Cabinet, which had radically modified a host of restrictive laws, was logically and politically bound to deal with the most important of them all—that which restrained the importation of food. By the law of 1815 corn could be imported when wheat had risen to eighty shillings a quarter. By the law of 1822 this was improved to the extent of permitting importation when the price of wheat was seventy shillings a quarter. The landlords vowed that this was the lowest rate at which the British farmer could live, and not a few of them cried out for total prohibition. They had powerful allies in the Cabinet, and even the Liberal wing in the Cabinet which was led by Canning, never dreamed of being able to push the landlords very hard. When pressed by a motion for extending to the case of grain the same principle which had just been so wisely glorified in the case of cotton, woollen, silk, linen, and glass, Huskisson resisted it on the too familiar ground that the motion was ill-timed. He did not deny that it would presently be necessary to revise the Corn Laws; and he added the important admission that several foreign countries were not only in distress, owing to our exclusion of their corn, but that in revenge they were proceeding to shut out our manufactures.[1]

Two years elapsed before the Ministry ventured to touch the burning subject. The new measure was not brought forward by Huskisson. It was officially given out as the reason for this that he was ill, but this was only one of the peculiar blinds that serve to open people's eyes. Everybody suspected that Huskisson's illness was in reality the chagrin of the good economist at a bad measure. It was Canning who, in the spring of 1827, introduced the new Corn Bill.[2] It proceeded on the plan of making

[1] April 28, 1825.

[2] March 1, 1827.

the duty vary inversely with the price of the grain in the home market. When the price of wheat in the home market reached sixty shillings a quarter, foreign wheat was to pay on importation a duty of one pound. For every rise of a shilling in the home price the duty was to go down two shillings; for every fall of a shilling in the home price the duty was to go up two shillings. The increase and decrease in the duty was always to be double the fall and rise in the price. In other words, when the average price reached seventy shillings, wheat might be imported with a nominal duty of one shilling; on the other hand, when the average price fell to fifty shillings, the duty on foreign wheat would be forty shillings.

After the Bill had passed the Commons, the Liverpool Ministry fell to pieces, and a season of odious intrigue was followed by the accession of Canning. The Corn Bill went up to the Lords in due course. The Duke of Wellington, though he had been a member of the Liverpool Cabinet by which the Bill had been sanctioned, now moved an amendment on it, and the new Ministry was defeated. Canning and Huskisson let the Bill drop. The event which so speedily followed is one of the tragic pages in the history of English statesmen. Canning died a few weeks after the close of the session; Lord Goderich's abortive Ministry flickered into existence for four or five months, when it flickered out again; and before the end of the year the Duke of Wellington was Prime Minister. The great soldier was a narrow and sightless statesman, and with his accession to power all the worse impulses of the privileged classes acquired new confidence and intensity. In every sphere the men of exclusion and restriction breathed more freely.

The Duke introduced a new Corn Bill. This

bad measure accepted Canning's principle, if we may give the name of principle to an empirical device; but it carried the principle further in the wrong direction. In the Bill of 1827, the starting-point had been the exaction of a twenty shilling duty, when the home price was sixty shillings the quarter. According to the Bill of 1828, when the price in the home market was sixty-four shillings, the duty was twenty-three shillings and eightpence. The variations in the amount of duty were not equal as in the previous Bill, but went by leaps. Thus, when wheat was at sixty-nine shillings, the duty was sixteen and eightpence; and when the home price rose to seventy-three, then the duty fell to the nominal rate of a shilling. This was the Corn Law which Cobden and his friends rose up to overthrow.[1]

So far back as 1815, when that important measure had been passed restraining the introduction of wheat for home consumption unless the average price had reached eighty shillings for the quarter, the mischief of such legislation had been understood and described in Parliament. In the House of Lords the dissentients from the measure, only ten in number, had signed a protest, drawn up, as it has always been believed, by that independent and hard-headed statesman, Lord Grenville. The grounds of dissent were these: That all new restraints on commerce are bad in principle; that such restraints are especially bad when they affect the food of the people; that the results would not conduce to plenty, cheapness, or steadiness of price; that such a measure levied a tax on the consumer, in order to give a bounty to the grower of corn. This was a just and unanswerable series of objections. Within

[1] 9 Geo. IV. c. 60.

six years (1821) a parliamentary committee was appointed to inquire into agricultural depression.

1828.

ÆT. 24.

If we turn to the effect of our regulations upon foreign countries, there too they brought nothing but calamity. When grain rose to a starvation price in England, we entered the foreign markets; the influx of our gold disturbed their exchanges, embarrassed their merchants, and engendered all the mischief of speculation and gambling. As it was put by some speaker of the day, the question was—"Are you to receive food from a foreign country quietly, reasonably, in payment for the manufactures which you send to them? Or are you to go to them only in the moment of perturbation, of anxiety, of starvation, and say, Now we must have food at any rate, and we will pay any price, though the very foundations of your society should be shaken by the transaction."

There was no essential bond between the maintenance of agricultural protection and Conservative policy. Burke, the most magnificent genius that the Conservative spirit has ever attracted, was one of the earliest assailants of legislative interference in the corn trade, and the important Corn Act of 1773 was inspired by his maxims.[1] There is no such thing, Burke said, as the landed interest separate from the trading interest; and he who separates the interest of the consumer from the interest of the grower, starves the country.[2] Five and twenty years after this, in a

[1] This was the most liberal piece of legislation until the Act of Repeal in 1846. When the home price was at or above 48s., imported wheat paid a nominal duty of 6d., and the bounty on exportation ceased when the home price was 44s. "The Act of 1773 should not have been altered," says McCulloch, "unless to give greater freedom to the trade."

[2] Feb 28, 1771.

luminous tract often praised by Cobden, he again attacked a new form of the futile and mischievous system of dealing with agriculture as if it were different from any other branch of commerce, and denounced tampering with the trade in provisions as of all things the most dangerous.[1] Although, however, Conservative policy was not necessarily bound up with protection, the Tory party were committed to it by all the ties of personal interest.

The Whigs ruled the country, save for a few months, for eleven years from 1830 to 1841. In Lord Melbourne's Cabinet, in 1839, the Corn Laws were, as we have already seen, an open question.[2] But two years later the financial position of the country had become so serious, and the credit and forces of the party had fallen so low, that it became necessary to enter upon a more decisive course. The expenditure had undergone a progressive increase, amounting in six years to four millions sterling on the annual estimates for the military and naval services alone, a rise of more than thirty per cent. For each of the last four years there had been a serious deficiency of income. In 1840 it was a million and a half. For 1841 it was given out as upwards of one million, eight hundred and fifty thousand. Nor was this the result merely of an absence of fiscal skill in the government of the day. It was the sign, confirmed by the obstinate depression of trade and the sufferings of the population, of an industrial and commercial stagnation which could only be dealt with by an economic revolution.

Besides such considerations as these, there were the considerations of party strength. Macaulay's biographer quotes a significant passage from his

[1] *Thoughts and Details on Scarcity*, 1795.
[2] Above, pp. 156 and 161.

diary. "The cry for free trade in corn," he wrote in 1839, and Macaulay was in the Cabinet, "seems to be very formidable. If the Ministers play their game well, they may now either triumph completely, or retire with honour. They have excellent cards, if they know how to use them."[1] Unluckily for themselves, they did not know how to use them; and everybody was quite aware that their conversion towards Free Trade was not the result of conviction, but was only the last device of a foundering party.

In 1840 a committee on import duties had sat, and produced a striking and remarkable report, recommending an abandonment of the illiberal and exclusive policy of the past, and a radical simplification of the tariff by substituting for a multitude of duties, imposts on a small number of the most productive articles, the amount of the impost being calculated with a view to the greatest consumption. This was in truth the base of Peel's great reform of 1842. But Lord Melbourne's Cabinet had no member of sufficient grasp and audacity in finance to accept boldly and comprehensively, as Peel afterwards did, the maxim that reduction of duties is one way to increase of revenue. The Whig Government made the experiment timidly, and they met the common fate of those who take a great principle with half-heartedness and mistrust. They picked it up for want of a better. "I cannot conceive," said Peel, "a more lamentable position than that of a Chancellor of the Exchequer, seated on an empty chest, by the side of bottomless deficiencies, fishing for a budget."

The proposals which the Government had hit upon were these. They returned to the general principle of the budget which Lord Althorp had

[1] Trevelyan's *Life*, ii. 87.

brought forward at the beginning of the Whig reign (1831)—the boldest budget, as it has justly been called, since the days of Pitt.[1] The main object of the commutation of duties, Lord Althorp had said, is the relief of the lower classes. "The best way of relieving them is by giving them employment; and this can only be secured by reducing the taxes which most interfere with manufacturing industry." Among other devices for carrying this principle into practice, Lord Althorp had proposed to regulate the timber duties.[2] He had failed to carry that measure against Peel's opposition, which was aided by a general opinion that the budget was unsound—an opinion mainly due to the startling proposal to levy a tax of a half per cent on transfers of funded property. Lord Althorp's successor now came back to some of his ideas. The question for the Cabinet to decide, as Lord John Russell describes the situation, "was whether they would lower duties of a protective character on a great number of small articles, or whether they would attack the giant monopolies of sugar, of timber, and of corn." They adopted the latter course, but in the spirit of Huskisson, and not of Cobden. They preferred an ineffectual approach to Free Trade, to a complete repeal of protective duties. To touch the differential duties on sugar was to attack one at least of the strongest protective interests in Parliament, and every other protected interest moved in sympathetic agitation. The more sanguine of the Ministers hoped to beat them by conciliating the manufacturing interest. This they expected to reach through the Corn Laws. Lord John Russell moved (May 7) to abolish the sliding scale of 1828, and to

[1] Walpole's *History of England*, ii. 634.

[2] The 10s. duty on Canadian timber was to be raised to 20s., and the 55s. duty on Norwegian and other European timber lowered to 20s.

establish instead a fixed eight-shilling duty upon wheat.[1] The battle turned upon the comparative merits of Free Trade and Protective duties, and in the special question of the Corn Laws upon the comparative merits of a graduated and a fixed duty.

In a debate on a vote of confidence in 1840, Peel seemed to have advanced a step from the position which had irritated the Leaguers in 1839. He still considered a liberal protection to domestic agriculture indispensable, both in the special interests of agriculture and the general interests of the community. He did not tie himself to the details of the existing law; but he maintained that a graduated duty, varying inversely with the price of corn, was far preferable to a fixed duty. He objected to a fixed duty on two grounds: first, on account of the great difficulty of determining the proper amount of it on any satisfactory data; secondly, and chiefly, because he foresaw that it would be impossible to maintain that fixed duty under a very high price of corn, and that if it were once withdrawn, there would be extreme difficulty in reimposing it.

He now, in 1841, repeated what he had said the previous year. "Notwithstanding the formidable combination which has been formed against the Corn Laws," he said, "notwithstanding the declarations that either the total repeal or the substitution of a fixed duty for the present scale, is the inevitable result of the agitation now going forward, I do not hesitate to avow my adherence to the opinion which I expressed last year, and now again declare, that my preference is decidedly in favour of a graduated scale rather than any fixed duty."

Lord Melbourne had foreseen the fate of his Chancellor's budget. He was shrewd enough to be

[1] 5s. on rye; 4s. 6d. on barley; 3s. 4d. on oats.

1841.
ÆT. 37.

sure that a half-measure could never raise up so many friends among the manufacturers as to outweigh the united force of the agricultural and colonial interests.[1] In fact, no friends were raised up. No great body was conciliated, nor attracted, nor even touched with friendly interest; and the chief reason for this stubborn apathy was, as Sir Robert Peel said, that nobody believed that the proposals of Ministers sprang from their spontaneous will, or that they had been adopted in consequence of the deliberate convictions of those who brought them forward. The conversion was too rapid. Only two years had gone since the Prime Minister had declared in his place that the repeal of the Corn Laws would be the most insane proposition that ever entered a human head. Lord Palmerston made a fine speech against the system of protective duties; but men remembered that, two years before, he had voted against Mr. Villiers's motion to hear the members of the Manchester Association at the bar of the House. And the motives of so speedy a change were too plain.

The first division as to the new budget was taken upon the sugar duties; the Ministers found themselves in a minority of thirty-six. They still held on, and instead of either resigning or dissolving immediately, astonished Parliament and the country by an announcement that they would go on with the old sugar duties, and would bring forward the question of the Corn Laws in the course of two or three weeks. Sir Robert Peel declined to give them the chance, brought forward a vote of want of confidence, and carried it by a majority of one.

The Ministers could not believe that the House of Commons represented the wishes of the country, and to the country they now appealed.

[1] Torrens's *Life of Melbourne*, ii. 358.

CHAPTER VIII

COBDEN ENTERS PARLIAMENT—FIRST SESSION

1841.

Æt. 37.

THE dissolution of Parliament took place at Midsummer. The League went actively into the campaign, though not with that inflexibility in electoral policy which afterwards marked their operations. They had to face the question which always perplexes the thorough-going advocates of any political principle, when they come to deal with political practice. In all such cases a section springs up which is prepared to go half-way. The Government had given to this section a cry. They were not prepared for total and immediate repeal, but they would go for a moderate fixed duty. The proposal of a fixed duty furnished the compromisers with a comfortable halting-place. They could thus claim to be Free Traders, without being suspected of the deadly sin of being extreme. The Council of the League were called upon to settle the proper attitude towards the men of the middle course. Were they to offer a fanatical resistance to the men of the middle party, thus shocking timid but reasonable sympathizers, and forfeiting their own character for prudence and discretion, qualities as essential to success as sincerity itself? They answered this question as might have been expected at that time. For themselves, they held to their own demand for the entire liberation of the provision trade. Wherever there was a constituency ripe for carrying a candidate of this colour, every exertion was to be made for securing a good candidate and ensuring his return. Where friends of the League were in a constituency not yet enlightened enough to return a candidate of League principles, then they ought to vote for a candidate who would support the measure of the Government. Considering both the moderate strength of the League at that time, and the state of the question in men's minds, it seems that this was the natural and judicious course.

Some of the more dogged, however, among members of the League were hurt by what they took for a Laodicean halting between two opinions, and talked of withdrawing or lessening their subscriptions. Subscriptions are always a very sensitive point in agitations; and Cobden found it worth while, after the elections were over, to write a letter to one of the more important of the protesters, explaining the principle on which the League had acted. "With reference to your complaint," he says, "that the League did not oppose the measure of the Government, I must remind you that the real governing power, the landed and other monopolists, held fast by the old law; *they* never attempted to force the fixed duty upon us. We regarded the Government proposal, not as an offer from a party strong enough to concede anything, but merely as a step in advance taken by a portion of the aristocracy. It was not our business to attack them, whilst another party, more powerful than the Government and the people, were resolutely opposed to any concession. To my humble apprehension, it is as unwise as unjust in any kind of political warfare to assail those who are disposed to co-operate, however slightly, in the attempt to overthrow a formidable and uncompromising enemy."

1841. Æt. 37.

In the elections in the north of England the Repealers were successful against both Whigs and Tories, and among those who succeeded was Cobden himself. "I am afraid," he wrote to his brother, "you will be vexed on landing in England to find me Member for Stockport. I had fully, as you know, determined not to go to Parliament. I stood out. The Bolton and Stockport folks both got requisitions to me ensuring my return. I declined. It was then that the Stockport people put the screw upon me, by a large deputation confessing their inability to agree amongst themselves upon any other man who could turn out the Major. They offered me *carte blanche* as to my attendance in London, and as to the time of my retaining the seat. I was over-persuaded by my Manchester partisans and have yielded, and the election is secure. You must not vex yourself, for I am quite resolved that it shall not be the cause of imposing either additional expense on my mode of living, or any increased call upon my time for public objects. I did not dream of this, as you very well know."[1]

"I have a right to expect other men of business," he wrote to a manufacturer at Warrington, urging a contest in that borough, "for I am doing it myself much against my wish. I offered to give a hundred pounds towards the expenses of another candidate in my stead for Stockport, and to canvass for him for a week; and it was only when the electors declared that they could not agree to another, and would not be able to oust the bread-taxers without me, that I consented to stand."

The League, in fact, put a strong pressure upon

[1] *To F. Cobden*, June 16, 1841.

1841.
Æt. 37.

him, and we may perhaps believe that Cobden's resistance to the urgency of his political friends was not very stubborn. He must have felt by invincible instinct that only through a seat in Parliament could he secure an effective hearing for his arguments. It is uncertain whether the opinion of the constituency which had rejected him in 1837 had really been excited by the Free Trade discussion, or whether the motives of the voters were merely personal. Shrewd electioneerers have a maxim that a candidate is sure to win any given seat in time, if he is only tenacious enough. Cobden was returned by a triumphant majority. "The Stockport affair," he wrote, "was carried with unexpected éclat. We drubbed the Major so soundly that at one o'clock he resigned. We could have beaten him easily by two to one. My committee worked to admiration. Two hundred electors were up all the night previous to polling, including the mill-owners . . . who neither changed their clothes nor closed their eyes for thirty-six hours. These men were against me at the former election. Upon the whole the elections will give Peel a majority of thirty or forty. So much the better. We shall do something in opposition."[1]

It proved that Sir Robert Peel had a majority, not of thirty or forty, but of more than ninety. Lord Melbourne, however, did not anticipate the practice of our own day by resigning before the meeting of the hostile Parliament. The Ministers put into the Queen's speech as good an account as they could of their policy, and awaited their fate. Cobden took his seat on the first day of the session. "Yesterday," he says, "I went down to the House to be sworn to renounce the Pope and the Pretender. Then I went into the Treasury, and heard Lord John deliver his

[1] *To F. Cobden*, July 3, 1841.

last dying speech and confession to his parliamentary minority. He gave us the substance of the Queen's speech, which is in the *Chronicle* to-day. I cannot learn what the Tories intend to do to-night, but I suppose they will try to avoid committing themselves against the Free Trade measures. It is allowed on all sides that they fear discussion as they do death. It is reported that the old Duke advises his party not to force themselves on the Queen, but to let the Whigs go on till the reins fairly drop out of their hands. The Queen seems to be more violently opposed than ever to the Tories."[1]

The Queen had no choice. An amendment was moved upon the address in both Houses, and carried in the Commons by the irresistible majority of ninety-one. The vote was taken at five in the morning (August 28), and in the afternoon of the same day, Lord Melbourne went down to Windsor to resign his post. Within a few days that great administration was formed which contained not only able Tories like Lord Lyndhurst, but able seceders from the Whigs like Lord Stanley and Sir James Graham; which commanded an immense majority in both Houses; which was led by a chief of consummate sagacity; and which was at last, five years afterwards, slowly broken to pieces by the work of Cobden and the League.

Cobden made his maiden speech in the debate which preceded this great official revolution. "I was induced," he writes to his brother, "to speak last night at about nine o'clock. We thought the debate would have been brought to a close. The Tories were doggedly resolved from the first not to enter upon any discussion of the main question, and the discussion, if it could be called one, went on as

[1] *To F. Cobden*, August 24, 1841.

flat as possible. My speech had one good effect. I called up a booby who let fly at the manufacturers, very much to the chagrin, I suspect, of the leader of his party. It is now thought that the Tories must come out and discuss in self-defence the Free Trade question, and if not, they will be damaged by the arguments on the other side. All my friends say I did well. But I feel it very necessary to be cautious in speaking too much. I shall be an observer for some time."[1]

We now see that Cobden's maiden speech was much more than a success in the ordinary sense of attracting the attention of that most difficult of all audiences. It sounded a new key, and startled men by an accent that was strange in the House of Commons. The thoughtful among them recognized the rare tone of reality, and the note of a man dealing with things and not words. He produced that singular and profound effect which is perceived in English deliberative assemblies, when a speaker leaves party recriminations, abstract argument, and commonplaces of sentiment, in order to inform his hearers of telling facts in the condition of the nation. Cobden reminded the House that it was the condition of the nation, and not the interests of a class, or the abstract doctrines of the economist, that cried for a relief which it was in the power of the legislature to bestow. This was the point of the speech. In spite of the strong wish of everybody on the side of the majority, and of many on the side of the minority, to keep the Corn Law out of the debate, Cobden insisted that the Corn Law was in reality the only matter which at that moment was worth debating at all. The family of a nobleman, he showed the House, paid to the bread-tax about one

[1] *To F. Cobden*, August 26, 1841.

halfpenny on every hundred pounds of income, while the effect of the tax on the family of the labouring man was not less than twenty per cent. A fact of this kind, as they said of Pericles's speeches, left a sting in the minds of his hearers. The results of the injustice were seen in the misery of the population. A great meeting of ministers of religion of all sects had been held in Manchester a few days before, and Cobden told the House something of the destitution throughout the country, to which these men had borne testimony.

"At that meeting," he said, "most important statements of facts were made relating to the condition of the labouring classes. He would not trouble the House by reading those statements; but they showed that in every district of the country . . . the condition of the great body of Her Majesty's labouring population had deteriorated woefully within the last ten years, and more especially within the last three years; and that, in proportion as the price of food increased, in the same proportion the comforts of the working classes had diminished. One word with respect to the manner in which his allusion to this meeting was received. He did not come there to vindicate the conduct of these Christian men in having assembled in order to take this subject into consideration. The people who had to judge them were their own congregations. There were at that meeting members of the Established Church, of the Church of Rome, Independents, Baptists, members of the Church of Scotland and of the Secession Church, Methodists, and indeed ministers of every other denomination; and if he were disposed to impugn the character of those divines, he felt he should be casting a stigma and a reproach upon the great body of professing Christians in his country.

1841.
Æt. 37

He happened to be the only member of the House present at that meeting; and he might be allowed to state that when he heard the tales of misery there described; when he heard these ministers declare that members of their congregations were kept away from places of worship during the morning service, and only crept out under cover of the darkness of night; when they described others as unfit to receive spiritual consolation, because they were sunk so low in physical destitution; that the attendance at Sunday Schools was falling off; when he heard these and such-like statements; when he who believed that the Corn Law, the provision monopoly, was at the bottom of all that was endured, heard those statements, and from such authority, he must say that he rejoiced to see gentlemen of such character come forward, and like Nathan, when he addressed the owner of flocks and herds who had plundered the poor man of his only lamb, say unto the doer of injustice, whoever he might be: 'Thou art the man.' The people, through their ministers, had protested against the Corn Laws. . . . When they found so many ministers of religion, without any sectarian differences, joining heart and hand in a great cause, there could be no doubt of their earnestness. . . . Englishmen had a respect for rank, for wealth—perhaps too much; they felt an attachment to the laws of their country; but there was another attribute in the minds of Englishmen—there was a permanent veneration for sacred things; and when their sympathy and respect and deference were enlisted in what they believed to be a sacred cause, you and yours [addressing the Protectionists] will vanish like chaff before the whirlwind."

One or two simpletons laughed at an appeal to evidence from such a source; but it was felt that, though they might jeer at the speaker as a Methodist parson, and look down upon him as a manufacturer, yet he represented a new force with which the old parties would one day have to deal. In the country his speech excited the deep interest of that great class, who are habitually repelled by the narrow passions and seeming insincerity of ordinary politics.

His friends in the north were delighted by the vigour and alacrity of their champion. With the sanguine assurance of all people who have convinced themselves of the goodness of their cause, and are very earnest in wishing to carry it, they were certain that Cobden's arguments must speedily convert Parliament and the Ministry. "It is pleasant," Cobden wrote to his brother, "to learn that my maiden effort has pleased our good friends. I have some letters from Manchester with congratulations. It is very pleasant, but I must be careful not to be carried off my legs. Stanley scowls and Peel smiles at me, both meaning mischief. There is no other man on the other side that I have heard, who is at all formidable. I observe there are a great many busy men of our party who like to see their names in print, and who therefore take up small matters continually; they are very little attended to by the House. With these men I shall not interfere, and they will all aid me in obtaining a fair hearing on my great question. We had a curious scene of jealousy and bickering to-day. Sharman Crawford brought on an amendment to the address without consulting anybody.[1] Roebuck, who is as wayward

[1] When the House met to receive the Report on the Amended Address, Mr. Crawford proposed an amendment, to the effect that the distress deplored in the Speech was to be attributed to the non-representation of the working classes in Parliament. The Radicals were not unanimous, and the amendment was defeated by 283 against 39.

and impulsive as he is clever, walked out of the House with a tail of four or five, whilst hearty old Wallace of Greenock cried out, 'Who cares for you? who cares?' amidst the roars of the House. I can see that Roebuck will never do any good for our Free Trade party. He does not see the importance of our principle, and therefore cannot feel a proper interest in it. He is a good deal in communication with Brougham, who, by the way, sent word by Sturge to-day that he wants to see me. I find myself beset by cliques, but my abstemious and ruminating turn will make me entirely safe from all such intrigues and influences."[1]

"From what I can hear," he wrote a month later, "it appears that Peel has no plan in view of any kind, with respect to the Corn question. The aristocracy and people are gaping at him, wondering what he is going to do, and his head will be at work with no higher ambition than to gull both parties. I am of opinion that there never was a better moment than at present for carrying the question out of doors. If there be determination enough in the minds of the people to make a vigorous demonstration during the recess, he will give way; if not, he will stick to his sliding scale and the aristocracy. There is a rumour very industriously spread in London that we are going to have a better trade. This is one in the chapter of accidents upon which Peel depends for an escape into smooth water."

Now, as throughout the whole of the struggle, Cobden kept up the closest relations with the local leaders of the movement in the north. One of the most baneful effects of the concentration and intensity of parliamentary life is that members cease to inspire themselves with the more wholesome air of the nation

[1] *To F. Cobden*, August 29, 1841.

outside. From the beginning to the end of his career, Cobden cared very little about the opinion of the House, and hoped very little from its disinterestedness. He never greatly valued the judgment of parliamentary coteries. It was the mind of the country that he always sought to know and to influence. And though he had proper confidence in the soundness of his own judgment, he was wholly free from the weakness of thinking that his judgment could stand alone. He was invariably eager to collect the opinions of his fellow-workers at Manchester, and not only to collect them, but to be guided by them.

"It is quite evident," he wrote to Mr. George Wilson, towards the end of September, "that Peel has made up his mind to prorogue without entering upon the consideration of the Corn Law. The business of the session will now be hurried on and brought to a close probably by the end of the week. Under these circumstances I wish to know the opinion of our friends in Manchester as to the course which it would be advisable for the few Anti-Corn Law members now in London to pursue. Will you be good enough at once to call together the whole of the Council, and consult with as many judicious people as you can, and determine whether you think anything, and what, can be done to promote the cause? The main question for you to decide is whether it be advisable for Mr. Villiers to give notice of a motion for discussing the question before the Houses are prorogued. The Tories would shirk the discussion in the same way as heretofore. Do you think under such circumstances that it would advance our cause by persisting in a one-sided debate? I think the general opinion up here is that the way in which Peel has hitherto evaded the question, has

1841. — Æt. 37.

done us good service by dissatisfying the public mind with the new Ministry. But we are not good judges of the public feeling, who are actors in a sphere of our own, where we are apt to be acted upon by our own preconceived opinions. You are in a better position for forming a correct judgment as to the state of the public mind. The question for you to decide really is whether the feeling out of doors would back a small party in the House struggling for a hearing of their cause now. Do you think there is a desire for us to make a pertinacious stand *now*? Be good enough to take the matter into your calm consideration, and give me the result of your deliberation by return. Mr. Villiers, who is now installed as our leader, would, I have no doubt, act upon your well-considered judgment. I would merely add that you would do well to take into consideration the probable amount of public demonstration to be made by memorials to the Queen during the next week. You will be able to form an estimate of the extent to which the example of Manchester will be followed in other places, and which must form a material consideration in deciding upon the course we ought to take in Parliament."[1]

Cobden made two other speeches in the course of the autumn session, after the re-election of the Ministers (September 16–October 7). Lord John Russell reproached the new Premier for asking for time to prepare his schemes for repairing the national finances. Peel justly asked him why, if they were so convinced of the urgency of the evils inflicted on the country by the Corn Laws, if they thought that commercial distress was to be attributed to them, and that these laws were at the root of the

[1] *To G. Wilson*, September 1841.

sufferings of the working class—why they had allowed them to remain an open question, and why they remained in office, allowing Lord Melbourne to hold opposite opinions. Cobden rose to protest against treating the subject as a party question, and against making the House a mere debating club. He insisted on trying to keep the mind of the House fixed on the privation and distress in the manufacturing districts, and he urged the Minister not to postpone the question of the Corn Laws over the coming winter.

". . . I sat through the voting of money, vastly edified and scandalized at the way in which the poor devils of tax-payers are robbed. The sum of £100,000 for arming and clothing militia in Canada, lighthouses in Jamaica, negro education, bishops all over the world, etc. etc., in goodly proportions. . . . The people are, I am afraid, fit for nothing better. I did not offer an objection, for it would have been ridiculous to do so. It did, however, cost me some efforts to hold my tongue. I am glad that you did not think my second speech too strong. I was not quite satisfied with it myself. It was, however, badly reported. I was rather better pleased with my third on Friday, when I found there was an effort made at first to annoy me, on the part of some young obscures, one of whom followed me with an evidently 'conned reply,' in which he had quotations from my speech at Manchester, about the Oxford education, the Ilissus, Scamander, etc. His speech was not reported. It was a mere prize-essay oration, which, thanks to the practical turn that has been given to subjects of debate, finds no relish in the House nowadays. It is quite clear that I am looked upon as a Gothic invader, and the classicals will criticize me unmercifully. But I have vitality enough to rise above

1841. — ÆT. 37.

the little trips which my heels may get at first. Ultimately these attacks will only give me a surer foothold. The part of my last speech that struck home the most was at the close. I had observed an evident disposition on the Tory side to set up as philanthropists. Old Sir Robert Inglis sat with his hands folded ready to sigh, and, if needful, to weep over a case of church destitution; he delivered a flaming panegyric upon Lord Ashley the other night, styling him *the friend of the unprotected*, after he had been canting about the sufferings of lunatics. Added to this, Peel has been professing the utmost anxiety for paupers, and Sir Eardley Wilmot is running after Sturge. When I told them at the close of my speech that I had been quietly observing all this, but it would not all do unless they showed their consistency by untaxing the poor man's loaf, there was a stillness and attention on the other side very much like the conduct of men looking aghast at the first consciousness of being found out. My style of speaking pleases the gallery people, and has attracted the notice of the Radicals out of doors. But the Tories, especially the young fry, regard me in no other way than as a petard would be viewed by people in a powder-magazine, a thing to be trampled on, kicked about, or put out in any way they can."[1]

When Cobden rose on this last occasion there were cries of impatience from the ministerial side of the House, but this did not prevent him from persevering with an argumentative remonstrance against the incredulity or apathy with which the Government treated the distress of the manufacturing towns. The point which he pressed most keenly was the interchange of food and manufactures between England and the United States that would

[1] *To F. Cobden*, Sept. 27, 1841.

instantly follow repeal. He quoted from a petition to the Congress of the United States. The petitioner argued that if the English landowners would only be satisfied with a moderate duty in lieu of the existing sliding scale, there would then be a constant market for wheat in England, and the whole of the return would be required in British manufactured goods; the consequence of which would be that every spindle, wheel, and hammer in the manufacturing district in this country would be set free.

"Suppose now," Cobden went on, "that it were but the Thames instead of the Atlantic which separated the two countries—suppose that the people on one side were mechanics and artisans, capable by their industry of producing a vast supply of manufactures; and that the people on the other side were agriculturists, producing infinitely more than they could themselves consume of corn, pork, and beef—fancy these two separate peoples anxious and willing to exchange with each other the produce of their common industries, and fancy a demon rising from the middle of the river—for I cannot imagine anything human in such a position and performing such an office—fancy a demon rising from the river, and holding in his hand an Act of Parliament, and saying, 'You shall not supply each other's wants'; and then in addition to that, let it be supposed that this demon said to his victim with an affected smile, 'This is for your benefit; I do it entirely for your protection!' Where was the difference between the Thames and the Atlantic?"

It was after a vigorous and persistent description of the privations of the people in the north, that he turned sharply round upon the men whom he denounced for drawing the attention of Parliament away from the real issues to vague questions of

1841.
—
ÆT. 37.

philanthropy. "When I go down to the manufacturing districts," he said, "I know that I shall be returning to a gloomy scene. I know that starvation is stalking through the land, and that men are perishing for want of the merest necessaries of life. When I witness this, and recollect that there is a law which especially provides for keeping our population in absolute want, I cannot help attributing murder to the legislature of this country: and wherever I stand, whether here or out of doors, I will denounce that system of legislative murder." He then turned to one member who was a great friend of negro slaves, and to another who was a great friend of Church Establishment, and who had lately complimented Lord Ashley as the great friend of humanity generally, and of factory children in particular. "When I see a disposition among you," he said, "to trade in humanity, I will not question your motives, but this I will tell you, that if you would give force and grace to your professions of humanity, it must not be confined to the negro at the antipodes, nor to the building of churches, nor to the extension of Church establishments, nor to occasional visits to factories to talk sentiment over factory children—you must untax the people's bread."

Cobden's intervention in debate was more than a parliamentary incident. It was the symbol of a new spirit of self-assertion in a great social order. The Reform Bill had admitted manufacturing towns to a share of representation. Cobden lost no time in vindicating the reality of this representation. The conflict of the next five years was not merely a battle about a customs duty; it was a struggle for political influence and social equality between the landed aristocracy and the great industrialists. Of this, an incident in the debates of the following session will furnish us with a sufficiently graphic illustration. It is only by reading the correspondence of that time, and listening to the men who still survive, without having left its passions behind them, that we realize the angry astonishment with which the old society of England beheld the first serious attempts of a new class to assert its claim to take a foremost place. Many years after the fight began, when Mr. Bright was unseated at Manchester, we shall find that Cobden laid most stress on the ingratitude of the manufacturers of the northern capital in forgetting that Mr. Bright had been the "valiant defender of their order."

CHAPTER IX

COBDEN AS AN AGITATOR

1841. — ÆT. 37.

IN the autumn of 1841 there happened what proved to be a signal event in the annals of the League, and in Cobden's personal history. He and Mr. Bright made that solemn compact which gave so strong an impulse to the movement, and was the beginning of an affectionate and noble friendship that lasted without a cloud or a jar until Cobden's death.

Mr. Bright, who was seven years younger than Cobden, had made his acquaintance some time before the question of the Corn Laws had come up. He had gone over in the year 1836 or 1837 to Manchester, to call upon Cobden, "to ask him if he would be kind enough to come to Rochdale, and to speak at an education meeting which was about to be held in the schoolroom of the Baptist chapel in West Street of that town. I found him in his office in Mosley Street. I introduced myself to him. I told him what I wanted. His countenance lit up with pleasure to find that there were others that were working in this question, and he without hesitation agreed to come. He came, and he spoke; and though he was then so young as a speaker, yet the qualities of his speech were such as remained with him so long as he was able to speak at all—clearness, logic, a conversational eloquence, a persuasiveness which, when conjoined with the absolute truth which there was in his eye and in his countenance—a persuasiveness which it was almost impossible to resist."

Then came the gradual formation of the League, Cobden's election to Parliament, and the close of his first session. "It was in September, in the year 1841," said Mr. Bright. "The sufferings throughout the country were fearful; and you who live now, but were not of age to observe what was passing in the country then, can have no idea of the state of your country in that year. . . . At that time I was at Leamington, and I was, on the day when Mr. Cobden called upon me—for he happened to be there at the time on a visit to some relatives—I was in the depths of grief, I might almost say of despair; for the light and sunshine of my house had been extinguished. All that was left on earth of my young wife, except the memory of a sainted life and of a too brief happiness, was lying still and cold in the chamber above us. Mr. Cobden called upon me as his friend, and addressed me, as you might suppose, with words of condolence.[1] After a time he looked up and said, 'There are thousands of houses in England at this moment where wives, mothers, and children are dying of hunger. Now,' he said, 'when the first paroxysm of your grief is past, I would advise you to come with me, and we will never rest till the Corn Law is repealed.' I accepted his invitation. I knew that the description he had given of the homes of thousands was not an exaggerated description. I felt in my conscience that there was a work which somebody must do, and therefore I accepted his invitation, and from that time we never

[1] Mr. Bright lost his wife on the 10th of September, and Cobden's visit to him was on the 13th.

ceased to labour hard on behalf of the resolution which we had made."

"For seven years," Mr. Bright says, "the discussion on that one question—whether it was good for a man to have half a loaf or a whole loaf—for seven years the discussion was maintained, I will not say with doubtful result, for the result was never doubtful, and never could be in such a cause; but for five years or more [1841-6] we devoted ourselves without stint; every working hour almost was given up to the discussion and to the movement in connexion with this question."[1]

This is an appropriate place for considering some of the qualifications that Cobden brought to the mission which he and his ally thus imposed upon themselves. In speaking of him I may seem to ignore fellow-workers whose share in the agitation was hardly less important than his own; without whose zeal, disinterestedness, and intelligence, the work of himself and Mr. Bright would have been of little effect, and could never have been undertaken. No history of the League could be perfect which did not commemorate the names and labours of many other able men, who devoted themselves with hardly inferior energy to the exhausting work of organization and propagandism. But these pages have no pretensions to tell the whole story; they only are concerned with so much of it as relates to one of its heroes. "We were not even the first," said Mr. Bright, "though afterwards, perhaps, we became the foremost before the public. But there were others before us." The public imagination was struck by

[1] This and the preceding passages are from the very beautiful address delivered by Mr. Bright, when he unveiled the statue of his friend at Bradford, July 25, 1877. The address is to be found in Mr. Thorold Rogers's volume of *Public Addresses of John Bright*, pp. 354-366.

the figures of the pair who had given themselves up to a great public cause. The alliance between them far more than doubled the power that either could have exerted without the other. The picture of two plain men leaving their homes and their business, and going over the length and breadth of the land to convert the nation, had about it something apostolic: it presented something so far removed from the stereotyped ways of political activity, that this circumstance alone, apart from the object for which they were pleading, touched and affected people, and gave a certain dramatic interest to the long pilgrimages of the two men who had only become orators because they had something to say, which they were intent on bringing their hearers to believe, and which happened to be true, wise, and just.

The agitator has not been a very common personage in English history. The greatest that has ever been seen was O'Connell, and I do not know of any other, until the time of the League, who may be placed even as second to him. In the previous century Wilkes had made a great figure, and Wilkes was a man of real power and energy. But he was rather the symbol of a strong popular sentiment, than its inspirer; and he may be more truly said to have been borne on the crest of the movement, than to have given to it force or volume.

Cobden seemed to have few of the endowments of an agitator, as that character is ordinarily thought of. He had no striking physical gifts of the histrionic kind. He had one physical quality which must be ranked first among the secondary endowments of great workers. Later in life he said, "If I had not had the faculty of sleeping like a dead fish, in five minutes after the most exciting mental effort, and with the certainty of having oblivion for six consecutive hours, I should not have been alive now." In his early days, he was slight in frame and build. He afterwards grew nearer to portliness. He had a large and powerful head, and the indescribable charm of a candid eye. His features were not of a commanding type; but they were illuminated and made attractive by the brightness of intelligence, of sympathy, and of earnestness. About the mouth there was a curiously winning mobility and play. His voice was clear, varied in its tones, sweet, and penetrating; but it had scarcely the compass, or the depth, or the many resources that have usually been found in orators who have drawn great multitudes of men to listen to them. Of nervous fire, indeed, he had abundance, though it was not the fire which flames up in the radiant colours of a strong imagination. It was rather the glow of a thoroughly convinced reason, of intellectual ingenuity, of argumentative keenness. It came from transparent honesty, thoroughly clear ideas, and a very definite purpose. These were exactly the qualities that Cobden's share in the work demanded. Any professor could have supplied a demonstration of the economic fallacy of monopoly. Fox, the Unitarian minister, was better able to stir men's spirits by pictures, which were none the less true for being very florid, of the social miseries that came of monopoly. In Cobden the fervour and the logic were mixed, and his fervour was seen to have its source in the strength of his logical confidence.

It has often been pointed out how the two great spokesmen of the League were the complements of one another; how their gifts differed, so that one exactly covered the ground which the other was predisposed to leave comparatively untouched. The differences between them, it is true, were not so

1841. Æt. 37.

many as the points of resemblance. If in Mr. Bright there was a deeper austerity, in both there was the same homeliness of allusion, and the same graphic plainness. Both avoided the stilted abstractions of rhetoric, and neither was ever afraid of the vulgarity of details. In Cobden as in Bright, we feel that there was nothing personal or small, and that what they cared for so vehemently were great causes. There was a resolute standing aloof from the small things of party, which would be almost arrogant, if the whole texture of what they had to say were less thoroughly penetrated with political morality and with humanity. Then there came the points of difference. Mr. Bright had all the resources of passion alive within his breast. He was carried along by vehement political anger, and, deeper than that, there glowed a wrath as stern as that of an ancient prophet. To cling to a mischievous error seemed to him to savour of moral depravity and corruption of heart. What he saw was the selfishness of the aristocracy and the landlords, and he was too deeply moved by hatred of this, to care to deal very patiently with the bad reasoning which their own self-interest inclined his adversaries to mistake for good. His invective was not the expression of mere irritation, but a profound and menacing passion. Hence he dominated his audiences from a height, while his companion rather drew them along after him as friends and equals. Cobden was by no means incapable of passion, of violent feeling, or of vehement expression. His fighting qualities were in their own way as formidable as Mr. Bright's; and he had a way of dropping his jaw and throwing back his head, when he took off the gloves for an encounter in good earnest, which was not less alarming to his opponents than the more sombre style of his colleague.

Still, it was not passion to which we must look for the secret of his oratorical success. I have asked many scores of those who knew him, Conservatives as well as Liberals, what this secret was, and in no single case did my interlocutor fail to begin, and in nearly every case he ended as he had begun, with the word *persuasiveness.* Cobden made his way to men's hearts by the union which they saw in him of simplicity, earnestness, and conviction, with a singular facility of exposition. This facility consisted in a remarkable power of apt and homely illustration, and a curious ingenuity in framing the argument that happened to be wanted. Besides his skill in thus hitting on the right argument, Cobden had the oratorical art of presenting it in the way that made its admission to the understanding of a listener easy and undenied. He always seemed to have made exactly the right degree of allowance for the difficulty with which men follow a speech, as compared with the ease of following the same argument on a printed page which they may con and ponder until their apprehension is complete. Then men were attracted by his mental alacrity, by the instant readiness with which he turned round to grapple with a new objection. Prompt and confident, he was never at a loss, and he never hesitated. This is what Mr. Disraeli meant when he spoke of Cobden's "sauciness." It had an excellent effect, because everybody knew that it sprang, not from levity or presumption, but from a free mastery of his subject.

If in one sense the Corn Laws did not seem a promising theme for a popular agitation, they were excellently fitted to bring out Cobden's peculiar strength, for they dealt with firm matter and demonstrable inferences, and this was the region where Cobden's powers naturally exercised themselves. In such an appeal to sentiment and popular passion as the contemporary agitation of O'Connell for Repeal, he could have played no leading part.[1] Where knowledge and logic were the proper instruments, Cobden was a master.

Enormous masses of material for the case poured every week into the offices of the League. All the day long Cobden was talking with men who had something to tell him. Correspondents from every quarter of the land plied him with information. Yet he was never overwhelmed by the volume of the stream. He was incessantly on the alert for a useful fact, a telling illustration, a new fallacy to expose. So dexterously did he move through the ever-growing piles of matter, that it seemed to his companions as if nothing apposite ever escaped him, and nothing irrelevant ever detained him.

A political or religious agitator must not be afraid of incessant repetition. Repetition is his most effective instrument. The fastidiousness which is proper to literature, and which makes a man dread to say the same thing twice, is in the field of propagandism mere impotency. This is one reason why even the greatest agitators in causes which have shaken the world, are often among the least interesting men in history. Cobden had moral and social gifts which invest him with a peculiar attraction, and will long make his memory interesting as that of a versatile nature; but he was never afraid of the agitator's art of repeating his formula, his principles, his illustrations, his phrases, with untiring reiteration.

Though he abounded in matter, Cobden can hardly be described as copious. He is neat and pointed, nor is his argument ever left unclenched;

[1] See Mr. McCarthy's *History of Our Own Times*, i. 340, 348.

but he permits himself no large excursions. What he was thinking of was the matter immediately in hand, the audience before his eyes, the point that would tell best then and there, and would be most likely to remain in men's recollections. For such purposes copiousness is ill-fitted; that is for the stately leisure of the pulpit. Cobden's task was to leave in his hearer's mind a compact answer to each current fallacy, and to scotch or kill as many protectionist sophisms as possible within the given time. What is remarkable, is that while he kept close to the matter and substance of his case, and resorted comparatively little to sarcasm, humour, invective, pathos, or the other elements that are catalogued in manuals of rhetoric, yet no speaker was ever further removed from prosiness, or came into more real and sympathetic contact with his audience. His speaking was thoroughly business-like, and yet it was never dull. It was not, according to the old definition of oratory, reason fused in passion, but reason fused by the warmth of personal geniality. No one has ever reached Cobden's pitch of success as a platform speaker, with a style that seldom went beyond the vigorous and animated conversation of a bright and companionable spirit.

After all, it is not tropes and perorations that make the popular speaker; it is the whole impression of his personality. We who only read them, can discern certain admirable qualities in Cobden's speeches; aptness in choosing topics, lucidity in presenting them, buoyant confidence in pressing them home. But those who listened to them felt much more than all this. They were delighted by mingled vivacity and ease, by directness, by spontaneousness and reality, by the charm, so effective and so uncommon between a speaker and his audience, of personal friendliness and undisguised cordiality. Let me give an illustration of this. Cobden once had an interview with Rowland Hill, some time in 1838, and gave evidence in favour of the proposed reform in the postage. Rowland Hill, in writing to him afterwards, excuses himself for troubling Cobden with his private affairs: "Your conversation, evidence, and letters, have created a feeling in my mind so like that which one entertains towards an old friend, that I am apt to forget that I have met you but once." It was just the same with bodies of men as it was with individuals. No public speaker was ever so rapid and so successful in establishing genial relations of respect without formality, and intimacy without familiarity. One great source of this, in Mr. Bright's words, was "the absolute truth that shone in his eye and in his countenance."

1841.

ÆT. 37.

I have spoken of Cobden's patience in acquiring and shaping matter. This was surpassed by his inexhaustible patience in dealing with the mental infirmities of those whom it was his business to persuade. He was wholly free from the unmeasured anger against human stupidity, which is itself one of the most provoking forms of that stupidity. Cobden was not without the faculty of intellectual contempt, and he had the gift of irony; but in the contempt was no presumption, and it was irony without truculence. There came a time when he found that he could do nothing with men; when he could hardly even hope to find an audience that would suffer him to speak. But during the work of the League, at any rate, he had none of that bias against his own countrymen to which the reformer in every nation is so liable, because upon the reformer their defects press very closely and obstructively, while he has no reason to observe the same or worse defects in other nations.

It has often been said that Cobden was a good Englishman, and he was so, in spite of finer qualities which our neighbours are not willing to allow to us. London society, and smart journalists who mistook a little book-knowledge for culture, were in the habit of disparaging Cobden as a common manufacturer, without an idea in his head beyond buying in the cheapest market and selling in the dearest. This was not the way in which he struck the most fastidious, critical, and refined man of letters in Europe, accustomed to mix with the most important personages of literature and affairs then alive. Prosper Mérimée saw a great deal of Cobden in 1860, when they both spent part of the winter at Cannes. "Cobden," he wrote to his intimate correspondent, "is a man of an extremely interesting mind; quite the opposite of an Englishman in this respect, that you never hear him talk commonplaces, and that he has few prejudices." It was just because he was not a man of prejudice, that he had none against his own countrymen. We saw how when he was travelling in America, he found his British blood up, as he said, and he dealt faithfully with the disparagers of the mother country.[1] Returning from France on one occasion, Cobden says in his journal, that they all remarked on the handsome women who were seen on the English platforms, and all agreed that they were handsomer than those whom they had left on the other side. "The race of men and women in the British Islands," Cobden goes on to himself, "is the finest in the world in a physical sense; and although they have many moral defects and some repulsive qualities, yet

[1] Above, pp. 37-8.

on the whole I think the English are the most outspoken, truthful men in the world, and this virtue lies at the bottom of their political and commercial greatness."

This conviction inspired him with a peculiar respect for his great popular audiences, and they instinctively felt the presence of it, making a claim to their good-will and their attention. Cobden differed from his countrymen as to what it is that will make England great, but he was as anxious that England should be great, and as proud of English virtues and energies, as the noisiest patriot in a London music-hall.

Cobden always said that it was an advantage to him as an agitator that he was a member of the Church of England. He used to tell of men who came up to him and declared that their confidence in him dated from the moment when they learnt that he was a Churchman. It was, perhaps, a greater advantage to him than he knew. However little we may admire a State establishment of religion, it is certain that where such an establishment happens to exist, those who have been brought up in it, and have tranquilly conformed to its usages, escape one source of a certain mental asperity and the spirit of division. This is no credit to them or to the institution; any more than the asperity is a discredit to those who do not conform to the institution. Nay, one strong reason why some disapprove of systems of ecclesiastical privilege, is exactly that in modern societies it necessarily engenders this spirit of division. But in itself the spirit of division is no element of strength, but rather of weakness, for one whose task is to touch doubtful or unwilling hearers.

Temperament, however, had a larger share than institutions in Cobden's faculty of moral sympathy.

1841.
Æt. 37.

There is scanty evidence of anything like an intense spirituality in his nature; he was neither oppressed nor elevated by the mysteries, the aspirations, the remorse, the hope, that constitute religion. So far as we can have means of knowing, he was not of those who live much in the Unseen. But for moral goodness, in whatever association he came upon it, he had a reverence that came from his heart of hearts. While leaning strongly towards those scientific theories of motive and conduct, of which, as has been already said, George Combe was in those days the most active propagandist, he felt no contempt, provided only their practical endeavour was towards good, for those who clung narrowly to older explanations of the heart of man. In a letter written to Combe himself, when the struggle against the Corn Laws was over, Cobden allows himself to talk freely on his own attitude in these high matters:—

. . . "With reference," he says, "to your remarks as to the evangelical dissenters and religionists generally, and their views of your philosophy of morals—I will confess to you that *I* am not inclined to quarrel with that class of my countrymen. I see the full force of what you urge, but am inclined to hope more from them in time than any other party in the State. Gradually and imperceptibly to themselves they are catching the spirit of the age, so far as to recognize the moral laws as a part of our natural organization. They do not accept your views to the *superseding* of their own, but, like geology, your science is forcing its way alongside of preconceived ideas, and they will for a time go together without perceptibly clashing.

"I do not quarrel with the religionists, for I find them generally enforcing or at all events recognizing and professing to act upon (they do not, I admit, sufficiently preach it) the morality of the New Testament, and you can do no more. The only difference is that John Calvin and George Combe act upon different theories, and rely upon different motives, and start from very different premises, but they recognize the self-same ends secularly speaking, and I cannot quarrel with either . . . I am by nature a religionist. I was much struck with your remark when you mapped my head eleven years ago,—'Why, if you had been born in the middle ages, you would have made a good monk, you have so much veneration!' That was a triumph for phrenology, for you could have formed no such notion from anything you had seen or heard of me. I have a strong religious feeling,—a sympathy for men who act under that impulse; I reverence it as the great leverage which has moved mankind to powerful action. I acknowledge that it has been perverted to infinite mischief. I confess it has been the means of degrading men to brutish purposes . . . . but it has also done glorious deeds for liberty and human exaltation, and it is destined to do still better things. It is fortunate for me that whilst possessing a strong logical faculty, which keeps me in the path of rationalism, I have the religious sympathy which enables me to co-operate with men of exclusively religious sentiment. I mean it is fortunate for my powers of usefulness in this my day and generation. To this circumstance I am greatly indebted for the success of the great Free Trade struggle, which has been more indebted to the organ of veneration for its success, than is generally known.

"I am not without hopes that the same fortunate circumstance in organization may enable me to co-operate efficiently with the most active and best spirits of our day, in the work of moral and intellectual EDUCATION. I could insist upon the necessity of secular teaching and training without wounding the religious prejudices of any man, excepting the grovelling bigots whether of the High Church party or the opposite extreme, against whom I could make war in the same spirit which has in the case of the Corn monopolists enabled me to deprive them of the pretence for personal resentment, even in the hour of their defeat and humiliation.

"I have said that I have a strong feeling of sympathy for the religious sentiment. But I sympathize with all moral men who are not *passive* moralists: with them it is difficult to sympathize, but I venerate and trust them. Especially do I sympathize with those who labour and make sacrifices for the diffusion of sound moral principles. I will own, however, that it is unpleasant to my feelings to associate with those who, whilst they indulge in coarse sceptical allusions to our faith, do not in their private life manifest that they impose a better restraint upon themselves than is to be found in the New Testament. My active public life has sometimes thrown me into such company, and with these *esprits forts*, as the French call them, I have no sympathy. My maxim is in such predicaments to avoid theological discussions (here again is my veneration over-riding causality), and to avow that I am resolved to follow Bonaparte's advice—to adhere to the religion of my mother, who was an energetically pious woman."[1]

No whisper was ever seriously raised against Cobden's transparent honesty. What is worth remarking is that his sincerity was not of that cheap

[1] *To George Combe*, Aug. 1, 1846.

and reckless kind, by virtue of which men sometimes in one wild outburst of plain speech cut themselves off from chances of public usefulness for the remainder of their lives. He laid down certain social ends, which he thought desirable, and which he believed that he could promote. And when one of these was fixed in his mind, and set definitely before him, he became the most circumspect of creatures. Being a man of action, and not a speculative teacher, he took care not to devote his energies to causes in which he did not see a good chance of making some effective mark, either on legislation or on important sections of public opinion. "I am cautious to a fault," he once wrote, "and nothing will be done by me that has not the wisdom of the serpent, as much as the harmlessness of the dove in it."[1]

This was only another way of saying that strong enthusiasm in him was no hindrance to strong sense. Instead of increasing the elements of friction—the besetting weakness of reformers and dissidents of all kinds—he took infinite trouble to reduce these elements to the lowest possible point. Hence he was careful not to take up too many subjects at once, because the antagonism generated by each would have been made worse by the antagonism belonging to every other, and he would have called up a whole host of enemies together, instead of leaving himself free to deal with one at a time. A correspondent once wrote to him on this point.

"You have opened a very important question," Cobden replied, "in respect to the duty of a public man to advocate all the changes to which he may be favourable. I have often reflected upon this. Bacon says, if you have a handful of truths, open

[1] *To S. Lucas*, Jan. 27, 1862.

but one finger at a time. He is not the safest moral guide, I admit, but I am not sure that he is not to some extent right in this view. If we are to declare our convictions upon all subjects, and if abstract reason is to be our guide, without reference to time and circumstance, why should not I, for instance, avow myself a republican? A republic is undeniably the most rational form of government for free men. But I doubt whether I should enhance my power of usefulness by advocating that form of government for England. But whilst I do not think I should act wisely by putting forth all I think, in a practical way I so far admit the principle that I would not advocate the opposite of what I am convinced is the truth abstractedly. And this brings me to my old ground of trying to do one thing at a time. By this I mean merely that I have an aptitude for certain questions. Other people have a talent for others, and I think a division of labour is necessary for success in political, as in industrial life."[1]

This wise economy brought its reward. Cobden did not carry the world with him in his own lifetime, but what he did by his method was to bring certain principles of human progress into line with the actual politics of the day. He did not create a majority, but he achieved the first difficult step of creating a strong minority, and this not merely of sympathizers in the closet, but of active followers in the nation.

It was what he called his wisdom of the serpent that gave Cobden his power in the other arts of a successful agitator, which are less conspicuous but hardly less indispensable, than commanding or persuasive oratory. He applied the same qualities in the actual business of the League which he

[1] *To the Rev. Thomas Spencer*, April 23, 1849.

brought to bear in his speeches. He was indefatigable in his industry, fertile in ingenious devices for bringing the objects of the League before the country, constantly on the alert for surprising a hostile post, never losing a chance of turning a foe or a neutral into a friend, and never allowing his interest about the end for which he was working, to confuse his vigilant concentration upon the means. The danger of great confederacies like the League is that they become mechanical. Machinery must of necessity play a large part. Circulars, conferences, subscriptions, advertisements, deputations, eternal movings and secondings—all these things are apt to bury the vital part of a movement under a dreary and depressing fussiness, that makes one sometimes wonder whether the best means of saving an institution might not be to establish a society for overthrowing it. A society of this kind seems often a short way for choking the most earnest spirits with dusty catch-words, that are incessantly being ground out by the treadmill of agitation. It was Cobden's fresh and sanguine temper that bore him triumphantly through this peril, though none of the energetic men with whom he worked was more busily intent on every detail of their organization. He had none of that fastidiousness which is repelled by the vulgarities of a proselytizing machine. He was like a general with a true genius for war. The strategy was a delight to him; in tactics he was one of the most adroit of men; he looked to everything; he showed the boldness, the vigilance, the tenacity, the resource, of a great commander. Above all, he had the commander's gift of encouraging and stimulating others. He had enthusiasm, patience, and good humour, which is the most valuable of all qualities in a campaign. There was as little bitterness in

1841. — ÆT. 37.

his nature as in any human being that ever lived: so little that he was able to say, at the end of seven years of as energetic an agitation as could be carried on, short of physical force, that he believed he had not made a single enemy, nor wounded a single man's personal feelings.

Critics usually singled out Cobden's logical faculty as his strongest trait, and it was so; but he was naturally inclined to think of the conclusions of his logic in poetized forms. He always delighted, in spite of the wretched simile with which they close, in the lines in which Cowper anticipated the high economic doctrine:—

> Again—the band of commerce was design'd,
> To associate all the branches of mankind,
> And if a boundless plenty be the robe,
> Trade is the golden Girdle of the globe.
> Wise to promote whatever end he means,
> God opens fruitful Nature's various scenes,
> Each climate needs what other climes produce,
> And offers something to the general use;
> No land but listens to the common call,
> And in return receives supply from all.
> This genial intercourse and mutual aid
> Cheers what were else an universal shade,
> Calls Nature from her ivy-mantled den,
> And softens human rock-work into men.

From Cowper, too, he was never weary of quoting the lines about liberty:—

> 'Tis liberty alone that gives the flower
> Of fleeting life its lustre and perfume,
> And we are weeds without it. All constraint
> Except what wisdom lays on evil men
> Is evil.

It was this association of solid doctrine with genial enthusiasm and high ideals, that distinguished Cobden from too many preachers of what our humorist has called the gospel according to McCrowdy. It was this kindly imaginativeness in him which caught men's hearts. His ideals were constantly sneered at as low, material, common, unworthy, especially by the class whose lives are one long course of indolence, dilettantism, and sensuality. George Combe tells how one evening in 1852 he was in the drawing-room of some great lady, who, amid the applause of her friends, denounced Cobden's policy as never rising beyond a mere "bagman's millennium."[1] This was the clever way, among the selfish and insolent, of saying that the ideal which Cobden cherished was comfort for the mass, not luxury for the few. He knew much better than they, that material comfort is, as little as luxury, the highest satisfaction of men's highest capacities; but he could well afford to scorn the demand for fine ideals of life on the lips of a class who were starving the workers of the country in order to save their own rents.

There is one more point on which it is worth while to say a word in connexion with Cobden's character as an agitator. The great danger of the career is that it may in time lessen a man's moral self-possession. Effect becomes the decisive consideration instead of truth; a good meeting grows into a final object in life; the end of existence is a paradise of loud and prolonged cheering; and character is gradually destroyed by the parasites of self-consciousness and vanity. On one occasion, in 1845, as we shall see, Cobden was betrayed, excusably enough, into some strong language about Sir Robert Peel. Miss Martineau, George Combe, and others, rebuked him rather sharply. He took the rebuke with perfect temper and humility, and in

[1] *Life of George Combe*, ii. 309.

1841. — ÆT. 37.

seeking to excuse himself, he described his feelings about public life in words of which it is impossible to doubt the exact truth. "You must not judge me," he said, "by what I say at these tumultuous public meetings. I constantly regret the necessity of violating good taste and kind feeling in my public harangues. I say advisedly *necessity*, for I defy anybody to keep the ear of the public for seven years upon one question, without studying to amuse as well as instruct. People do not attend public meetings to be taught, but to be excited, flattered, and pleased. If they are simply lectured, they may sit out the lesson for once, but they will not come again ; and as I have required them again and again, I have been obliged to amuse them, not by standing on my head or eating fire, but by kindred feats of jugglery, such as appeals to their self-esteem, their combativeness, or their humour. You know how easily in touching these feelings one degenerates into flattery, vindictiveness, and grossness. I really sometimes wonder how I have escaped so well as I have done. By nature I am not a mob orator. It is an effort for me to speak in public. The applause of a meeting has no charm for me. When I address an audience, it is from a sense of duty and utility, from precisely the motive which impels me to write an article in the *League* newspaper, and with as little thought of personal *éclat*. Do not, therefore, be alarmed with the idea that my head will be turned with applause. It would be a relief to me if I knew there was no necessity for my ever appearing again at a public meeting."[1]

[1] *To George Combe*, Dec. 29, 1845.

CHAPTER X

THE NEW CORN LAW

1842.

ÆT. 38.

In the interval between the prorogation and the great session of 1842 it was commonly understood that the Government would certainly do something with the Corn Law. Expectation was not sanguine among the men in the north. Some of the more impatient were so irritated by the delay, that they even wished to agitate for the overthrow of a Government which had just been appointed, and which commanded an overwhelming majority. Cobden was wiser. To one of the shrewdest of his allies he wrote some useful truth:—

"I do not like your idea," he said, "of getting the deputies to pass a vote for dismissing the Ministry. That would be taken as a partisan movement—which it really would be—and we should lose moral influence by it. Let us not forget that we were very tolerant of the Whig Ministers, even after Melbourne had laughed in our faces and called us madmen. The present Government will do something. It is the House of Commons, and not the Ministers, that we ought to attack. I do not see how with decency we can worry the Queen to change her Ministers, whilst the *people's* representatives have made her take to Peel against her consent. And amongst the representatives who have done this are

1842. — ÆT. 38.

those from Liverpool, Warrington, Wigan, Leeds, Blackburn, Lancaster, et cetera. Really when we think of these places, it ought to make us modest.

"I have been thinking a good deal of the plan of district meetings alluded to in a former letter to Mr. Rawson, and am more and more favourable to it. I am convinced that spontaneous efforts through the country would tell more powerfully upon the aristocracy, than another great meeting in Manchester. The question has been too much confined to Manchester. The cotton lords are not more popular than the landlords."[1]

Although he deprecated the agitation of impatience, Cobden was as eager and as active as anybody else in the agitation of persuasion. He spoke at a great conference, held at Derby, of the merchants of Derbyshire, Nottinghamshire, and Leicestershire, where he made a vigorous onslaught upon what he called the Land-tax fraud. From the Trent he found his way to the Clyde, while Mr. Bright went to Dublin, as well as to every place nearer home where he could get men to listen to him. In all the centres of industry people were urged to form associations, to get up petitions, and to hold district meetings of deputies. They were to collect information as to the state of trade, the rate of wages, the extent of pauperism, and other facts bearing upon the food monopoly, as all these things affected their local industry; the woollen trade at Leeds, the iron trade at Wolverhampton, the earthenware trade in the Potteries, the flax trade at Dundee, the cotton trade at Manchester and Glasgow.

The lecturers continued their work. One of them went among the farmers and labourers on Sir James Graham's estate, where he did not forget the land-

[1] *To G. Wilson*, Leamington, Oct. 12, 1841.

lord's idyllic catalogue of the blessings of the rural poor. "What!" cried the lecturer, "six shillings a week for wages, and the morning's sun, and the singing of birds, and sportive lambs, and winding streams, and the mountain breeze, and a little wholesome labour—six shillings a week, and all this! And nothing to do with your six shillings a week, but merely to pay your rent, buy your food, clothe yourselves and your families, and lay by something for old age! Happy people!" In many rural districts the only arguments which the lecturers were called upon to resist were stones and brickbats; and even in some of the towns they still encountered rough and unfair treatment from members of the respectable classes, and their hired ruffians. The Chartists were for the time less violently hostile.

Among other devices this autumn was that of a great bazaar, which should both add to the funds of the League, and bring the friends of its objects into closer personal contact. The bazaar was held in the beginning of the following February, in the Royal Theatre at Manchester. It was a great success, and produced nearly ten thousand pounds. The following may serve to show Cobden's eye for the small things of agitation, and the unconsidered trifles that affect public opinion:—

"I have just got your letter, and am delighted that you are satisfied with the bazaar prospects. Really I wonder how you and your four coadjutors endure the immense exertions called for in this undertaking. You must not look upon the mere money return as the sole test of success. It will give us a position in the public eye worth all the outlay. I remember twelve months ago feeling apprehensive that the monopolist papers would have deterred the ladies from appearing as sellers at the

1842.
Æt. 38.

stalls by their blackguardism. Certainly three years ago that would have been the tone of the *Herald*, *Post*, and *Bull*. Now what a marked change is seen in those papers; not a joke or attempt at ribald wit. All is fair and even laudatory. In this fact alone I see the evidence of a great moral triumph of the League. Could you not get a succession of notices in the papers similar to the *Globe* last evening? Might not R. employ his pen in that way? Tell him not to be too rhapsodical or eulogistic in his descriptions, but to give from day to day a few facts and scraps of information which would induce the papers to insert the articles as news. There should be a description of the arrivals of the great trains filled with country Leaguers. In the next *League* let as long a list as possible of the people of rank who have attended be given—this is very important."[1]

Their newspaper deserves a word. Its energy was as striking as the energy of their speakers. Its leading articles, many of them written by Cobden and Bright themselves, were broad and weighty statements of the newest aspect of their case. Any unlucky phrase that fell from a monopolist was pounced upon and made the text of a vivacious paragraph. No incautious admission from the other side was ever allowed to escape, until all the most damaging conclusions that could be drawn from it had been worked out to the very uttermost. All the news of the day was scanned with a vigilant eye, and no item that could be turned into an argument or an illustration was left unimproved. This ingenuity and verve saved the paper from the monotony of most journals of a single purpose. Its pages were lighted up by reports of the speeches of Cobden, Bright, and

[1] *To G. Wilson*, November 1841.

Fox. The pictures with which it abounds of the condition of the common people, are more graphic than the most brilliant compositions of mere literary history. It does not affect us as the organ of a sect; though it preaches from one text, it is always human and social. There were Poor Men's Songs, Anti-Corn-Law Hymns, and Anti-Bread-Tax Collects. Nor did the editor forget Byron's famous lines from the *Age of Bronze*, a thousand times declaimed in this long war:—

See these inglorious Cincinnati swarm,
Farmers of war, dictators of the farm;
Their ploughshare was the sword in hireling hands,
Their fields manured by gore of other lands;
Safe in their barns, these Sabine tillers sent
Their brethren out to battle—why? for rent!
Year after year they voted cent per cent,
Blood, sweat, and tear-wrung millions—why? for rent!
They roar'd, they dined, they drank, they swore they meant
To die for England—why then live? for rent!
The Peace has made one general malcontent
Of these high-market patriots; war was rent!
Their love of country, millions all misspent,
How reconcile? by reconciling rent!
And will they not repay the treasures lent?
No: down with every thing, and up with rent!
Their good, ill, health, wealth, joy, or discontent,
Being, end, aim, religion—rent, rent, rent!

A volunteer in Preston this winter began to issue on his own account a quaint little sheet of four quarto pages, called *The Struggle*, and sold for a halfpenny. It had no connexion with any association, and nobody was responsible for its contents but the man who wrote, printed, and sold it. In two years eleven hundred thousand copies had been circulated. *The Struggle* is the very model for a plain man who wishes to affect the opinion of the humbler class, without the wasteful and, for the most part, ineffectual

1842. — ÆT. 38.

machinery of a great society. It contains in number after number the whole arguments of the matter in the pithiest form, and in language as direct if not as pure as Cobbett's. Sometimes the number consists simply of some more than usually graphic speech by Cobden or by Fox. There are racy dialogues, in which the landlord always gets the worst of it; and terse allegories in which the Duke of Buckingham or the Duke of Richmond figures as inauspiciously as Bunyan's Mr. Badman. The Bible is ransacked for appropriate texts, from the simple clause in the Lord's Prayer about our daily bread, down to Solomon's saying: "He that withholdeth the corn, the people shall curse him; but blessings shall be upon the head of him that selleth it." On the front page of each number was a woodcut, as rude as a schoolboy's drawing, but full of spirit and cleverness, whether satirizing the Government, or contrasting swollen landlords with famine-stricken operatives, or painting some homely idyll of the industrious poor, to point the greatest of political morals, that "domestic comfort is the object of all reforms."

Cobden had, at the beginning of the movement, been very near to securing the services, in the way of pictorial illustration, of a man who afterwards became very famous. This was Thackeray, then only known to a small public as the author of the *Hoggarty Diamond*. "Some inventor of a new mode of engraving," Mr. Henry Cole wrote to Cobden, "told Mr. Thackeray that it was applicable to the designs for the Corn Laws. Three drawings of your Anglo-Polish Allegory have been made and have failed. So Thackeray has given up the invention, and wood engraving must be used. This will materially alter the expense. . . . I hope you will think as well of the accompanying sketch—very rough, of course—as all I have shown it to, do. It was the work of only a few minutes, and I think, with its corpses, gibbet, and flying carrion crow, is as suggestive as you can wish. We both thought that a common soldier would be better understood than any more allegorical figure. It is only in part an adaptation of your idea, but I think a successful one. Figures representing eagerness of exchange, a half-clothed Pole offering bread, and a weaver manufactures, would be idea enough for a design alone. Of course, there may be any changes you please in this present design. I think for the multitude it would be well to have the ideas very simple and intelligible to all. The artist is a genius, both with his pencil and his pen. His vocation is literary. He is full of humour and feeling. Hitherto he has not had occasion to think much on the subject of Corn Laws, and therefore wants the stuff to work upon. He would like to combine both writing and drawing when sufficiently primed, and then he would write and illustrate ballads, or tales, or anything. I think you would find him a most effective auxiliary, and perhaps the best way to fill him with matter for illustrations, would be to invite him to see the weavers, their mills, shuttles, et cetera. If you like the sketch, perhaps you will return it to me, and I will put it in the way of being engraved.

"He will set about Lord Ashley when we have heard your opinion of the present sketch. Thackeray is the writer of an article in the last number of the *Westminster Review*, on French caricatures, and many other things. For some time he managed the *Constitutional* newspaper. He is a college friend of Charles Buller. We think the idea of an ornamental emblematical heading of the Circular good. The lower class of readers do not like to have to cut the leaves of a paper. Another, but a smaller class, like a small-sized page, because it is more convenient for binding. Corn Law readers lie, I suppose, chiefly among the former. Will you send your Circular to Thomas Carlyle, Cheyne Street, Chelsea? He was quoted in last week's Circular, and is making studies into the condition of the working class."[1]

The approach of the time for the assembling of Parliament drew men's minds away from everything else, and expectation became centred with new intensity on the scheme which the Minister would devise for the restoration of national prosperity. The retirement of an important member of the Cabinet during the recess had greatly quickened public excitement among both Protectionists and Free Traders. Both felt that their question was at stake, and that the Prime Minister would not allow the duty on corn to stand as it was. Peel has told us, in the *Memoirs* published after his death, exactly what happened during the autumn of 1841. In conformity with his general practice, he brought the subject under the consideration of his colleagues in written memoranda. These memoranda, he said, afforded the best opportunity for mature consideration of facts and arguments, and were most effectual against misconstruction and hasty, inconsiderate decision.[2] In them he now pointed out with unanswerable force the evils of the existing system. He dwelt more especially on the violent fluctuations in the corn duty, and the consequent derangements and unsteadiness of the markets. He showed how little the duties on importation could do towards keeping up a permanent high price. All that law could effect was to provide that, so long as corn

[1] *H. Cole to R. Cobden*, June 22, 1839.
[2] *Memoirs*, ii. 29.

grown in this country should not exceed a certain price, there should be no serious danger from competition with corn grown in other countries. What was that price? The law of 1815 had assumed that wheat could not be profitably grown at a lower price than eighty shillings a quarter. Events had shown that this was absurd; the averages of a number of years came to fifty-six shillings. It seemed wise, then, so to readjust the machinery of the sliding scale as to tend to secure that price.

The Duke of Buckingham, whose name figures so often in the sarcasms and invectives of the League, at once resigned his seat in the Cabinet rather than be a party to any meddling with the Corn Law of 1828. Even those who remained, seem to have pressed for an understanding, as was afterwards openly done in Parliament, that whatever amount of protection was set up by the new law should be permanently adhered to. This guarantee, Peel was far too conscientious to consent in any form to give. The Cabinet at length, with many misgivings, assented to their chief's arguments, and for the time the party was saved.

I may as well quote here a passage from one of Cobden's familiar letters to his brother, which describes the episode to much the same effect as Peel's more dignified narrative:—

"Whilst I was with McGregor, he showed me a copy of the scale of duties which he had prepared under Peel's directions, and which he proposed to the Cabinet, causing Buckingham's retirement, and nearly leading to a break-up altogether. The scale was purposely devised to be as nearly as possible equal to an 8s. fixed duty. It was 8s. at 56s., rising a shilling of duty with a shilling fall of prices till it reached 16s., which was the maximum duty, and falling a shilling in duty with the rise of a shilling in price. With the exception of Ripon, he could get no support in the Cabinet. Lyndhurst, like an old fox, refused to vote (as I am told), not knowing whether Peel or the monopolists might be conqueror, and being himself equally happy to serve God or Mammon. The Duke of Bucks got hold of Richmond, who secured Wellington, who by the aid of Stanley and Graham frustrated Peel's intentions. The latter told them that no other Prime Minister after him would ever take office to give the landlords even an 8s. maximum duty. I learn from several quarters that Stanley is one of Peel's stoutest opponents against any alterations of a beneficial character in the monopolies. Last autumn I remember writing to Langton (at Heywood's) a letter for Birley's eye, in which I told him that if Peel's Cabinet were pressed for a liberal Corn Law by the Lancashire Conservatives, it would aid Peel in forcing his colleagues to go along with him, and be the very thing he would like. McGregor now confirms my view."[1]

The League resolved that they at any rate would leave nothing undone to support or overawe the Prime Minister. On the eve of the session several hundreds of delegates, including Cobden, O'Connell, Mr. Bright, Mr. Villiers, and Mr. Milner Gibson, assembled at the Crown and Anchor. They learned that the Prime Minister had that morning refused to receive a deputation from them, on the ground of his numerous engagements. The *Times* had a contemptuous article, mocking at them for the presumption and impertinence of their conduct. These deputies from country associations and religious

[1] *To F. Cobden,* June 22, 1842.

congregationalists, instead of settling their differences with one another, had yet on one single point, forsooth, discovered a system so pure that in a single interview the greatest and most experienced of statesmen would be thrown on his haunches. Perhaps these gentlemen would be willing to offer their services as members of Her Majesty's Privy Council. And so forth, in that vein of cheap ridicule with which the ephemera of the leading article are wont to buzz about all new men and unfamiliar causes. Ridicule notwithstanding, the deputies thronged down to the House of Commons with something so like tumult, that the police turned them out and cleared the lobbies. As they crowded round the approaches to the House, the irritated men hailed with abusive names those whom they knew to be champions of the abhorred monopoly. It was noticed that they did not agree in their cries. While all shouted out, "*No sliding scale*," some called for a fixed duty, and others clamoured for "*Total and immediate repeal.*"

The ministerial plan was soon known, and brought scanty comfort to the men of the north, as their friends rushed down the corridors to tell them what it was to be. Sir Robert Peel could not accept their explanation of the prevailing depression and distress. That was due, he contended, to over-investment of borrowed capital in manufactures; to the displacement of hand-loom weaving by steam power; to monetary difficulties in the United States, and consequent diminution of demand for our manufactures; to interruption of the China trade; finally, to alarms of war in Europe, and the stagnation of commerce which always follows such alarms. To alter the Corn Law would touch none of these sources of the mischief, and would be no remedy. At the same time he thought that the Corn Law, as it stood, was capable of improvement. The working of the sliding scale of 1828[1] was injurious to the consumer, because it kept back corn until it was dearer; to the revenue, by the forced reduction of duty; to the agriculturist, by withholding corn until it reached the highest price, which was then suddenly snatched from him, and his protection defeated; and to commerce, because it introduced paralysing uncertainty. How, then, ought the Corn Law to be improved? Not by changing a variable into a fixed duty, because a fixed duty could not bear the strain of a time of scarcity and distress, and could not be permanent. It must be by modifying the existing principle of a duty varying inversely with the price. Now what was the price which would encourage the home-growth of corn? On the whole it was for the interest of the agriculturist that the price of wheat, allowing for its natural oscillations, should range between fifty-four and fifty-eight shillings. The legislature could not guarantee that or any other price, but the scale might best be constructed with a view to this range of prices. What he proposed, then, was a new scale, considerably decreasing the protection hitherto afforded to the home-grower.[2]

[1] See above, p. 180.

[2] As this became the Corn Law denounced by Cobden during the agitation from 1842 to 1846, it is well to describe the difference between the new scale and that of the Act of 1828 in Peel's own words:—"When corn is at 59s. and under 60s., the duty at present is 27s. 8d. When corn is between those prices, the duty I propose is 13s. When the price of corn is at 50s., the existing duty is 36s. 8d., increasing as the price falls; instead of which I propose, when corn is at 50s., that the duty shall only be 20s., and that that duty shall in no case be exceeded. (Hear, hear.) At 56s. the existing duty is 30s. 8d.; the duty I propose at that price is 16s. At 60s. the existing duty is 26s. 8d.; the duty I propose at that price is 12s. At 63s. the existing duty is 23s. 8d.; the duty I propose is 9s. At 64s. the existing duty is 22s. 8d.; the duty I

Peel concluded a long exposition with a statement of those general ideas about an economic and national system on which his proposals rested. They were these. It is of the highest importance to the welfare of all classes in this country, that care should be taken that the main sources of your supply of corn should be derived from domestic agriculture. The additional price which you may pay in effecting that object cannot be vindicated as a bonus or premium to agriculture, but only on the ground of its being advantageous to the country at large. The agriculturist has special burdens, and you are entitled to place such a price on foreign corn as is equivalent to these special burdens. Any additional protection to them can only be vindicated on the ground that it is for the interest of the country generally. And it is for the interest of all classes that we should be paying occasionally a small additional sum upon our own domestic produce, in order that we may thereby establish a security and insurance against the calamities that would ensue if we became altogether, or in a great part, dependent upon foreign countries for our supply.[1]

When the Minister sat down, Lord John Russell said a few formal words, and Peel added some explanation which took a moment or two. Cobden, according to a hostile reporter, had been "looking very lachrymose all the evening," and he now rose—it is interesting to notice contemporary estimates of important men whose importance has not yet been stamped—"for the purpose of inflicting one of his stereotyped harangues on the House." He did not do this, but he wound up the proceedings by a short

propose is 8s. At 70s. the existing duty is 10s. 8d.; the duty I propose is 5s."

[1] February 9, 1842.

and vehement declaration that he could not allow a moment to pass in denouncing the proposed measure as a bitter insult to a suffering nation.

Cobden's reception of the Ministerial plan was loudly re-echoed in the north of England. The news of the retention of the sliding scale was received with angry disgust throughout the manufacturing districts. Thousands of petitions, with hundreds of thousands of signatures, were sent up to Cobden and other members to lay before Parliament. The ordinary places of public meeting were not large enough to hold the thousands of exasperated men, who had just found from the newspapers that the Government would not give way. In cold and rain they assembled in the open spaces of their towns to listen to speeches, and to pass resolutions, denouncing Sir Robert Peel's measure as an insult and a mockery to a distressed population. The Prime Minister was formally accused of offering indignity and contempt to the working classes; of sacrificing the rights of the poor to the selfish interests of an unfeeling and avaricious aristocracy; of creating wealth, luxury, and splendour for a class, out of the abject misery of the millions. His effigy was carried on gibbets in contumely through the streets of towns like Stockport and Rochdale, to the sound of drums and fifes, and then, amid the execration of multitudes, hurled into the flames. In some places the fierce ceremony was preceded by a mock trial, in which the criminal was swiftly condemned, sentenced, and thrown into the bonfire as a traitor to his country, while the crowd shouted their prayer that so might all oppressors of the people perish.

Considering Cobden's untiring promptitude in seizing every occasion of enforcing his cause upon the House, it is odd that he should not have spoken in the debate in which the new plan was most directly under discussion. The debate ended in a majority for the Minister of one hundred and twenty-three. Mr. Villiers, however, with the judicious neglect of tact that is always so provoking to neutrals, and without which no unpopular cause ever prospers, immediately after the House had decided that corn should be subject to a variable and not a fixed duty, proceeded to invite the same House to decide that it should be subject to no duty at all (Feb. 18). The first debate had lasted for four nights, and the second upon the same topics now lasted for five more. On the last of them (Feb. 24) Cobden made his speech.[1] He dealt with the main propositions which Peel had laid down as the defence of the new Bill. The Minister had confessed, and he now repeated it in reply to a direct challenge, that it was impossible to fix the price of food by legislative enactment. Then for what were they legislating? At least to keep up the price of food. Why not try in the same way to keep up the price of cottons, woollens, and silks? The fact that they did not try this, was the simple and open avowal that they were met there to legislate for a class, against the people. The price of cotton had fallen thirty per cent in ten years, and the price of ironmongery had fallen as much. Yet the iron-monger was forced to exchange his goods with the agriculturist for the produce of the land, at the present high price of corn. Was this fair and reasonable? Could it be called legislation at all? Assuredly it was not honest legislation. Why should there not be a sliding scale for wages? If they admitted that wages could not be artificially sustained

[1] *Cobden's Speeches*, Mr. Rogers's edition, vol. i. 15-28. [Edition of 1870.]

at a certain price, why should a law be passed to keep up the price of wheat? But the land, they said, was subject to heavy burdens. For every one special burden, he could show ten special exemptions. Even if the exclusive burdens on land were proved, the proper remedy was to remove them, and not to tax the food of the people.

An excellent point was made by the exposure of the fallacy, that low wages are the same thing as cheap labour. And this proved to be of the highest importance, as an element in Sir Robert Peel's conversion. He admitted afterwards that he had accepted this fallacy without proper examination, and that its overthrow was one of the things which most powerfully affected his opinions on a protective system. Apart from his general demonstration of the truth in this respect, Cobden now showed that the highly paid labour of England was proved to be the cheapest labour in the world. The manufacturers might have credit for taking a more enlightened view of their own interest than to suppose that the impoverishment of the multitude—the great consumers of all that they produce—could ever tend to promote the prosperity of the manufacturers. "I will tell the House, that by deteriorating the population, of which they ought to be so proud, they will run the risk of spoiling, not merely the animal, but the intellectual creature. It is not a potato-fed race that will ever lead the way in arts, arms, or commerce."

In the course of his speech, which was not in the strong vein that greater experience soon made easy to him, Cobden had talked of the ignorance on the question which prevailed among the Tory members. "Yes," he exclaimed, when his adversaries cried out against this vigorous thrust, "I have never seen their ignorance equalled among any equal number of working men in the north of England." And he reminded them that when the Corn Law of 1815 was passed, and when eminent men of both parties honestly thought that wages followed the price of corn, the great multitude of the nation, without the aid of learning, "with that intuitive sagacity which had given rise to the adage, 'The voice of the people is the voice of God,'" foresaw what the effect of the measure would be upon wages, and from 1815 to 1819 there never was a great public meeting at Manchester at which there was not some banner inscribed with the words, *No Corn Laws.*

For these taunts, the House took a speedy revenge. When Cobden sat down, the benches were crowded, and the member for Knaresborough got up. In a speech ten days before, Mr. Ferrand had said that the member for Stockport had during the last twelve years accumulated half a million of money; and that when night after night, during the last session, he was asserting that the Corn Laws had ruined the trade in Lancashire, he was actually at that very time running his works both night and day. This was only one item in a gross and violent attack on the whole class of northern manufacturers. He now returned to the charge with greater excitement than before. He quoted a great number of instances, where the system of truck was forced upon the helpless workmen. The artisans, he said, were compelled to live in cottages belonging to the employer, and to pay rent higher by one-tenth than their proper value. They were poisoned by the vile rags and devil's dust with which they had to work, and which the masters used for the fraudulent adulteration of their cloths. As for scarcity of flour, it arose from the consumption of that article by the manufacturers, in a paste with which they dishonestly daubed the face of their calicoes.

1842.
ÆT. 38.

The country gentlemen shouted with exultation. They were ill qualified to judge the worth of these extravagant denunciations. The towns of Lancashire were more unfamiliar to them in those days than Denver or Omaha are in our own, and any atrocity was credible of those who lived and worked within them. The whole conception of modern manufacturing industry was as horrible as it was strange in their eyes. We have already seen Sir James Graham's description of them as more cruel than the icy wastes of Siberia, or the burning shores of Mauritius. The chief newspaper of the country party boldly declared that England would be as great and powerful, and all useful Englishmen would be as rich as they are, though all the manufacturing houses in Great Britain should be engulfed in ruin. The same paper pleased the taste of its subscribers by saying that there was not a single mill-owner who would not compound for the destruction of all the manufacturing industry of England, on condition that during that period he should have full work and high profits for his mill, capital, and credit.[1] It is no exaggeration to say that by the majority of the Parliament of 1841, the cotton-spinners of the north were regarded with the same abhorrence as was common twenty years ago towards such representatives of Trade Unionism as were discovered in Sheffield.

Cobden was not cowed by the furious scene. Amid cries of "explain," he rose to tell the House very quietly, that it was not his mission to indulge in gross personalities. He assured the members who desired a partisan warfare of this kind, that nothing should drive him into a personal altercation; and he considered the dignity of the House in some danger when he found language such as they had been listen-

[1] Quoted in Prentice's *History of the League*, i. 284.

ing to for the last half-hour, received with so much complacency by the Ministers, and with such cheers by the party at their back.

1842.

ÆT. 38.

There was violent irritation among his friends at the attack on him and their class, caused less by the exaggeration of the attack itself, than by the exultant spirit in which it was received by the House. Neighbours in Lancashire came forward to testify that both at Sabden and at Crosse Hall he had set up a school, a library, and a news-room for the benefit of old and young in his employ; that the workmen of his district were eager for a place in his works; and that to no one did Mr. Ferrand's remarks apply with less truth than to Cobden and his partners for the last ten years. Cobden cared little for what had been said about him, but he seems to have felt some dissatisfaction with the momentary hesitation of the League as to the larger question of the new law. He wrote to his brother:—

"You never witnessed such a scene as that in the House of Commons when Ferrand was speaking the other night. The Tories were literally frantic with delight. Every sentence he uttered was caught up and cheered by a large majority, far more vehemently than anything that ever fell from Peel or Macaulay. It was not ironical cheering, but downright hearty approbation. I have not the least doubt that the M.P. for Knaresborough spoke the honest convictions of a majority of the members present. The exhibition was premeditated and got up for the occasion. I was told several days before at the club that Ferrand was to follow me in the debate. He was *planted* (to use a vulgar phrase) upon me by his party. I finished speaking at about a quarter past eleven, and it was remarked by two or three on our side that just before I sat down, Sir George Clerk of the Treasury went and

1842.
Ært. 38.

whispered to Green, the Chairman of Committee, and directed his eye towards Ferrand, so that notwithstanding that others tried to follow me, he called straight for the Knaresborough hero. Away he went with the attitudes of a prize-fighter, and the voice of a bull. . . . Just at the time when I was speaking the members swarmed into the House from the dinner-tables, and they were in a right state for supporting Master Ferrand. Colonel S—— plied the fellow with oranges to suck, in an affectionate way that resembled a monkey fondling a bear. What do your Tories think of their party in the House? I find that nothing seems to be considered so decided a stigma, as to brand a man as a mill-owner. Thus you see that the charge against me of working a *mill* at night would not be given up, even although it was proved to be a print works. I hope Ferrand by getting rope enough will settle himself soon. Tory praise will soon carry him off his legs.

"From all that I hear, your people in Lancashire seem to be swayed to and fro like the grass by a summer's wind, without any particular progress. I suppose it will settle down into more quiet work in the way of tracts and lectures. I should like to have carried it by a *coup*, but that is not possible. It seems generally admitted up here by all parties that it is now only a question of time. Lord Lowther said to a friend of Villiers the other day, after the division of ninety, that he did not think it would take more than three years to *abolish* the Corn Laws; and Rawson and I were taking tea at Bellamy's, when a party of Tory members at another table agreed that it would come to a 5s. fixed duty in about three years. The Tories have not liked the debate. Peel feels that he has not come out of it well. He looks dissatisfied with himself, and I am told he is not in good health. What will he be by the end of the session?"[1]

1842. Æt. 38.

The truth seems to be that the Leaguers, in spite of their moderate expectations, were taken aback by the heavy blow which the Minister had just dealt them. They had hoped against hope, and had been too full of faith in their own arguments to doubt their effect upon others. The ways of parliaments were as strange to them as the ways of mill-owners were to the House of Commons. For a single moment they were staggered; Cobden was for an instant or two fired by a violent impulse, which soon, however, yielded to his usual good sense. "I feel some little difficulty," he wrote to Mr. George Wilson, "in offering my advice as to the course which the League should henceforth pursue. That course depends very much upon the spirit of the people who are acting with us. If they were all of my temper in the matter, we would soon bring it to an issue. I presume, however, that your friends are not up to the mark for a general *fiscal revolt*, and I know of no other plan of peaceful resistance. The question is, then, as to the plan of agitation for the future. The idea of ever petitioning the present House of Commons again upon the Corn Laws should be publicly renounced. It involves great trouble and expense, and will do no good. If we had another election, the case would be different, but there is no use in petitioning the present House. I think our lecturers should be thrown upon the boroughs, particularly in the rural districts where we have been opposed. A well-prepared account should be taken of the state of all the boroughs in the kingdom in reference to our question. They should be classified, and put into lists of *safe*, *tolerably safe*, *doubtful*,

[1] *To F. Cobden*, Feb. 28, 1842.

1842.
Æt. 38.

desperate, hopeless. Our whole strength should be then thrown upon the doubtfuls. Electoral Committees should be formed in each borough to look after the registration, and we ought, if needful, to incur some expenditure in this department. Much will depend on our getting a good working Committee in every borough to look after the register, and to agitate our question.

"Now as respects any great demonstration of *numbers* against the passing of the present law. It has been suggested that we ought to hold a meeting on Kersall Moor. But I presume that would be a joint Suffrage and Corn Law meeting, which would not aid our cause at present. The middle class must be still further pinched and disappointed before they will go to that. I quite agree with you that we must keep the League as a body wholly distinct from the Suffrage movement. But at the same time I think the more that individuals connected prominently with the League join the Suffrage party the better. I shall take the first opportunity in the House of avowing myself for the suffrage to every man.

"After all, I hardly entertain a hope that we shall effect our object by old and regular methods; accidents may aid us, but I do not see my way in the ordinary course of things to beating down the power of the aristocracy."[1]

Mr. Bright made various suggestions, and Cobden replied to them with provisional assent:—

"I am afraid you must not calculate on my attending at your tea-party. During the recess I shall have some private matters to attend to, and I shall endeavour to avoid public meetings as far as possible. I have been thinking of our future plans, and am more and more convinced of the necessity

[1] *To G. Wilson*, Feb. 27, 1842.

of keeping ourselves free from all other questions. I am much more of opinion upon reflection, of the necessity of some such bold demonstration in the way of organization and the securing a large fund, as you were alluding to. Something must be done to secure the ground, and thus prevent its being occupied by any other party. Nothing would so much attain that object as to get a large fund secured. I like the idea of an Anti-Corn-Law *rent*. Unless some such demonstration of renewed life and resolution be made immediately after the passing of the Corn Law, it will be suspected that we are giving up the cause."[1]

Cobden seems to have cooled down to a sober view of the situation when he wrote to his brother, a fortnight after the affair of Mr. Ferrand:—

"There is a curious symptom breaking out in the Tory ranks. Several of the young aristocrats are evidently more liberal than their leaders, and they have talked rationally about an ultimate Free Trade. I hear a good deal of this talk in the tea and dining-rooms. In fact the Tory aristocracy are Liberals in *feeling*, compared with your genuine political bigot, a cotton-spinning Tory. I see no other course for us but a renewed agitation of the agricultural districts, where I expect there will be a good deal of discontent ere long. I mean in the small rural towns. Bad trade in the manufacturing towns will, I suspect, very soon convert the Tories, or break them, the next best thing."[2]

No new line of action was hit upon until the end of the session. In the meantime, so far as the agitation out of doors went, Cobden's mind was

[1] *To Mr. Bright*, March 7, 1842.
[2] *To F. Cobden*, March 10, 1842.

1842. — Æt. 38.

incessantly turning over plans for strengthening the connexions of the League. To Mr. Ashworth he wrote:—

"It has struck me that it would be well to try to engraft our Free Trade agitation upon the Peace movement. They are one and the same cause. It has often been to me a matter of the greatest surprise that the Friends have not taken up the question of Free Trade as the means—and I believe the only human means—of effecting universal and permanent peace. The efforts of the Peace Societies, however laudable, can never be successful so long as the nations maintain their present system of isolation. The colonial system, with all its dazzling appeals to the passions of the people, can never be got rid of except by the indirect process of Free Trade, which will gradually and imperceptibly loose the bands which unite our Colonies to us by a mistaken notion of self-interest. Yet the Colonial policy of Europe has been the chief source of wars for the last hundred and fifty years. Again, Free Trade, by perfecting the intercourse, and securing the dependence of countries one upon another, must inevitably snatch the power from the *governments* to plunge their people into wars. What do you think of changing your plan of a prize essay, from the Corn Law to 'Free Trade as the best human means for securing universal and permanent peace.' This would be a good and appropriate prize to be given by members of the Society of Friends. At all events, in any way possible I should like to see the London Friends interested in the question of the Corn Law and Free Trade. They have a good deal of influence over the City moneyed interest, which has the ear of the Government."[1]

Besides these tentative projects of new alliances, he watched vigilantly every chance of suggesting a

[1] *To Henry Ashworth*, April 12, 1842.

point to his allies outside. To Mr. Bright he wrote:—

"If you have a leisure hour, I wish you would write an article upon the subject of the Queen's Letter to the parsons, ordering collections in the churches for the distressed. Here is a good opportunity for doing justice to the Dissenting ministers, who met last year to proclaim the miseries of the people, and to propose a better remedy than almsgiving. The Church clergy are almost to a man guilty of causing the present distress by upholding the Corn Law, they *having themselves an interest in the high price of bread*, and their present efforts must be viewed as tardy and inefficient, if not hypocritical.

"Again, show how futile it must be to try to subsist the manufacturing population upon charitable donations. The wages paid in the cotton trade alone amount to twenty millions a year. Reduce that amount even ten per cent, and how could it be made up by charity? If you have also leisure for another article, make a swingeing assault upon the last general election, and argue from the disclosures made by the House of Commons itself, that we the Anti-Corn-Law party were not defeated, but virtually swindled and plundered of our triumph at the hustings."[1]

[1] *To Mr. Bright*, May 12, 1842. In the following number of the *Anti-Bread-Tax Circular* (May 19), articles on the two subjects here suggested by Cobden, duly appeared. "The clergy of the establishment," says the writer, with good strong plainness of speech, "would do well to reflect upon their position in this matter. They have, with very few exceptions, upheld to he uttermost the unnatural system, which, after working during a period of twenty-seven years, causing more or less of suffering throughout the whole of its existence, has at length brought the nation to the verge of ruin. They have almost to a man been the ever-active agents and allies of the monopolist party, and their restless energy in the worst of causes has been mainly instrumental in carrying into office a

1842.
ÆT. 38.

With reference to the first of the two themes which is here suggested, Cobden always felt keenly the wrong part taken throughout the struggle by the clergy of the Establishment. The rector of the church which he was in the habit of attending, Saint John's, in Deansgate, appealed to him for help towards an Association for providing ten new churches in Manchester. Cobden in reply expressed his opinion of the project with wholesome frankness:—

"It will be always very gratifying to me to second your charitable efforts to relieve the distresses of our poor neighbours; and if I do not co-operate in the plan for benefiting the destitute population on a large scale by erecting ten new churches, it is only because, in the words of the appeal, I 'differ about the means to be adopted.' You, who visit the abodes of poverty, are aware that a great portion of the working population of Manchester are suffering from an insufficiency of wholesome nourishment. The first and most pressing claim of the poor is for food: all other wants are secondary to this. It is in vain to try and elevate the moral and religious character of a people whose physical condition is degraded by the privation of the first necessaries of life; and hence we are taught to pray for 'our daily bread' before spiritual graces. There is a legislative enactment which prevents the poor of this town from

Ministry whose only pledge was that the interests of the nation should be held subservient to the interests of the land and colonial monopolists. . . . We fear that any attempt to raise contributions from the clergy, or by their agency, can only subject that body to the charge of gross ignorance or gross hypocrisy. . . . Their conduct contrasts strongly with the noble efforts of the Christian ministers who last year assembled in Manchester, in Carnarvon, and in Edinburgh, to declare their entire abhorrence of the unjust and murderous system by which multitudes of honest and industrious men are made to suffer wrongs more grievous than can easily be described."

obtaining a sufficiency of wholesome food, and I am sure the law only requires to be understood by our clergy to receive their unanimous condemnation. Surely a law of this kind, opposed alike to the laws of nature, the obvious dispensations of divine providence, and the revealed word of God, must be denounced by the ministers of the Gospel. So convinced am I that there is no other mode of raising the condition of the working classes in the scale of morality or religion, whilst they are denied by Act of Parliament a sufficiency of food, that I have set apart as much of my income as I can spare from other claims for the purpose of effecting the abolition of the Corn Law and Provision Law. Until this object be attained I shall be compelled to deny myself the satisfaction of contributing to other public undertakings of great importance in themselves, and secondary only to the first of all duties—*the feeding of the hungry*. It is for this reason that I am reluctantly obliged to decline to contribute to the fund for building ten new churches. My course is, I submit, in strict harmony with the example afforded us by the divine author of Christianity, who preached upon the mountain and in the desert, beneath no other roof than the canopy of heaven, and who yet, we are told, was careful to feed the multitude that flocked around Him. You will, I am sure, excuse me troubling you at such length upon a subject which I conscientiously believe to be the most important in relation to the poor of any that can engage your attention."[1]

[1] February 1841.

CHAPTER XI

SIR ROBERT PEEL'S NEW POLICY

1842. — ÆT. 38.

THE new Corn Bill was the first of three acts in the great drama which Peel now unfolded to Parliament and the nation. Things looked as if the country were slowly sinking into decay. The revenue, which had been exhibiting deficits for several years, now fell short of the expenditure for the year current by two millions and a half. The working classes all over the land were suffering severe and undeniable distress. Population had increased to an extent at which it seemed no longer possible to find employment for them. To invite all the world to become our customers, by opening our ports to their products in exchange, was the Manchester remedy. It would bring both work and food. The Prime Minister believed that the revenue could be repaired, and the springs of industry relieved, without that great change in our economic policy. But he knew that the crisis was too deep for half-measures, and he produced by far the most momentous budget of the century.

The Report of the Committee of 1840 on Import Duties was, as I have already mentioned, the starting-point of the revolution to which Peel now proceeded. It passed a strong condemnation on the existing tariff, as presenting neither congruity nor unity of purpose, and conforming to no general principles.

Eleven hundred and fifty rates of duty were enumerated as chargeable on imported articles, and all other articles paid duty as unenumerated. In some cases the duties levied were simple and comprehensive; in others they fell into vexatious and embarrassing details. The tariff often aimed at incompatible ends. A duty was imposed both for revenue and protection, and then was pitched so high for the sake of protection as to produce little or nothing to revenue. A great variety of particular interests were protected, to the detriment of the public income, as well as of commercial intercourse with other countries. The same preference was extended by means of discriminating duties to the produce of the colonies; great advantages were given to the colonial interests at the expense of the consumers in the mother country.

It was pointed out that the effect of prohibitory duties was to impose on the consumer an indirect tax often equal to the whole difference of price between the British article and the foreign article which the duty kept out. On articles of food alone the amount taken in this way from the consumer exceeded the amount of all the other taxes levied by the Government. The sacrifices of the community did not end here, but were accompanied by injurious effects upon wages and capital. The duties diminished greatly the productive powers of the country; and they limited our trade. The action of duties which were not prohibitory, but only protective, was of a similar kind. They imposed upon the consumer a tax equal to the amount of the duty levied on the foreign article; but it was a tax which went not to the public treasury, but to the protected manufacturer.

Evidence was taken to show that the protective

1842. — Æt. 38.

system was not on the whole beneficial to the protected manufactures themselves. The amount of duties levied on the plea of protection to British manufactures did not exceed half a million sterling. Some even of the manufacturers supposed to be most interested in retaining the duties, were quite willing that they should be abolished.

With reference to the influence of the protective system on wages, and on the condition of the labourer, the Report was equally decided. As the pressure of foreign competition was heaviest on those articles in the production of which the rate of wages was lowest, so it was obvious in a country exporting so largely as England, that other advantages might more than compensate for an apparent advantage in the money price of labour. The countries in which the rate of wages is lowest, are not always those which manufacture most successfully. The Committee was persuaded that the best service that could be rendered to the industrious classes of the community, would be to extend the field of labour by an extension of our commerce.

The conclusion was a strong conviction in the minds of the Committee, of the necessity of an immediate change in the import duties of the kingdom. By imposts on a small number of those articles which were then most productive[1]—the amount of each impost being carefully considered with a view to the greatest consumption of the article, and therefore the highest receipts at the customs—the revenue would not only suffer no loss, but would be considerably augmented.[2]

[1] Seventeen articles produced 94½ per cent of the total revenue, and these with twenty-nine other articles, or forty-six articles in all, produced 98⅗ per cent.

[2] Much of the evidence which led to this Report is, in the present recrudescence of bad opinions, as well worth reading

This Report was the charter of Free Trade. The Whig Government, as we have seen, had taken from it in a timid and blundering way a weapon or two, with which they hoped that they might be able to defend their places. Their successor grasped its principles with the hand of a master. "My own conviction," said Cobden many years afterwards, "is that Peel was always a Free Trader in theory; in fact, on all politico-economical questions, he was always as sound in the abstract as Adam Smith or Bentham. For he was peculiarly a politico-economical, and not a Protectionist, intellect. But he never believed that absolute Free Trade came within the category of practical House of Commons measures. It was a question of numbers with him; and as he was yoked with a majority of inferior animals, he was obliged to go their pace, and not his own."[1]

This is true of Sir Robert Peel's mind throughout from 1843 to 1846. But it seems only to be partially true of the moment when he brought in the great budget of 1842. Notwithstanding its fatal omission of the duties on corn, it was a Free Trade budget. Corn was excluded partly from the leader's fear of the "inferior animals" whom it was his honourable but unhappy mission to drive, but partly also by an honest doubt in Peel's own mind, whether it was safe to depend on foreign countries for our supplies. The doubt was strong enough to warrant

to-day as it was forty years ago—especially the evidence of Mr. J. Deacon Hume, who is not to be confused, by the way, with Joseph Hume, the Chairman of the Committee. Cobden said that if the Committee had done nothing else but elicit this evidence, "it would have been sufficient to produce a commercial revolution all over the world." Mr. Hume's answers were largely circulated as one of the League tracts. This important blue-book, *Import Duties*, No. 601, was ordered to be printed, Aug. 6, 1840.

[1] *To J. Parkes*, May 26, 1856.

him, from his own point of view, in trying an experiment before meddling with corn; and a magnificent experiment it was. The financial plan of 1842 was the beginning of all the great things that have been done since. Its cardinal point was the imposition of a direct tax, in order to relax the commercial tariff. Ultimately the effect of diminishing duties was to increase revenue, but the first effect was a fall in revenue. It was expedient or indispensable for the revival of trade to lower or remit duties, and to purge the tariff. To bridge over the interval before increased trade and consumption made up for the loss thus incurred, the Government proposed to put on the Income Tax at the rate of sevenpence in the pound. They expected that the duration of the impost would probably be about five years. At the end of that time the loss caused by remissions would, they hoped, have been recovered.

The new tariff was not laid before Parliament for some weeks.[1] The labour of preparation was enormous. Mr. Gladstone, who was then at the Board of Trade, and on whom much of the labour fell, said many years afterwards that he had been concerned in four revisions of the tariff, namely in 1842, in 1845, in 1854, and in 1860; and he told Cobden that the first cost six times as much trouble as all the others put together. There was an abatement of duty on seven hundred and fifty articles. The object, as set forth by the Minister himself, speaking generally, was to reduce the duties on raw materials, which constituted the elements of manufactures, to an almost nominal amount; to reduce the duties on half-manufactured articles, which

[1] The speech proposing the Income Tax was March 11. It was May 5 when Sir Robert Peel moved to go into Committee on the tariff.

entered almost as much as raw material into domestic manufactures, to a nominal amount. In articles completely manufactured, their object had been to remove prohibitions and reduce prohibitory duties, so as to enable the foreign producer to compete fairly with the domestic manufacturer. The general principle Sir Robert Peel went upon, was to make a considerable reduction in the cost of living. It is true that the duty on the importation of fresh and salted meat was lowered. It is true, too, that he could point to the new Corn Bill as having reduced the duty on wheat by more than a half. While he spoke, it was nine shillings under the new law, and twenty-three under the old one. But the sugar duties were untouched. It seemed a fatal, absurd, miserable flaw in the new scheme to talk of the main object being to lessen the charge of living, and then to leave bread and sugar, two great articles of universal consumption, burdened with heavy protective taxation. Many a League meeting in the next three years rang with fierce laughter at the expense of a Minister who talked of relieving the consumer, when he had taken the tax off dried fruits, cosmetics, satins, caviare, and left it upon the loaf of bread.

The Tories followed reluctantly. The more acute among the Protectionists felt that the colonial interest would speedily be forced to surrender its advantage over the sugar of Cuba and Brazil; and one member warned sympathetic hearers that, when the tariff was passed, the next step to be expected was the repeal of the Corn Laws. The Minister found one remarkable champion on his own side, whose genius he failed to recognize. Mr. Disraeli laughed at the Whigs for pretending to be the originators of Free Trade. It was Mr. Pitt, he said, who first promulgated its doctrines; and it was Fox, Burke, and Sheridan who then denounced the new commercial principles. The principles of Free Trade were developed, and not by Whigs, fifty years before; and the conduct now pursued by Sir Robert Peel was in exact accordance and consistency with the principles for the first time promulgated by Mr. Pitt. So far as it went, Mr. Disraeli's contention was perfectly correct.

If the Protectionists were puzzled as well as annoyed by the new policy, so were the Free Traders. The following extracts from letters to his brother convey one or two of Cobden's earlier impressions about Peel. Of the measure he always thought the same, and the worst. By the end of the session Cobden had clearly discerned whither Peel's mind was turning. We who live a generation after the battle was won, may feel for a moment disappointed that Cobden did not at once judge the Minister's boldness in imposing the Income Tax as a means of reforming the tariff, in a more appreciative spirit. It is just, however, to remember that in his letters we seize the first quick impressions of the hour; that these first impressions were naturally those of chagrin in one who saw that the new scheme, however good in its general bearings, omitted the one particular change that was needful. We must not expect from an energetic and clear-sighted actor, committed to an urgent practical cause, the dispassionateness of a historian whose privilege it is to be wise after the event.

"What say the wise men to Sir Robert's Income Tax? In other words, how do our mill-owners and shopkeepers like to be made to pay £1,200,000 a year out of their profits, to insure the continuance of the corn and sugar monopolies? I should think that the proposal to place profits upon a par with rent before the tax-collector will not be vastly popular, unless the law can contrive to keep up the former as it does the latter. The only important change after all, announced last night, was timber. . . . Peel delivered his statement in a clear and clever way, never faltering nor missing a word in nearly a four hours' speech. This has gone far to convince our noodles on the Whig side that there is a great deal of good in his budget; and I find even our friend J—— is inclined to praise the budget. But I fully expect that it will do much to render Peel vastly unpopular with the upper portion of the middle class, who will see no compensation in the tariff for a tax upon their incomes and profits. If this be the result of the measure, it will do good to the Corn Law cause, by bringing the discontented to our ranks. Let me know what your wiseacres say about it."[1]

"Both the Corn and Income Tax will be thrown over Easter I expect. Peel is very anxious to force on both measures, which I am not surprised at, seeing how he is badgered both in the House and out of doors. He gets at times very irritable, as you will have seen. It is a hard task to govern for a class, under the pretence of governing for the people. If he should be killed in the vain attempt to serve two such opposite masters, it is to be hoped he will be the last man foolish enough to make the attempt. He is certainly looking very fagged and jaded. The Income Tax will do more than the Corn Law to destroy the Tories. The class of voters in the towns upon which they rely, are especially touched by his schemes. The genteel shopkeepers

[1] *To F. Cobden*, March 12, 1842.

1842. — ÆT. 38.

and professional men who depend upon appearances, and live by a false external, will never forgive him for exposing their tinsel. You will not hear of any public demonstration against the tax, but a much more effective resistance is being offered by the private remonstrance of Tory voters. There is very little feeling in the manufacturing districts compared with that of the southern boroughs. Peel is also undermining his strength in the counties by displeasing everybody, and putting everything in disorder without settling anything. The worst danger is of the Whigs coming in again too soon. The hacks would be up on their hind legs, and at their old prancing tricks again, immediately they smelt the Treasury crib."[1]

"The truth is, your accounts make me feel very uneasy at my position. No earthly good can I do here. The thing must be allowed to work itself into some new shape—time only can tell what. We are *nowhere* on the opposition side at present. Peel must head a milieu party soon. If the old Duke were dead, he would quarrel with the ultra-Tories in a month. He is no more with them in heart than you or I, and I suspect there is now an accumulation of grudges between him and the more violent of his party, that can hardly be suppressed."[2]

"Peel is a Free Trader, and so are Ripon and Gladstone. The last was put in by the Puseyites, who thought they had insinuated the wedge, but they now complain that he has been quite absorbed by Peel, which is the fact. Gladstone makes a very clever aide-de-camp to Peel, but is nothing without

[1] *To F. Cobden*, March 22, 1842.
[2] *Ibid.* April 11, 1842.

him. The Government are at their wits' end about the state of the country. The Devonshire House Whigs are beginning to talk of the necessity of supporting the Government in case of any serious troubles, which means a virtual coalition; a point they are evidently being driven to by the force of events. Peel will throw overboard the bigots of his party, if he have the chance. But the real difficulty is the present state of the country. The accounts from every part are equally bad, and Chadwick says the poor-rates in the agricultural districts are rising rapidly. A great deal of land has been offered for sale during the last three months, and everything seems working beautifully for a cure in the only possible way, viz. distress, suffering, and want of money. I am most anxious to get away and come to Manchester; I know the necessity of my presence, and shall let nothing but the Corn question keep me."[1]

"The last fortnight has done more to advance our cause than the last six or twelve months. The Peel party are fairly beaten in argument, and for the first time they are willing to listen to us as if they were anxious to learn excuses for their inevitable conversion. If I were disposed to be vain of my talk, I have had good reason, for both sides speak in praise of my two last efforts. The Reform and Carlton Clubs are both agreed as to my having pleaded the cause successfully. The real secret, however, is the irresistible pressure of the times, and the consciousness that the party in power can only exist by restoring the country to something like prosperity. If nothing happens to revive trade, the Corn Law goes to a certainty before spring."[2]

[1] *To F. Cobden*, June 22, 1842.
[2] *Ibid.* July 14, 1842.

"Peel and his squad will be right glad to get rid of the House, and I suspect it will not be his fault if he does not get a measure of Corn Law repeal ready before next session, to stop the mouths of the League men. He has been excessively worried by *our* clique in the House, and I have reason to flatter myself with the notion that I have been a frequent thorn in his side. If distress should continue to favour us, we shall get something substantial in another twelve months, and I suspect we may bargain for the continuance of bad trade for that length of time at least."[1]

Something must be said of the two speeches of which Cobden speaks so lightly in one of these extracts. It was July before he made any prominent attack on the financial scheme. In March, when Peel had wished to press the Income Tax Bill forwards, Cobden had been one of a small group who persisted in obstructive motions for adjournment, until Peel was at length forced to give way. He had also made remarks from time to time in Committee. But the session was far advanced before he found a proper occasion for putting forward all the strength of his case.

On July 1 a great debate was opened by Mr. Wallace of Greenock, upon the distress of the country. Mr. Disraeli pointed out, with much force and ingenuity, that the languid trade from which they were suffering would receive a far more powerful stimulus than the repeal of the Corn Laws could give, if Lord Palmerston had not, by a mischievous political treaty, put an end to a treaty of commerce with France, which would have opened new markets for all the most heavily stricken industries of

[1] *To F. Cobden,* July 20, 1842.

England. Joseph Hume urged that the Government should either agree to an inquiry, or else adopt the remedy of a repeal of the Corn Laws. Lord John Russell lamented the postponement of remedies, but would leave to the Government the responsibility of choosing their own time. The Prime Minister followed in a speech in which he confined himself to very narrow ground. It was rather a defence of his financial policy, than a serious recognition of the state of the country.

This provoked Cobden to make his first great speech in the House (July 8). Mr. Roebuck, who spoke the same evening, described it as "a speech fraught with more melancholy instruction than it had ever been his lot to hear. A speech, in the incidents which it unfolded, more deeply interesting to the people of this country, he had never heard in his life; and these incidents were set forth with great ability and great simplicity." As a debating reply to the Prime Minister, it was of consummate force and vivacity. The facts which Cobden adduced supported his vigorous charge that Peel viewed the matter too narrowly, and that circumstances were more urgent than he had chosen to admit. It was exactly one of those speeches which the House of Commons naturally delights in. It contained not a single waste sentence. Every one of Peel's arguments was met by detail and circumstance, and yet detail and circumstance the most minute were kept alive by a stream of eager and on-pressing conviction. Peel had compared the consumption of cotton in two half-years; Cobden showed that for purposes of comparison they were the wrong half-years. Peel had talked of improved machinery for a time turning people out of employment; Cobden proved with chapter and verse how gradual the improve-

1842.
Æt. 38.

ment in the power-looms had been, and pointed out that Manchester, Bolton, Stockport, and other towns in the north, were really the creation of labour-saving machines. Peel had spoken as if it were merely a cotton question and a Manchester question: Cobden, out of the fulness of his knowledge, showed that the stocking-frames of Nottingham were as idle as the looms of Stockport, that the glass-cutters of Stourbridge and the glovers of Yeovil were undergoing the same privation as the potters of Stoke and the miners of Staffordshire, where five-and-twenty thousand were destitute of employment. He knew of a place where a hundred wedding-rings had been pawned in a single week to provide bread; and of another place where men and women subsisted on boiled nettles, and dug up the decayed carcass of a cow rather than perish of hunger. "I say you are drifting to confusion," he exclaimed, "without rudder and without compass. . . . Those who are so fond of laughing at political economy forget that they have a political economy of their own: and what is it? That they will monopolize to themselves the fruit of the industry of the great body of the community—that they allow the productions of the spindle and the loom to go abroad to furnish them with luxuries from the farthest corners of the world, but refuse to permit to be brought back in exchange what would minister to the wants and comforts of the lower orders. What would the consequence be? We are sowing the seeds broadcost for a plentiful harvest of workmen in the western world. Thousands of workmen are delving in the mines of the western continent, where coals can be raised for a shilling a ton. We are sending there the labourers from our cotton manufactories, from our woollen, and from our silk. They are not going by dozens or by scores to teach the people of other countries the work they have learnt—they are going in hundreds and thousands to those states to open works against our own machines, and to bring this country to a worse state than it is now in. There is nothing to atone for a system which leads to this; and if I were to seek for a parallel, it would be only in the Revocation of the Edict of Nantes by Louis XIV., or the decree of Alva in Belgium, where the best men were banished from their country."

Cobden gave additional strength to his appeal by showing that its eagerness was not due to a merely official partisanship. He saw no reason, he declared, why they should not take good measures from Sir Robert Peel, or why they should prefer those of Lord John Russell. "The noble Lord is called the leader on this side of the House, and I confess that when I first came into the House I was inclined to look upon him as a leader; but from what I have seen, I believe the right hon. Baronet to be as liberal as the noble Lord. If the noble Lord is my leader, I can only say that I believe that in four out of five divisions I have voted against him. He must be an odd kind of leader who thus votes against those he leads. I will take measures of relief from the right hon. Baronet as well as from the noble Lord, but upon some measure of relief I will insist. . . . I give the Prime Minister credit for the difficulties of his situation; but this question must be met, and met fully; it must not be quibbled away; it must not be looked upon as a Manchester question; the whole condition of the country must be looked at and faced, and it must be done before we separate this session."

Three nights later (July 11), Sir Robert Peel

took occasion to deal with some of Cobden's economic propositions, especially an assertion that in prosperous times improvements in machinery do not tend to throw labourers out of employment. At the close of his speech the Minister revealed the tentative spirit in which his great measures had been framed, and the half-open mind in which he was beginning to stand towards the Corn Law. If these measures should not prove adequate to meet the distress of the country, in that case, he said, "I shall be the first to admit that no adherence to former opinions ought to prevent their full and careful revision."

Cobden, in the course of a vigorous reply, pointed to a historic parallel which truly described the political situation. He warned the aristocracy and the landowners never to expect to find another Prime Minister who would take office to uphold their monopoly. "They had killed Canning by thwarting him, and they would visit the same fate on their present leader, if he persevered in the same attempt to govern for the aristocracy, while professing to govern for the people." At this there were loud groans from some parts of the House. "Yes," repeated Cobden, undaunted, "they had killed Canning by forcing him to try and reconcile their interests with those of the people, and no human power could enable the right hon. Baronet to survive the same ordeal."

CHAPTER XII.

RENEWED ACTIVITY OF THE LEAGUE—COBDEN AND SIR ROBERT PEEL—RURAL CAMPAIGN

1842.
—
Æt. 38.

At the close of the session, Cobden hastened back to Manchester, where his business, as he too well knew, urgently required his presence. As we have seen, his brother's letters had begun to make him seriously uneasy as to his position. Affairs were already beginning to fall into disorder at Chorley and in Manchester, and in telling the story of Cobden's public activity, we have to remember that almost from the moment of entering Parliament he began to be harassed by private anxieties of a kind which depress and unnerve most men more fatally than any other. Cobden's buoyant enthusiasm for his cause carried him forward; it drove these haunting cares into the background, and his real life was not in his business, but in the affairs of the nation.

In September he made an important speech to the Council of the League, at Manchester. It explains their relations to political parties, and to social classes. They had been lately charged, he said, with having been in collision with the Chartist party. But those who made this charge had themselves been working for the last three years to excite the Chartist party against the League, and that, too, by means that were not over-creditable. These intriguers had succeeded in deluding a considerable portion of the working classes upon the subject of the Corn Laws. "And I have no objection in admitting here," Cobden went on to say, "as I have admitted frankly before, that these artifices and manœuvres have, to a considerable extent, compelled us to make our agitation a middle-class agitation. I do not deny that the working classes generally have attended our lectures and signed our petitions; but I will admit, that so far as the fervour and efficiency of our agitation has gone, it has eminently been a middle-class agitation. We have carried it on by those means by which the middle class usually carries on its movements. We have had our meetings of dissenting ministers; we have obtained the co-operation of the ladies; we have resorted to tea-parties, and taken those pacific means for carrying out our views, which mark us rather as a middle-class set of agitators. . . . We are no political body; we have refused to be bought by the Tories; we have kept aloof from the Whigs; and we will not join partnership with either Radicals or Chartists, but we hold out our hand ready to give it to all who are willing to advocate the total and immediate repeal of the Corn and Provision Laws."

In another speech, he said the great mass of the people stuck to the bread-tax because it was the law. "He did not charge the great body of the working classes with taking part against the repeal of the Corn Laws, but he charged the great body of the intelligent mechanics with standing aloof, and allowing a parcel of lads, with hired knaves for leaders, to interrupt their meetings." As time went on, the share of the working class in the movement became more satisfactory. Meanwhile, it is important to notice that they held aloof, or else opposed it as interfering with those claims of their own to political power, which the Reform Act had so unexpectedly baulked.

1842.
Æt. 38.

Recovering themselves from the disappointment and confusion of the spring, the agitators applied themselves with invigorated resolution to their work.

They had been spending a hundred pounds a week. They ought now, said Cobden, to spend a thousand. Up to this time the Council of the League had had twenty-five thousand pounds through their hands, of which by far the larger portion had been raised in Manchester and the neighbouring district. About three times that sum had been raised and expended by local associations elsewhere. In all, therefore, a hundred thousand pounds had gone, and the Corn Laws seemed more immovable than ever. With admirable energy, the Council now made up their minds at once to raise a new fund of fifty thousand pounds, and, notwithstanding the terrible condition of the cotton trade, the amount was collected in a very short time. Men contributed freely because they knew that the rescue of their capital depended on the opening of markets from which the protection on corn excluded them.

"You will have observed," Cobden wrote to Mr. Edward Baines, "that the Council of the League are determined upon a renewed agitation upon a great scale, provided they can get a commensurate pecuniary help from the country, and my object in troubling you is to beg that you will endeavour to rouse the men of the West Riding to another effort.

"The scheme which we especially aim at carrying out is this:—To make an attack upon every registered elector of the kingdom, county and borough, by sending to each a packet of publications embracing the whole argument as it affects both the agricultural and trading view of the question. We are procuring the copies of the registers for the purpose. *But the plan involves an expense of £20,000.* Add to this our increased expenditure in lectures, etc., and the contemplated cost of the spring deputations in London, and we shall require £50,000 to do justice to the cause before next June. And we have a Spartan band of men in Manchester who are setting to work in the full confidence that they will raise the money. The best way to levy contributions on the public for a common object is *to set up a claim*, and therefore Manchester men must not in public declare the country in their debt. But between ourselves this is the case to a large extent. The agitation, though a national one, and for national objects, has been sustained by the pockets of the people here to the extent of 10 to 1 against the whole kingdom!

"A vast proportion of our expenditure has been of a kind to bring no éclat, such as the wide distribution of tracts in the purely agricultural districts, and the subsidizing of literary talent which does not *appear* in connexion with the League. If I had the opportunity of a little gossip with you, I could give you proof of much efficient agitation for which the League does not get credit publicly. There is danger, however, in the growing adversity of this district, that we may pump our springs dry, and it is more and more necessary to widen the circle of our contributors. We confidently rely on your influential co-operation.

"Recollect that our primary object is to work the printing-press, not upon productions of our own, but producing the *essence* of authoritative writers, such as Deacon Hume, Lord Fitzwilliam, etc., and scattering them broadcast over the land. Towards such an object no Free Trader can scruple to commit himself. And in no other human war that I am acquainted with, can we accomplish our end by moral and peaceable means. There is no use in blinking the real difficulties of our task, which is the education of twenty-seven millions of people, an object not to be accomplished except by the cordial assistance of the enlightened and patriotic in all parts of the kingdom."[1]

The staff of lecturers was again despatched on its missionary errand. To each elector in the kingdom was sent a little library of tracts. Tea-parties followed by meetings were found to be more attractive in the northern towns than meetings without tea-parties. Places where meetings had been thinly attended, now produced crowds. Cobden, Mr. Bright, Mr. Ashworth, and the other chief speakers, again scoured the country north of the Trent; and at the end of the year, the first two of these, along with Colonel Perronet Thompson—the author of the famous *Catechism of the Corn Laws*, and styled by Cobden, the father of them all—proceeded on a pilgrimage to Scotland.

"Our progress ever since we crossed the border," Cobden writes, "has been gratifying in the extreme. Had we been disposed to encourage a display of enthusiasm, we might have frightened the more nervous of the monopolists with our demonstrations. As it is, we have been content to allow honours to be thrust upon us in our own persons, or rather mine, by the representatives of the people. Glasgow, Edinburgh, Kirkcaldy, Dundee, Perth, and Stirling, have all presented me with the freedom of their burghs, and I have no doubt I could have become a free citizen of every corporate town in Scotland by

[1] *To Edward Baines*, Oct. 25, 1842.

1843.
ÆT. 39.

paying them a visit.[1] All this is due to the principles we advocate, for I have done all I could to discourage any personal compliments to myself. Scotland is fairly up now, and we shall have more in future from this side of the Tweed upon the Corn Law. We go to-day to Glasgow to attend another Free Trade banquet. To-morrow we proceed to Edinburgh, where I shall remain a few days to go through the ceremony of becoming a citizen of Auld Reekie, and then go forward to Newcastle to join Colonel Thompson and Bright (who have both been working miracles), who will take Hawick by the way for a meeting on Thursday evening."[2]

"I shall be with you at the end of the week. The work has been too heavy for me, and I have been obliged to throw an extra share upon Bright and the old veteran Colonel. I caught cold in coming from Carlisle to Glasgow by night, and have not got rid of it. To-day has, however, been very fine, and I have enjoyed a long walk with George Combe into the country, looking at the farm-houses, each of which has a tall chimney attached belonging to the engine-house. I am obliged to come from Glasgow here on Thursday to go through the ceremony of receiving the freedom of this city. Upon the whole, I am satisfied with the aspect of things in Scotland. I am not afraid of their going back from their convictions, and there is scarcely a man who is not against the present law, and nearly all are going on to total repeal. Fox Maule's con-

[1] It is worth noticing that in Glasgow this honour was conferred upon him, not merely on the ground of his public action, but because, in the words of his proposer, by his ingenuity as a calico printer, he had brought that manufacture to such a state of perfection that we were now able to compete with the printers of France and Switzerland.

[2] *To George Wilson*, Stirling, Jan. 18, 1843.

version is important. He is heir to £80,000 a year in land, 40,000 acres under the plough."[1]

1843.
ÆT. 39.

From Dundee, through Hawick, the deputation crossed the border to Newcastle, Sunderland, Darlington, and other towns of that region. On their return to head-quarters, Mr. Bright recounted to a crowded meeting at Manchester what they had done, and he summed up their impressions of Scotland in words that deserve to be put on record. There were some general features, Mr. Bright said, which struck him very strongly in their tour through Scotland. "In the first place, I believe that the intelligence of the people in Scotland is superior to the intelligence of the people of England. I take it from these facts. Before going to the meetings, we often asked the committee or the people with whom we came in contact, 'Are there any fallacies which the working people hold on this question? Have they any crotchets about machinery, or wages, or anything else?' And the universal reply was, 'No; you may make a speech about what you like; they understand the question thoroughly; and it is no use confining yourself to machinery or wages, for there are few men, probably no man here, who would be taken in by such raw jests as those.' Well, if the working men are so intelligent in Scotland, how are the landowners? You find, in that country, that the science of farming is carried to a degree of perfection which is almost unknown in England. You find them with a climate not so kind and genial as ours, for they often fail in gathering in wheat when the farmers in the south of England succeed; they have land not naturally so fertile as ours, and many are not so near a market to take off the whole of their produce as our farmers are; but we find there that the land-

[1] *To F. Cobden*, Jan. 15, 1843.

owners are intelligent enough to know that the monopolists themselves rarely thrive under the monopolies they are so fond of, and that it would be much better for them to be subjected to the same wholesome stimulus which persons in other pursuits feel, and which is alike beneficial to the people so engaged, and to those who purchase the articles they produce. . . . Well, then, as to the middle classes of Scotland, I hold that the municipalities of Scotland represent the opinion of the middle classes. In Glasgow, Edinburgh, Perth, and other towns, we found that the members of the corporations were a true index to the opinion of the main body of the inhabitants of the town in which it was situate. Now, in Glasgow, Edinburgh, Kirkcaldy, Dundee, Perth, and Stirling, the highest honour which the municipal authorities of these cities and towns can give, has been conferred upon that man who is in all parts of the country, and throughout the world, recognized as the impersonation of Free Trade principles, and of the Anti-Corn-Law League.

"Scotland, in former ages, was the cradle of liberty, civil and religious. Scotland, now, is the home of liberty; and there are more men in Scotland, in proportion to its population, who are in favour of the rights of man than there are in any other equal proportion of the population of this country. . . . I told them that they were the people who should have repeal of the Union; for that, if they were separate from England, they might have a Government wholly popular and intelligent, to a degree which I believe does not exist in any other country on the face of the earth. However, I believe they will be disposed to press us on, and make us become more and more intelligent; and we may receive benefit from our contact with them, even though, for some ages to come, our connexion with them may be productive of evil to themselves."

In England, at least, it is certain that the amazing vigour and resolution of the League were regarded with intense disfavour by great and important classes. The League was thoroughly out of fashion. It was regarded as violent, extreme, and not respectable. A year before, it had usually been described as a selfish and contemptible faction. By the end of 1842 things had become more serious. The notorious pamphleteer of the *Quarterly Review* now denounced the League as the foulest and most dangerous combination of recent times. The *Times* spoke of Cobden, Bright, and their allies as "capering mercenaries who go frisking about the country"; as authors of incendiary clap-trap; as peripatetic orators puffing themselves into an easy popularity by second-hand arguments. They were constantly accused of retarding their own cause, and frightening away respectable people, by their violence. Violence, as usual, denoted nothing more than that they knew their own minds, and pressed their convictions as if they were in earnest. In the earlier part of the autumn there had been a furious turn-out of the operatives in the mills, and later on in the season ricks had been burnt in the midland and southern counties. The League, in spite of the fact that its leaders were nearly all mill-owners, or connected with manufactures, was accused of promoting these outrages. There were loud threats of criminal proceedings against the obnoxious confederacy. It was rumoured on the Manchester Exchange that the Government had resolved to put down the League as an association constituted against the law of the land. If necessary, a new law would be made to enable them to suppress a body so seditious. This heat in the minds of the ruling class made them anxious at almost any cost to destroy Cobden, who was now openly recognized as the foremost personage in the detested organization. This partly explains what now followed.

The session of 1843 opened with the most painful incident in Cobden's parliamentary life. It is well to preface an account of it, by mentioning an event that happened on the eve of the session. Mr. Drummond, the private secretary of the Prime Minister, was shot in Parliament Street, and in a few days died from the wound. The assassin was Daniel M'Naghten, a mechanic from Glasgow, who at the trial was acquitted on the ground of insanity. From something that he said to a police inspector in his cell, the belief got abroad that in firing at Mr. Drummond he supposed that he was dealing with Sir Robert Peel. The evidence at the trial showed even this to be very doubtful, and in any case the act was simply that of a lunatic. But it shook Sir Robert Peel's nerves. He was known by those who were intimate with him to have a morbid sensibility to whatever was physically painful or horrible. It has always been believed that his distress at the circumstances of Mr. Drummond's death was the secret of the scene with Cobden which we have now to describe.

Lord Howick on an early night in the session moved that the House should resolve itself into a Committee to consider a passage in the Queen's speech, in which reference had been made to the prevailing distress. The debate on the motion was a great affair, and extended over five nights. It was a discussion worthy of the fame of the House of

Commons—a serious effort on the part of most of those who contributed to it, to shed some light on the difficulties in which the country was involved. Cobden spoke on the last night of the debate (Feb. 17). He answered in his usual dexterous and argumentative way the statements of Lord Stanley, Mr. Gladstone, and other opponents of a repeal of the Corn Law, and then he proceeded to a fervent remonstrance with the Prime Minister. I quote some of the sentences which led to what followed: "If you (Sir Robert Peel) try any other remedy than ours, what chance have you for mitigating the condition of the country? You took the Corn Laws into your own hands after a fashion of your own, and amended them according to your own views. You said that you were uninfluenced in what you did by any pressure from without on your judgment. You acted on your own judgment, and would follow no other, and you are responsible for the consequences of your act. You said that your object was to find more employment for the increasing population. Who so likely, however, to tell you what markets could be extended, as those who are engaged in carrying on the trade and manufactures of the country? . . . You passed the law, you refused to listen to the manufacturers, and *I throw on you all the responsibility of your own measure.* . . . The right hon. Baronet acted on his own judgment, and he retained the duty on the two articles on which a reduction of duty was desired, and he reduced the duties on those on which there was not a possibility of the change being of much service to the country. It was folly or ignorance (*Oh! Oh!*). Yes, it was folly or ignorance to amend our system of duties, and leave out of consideration sugar and corn. The reduction of the duties on drugs and such things

1843.
—
ÆT. 39.

was a proper task for some Under-Secretary of State, dealing with the sweepings of office, but it was unworthy of any Minister, and was devoid of any plan. It was one of the least useful changes that ever was proposed by any Government. . . . It is his duty, he says, to judge independently, and act without reference to any pressure; and I must tell the right hon. Baronet that *it is the duty of every honest and independent member to hold him individually responsible for the present position of the country*. . . . I tell the right hon. gentleman that I, for one, care nothing for Whigs or Tories. I have said that I never will help to bring back the Whigs; but I tell him that the whole responsibility of the lamentable and dangerous state of the country rests with him. It ill becomes him to throw that responsibility on any one at this side. I say there never has been violence, tumult, or confusion, except at periods when there has been an excessive want of employment, and a scarcity of the necessaries of life. The right hon. Baronet has the power in his hands to do as he pleases."

When Cobden sat down, the Prime Minister rose to his feet, with signs of strong agitation in his usually impassive bearing. "Sir," he said, "the honourable gentleman has stated here very emphatically, what he has more than once stated at the conferences of the Anti-Corn-Law League, that he holds me individually——" Here the speaker was interrupted by the intense excitement which his emphasis on the word, and the growing passion of his manner, had rapidly produced among his audience. "Individually responsible," he resumed, "for the distress and suffering of the country; that he holds me personally responsible. But be the consequences of these insinuations what they may, never will I be influenced by menaces, either in this House or out of this House, to adopt a course which I consider——" The rest of the sentence was lost in the shouts which now rose from all parts of the House. Cobden at once got up, but to little purpose. "I did not say," he began, "that I hold the right hon. gentleman personally responsible." Vehement cries arose on every side: "Yes, yes"—"You did, you did"—"Order"—"Chair." "You did," called out Sir Robert Peel. Cobden went on, "I have said that I hold the right hon. gentleman responsible by virtue of his office, as the whole context of what I said was sufficient to explain."

The enraged denials and the confusion with which the Ministerial benches broke into his explanation, showed Cobden that it was hopeless for the moment to attempt to clear himself. Sir Robert Peel resumed by reiterating the charge that Cobden had twice declared that he would hold the Minister individually responsible. This inauspicious beginning was the prelude of a strong and careful speech; as strong a speech as could be made by a Minister who was not prepared to launch into the full tide of Cobden's own policy,[1] and had only doubtful arguments about practical convenience to bring against the stringent pleas of logical consistency. What astonishes us is that such a performance should have followed such a preface. Those who have written

[1] The peroration of this speech is an admirably eloquent comparison between the pacific views of Wellington and Soult—"men who have seen the morning sun rise upon living masses of fiery warriors, so many of whom were to be laid in the grave before that sun should set"—and "anonymous and irresponsible writers in the public journals, who are doing all they can to exasperate the differences that have prevailed; and whose efforts were not directed by zeal for the national honour, but employed for the base purposes of encouraging national animosity, or promoting personal or party interest."

1843. — ÆT. 39.

about Sir Robert Peel's character have always been accustomed to say that, though there was originally a vein of fiery temper in him, yet he had won perfect mastery over it; and his outburst against Cobden was the only occasion when he seemed to fall into the angry impetuosity that was familiar enough on the lips of O'Connell, or Stanley, or Brougham. He was taunted before long by Mr. Disraeli with imitating anger as a tactical device, and taking the choleric gentleman for one of his many parts. Whether his display of emotion against Cobden was artificial or a genuine result of overstrung nerves, was disputed at the time, and it is disputed to this day by those who witnessed the scene. The display was undoubtedly convenient for the moment in damaging a very troublesome adversary.

Lord John Russell, who spoke after the Minister, had no particular reason to be anxious to defend so dubious a follower as Cobden, but his honourable spirit revolted against the unjust and insulting demeanour of the House. "I am sure," he said, "that for my own part, and I believe I can answer for most of those who sit round me, that the same sense was not attached to the honourable member for Stockport's words, as has been attached by the right honourable Baronet and honourable members opposite." When Lord John Russell had finished a speech that practically wound up the debate, Cobden returned to his explanation, and amid some interruptions from the opposite benches, as well as from the Speaker on a point of order, again insisted that he had intended to throw the responsibility of the Minister's measures upon him as the head of the Government. In using the word "individually," he used it as the Minister himself used the personal pronoun when he said "I passed the tariff." "I treat him," Cobden concluded, "as the Government, as he is in the habit of treating himself."

Very stiffly Peel accepted the explanation. "I am bound to accept the construction which the honourable member puts upon the language he employed. He used the word 'individually' in so marked a way, that I and others put upon it a different explanation. He supposes the word 'individually' to mean public responsibility in the situation I hold, and I admit it at once. I thought the words he employed, 'I hold you individually responsible,' might have an effect, which I think many other gentlemen who heard them might anticipate."

The sitting was not to end without an assault on Cobden from a different quarter. Sir Robert Peel had no sooner accepted one explanation, than Mr. Roebuck made a statement that demanded another. He taxed Cobden with having spoken of Lord Brougham as a maniac; with having threatened his own seat at Bath; and with having tolerated the use of such reprehensible and dangerous language by members of the League, as justified Lord Brougham's exhortation to all friends of Corn Law Reform to separate themselves from such evil advisers. This incident sprang from some words which Brougham had used in the House of Lords a week before. They are a fine example of parliamentary mouthing, and of that cheap courage which consists in thundering against the indiscretions of an unpopular friend. If anything could retard the progress of the doctrines of the League, he had said, "it would be the exaggerated statements and violence of some of those connected with their body—the means adopted by them at some of their meetings to excite—happily they have not much succeeded—to excite discontent and breakings-out into violence in different parts of the country; and, above all, I cannot discharge my duty to your Lordships and to my own conscience, if I do not express the utter abhorrence and disgust with which I have noted some men—men clothed with sacred functions, though I trust unconnected with the League, who have actually in this very metropolis of a British and Christian community, and in the middle of the nineteenth century of the gospel of grace and peace, not scrupled to utter words to which I will not at present more particularly allude, but which I abhor, detest, and scorn, as being calculated to produce fatal effects—I will not say have produced them — but calculated to produce the taking away of innocent life."

Cobden, as we might expect, had spoken freely of this rebuke as the result of a reckless intellect and a malignant spirit, or words to that effect.[1] Nobody can think that Mr. Roebuck had chosen his moment very chivalrously. Even now, when time and death are throwing the veil of kindly oblivion over the struggle, we read with satisfaction the denunciation by Mr. Bright, of the "Brummagem Brougham, who, when the whole Ministerial side of the House was yelling at the man who stood there, the very impersonation of justice to the people, stood forward and dared to throw his puny dart at Richard Cobden." There is hardly an instance which illustrates more painfully the ungenerous, the unsparing, the fierce treatment for which a man must be prepared who enters public life in the House of Commons. The sentiment of the House itself was against Cobden. It always is more or less secretly against any one of its members who is known to have a serious influence

[1] Mr. Bright also took the matter up in correspondence with Lord Brougham, and the language on both sides is as pithy as might be expected. (Feb. 15-24.)

outside, and to be raising the public opinion of constituencies to an inconveniently strong pitch. Cobden was scarcely allowed to explain what he had really said to Mr. Roebuck. It was simply this:—"If you justify Lord Brougham in this attack on the ministers who attend the conference of the Anti-Corn-Law League, you will get into trouble at Bath, and you will be considered the opponent of that body, and you will have your Anti-Corn-Law tea-parties, and some members of the League visiting Bath. So far from wishing to see Mr. Roebuck out of Parliament," Cobden concluded, "he is the last man I should wish to see removed from the seat which he now holds."

Cobden's own remarks on this unhappy evening are better than any that an outsider can offer. To his brother Frederick he wrote as follows:—

"The affair of last Friday seems to be working more and more to our advantage. It has been the talk of everybody here, from the young lady on the throne, down to the back-parlour visitors of every pot-house in the metropolis. And the result seems to be a pretty general notion that Peel has made a great fool of himself, if not something worse. He is obliged *now* to assume that he was in earnest, for no man likes to confess himself a hypocrite, and to put up with the ridicule of his own party in private as a coward. Lord —— was joking with Ricardo in the House the other night about him; pointing towards Peel as he was leaning forward, he whispered, 'There, the fellow is afraid somebody is taking aim at him from the gallery.' Then the pack at his back are not very well satisfied with themselves at having been so palpably dragged through the mud by him, for they had evidently not considered that I was threatening him. Indeed the fact of their having called for Bankes to speak after I sat down, and whilst Peel was on his legs, clearly showed (and they cannot escape from the unpleasant reflection) that they were unconscious of any grievance being felt by the latter, and that they considered the personality to refer to the former. They now feel themselves convicted of having taken the cue from Peel and joined *en masse* (without a conviction in their own minds to sanction the course they took), in hunting me down as an assassin. They will hear more of it. But the best part of the whole affair is that everybody of every shade of politics has read my speech carefully, in order to be able to judge of Peel's grounds of attack upon me. The consequence is that all the Tories of Oxford, as I learn, have been criticizing every word of it, and the result, I am told, is unfavourable to Peel. . . . He is looking twenty per cent worse since I came into the House, and if I had only Bright with me, we could worry him out of office before the close of the session.[1]

"The *thing* is on its last legs. The wholesale admissions of our principles by the Government must prove destructive to the system in no very long time. The whole matter turns upon the possibility of their finding a man to fill the office of executioner for them, and when Peel bolts or betrays them, the game is up. It is this conviction in my mind which induced me after some deliberation to throw the responsibility upon Peel, and he is not only alarmed at it, but indiscreet enough to let everybody

[1] Mr. Bright, as it happened, was returned to Parliament before the end of the session. He contested Durham in April 1843, and was beaten by Lord Dungannon. The new member was unseated on petition, on the ground of bribery. Mr. Bright again offered himself, and was elected (July 1843).

know that he is so. . . . Our meeting last night was a wonderful exhibition. In the course of a couple of months we will have entire possession of the metropolis. Nothing will alarm Peel so much as exhibitions of strength and feeling at his own door. I am overdone from all parts with letters and congratulations, and can hardly find time to say a word to my friends."[1]

1843.

ÆT. 39.

The enemies of the League made the most of what had happened. They spoke of Cobden as politically ruined, and ruined beyond retrieval. Brougham, with hollow pity, wrote about the "downfall of poor Mr. Cobden." It soon appeared that there was another side to the matter. Meetings were held to protest against the treatment which Cobden had received from the Minister and the House; sympathetic addresses were sent to him from half the towns in England, and all the towns in Scotland; and for many weeks afterwards, whenever he appeared in a public assembly, he was greeted with such acclamations as had seldom been heard in public assemblies before. We may believe that Cobden was perfectly sincere when he said to one of his friends:—"I dislike this personal matter for many good reasons, public and private. We must avoid any of this individual glorification in the future. My forte is simplicity of action, hard working behind the scenes, and common sense in council; but I have neither taste nor aptitude for these public displays."[2]

At Manchester some eight thousand men and women met to hear stirring speeches on the recent affair. Mr. Bright moved a resolution, for an address

[1] *To F. Cobden*, Feb. 23, 1843.
[2] *To E. Baines*, March 8, 1843.

1843. — Æt. 39.

pernicious system would do more at the present moment than all the efforts of the friends of Free Trade to effect the downfall of monopoly has been proclaimed upon high authority from his own side of the House. 'If the right hon. Baronet,' said Mr. Liddell, member for North Durham, in the debate, Feb. 3, 'had shown any symptoms of wavering in the support of the Corn Law, which he had himself put upon a sound footing last year, such conduct would have been productive of a hundred times more mischief than all the denunciations of the Anti-Corn-Law League.' With such evidences of the power possessed by the First Minister of the Crown, I should have been an unworthy representative of the people, and a traitor to the suffering interests of my constituents, had I failed in my duty of reminding him of his accountability for the proper exercise of his power.

"Sanctioned and sustained as I have been by the approving voice of the inhabitants of Manchester, and of my countrymen generally, I shall go forward undeterred by the arts or the violence of my opponents, in that course to which a conscientious sense of public duty impels me; and whilst studiously avoiding every ground of personal irritation—for our cause is too vast in its objects, and too good and too strong in its principles, to be made a mere topic of personal altercation—I shall never shrink from declaring in my place in Parliament the constitutional doctrine of the inalienable responsibility of the First Minister of the Crown for the measures of his Government."[1]

A few days after the scene in the House of Commons, the first of those great meetings was held,

[1] *To Sir Thomas Potter*, March 1, 1843.

1843.
Æt. 39.

which eventually turned opinion in London in good earnest to the views of the League. The Crown and Anchor and the Freemasons' Tavern had become too small to hold the audiences. Drury Lane Theatre was hired, and here seven meetings were held between the beginning of March and the beginning of May. The crowds who thronged the theatre were not always the same in keenness and energy of perception, but their numbers never fell short, and their enthusiasm grew more intense as they gradually mastered the case, and became better acquainted with the persons and characters of the prominent speakers. In the following letter to his brother, Cobden hints at the special advantage which he expected from these gatherings:—

"There is but one of their lies," he says, referring to the gossip of the Tories, "that I should care to make them prove; that is that our business is worth £10,000 a year! By the way, it is a wholesome sign that my middle-class popularity seems rather to be increased by my avowal of my origin; and for the first time probably a man is served by that aristocratic class, who owes nothing to birth, parentage, patronage, connexions, or education. Don't listen to the nonsense about our being prosecuted. The enemy has burnt his fingers already by meddling with the Leaguers. Wait till we have held two or three weekly meetings in Drury Lane Theatre, and you will see that we are not the men to be put to the ordeal of a middle-class jury. Our metropolitan gatherings are *bona fide* demonstrations of earnest energetic men of the shopkeeping class, a large proportion under thirty years of age. There is this advantage from a middle-class movement in London, that it always carries with it the working men, who are all intermingled by their occupation with the

1843.
ÆT. 39.

class above them more completely than in any other large town. I observe what you say about the spirit of our Manchester Tories. The baseness of that party exceeds anything since the time of the old Egyptian worshippers of Bulls and Beetles. But depend upon it, the hostility to the League is confined pretty much to the leaders, and you will see when a general election turns upon the Corn Laws (and we must have a dissolution upon the question before settling it), that the rank and file of the party, the shopkeepers and owners of small cottage property, will either desert the Tory masters, or fold their arms and refuse to go into action at their bidding. But our salvation will come from the rural districts. The farmers are already half alienated from the landlords, and the schism will widen every rent-day. Amidst the deluge of letters that I have received since the Peel blunder, are lots of communications from farmers. My declaration that I am a farmer's son, seems to have told as I expected, and it is a point of too much importance not to be made the most of, even at the risk of being egotistical."[1]

"The meeting at Taunton was a *bona fide* farmers' gathering from all parts of the division of Somerset, and there was but one opinion in the town amongst all parties who attended the market, that the game of the 'political landlords' is all up. I find our case upon agricultural grounds far stronger and easier than in relation to the trading interests. Now, depend upon it, it will be just as we have often predicted, the agricultural districts of the south will carry our question. They are as a community in every respect, whether as regards intelligence, morality, politics, or public spirit, superior to the folks that surround you in Lancashire. I intend

[1] *To F. Cobden*, March 11, 1843.

to hold county meetings every Saturday after Easter."[1]

The year 1843 was famous for a great agitation in each of the three kingdoms. O'Connell was rousing Ireland by the cry of Repeal. Scotland was kindled to one of its most passionate movements of enthusiasm by the outgoing of Chalmers and his brethren from the Establishment. In England the League against the Corn Law was rapidly growing in flood and volume. If ever the natural history of agitations is taken in hand, it will be instructive to compare the different methods of these three movements, two of which succeeded, while the third failed.

Cobden never disdained large popular meetings, to be counted by thousands. These gatherings of great multitudes were useful, not merely because they were likely to stir a certain interest more or less durable in those who attended them, but also because they impressed the Protectionist party with the force and numbers that were being arrayed against them. But he did not overrate either their significance or their value. Chalmers, in his great work of reorganizing the broken Church, always expressed strong distaste for large meetings, compared with small conferences attended by none but those who could be persuaded to do what he commended. He wanted, he used to say, not the excitement of emotion, but the sturdiness and endurance of good working principles. It was the same kind of feeling which made Cobden always look back with peculiar satisfaction to his share in the education of the farmers in sound economic principles by dialectical disputes from waggons, and close debate over the beef and ale at market ordinaries.

[1] *To F. Cobden*, April 10, 1843.

1843. — ÆT. 39.

The League had shown the evil effects of the Corn Law upon operatives, shopkeepers, manufacturers, and merchants. They now turned to another quarter, and set to work to prove that the same law inflicted still greater injuries upon the tenant farmers and the labourers. The towns were already convinced, and the time was a good one for an invasion of the agricultural districts. The farmers were getting low prices. They were disgusted at the concessions to Free Trade which had been made in the budget, especially in the article of meat. They suspected their parliamentary friends of trickery, and a selfish deference to a plausible Minister.

The meetings in the counties were highly successful for their immediate purpose, and they are full of interest to look back upon. They are, perhaps, the most striking and original feature in the whole agitation. There was true political courage and profound faith, in the idea of awakening the most torpid portion of the community, not by any appeal to passion, but by hard argumentative debate. It was generally accepted that the controversy was one to be settled by arguments and not by force. Sir George Lewis said that if the proposal had been to annihilate rents instead of reducing them, the Protectionists would as certainly have gone from words to blows, as the American slaveholders afterwards did when their peculiar institution was touched. One reason why the shock, when it came, was accepted without disorder, was that the League had succeeded in thoroughly loosening, if not in overthrowing, the prejudices of those who expected to be immediately ruined by the change. The discussion was usually conducted in a fair and manly spirit on both sides. The speakers for the League told their hearers that they did not wish to say anything personally offensive to anybody; that they were simply anxious that what was true on the subject of protection should be discovered; and that they gave the gentlemen in the opposition waggon credit for anxiety to do the same thing. As a rule, things were conducted with order and good temper. Land agents, valuers, and auctioneers were angrier disputants than either farmers or squires. At Dorchester there was an attempt to storm the hustings, but the Leaguers were prepared, and a stout party of their friends, aided by the labourers, repulsed the attack. At Canterbury, where the cause of protection was advocated oddly enough by Mr. G. P. R. James, the renowned novelist, one or two corn-factors insulted Cobden and Mr. Bright, and there was some uplifting of sticks. There were occasional threats of violence, tossing in a blanket, and so forth, beforehand. But when the time came, all passed off peaceably.[1]

Farmers who were afraid of attending meetings in their own immediate district, used to travel thirty or forty miles to places where they could listen to the speakers without being known. Enemies came to the meetings, and began to take notes in a very confident spirit, but as the arguments became too strong for them, the pencil was laid aside, and the paper was torn up. At Norwich, the leading yeoman of the county put a number of questions to Cobden, which were so neatly and conclusively answered, that the farmers who were listening to the controversy burst out into loud applause. The terse sentences in which Cobden condensed his matter carried conviction home. Though it was impossible

[1] When a visit from Mr. Bright was announced at Alnwick, the *Newcastle Journal* had a most brutal paragraph to the effect that some stalwart yeoman should take the matter into his hands.

for him to invent new arguments or discover unfamiliar facts every day, yet even those who were best acquainted with the facts and the arguments, were struck at every meeting by his power of selecting and concentrating the important points, with a conversational strength that brought every word within the easy comprehension of the most careless listener. Antagonists were sometimes astute, but were often stupid even to impenetrability. In one place, a clergyman firmly contended that scarcity had nothing to do with dearness. In that case, Mr. Bright replied, he need not be afraid of repeal, for of course on his principles abundance could not produce cheapness.

At Hertford the Shire Hall was so crowded, that the meeting was held in the open air. The multitude was mainly composed of farmers, and on the skirts of the multitude some of the most important squires in the county sat on horseback to hear the discussion. Cobden spoke for two hours, and obtained a sympathetic hearing by his announcement that he was the son of a Sussex farmer, that he had kept his father's sheep, and had seen the misery of a rent-day. It was at this meeting at Hertford that he first met Mr. Lattimore, the well-known farmer of Wheathampstead, to whom he was in the subsequent course of the movement greatly indebted for agricultural facts bearing on Free Trade.[1]

[1] "I have not forgotten the trouble you took to instruct me in the agricultural view of the question; how you visited me in London for that purpose. I recollect after making my speech in the House on the agricultural view of the Free Trade question—the most successful speech I ever made—that several county members asked me where my land lay, thinking I must be an experienced proprietor and farmer. I told them I did not own an acre, but that I owed my knowledge to the best farmer of my acquaintance, which I have always considered you to be."—*Cobden to R. Lattimore*, April 20,

At Aylesbury, which was the stronghold of the Duke of Buckingham, after his address, Cobden was confronted by a long list of questions from an anonymous inquirer. Would not Free Trade lower the price of corn and the means of employing labour, from thirty to fifty per cent? Did the members of the League think the existing price of the quartern loaf, which was then fivepence, too high for either producer or consumer? Cobden answered them with his usual dexterity, and wound up with the crucial question on his own part; namely, in what way farmers and farm-labourers had profited by the Corn Laws since 1815? A resolution approving of the principles of Free Trade was then put and carried with a few dissentients—so few, that Lord Nugent, who was in the chair, said they were about as many as would have held up their hands in favour of Free Trade five and twenty years before. At Uxbridge, the farmers who usually attended the corn-market, invited Cobden to explain his views to them. The arrangements for the meeting were left entirely in their own hands. The tickets of admission were issued by the farmers, and disposed of by them; the county was ransacked for supporters of monopoly, and the discomfiture of the prophet of the League was confidently predicted. The audience was more exclusively composed of farmers than any that had yet been held. When the time came, four gentlemen, one after another, advocated the cause of monopoly as ably as they could, and the discussion between them on the one hand, and Cobden and Joseph Hume on the other, lasted for four hours and a half. In the end, the arguments of the Free Traders were felt to be so

1864. The speech referred to as the most successful he ever made, I presume to be that of March 13, 1845, No. xv. in the collected speeches.

absolutely unanswerable, that a resolution in favour of total and immediate repeal was carried by five to one. The circumstances were much the same, and the result was the same at Lincoln, where Cobden was accompanied by Mr. Bright. At Taunton, the church bells were rung, flags with Free Trade mottoes were hung from the windows, and a brass band insisted on accompanying the deputation from the railway to the place of meeting. Cobden, Mr. Bright, and Mr. Moore were listened to with unwearied attention for more than four hours. The farmers listened at first with doubt and suspicion. Gradually their faces cleared, conviction began to warm them, and at last such an impression had been made, that eight hundred farmers out of a meeting of twelve hundred persons, voted in favour of total and immediate repeal.

In Bedford Cobden had not a single friend or acquaintance. He had simply announced as extensively as he could by placards, that he meant to visit the town on a given day. The farmers had been canvassed far and wide to attend to put down the representatives from the Anti-Corn-Law League. The Assembly Rooms could not hold half the persons who had come together, and they adjourned to a large field outside the town. Three waggons were provided to serve as hustings, but the monopolist party rudely seized them, and Cobden had to wait while a fourth waggon was procured. Lord Charles Russell presided, and the discussion began. The proceedings went on from three o'clock in the afternoon until nine o'clock in the evening, in spite of heavy showers of rain. At first Cobden was listened to with some impatience, but as he warmed to his subject, and began to deliver telling strokes of illustration and argument, the impression gradually spread that he was right. The chairman was unwillingly obliged to declare that an amendment in favour of Free Trade was carried by a large majority.

"We fought a hard battle at Bedford," Cobden writes to his brother, "against brutish squires and bull-frogs, but carried it two to one, contrary to the expectations of every man in the county. Lord Charles Russell is the man who opposed even his brother John's fixed duty, declaring at the time that it was to throw two millions of acres out of cultivation. After Bedford, we can win anywhere; and it is giving great moral power to my movements in the rural districts to be *always* successful. The aristocracy are becoming savage and alarmed at the war going on in their own camp."[1]

"On Saturday next," he continues, "I shall be at Rye, where there will be a grand muster from all the eastern part of our county and from parts of Kent. These county meetings are becoming provokingly interesting and attractive, so far as the landlords are affected. They begin to feel the necessity of showing fight, and yet when they do come out to meet me, they are sure to be beaten on their own dunghill. The question of protection is now an open one at all the market tables in the counties where I have been, and the discussion of the question cannot fail to have the right issue."[2]

This discussion sometimes broke down for lack of representatives of the opposite cause:—

"Our meeting at Rye was a very tame affair for want of any open spirit of opposition. The audience was almost as quiet as a flock of their own Southdowns. I fear the squires and parsons will give up the old game of opposition, and try to keep the farmers away.

[1] *To F. W. Cobden*, London, June 5, 1843.
[2] Tunbridge Wells, June 7, 1843.

1843. — ÆT. 39.

However, we have sown the seeds in the south of England which nothing will eradicate. Wherever I go, I make the Corn question an open question at all the market tables. And everywhere are strong-headed men who take up our cause. At Winchester I found many intelligent farmers. Mr. M., who moved the Free Trade resolution, is, with his brother, the largest occupier in the county. A very quiet man, highly respected: his very name a passport. A Mr. E. was at the meeting, who rents 3000 acres. After hearing our statements, he remarked, 'These facts and arguments are quite unanswerable. Every word is true.'"[1]

At Penenden Heath (June 29), three thousand of the men of Kent assembled to hear a close argumentative debate between Cobden and a local landowner. Two days later there was an open-air meeting at Guildford, where Cobden stated his case, tided over interruptions, and met objections from all comers for several hours. We need not further prolong the history of this summer's campaign. Hereford, Lewes, Croydon, Bristol, Salisbury,[2] Canterbury, and Reading were all visited before the end of the session by Cobden and Mr. Bright, or some other coadjutor. In all of them, amid great variety of illustrations, and with a constantly increasing stock of facts, he pinned his opponents to the point, How, when, or where, have farmers and farm-

[1] *To F. W. Cobden*, London, July 20, 1843.

[2] It was at Salisbury, on a second visit later in the year, that Cobden was reported to have pointed to the cathedral and said: "He thought the best thing that could happen would be to see that huge monster turned into a good factory." Even his foes admitted that this story was a gross fabrication, but it was often revived against him in the days of the Crimean War. Probably some one said that this was what he was capable of saying, and then by well-known mythopœic processes, it was believed that he actually had said it.

labourers benefited by the Corn Law? His greatest victory was at Colchester, the chief town of a county which kept its parliamentary representation unsullied by a single Liberal. The whole district had been astir with angry expectation for many days; the drum ecclesiastic had been vigorously beaten all over the county; Sir John Tyrrell, at this time one of the doughtiest followers of Peel, promised or threatened to attend; passions waxed very high; special constables were sworn in; and the violent and the timid alike declared that the agitators would find themselves in no small bodily peril. Hustings were erected in a large field, and when the day came, several thousands of people assembled from all parts of the county. At the appointed hour Cobden and Charles Villiers were at their posts, and they were soon followed by Sir John Tyrrell and Mr. Ferrand. Then the tournament began. The battle raged for six hours, and the League champions achieved a striking victory. The amendment to his resolution was put to utter rout, and when night fell, Sir John Tyrrell was found to have silently vanished. At one point in the controversy, he had irrelevantly defied Cobden to do further battle with him at Chelmsford. Cobden instantly took up the glove, and on the appointed day to Chelmsford he went. Sir John, however, had already had enough of an unequal match, and Cobden carried on the controversy in the usual way and with his usual success.

"Will these repeated discomfitures," cried the *Morning Post*, "induce the landowners of England to open their eyes to the dangers that beset them? What may be the causes of Mr. Cobden's success? The primary cause is assuredly that which conduces to the success of Sir Robert Peel. Why, indeed, if parliamentary landowners deem it honest and wise to support the author of the tariff and the new Corn Law, should not the tenant farmers of England support Sir Robert Peel's principles when enunciated by Mr. Cobden? With what pretensions to consistency could Sir John Tyrrell oppose Mr. Cobden on the hustings at Colchester, after having supported all the Free Trade measures that had made the session of 1842 infamous in the annals of our legislation? . . . Mr. Cobden's speech is by no means unanswerable. But Sir John Tyrrell assuredly made no attempt to answer it. He uttered some things not devoid of shrewdness, but they bore as slight reference to the fallacies on which Mr. Cobden traded, as they did to the false doctrines of the Koran. It is not, we fear, by such men as the present race of the parliamentary landowners that the deadly progress of the League is to be arrested."

Mr. Bright once said at a public meeting,[1] that people had talked much more than was pleasant to him about his friend Cobden and himself, and he would tell them that in the Council were many whose names were never before the public, and yet who deserved the highest praise. He was sorry that it should for a moment be supposed, that they who were more prominently before the public, and who were but two or three, should be considered the most praiseworthy. Nor was he singular. Cobden took every opportunity quietly and modestly of saying the same thing. The applause of multitudes never inflated him into a demagogue, as it was truly observed, any more than the atmosphere of Parliament and of London society ever depressed him into conventionality.[2] I cannot find a trace or

[1] October 1843.

[2] "Members were subject to great temptations in London, and

a word in the most private correspondence, betraying on the part of any prominent actor in the League a symptom of petty or ignoble egotism. They were too much in earnest. Never on a scene where the temptations to vanity were so many, was vanity so entirely absent.

Cobden's incessant activity, his dialectical skill, the scandal of the recent scene in the House, and perhaps the fact that he was a member of the House, all contributed to make his position at this time conspicuous and unique, but his simplicity of spirit filled men with an affection and love for him, which made his success their own. As a speaker, nobody knew better than he did the more stately genius of his chief friend and ally. He once told an audience at Rochdale that at this time, for reasons which they would be at no loss to guess, he always stipulated that Mr. Bright should let him speak first. From Winchester Mr. Bright wrote to him, that they had promised faithfully that he should attend the meeting, and that if the train failed to bring him, they should run the country. If Cobden's name was mentioned at a meeting, the audience would rise and give three times three for the member for Stockport, the friend of the people. At Manchester, an immense gathering assembled to present an address to him, formally describing him as the leader of the movement; and the cheers grew more enthusiastic when a letter from Lord Ducie was read, declaring that there was no man alive to whom the country was more indebted than

those who had not been behind the scenes little knew the perils and dangers they had to go through. It was very difficult for a man, however clothed in the panoply of principle, to go through the ordeal of a London season, without finding his coat of mail perforated from one quarter or another."—*Cobden, at Ashton-under-Lyne*, January 1843.

1843.
Æt. 39.

to Richard Cobden. In the same way the men on the other side singled him out for special vituperation; and people who had never seen a print-works in their lives, excited agricultural audiences by asserting that Cobden was making enormous wealth at the expense of the strength, the happiness, the limbs, and the very lives of little children.

As he said afterwards, Cobden lived at this time in public meetings. Along with the county meetings, there was for some time a weekly gathering at the Commercial Rooms in Threadneedle Street, where the League speakers reiterated their arguments to crowded audiences of merchants and bankers. There were the enthusiastic assemblies at Drury Lane and afterwards at Covent Garden, in which the interest of the London public was so great that the report of them doubled and trebled the ordinary sale of the newspapers on the following morning. Besides all this, Cobden attended to everything that in any way concerned his own great subject in the House of Commons. There his position by this time had become really formidable to the Minister. His complete knowledge of every aspect of the case, his tenacity, his skill in debate, and the immense influence which it was perceived that he was acquiring out of doors, had brought him to a front place; and the man who in February had been spoken of as politically ruined, was by August exercising a pressure on the mind of Sir Robert Peel, as strong on the one side, as the pressure of a whole group of insurgent dukes on the other.

The serious subjects of discussion in Parliament were all related to the social condition of the people, and men noticed how at one point or another they all touched the question of Free Trade. The Government brought in their famous measure of national education, as we shall afterwards see. The League, though not formally opposed to the measure, pointed out the folly of first by the Corn Law taxing the people into poverty, and then taxing the impoverished to pay for the instruction of the starving. Charles Buller pressed his scheme of State-aided emigration.[1] The League retorted that if the Corn Law were repealed, there would be no need for emigration. A Free Trader moved for a committee to inquire into the burdens and exemptions peculiar to the landed interest. A county member proposed an amendment that the House should direct its attention to Associations which, in matters affecting agriculture and commerce, pretended to influence the Legislature, and which by their combination and proceedings were dangerous

[1] In his speech, Buller reproached Cobden with condescending to practise on the ignorance of his audience by resort to stale theatrical clap-trap, which must have been suggested to him by the genius of Drury Lane—where he was speaking. As this particular passage has been much applauded by Cobden's admirers, both abroad and at home, I venture to reproduce it: "Did the men who signed that memorial ever go down to St. Catherine's Dock, and see an emigration ship about to start on its voyage? Had they seen these poor emigrants sitting till the moment of departure on the stones of the quay, as if they would cling to the last to the land of their birth? They need not inquire what were their feelings; they would read their hearts in their faces. Had they ever seen them taking leave of their friends? He had watched such scenes over and over again. He had seen a venerable woman taking leave of her grandchildren, and he had seen a struggle between the mother and the grandmother to retain possession of a child. As these emigrant-vessels departed from the Mersey to the United States, the eyes of all on deck were directed back to the port whence they had started, and the last objects which met their gaze, as their native land receded from their view, were the tall bonding-houses of Liverpool, where under the lock—he was going to say the Queen's lock, but under the lock of the aristocracy—were shut up some hundreds of thousands of barrels of the finest flour of America—the only object that these unhappy wanderers were going in quest of." His friends, he was told, did not know he had so much sentiment and eloquence in him.

1843.
—
ÆT. 39.

to the public peace and inconsistent with the spirit of the constitution. Cobden retaliated with a vigorous account of the state of the labourers on the county member's own estates, and by the telling fact that in that very county of Dorset one out of every seven of the population was a pauper. On the occasion of Mr. Villiers's annual motion for a committee to consider the duties on foreign corn with a view to their immediate abolition, Cobden made one of the most spirited of his speeches on a subject on which it appeared that everything had been said.[1] It was circulated by hundreds of thousands of copies, and produced a great effect upon opinion. The Government introduced a Bill for the repeal of the restrictions on the export of machinery. Cobden supported the removal of this last prohibition on the Statute Book. Later in the session, he made a vigorous attack on the Sugar Duties, and the policy of giving a preference to the produce of the British colonies, when the colonies contributed nothing to the revenue, and burdened us with civil and military expenses. The whole colonial trade amounted only to £10,000,000 a year, and to maintain this, £5,000,000 were spent by the mother country. The West Indian sugar-grower was the natural ally of the British corn-grower,[2] and with equal zeal the Protectionist

[1] No. IV. in the collected speeches.

[2] The following extract from one of Cobden's speeches at Covent Garden states his argument, and is a characteristic illustration of his style:—

"Now, what is the pretence for monopoly in sugar? They cannot say that it benefits the revenue; neither is it intended to benefit the farmer in England, or the negro in the West Indies. What, then, is the pretence set up? Why, that we must not buy slave-grown sugar! I believe that the ambassador from the Brazils is here at present, and I think I can imagine an interview between him and the President of the Board of Trade. He delivers his credentials; he has come to arrange a treaty of commerce. I think I see the President of the Board of Trade calling

organs took up both causes against Cobden's penetrating attacks. These organs persisted in reproaching their party in the two Houses with weakness in defence of the sacred cause. There was disunion and want of confidence throughout the party. Mr. Gladstone eloquently expounded the principles of Free Trade, though it was true that he gave the adroitest reasons for not applying them. Mr. Cobden, they said, was a man of great energy, shrewdness, and strength of will, but the true cause of his successes in debate was the want of spirit in those who should have been his active adversaries. Was it not melancholy and even insufferable to

up a solemn, earnest, pious expression, and saying, 'You are from the Brazils—we shall be happy to trade with you, but we cannot conscientiously receive slave-grown produce!' His Excellency is a good man of business; so he says, 'Well, then, we will see if we can trade together in some other way. What have you to sell us?' 'Why,' returns the President of the Board of Trade, 'cotton goods; in these articles we are the largest exporters in the world!' 'Indeed!' exclaims his Excellency; 'cotton, did you say? Where is cotton brought from?' 'Why,' replies the Minister, 'hem—chiefly from the United States,' and at once the question will be, 'Pray, is it free-grown cotton or slave-grown cotton?' Now, I leave you to imagine the answer, and I leave you also to picture the countenance of the President of the Board of Trade. . . . Now, have any of you had your humanity entrapped and your sympathies bamboozled by these appeals against slave-grown produce? Do you know how the law stands with regard to the sugar trade at present? We send our manufactures to Brazil as it is; we bring back Brazilian sugar; that sugar is refined in this country—refined in bonding warehouses, that is, warehouses where English people are not allowed to get at it—and it is then sent abroad by our merchants, by those very men who are now preaching against the consumption of slave-grown sugar. Ay, those very men and their connexions who are loudest in their appeals against slave-grown sugar, have bonding warehouses in Liverpool and London, and send this sugar to Russia, to China, to Turkey, to Poland, to Egypt; in short, to any country under the sun—to countries, too, having a population of 500,000,000; and yet these men will not allow you to have slave-grown sugar here."

1843. — ÆT. 39.

witness "the landholders of England, the representatives of the blood of the Norman chivalry, shrinking under the blows aimed at them by a Manchester money-grubber"?

Unhappily there was nobody in Manchester to whom this evil designation was less applicable. Only a week before the close of the session, Cobden wrote to his brother:—

"Your account is surely enough a bad turn up. There must be something radically fallacious in our mode of calculating cost or fixing prices. Not that I expected very much this year, because our last autumn must have been a serious loss, and the spring business squeezed into too small a space of time to do great things in. We must have a rigid overhauling of expenses, and see if they can be reduced; and if not, we must at all events fix our prices to cover all charges. I rather suspect we made a blunder in fixing them too low last spring. But with our present reputation, we must not give our goods away. The truth is, a great portion of our Manchester trade has always been done at no profit or at a loss. Still I do not fall into your despair. We have the chance of righting ourselves yet. For after all, our great losses have always arisen from fluctuations in the value of the stock, and there is no risk in that way for some years to come. As to other matters hanging over us, they can only be righted by a general revival of the district, and we shall get Free Trade from the necessities of the Exchequer."[1]

The session came to an end; it does not appear, however, that he suffered himself to be long detained from the great work by private affairs. He went for two or three weeks with his family to the south of

[1] *To F. W. Cobden*, London, Aug. 17, 1843.

England for a breath of calm. By the middle of September, he and Mr. Bright were again at work at Oxford, Lancaster, and elsewhere. They were ubiquitous; to-day at Manchester, to-morrow at Lincoln, this week at Salisbury, the next in Haddingtonshire. A day without a meeting was said to be as deplorable to them, as the merciful emperor's day without a good deed. The following extracts from letters to his wife and his brother, from October to January (1844), will serve to show how Cobden passed the autumn and winter.

"I have been incessantly occupied travelling or talking since I saw you, having made the journey across Northumberland, Cumberland, and Haddingtonshire twice. We go to-morrow to Kendal to give Warburton a lift, and I shall be home on Tuesday. I have seen much to gratify and instruct me. We spent a couple of days with Hope, and his neighbours the East Lothian farmers. They are a century before our Hants and Sussex chawbacons. In fact, they are, by comparison, educated gentlemen and practical philosophers, and their workpeople are more like Sharp and Roberts's skilled mechanics than our round-frocked peasantry. Our farmers cannot be brought to the Scotch standard by Lord Ducie or a hundred Lord Ducies. The men are wanting. We have better soil and climate, and the live and dead stock may be easily brought to match them, but the two-legged animals will not do in the present generation. We have seen much to encourage us. I have no doubt the Haddingtonshire farmers will commence an agitation against the Corn Laws, which will be a nucleus for independent action amongst their class elsewhere. The Northumberland farmers especially in the north are nearly upon a par with them, and they are just as likely to aid us.

Altogether I am full of hope from the experience of the last week. I feel no doubt that we shall, before Parliament meets, get a declaration signed by 1000 farmers in all parts of the kingdom, declaring the Corn Law to have been a cheat upon the tenantry."[1]

"*Aberdeen, Jan.* 14, 1844.—Here we are happily at the far end of our pilgrimage, and on Tuesday morning we hope to turn our faces homeward. It has been a hard week's work. After finishing our labours at Perth, I expected to have had a quiet day yesterday. We started in the morning by the coach for this place, but in passing through Forfar we found all the inhabitants at their doors or in the streets. They had heard of our intended passage through their town, and a large crowd was assembled at the inn where the coach stopped, which gave us three cheers; and nothing would do but we must stop to give them an address. We consented, and immediately the temperance band struck up, and paraded through the town, and the parish church bells were set a-ringing, in fact the whole town was set in a commotion. We spoke to about two thousand persons in the parish church, which, notwithstanding that it was Saturday evening, was granted to us. It was the first time we ever addressed an Anti-Corn-Law audience in a parish church. Forfar is a poor little borough with a great many weavers of coarse linens, and their enthusiasm is nearly all we can expect from them. A subscription of about a hundred and fifty pounds will, however, be raised. We expect better things in the way of money here. Aberdeen is a fine large town with several extensive manufactories, and a good shipping port. But strange to say it is almost the only place in Scotland where the capitalists seem

[1] *To F. W. Cobden*, Carlisle, Oct. 27, 1843.

to have taken no part in the Free Trade movement. But I hope we shall be able to stir them up to-morrow. We shall depart from this on Tuesday morning at half-past five for the south, stopping at Montrose for a mid-day meeting, and then proceeding on to Dundee for a great meeting in the evening. Thus you see we are working double tides, travelling miles by coach and holding two meetings a day. I hope we shall last it out for another week. We are to have two large meetings here to-morrow. The deputation separated into two parties at Edinburgh. Moore and I came north, and Bright and Colonel Thompson went to the west of Scotland, taking Paisley, Kilmarnock, and Greenock, and we shall all meet again at Newcastle on Saturday next. We find a great change in the temperature in these northern regions. There is a hard frost, and the highlands are covered with snow. I have thus far escaped a cold, and find my health good; in fact, notwithstanding my hard work, I have been better this winter than ever, having escaped my usual fit of inflammation in my eyes. I think there is a special Providence watching over the Leaguers."

"*Dundee, Jan.* 17, 1844.—I am nearly overdone with work, two meetings at Aberdeen on Monday, up at four on Tuesday, travelled thirty-five miles, held a meeting at Montrose, and then thirty-five miles more to Dundee, for a meeting the same evening. To-morrow we go to Cupar Fife, next day, Leith, the day following, Jedburgh."

"*Newcastle-on-Tyne, Jan.* 22.—I got here last night from Jedburgh, where we had the most extraordinary meeting of all. The streets were blocked up with country people as we entered the place, some of whom had come over the hills for twenty miles. It is the Duke of Buccleuch's country, but he would be puzzled to find followers on his own lands to fight his battles as of old. To-night we meet here, to-morrow at Sunderland, the day after at Sheffield, where you will please address me to-morrow, on Thursday we shall be at York, and on Friday at Hull, and in Manchester on Saturday evening."[1]

"*Hull, Jan.* 26, 1844.—I shall leave this place to-morrow by the train at half-past ten, and expect to reach Manchester by about five o'clock. I am, I assure you, heartily glad of the prospect of only two days' relaxation after the terrible fagging I have had for the last three weeks. To-day we have two meetings in Hull. I am in the Court-House with a thousand people before me, and Bright is stirring up the lieges with famous effect. He is reminding the Hull people of the conduct of their ancient representative, Andrew Marvell, and talking of their being unworthy of the graves of their ancestors over which they walk. We shall have another meeting this evening."

There was one drawback to the Scotch. Before they crossed the border, the Leaguers had held meetings in Leicester, Nottingham, Sheffield, Leeds, where they got a couple of thousand pounds before they left the room. At a Scotch meeting, Cobden tells Mrs. Cobden, "we found that to name money was like reading the Riot Act, for dispersing them. They care too much for speeches by mere politicians and Whig aristocrats." But the results of the campaign were in the highest degree valuable. The deputation strengthened the faith in all the places that they visited, revived interest and conviction, and brought back to Manchester a substantial addition to the funds of their association.

[1] *To F. W. Cobden*, Newcastle-on-Tyne, Jan. 22, 1844.

The following letter to Mr. George Wilson belongs to this date, and illustrates a point on which Cobden and his friends were always most solicitous. It is written from Durham, for which Mr. Bright had been returned as member in the previous July:—

"You will remember that when Bright won this place, the Whigs (that is, the *Chronicle*) tried to make it a Whig triumph, which Bright spoilt by his declaration at the Crown and Anchor, 'that it was not a party victory.' Now your best plan at Covent Garden on Thursday will be to prevent the Whigs playing us off against the Tories, by declaring that the City election was a trial of strength not between the League and the Ministry, or between the League and the Tory party, but between Free Trade and Monopoly. There is no way so certain of bringing the Whigs to our ranks, as by showing them that they will not be allowed to make a sham fight with the Tories at our expense. Depend on it the Whigs are now plotting how they can use us and throw us aside. The more we show our honesty in refusing to be made the tools of a party, the more shall we have the confidence of the moderate and honest Tories. You have now an opportunity of putting us right with both parties, and I hope you will give the right tone to the speaking at Covent Garden."[1]

[1] *To George Wilson*, Durham, October 24, 1843.

CHAPTER XIII

THE SESSION OF 1844—FACTORY LEGISLATION—THE CONSTITUENCIES

1844.

Æt. 40.

THE statistics of agitation sometimes raise a smile. The nice measurement of argumentative importunity in terms of weight and bulk, seems incongruous in connexion with anything so complex, so volatile, so invisibly rooted as opinion. We all know how at each annual meeting the listeners receive these figures of tracts, pamphlets, and leaflets with the same kind of enthusiasm with which a farmer surveys his mountains of quickening manure. At Manchester, in the autumn of 1843, the report was stupendous. Five hundred persons had been employed in distributing tracts from house to house. Five millions of such tracts had been delivered to parliamentary electors in England and Scotland; and the total distributed to non-electors and others had been upwards of nine millions. The weight of papers thus circulated was no less than one hundred tons. One hundred and forty towns had been visited, and there had been five and twenty meetings in the agricultural districts. It was resolved that the new campaign should be conducted with redoubled vigour. In October (1843), after a vehement contest, in which the Monopolist candidate was backed by all the influence of the Government, a Free Trader was returned for the city, and this great victory gave new heart to the movement throughout the country. Fifty thousand pounds had been expended in the current year. A fund of a hundred thousand pounds was demanded for the year to come; and before the end of 1844 nearly ninety thousand pounds of that sum had actually been raised. Of this amount, nearly fourteen thousand pounds were subscribed at a single meeting in Manchester. Cobden had, at that time at any rate, supreme faith in the potency of this vast propagandism. He still believed that if you brought truth to people's doors, they must embrace it. Projects for the establishment of newspapers for the spread of the views of his school, always interested him keenly. The following letter to Mr. Bright describes the beginnings of one of the most excellent journals of the time:—

"I wish I could have a little talk with you and Wilson about the removal of the *Circular* to London. James Wilson[1] has a plan for starting a weekly Free Trader by himself and his friends, to be superintended by himself. But he does not intend this unless he can have the support of the League, or at least its acquiescence. He has a notion that a paper would do more good if it were *not* the organ of the League, but merely their independent supporter. But then what is the League to do for an organ? If we start another weekly paper, it would clash with his. Villiers seems to have been rather taken with James Wilson's plan, and it would undoubtedly be desirable to have Wilson's pen at work. It is quite clear that

[1] Afterwards Secretary to the Treasury, and Financial Member of the Council of India. A most interesting account of Mr. Wilson is to be found in the *Literary Studies* of the late Walter Bagehot (vol. i. pp. 367-406).

the League must have its organ. The question for us to decide is what kind of paper shall we have? Is it to be simply a removal of the *Anti-Bread-Tax Circular* to London with the change of the title to the *League Circular* and to be still confined exclusively to the one object and movement of the League, or must we enlarge to a sixpenny paper, and whilst keeping corn prominent, attack collaterally sugar, and coffee? If we stick to the *Circular* in its present character, then another Free Trade paper might be started; if we adopted the enlarged paper, then it would be folly in James Wilson to undertake another, and he would not attempt it."[1]

In the long-run Mr. Wilson started his own newspaper, which he called the *Economist*. The *Circular* was suppressed, and the *League* was published in its stead, conveying, as Cobden said, every syllable of their speeches to twenty thousand people in all the parishes of the kingdom. Before describing a more important move in the Manchester tactics, I have to say something of Cobden's action in Parliament, where a very momentous subject presently engaged attention.

In the session of 1844 the Corn Laws fell into the background. Mr. Cardwell, in seconding the motion on the Address, made a marked impression by a collection of evidence that trade was reviving. The revival of trade weakened the strongest argument of the agitators, because it diminished the practical urgency of their question. Parliament is always glad of an excuse for leaving a question alone, and the slightest improvement in the markets was welcomed as a reason for allowing the Corn Law to slumber. The Prime Minister took advantage of such a state of things to quell the sullen suspicion of the agricultural

[1] *To Mr. Bright*, June 21, 1843.

party, by emphatic declarations that the Government had never contemplated, and did not then contemplate, any alteration in the existing law. Repeal he hardly deigned to notice; it would, he said, produce the greatest confusion and distress. There was, no doubt, the alternative of a fixed duty; but if it should happen that the agriculturists should come to prefer that to his sliding scale, then he was inclined to think that, not he, but Lord John Russell would be the proper person to make the change. So closely did Peel habitually trim his sails to suit the shifting of the winds.

In consequence of this declaration of the Minister, and of the improvement in the condition of the population, comparatively slight attention was paid to the discussion on Mr. Villiers's annual Motion (June 25). The League was violently abused by the Mileses, Bankeses, Ferrands, and Sir John Trollopes. It was again and again asserted that the rate of wages was regulated by the price of corn, and that the avowed object of the agitators was to lower wages by lowering corn. Cobden replied to such serious arguments as he could find in the course of the debate, but the front bench on the side of the Opposition was empty for most of the evening; Lord John Russell declined to vote; Mr. Bright was listened to with so much impatience that he was forced to sit down; and a very hollow performance ended with a majority of 204 against the Motion.[1]

In the earlier part of the session (March 12), Cobden had moved for a Select Committee to inquire into the effects of protective duties on agricultural tenants and labourers. This was a new approach. The main argument for repeal had hitherto been

[1] 328 against 124.

from the side of the manufacturing population. In what way, save by the admission of foreign corn in exchange for British manufactures, could we secure extended markets; or, in other words, extended demand for the industry of the people? Cobden now turned to the agricultural side of the question, and asked the House of Commons, as he had asked the farmers during the previous year, to examine what advantage the Corn Law had brought to the agriculturists themselves. He described the condition of the labourer, morally, socially, and economically; said that it was the fear of falling into this condition which caused the strikes of the workmen in the towns; and asked how a starved population of this kind could form that valuable class of domestic consumers, who were held out by the landlords to the manufacturers as adequate compensation for loss of customers abroad. The official duty of reply fell to Mr. Gladstone. His answer turned mainly on the inexpediency of assenting to a motion which would imply that the Corn Law was an open question, and which would therefore tend to unsettle trade, disturb the revenue, and increase the excitement in people's minds. At present, Mr. Gladstone said, the League was thought to be a thing of no great practical moment: its parade and ceremonial were perhaps the most important features about it; but if Parliament should take up the subject, then assuredly the League would acquire a consequence to which it had really no title. Cobden's motion was rejected by a vote of two hundred and twenty-four against one hundred and thirty-three, being a majority of ninety-one.

This bad division had perhaps less than the general feeling of the House, as gathered from talk in the lobbies, to do with the changed view which Cobden now took of the prospects of the cause.

The ardour of his hopes was relaxed, though not the firmness of his resolution. He gave expression to this in writing to his brother:—

"It is now quite certain that our Free Trade labours must be spread over a larger space of time than we contemplated at one time. The agitation must be of a different kind to what we have hitherto pursued. In fact we must merely have just so many demonstrations as will be necessary to keep hold of public attention, and the work must go on in the way of registration labours in those large constituencies where we can hope to gain anything by a change of public opinion. The little pocket boroughs must be absolutely given over. They will not weigh as a feather in the settlement of the question. *Time* can alone effect the business. It cannot be carried by storm. We were wrong in thinking of it. In the meantime Peel's unsettlements are making enemies in the ranks of the united Monopolists, and everybody is making up his mind to more change. As my labours must henceforth be less intense than heretofore, I shall be able to give more attention to my private affairs, which, Heaven knows, have been neglected enough."[1]

The following passage relates to a subject which kindled more excitement in the country than any other question before Parliament. It was an episode in the endless battle between bigotry and the sense of justice. The judgment in the famous case of Lady Hewley's bequest, finally delivered after fourteen years of litigation, exposed endowments which had been for several generations in the hands of Unitarians, to the risk of appropriation by Trinitarian Dissenters. The Ministry brought in a Bill to confirm religious bodies, whether Trinitarian or

[1] *To F. W. Cobden*, London, June 4, 1844.

Unitarian, in the possession of property of which they had been in the enjoyment for twenty years. This measure was regarded by fanatics, alike of the Episcopalian and the independent churches, as favouring the deadly heresy of Unitarianism. The storm raged with furious violence; but the Ministry held firm, and the Bill, which was conservative of the rights of property in the right sense, happily became law. Sir W. Follett's speech broke down the opposition. We may be sure on which side in the controversy Cobden was found.

"I never entertained an idea of voting for the Monopolists in matters of faith. Nor have I had a line from anybody at Stockport to ask me to do so. As at present advised, I shall certainly vote for the Bill. What a spectacle we shall present, if the intolerance of the Commons should reject a measure which the Lords and the Bishops have passed! It would confirm one's notion that the Government of this country is in advance of the people.

"Lord Duncan's reply to a deputation was not amiss. He told them drily, 'It may be a question whether the founders of the chapels in question intended them for the benefit of Unitarians or Trinitarians, but one thing is certain, they did not intend them for the *lawyers*, who will have every kick of them, unless the Bill is passed into a law.' This young chip of the old block who stood such hard knocking at Camperdown, said an equally good thing to the short-time delegates who called on him to abuse the factory masters. He told them to go home and thank God they had not the landlords for masters, for if they had, their wages would be reduced one-half."[1]

It is now time to turn briefly to a subject which

[1] *To F. W. Cobden*, London, June 5, 1844.

sprang as directly as Free Trade itself from the great Condition of England Question. Throughout this memorable Parliament, which sat from 1841 to 1847, we are conscious of a genuine effort, alike on the part of the Prime Minister and of independent reformers and philanthropists of all kinds, to grapple with a state of society which threatened to become unmanageable. We see the Parliament diligently feeling its way to one piece after another of wise and beneficent policy, winding up with the most beneficent of all. The development of manufactures, and the increase and redistribution of population which attended it, forced upon all the foremost minds of that time a group of difficulties with which most of them were very inadequately prepared to deal. One fact will be enough to illustrate the extent of the change. In 1818 it was computed that 57,000 persons were employed in cotton factories. Within twenty-one years their numbers had increased to 469,000. How was this vast and rapid influx of population into the cotton towns, with all the new conditions which it implied, to be met? Or was it to the statesman indifferent? The author of *Sybil* seems to have apprehended the real magnitude and even the nature of the social crisis. Mr. Disraeli's brooding imaginativeness of conception gave him a view of the extent of the social revolution as a whole, which was wider, if it did not go deeper, than that of any other contemporary observer. To accidents of his position in society and necessities of personal ambition, it must, I suppose, be attributed that one who conceived so truly the seriousness of the problem, should have brought nothing better to its solution than the childish bathos of Young England. Mr. Carlyle, again, had true vision of the changes that were sweeping the unconscious nation away from the

1844. — ÆT. 40.

bonds and principles of the past into an unknown future. But he had no efficient instruments for controlling or guiding the process. He was right enough in declaring that moral regeneration was the one thing needful to set the distracted nation at ease. In a particular crisis, however, moral regeneration is no more than a phrase.

Cobden answered the question on the economic side. You must, he said, accept and establish the conditions of free exchange. Only on these terms can you make the best use of capital, and ensure the highest attainable prosperity to labour. But at this point—they were then close upon the ever-memorable date of '48—the gigantic question of that generation loomed on the horizon. How are you to settle the mutual relations of capital and labour to one another? Abolition of restriction may be excellent in the sphere of commodities. Is it so clear that the same condition suffices for the commonwealth, when the commodity to be exchanged is a man's labour? Or is it palpably false and irrational to talk of labour as a commodity? In other words, can the relations between labour and capital be safely left to the unfettered play of individual competition? The answer of modern statesmanship is, that unfettered individual competition is not a principle to which the regulation of industry may be entrusted. There may be conditions which it is in the highest degree desirable to impose on industry, and to which the general opinion of the industrial classes may be entirely favourable. Yet the assistance of law may be needed to give effect to this opinion, because—in the words of the great man who was now preparing the exposition of political economy that was to reign all through the next generation—only law can afford to every individual a guarantee that his competitors will pursue the same

1844.
ÆT. 40.

course as to hours of labour and so forth, without which he cannot safely adopt it himself.[1]

Cobden, as we have already seen (pp. 125-126), when he was first a candidate for Stockport, dissented from these theories. He could not adjust them to his general principle of the expediency of leaving every man free to carry his goods to whatever market he might choose, and to make the best bargain that he could. The man who saw such good reasons for distrusting the regulation of markets by Act of Parliament, was naturally inclined to distrust parliamentary regulation of labour. In the case of children, Cobden fully perceived that freedom of contract is only another name for freedom of coercion, and he admitted the necessity of legislative protection. He never denied that restrictions on the hours of labour were desirable, and he knew by observation, both at home and abroad, that the hours of labour are no measure of its relative productiveness. What he maintained was that all restrictions, however desirable, ought to be secured by the resolute demands and independent action of the workmen themselves, and not by intervention of the law.[2]

Singularly enough, while he thus trusted to the independence of the workmen, he objected to workmen's combinations. "Depend upon it," he said to his brother, "nothing can be got by fraternizing with Trades Unions. They are founded upon principles of brutal tyranny and monopoly. I would rather live under a Dey of Algiers than a Trades Committee."[3] Yet without combination it is difficult to see how, on the great scale of modern industries, the workmen can

[1] J. S. Mill's *Political Economy* was not begun until 1845, but it bears abundant traces how closely he watched the course of legislation during the years immediately preceding.

[2] See Appendix A, at the end of the volume.

[3] *To F. W. Cobden,* August 16, 1842.

exert any effective influence on the regulation of their labour. That in the first forms of combination there was both brutality and tyranny, is quite true. That these vices have almost disappeared is due in no small degree to an active fraternization, to use Cobden's own word, with the leaders of the workmen by members of the middle class, who represented the best moral and social elements in the public opinion of their time.

The protection of the labouring population had in various forms engaged the serious attention of Parliament for several years. So far back as 1802 there was a Factory Act, which was sanitary in its main intention, but also contained clauses regulating hours. Others followed in 1819 and 1825, and a very important Factory Law, containing the earliest provisions for education, was passed in 1833, by which time the workmen were partially able to make themselves heard in Parliament. In 1842 Lord Ashley had procured the passing of the Mines and Collieries Act, a truly admirable and beneficent piece of legislation, excluding women from labour underground, and rescuing children from conditions hardly less horrible than those of negro slavery. In 1843, still under the impulse of Lord Ashley, Sir James Graham brought in a Factory Bill, not only regulating the hours of labour, but proposing a system for the education of the children of the industrial class in the manufacturing towns. Cobden took an early opportunity of saying a friendly word for the education clauses of the measure, as being a step in the right direction. Popular education had been the most important of all social objects in his mind from the first; and in spite of drawbacks, which he did not despair of seeing amended, he saw more good than harm in the new proposals. These clauses, however, beyond doubt conferred advantages on the Established Church, in which the Dissenters justly and wisely refused to acquiesce.[1] It might well seem to be better that popular instruction should still be left to voluntary machinery for some time longer, than that new authority and new fields of ecclesiastical control should be opened to the privileged Church. The opposition was so vehement that the education clauses were dropped, and the Bill withdrawn.

1844.

Æt. 40.

In 1844 Sir James Graham reintroduced it, without the education clauses, simply as a Bill for regulating the labour of children and young persons. The definition of a child was extended to mean children between nine and thirteen; a child was only to be employed half time, that is to say, not more than six and a half hours each day. The definition of young persons remained as it was, covering persons from thirteen to eighteen; their hours in silk, cotton, wool, and flax manufactories were not to exceed thirteen and a half in each day; and of these one hour and a half were to be allowed for meals and rest, leaving twelve hours as the limit of actual labour. Lord Ashley moved that the hours should be not twelve but ten, and on this issue the battle was fought. The factory question from this time, down to the passing of the Ten Hours Act, was part of the wider struggle between the country gentlemen and the manufacturers. The Tories were taunted with the condition of the labourers in the fields, and they retorted by tales of the condition of the operatives in factories. The manufacturers rejoined by asking, if they were so anxious to benefit the workman, why they did not, by repealing the Corn Law, cheapen his bread. The

[1] The provisions for trustees of the schools were undeniably and deliberately calculated to give the clergy of the Established Church a predominant power on every board.

landlords and the mill-owners each reproached the other with exercising the virtues of humanity at other people's expense. This was not Lord Ashley's own position. He was at this time in favour of the Corn Law, but his exertions for the factory population were due to a disinterested and genuine interest in their welfare. In 1842[1] Cobden took a more generous, or rather a more just, view of Lord Ashley's character than he had been accustomed to express in his letters and conversation. "He would confess very frankly that before he entered that House, he had entertained doubts, in common with many of the employers in the north, whether those advocates of the Short Hours Bill who supported the Corn Law were really sincere. But since he had had an opportunity of a closer observation of the noble lord, he was perfectly convinced of his genuine philanthropy." That, however, was no reason why Lord Ashley should not be resisted, if his philanthropy led him wrong; and Mr. Bright, while not denying that the hours of labour were longer than they ought to be, made a vigorous onslaught on him. "It was a perilous effort," Cobden wrote, "especially in the canting tone of the country, but our friend came off well, and there is much credit due to him for taking the bull by the horns. The Tories have gained nothing by the last week's debate."[2]

Charles Buller defended Lord Ashley's proposal in what was a very wise speech, though it may have been made as a party move against Peel. Brougham poured out a torrent of invective in the House of Lords against all interference with labour. Most of the official Whigs, on the contrary, went for the limitation of ten hours, though they had stoutly opposed the same proposal when they were in power;

[1] July 8. [2] *To F. W. Cobden*, London, March 16, 1844.

but in the end the Government carried their Act for twelve hours.

1844.

ÆT. 40.

"I did not vote upon the Factory question," Cobden wrote. "The fact is the Government are being whipped with a rod of their own pickling. They used the Ten Hours cry, and all other cries, to get into power, and now they find themselves unable to lay the devil they raised for the destruction of the Whigs. The trickery of the Government was kept up till the time of Ashley's motion, in the confident expectation that he would be defeated by the Whigs and Free Traders. They (the Government) were calculating upon this support, and so they gave liberty to Wortley and others of their party to vote against the Cabinet in order to get favour at the hustings. The Whigs very basely turned round upon their former opinions to spite the Tories. The only good result is that no Government or party will in future like to use the Factory question for a cry. The last year's Education question, and this year's Ten Hours Bill, will sicken the factions of such a two-edged weapon. One other good effect may be that men like Graham and Peel will see the necessity of taking anchor upon some sound principles, as a refuge from the Socialist doctrines of the fools behind them. But at all events good must come out of such startling discussions."[1]

It cannot be seriously denied that Cobden was fully justified in describing the tendencies of this legislation as socialistic. It was an exertion of the power of the State in its strongest form, definitely limiting in the interest of the labourer the administration of capital. The Act of 1844 was only a rudimentary step in this direction. In 1847 the Ten

[1] *To F. W. Cobden*, March 23, 1844.

Hours Bill became law. Cobden was abroad at the time, and took no part in its final stages. In the thirty years that followed, the principle has been extended with astonishing perseverance. We have to-day a complete, minute, and voluminous code for the protection of labour: buildings must be kept pure of effluvia; dangerous machinery must be fenced; children and young persons must not clean it while in motion; their hours are not only limited but fixed; continuous employment must not exceed a given number of hours, varying with the trade, but prescribed by the law in given cases; a statutable number of holidays is imposed; the children must go to school, and the employer must every week have a certificate to that effect; if an accident happens, notice must be sent to the proper authorities; special provisions are made for bakehouses, for lace-making, for collieries, and for a whole schedule of other special callings; for the due enforcement and vigilant supervision of this immense host of minute prescriptions, there is an immense host of inspectors, certifying surgeons, and other authorities, whose business it is "to speed and post o'er land and ocean" in restless guardianship of every kind of labour, from that of the woman who plaits straw at her cottage door, to the miner who descends into the bowels of the earth, and the seaman who conveys the fruits and materials of universal industry to and fro between the remotest parts of the globe. But all this is one of the largest branches of what the most importunate Socialists have been accustomed to demand; and if we add to this vast fabric of Labour legislation our system of Poor Law, we find the rather amazing result that in the country where Socialism has been less talked about than any other country in Europe, its principles have been most extensively applied.

If the Factory Law was in one sense a weapon with which the country party harassed the manufacturers, it was not long before Cobden hit upon a plan for retaliating. For two or three years the League had confined its operations to the creation of an enlightened public opinion on the subject of the Corn Laws. Then it began to work in the boroughs, and Cobden was able to say that never at any previous date had so much systematic attention, time, and labour been given to the boroughs in the way of registration. The power which had thus been given to the Free Trade party in nearly one hundred and fifty boroughs, was expected to make an immense, if not a decisive, difference in the next Parliament. In the great county of Lancashire alone, such changes had been wrought by attention to the register, that it was calculated that a new election would only leave the Monopolists five out of the six-and-twenty members for the entire province. It now occurred to Cobden that these constituencies could be dealt with even more effectually. In the last division, not a single county member had gone into the lobby with Mr. Villiers. Cobden's thought was to turn the counties by an indefinite increase of the constituencies. They were to be won through that section of the Reform Act which conferred the franchise in counties upon possessors of freehold property of the value of forty shillings a year. The landlords had already availed themselves to an immense extent of the Chandos clause. By the Chandos clause tenants at will, occupying at a yearly value of fifty pounds, had the franchise. The Monopolists, in Cobden's words, worked this clause out; they applied themselves to qualifying their tenant-farmers for the poll, "by making brothers, sons, nephews, uncles—ay, down to the third generation, if they happened to live upon

1844. Æt. 40.

the farm—all qualify for the same holding, and swear, if need be, that they were partners in the farm, though they were no more partners than you are. This they did, and successfully, and by that means gained the counties." "But," Cobden continued, "there was another clause in the Reform Act, which we of the middle classes—the unprivileged, industrious men, who live by our capital and labour—never found out, namely, the forty-shilling freehold clause. I will set that against the Chandos clause, and we will beat them in the counties with it. . . . There is a large class of mechanics who save their forty or fifty pounds; they have been accustomed perhaps to put it in the Savings Bank. I will not say a word to undervalue that institution; but cottage property will pay twice as much interest as the Savings Bank. Then what a privilege it is for a man to put his hands in his pockets, and walk up and down opposite his own freehold, and say, 'This is my own; I worked for it, and I have won it.' There are many fathers who have sons just ripening into maturity, and I know that parents are very apt to keep their property and the state of their affairs from their children. My doctrine is that you cannot give your son your confidence, or teach him to be entrusted with property, too early. When you have a son just coming to twenty-one years of age, the best thing you can do, if you have it in your power, is to give him a qualification for the county; it accustoms him to the use of property, and to the exercise of a vote, whilst you are living and can have some little judicious control over it if necessary."[1]

The reader will observe that Cobden's design was free from the sinister quality of manufactured voting. He supposed that men would acquire property in

[1] Speech at Covent Garden, Dec. 11, 1844.

their own neighbourhood, the natural seat of their political interests and activity. What is politically mischievous in this franchise only happens when a number of strangers in possession of a factitious qualification invade a district and help to nullify the wishes and opinions of the majority of those who reside in it. Such a practice as this seems at no time to have been in Cobden's contemplation. Still many people demurred. The plan wore the look of manufacturing votes; it seemed, they said, mechanical, unworthy, and barely legitimate. No, replied Cobden, there is nothing savouring of trick or finesse of any kind in it; the law and the constitution prescribe the condition; you have a *bona fide* qualification, and are conforming to the law both in spirit and in fact. This was quite true, and no plan ever proposed by the League met with so unanimous a response from all parts of the kingdom. It took two hours a day to read the letters that came from every part of the country, all applauding the scheme. By the beginning of 1845 between four and five thousand new electors had been brought upon the lists in Yorkshire, Lancashire, and Cheshire. Not less than two hundred and fifty thousand pounds were invested in these counties in the forty-shilling qualification. It was believed that eight or ten times as many persons in other parts of the country had taken Cobden's hint to qualify.

It was to be an immense enfranchisement, on old constitutional lines and secured by the spontaneous effort and civil spirit of the population itself. "Wherever there is a man above the rank of an unskilled labourer, whether a shopkeeper, a man of the middle class, or of the skilled working class that has not got a county vote, or is not striving to accumulate enough to get one, let us point the finger of scorn at

1844.
Æт. 40.

him; he is not fit to be a freeman. It is an avenue by which we may reach the recesses of power, and possess ourselves of any constitutional rights which we are entitled to possess." In one of his speeches of that date, Cobden allowed it to be perceived that this great process had come into his mind not simply as a means of quickening the triumph of Free Trade, but as an agency for effecting a deep and permanent political transformation. "Some people," he said, "tell you that it is very dangerous and unconstitutional to invite people to enfranchise themselves by buying a freehold qualification. I say, without being revolutionary, or boasting of being more democratic than others, that the sooner the power in this country is transferred from the landed oligarchy, which has so misused it, and is placed absolutely—mind, I say absolutely—in the hands of the intelligent middle and industrious classes, the better for the condition and destinies of this country."[1]

Cobden's eloquent colleague, Fox, placed the movement deeper still, by dwelling on the moral elements that lay beneath it. If it was wise and good, he said, to endeavour to make all who could save their pittance become fundholders, it must be at least as prudent and just to induce them according to their proportion to become landholders also—joint shareholders in this lovely and fruitful country, which is their country as much as it is that of the wealthiest nobleman whose lands cover half a county. It would give them a tangible bond of connexion with society; it would put them in a position which was deemed necessary to citizenship in the republics of ancient days; and it was better adapted than anything else to cherish in them those emotions which best accord with consistency and dignity of character.

[1] *Speeches*, i. 256, Jan. 15, 1845.

CHAPTER XIV

BASTIAT—NEW TACTICS—ACTIVITY IN PARLIAMENT —MAYNOOTH GRANT—PRIVATE AFFAIRS

1845.
Æt. 41.

It was in this year that Cobden made the acquaintance of a French thinker who has done more than any other of his countrymen to give vivid and imaginative colour to the principles which in England we usually call Cobden's. Bastiat was born in 1806. He lived on a meagre ancestral property on the banks of the Adour, in the remote obscurity of the Landes. For twenty years he had been almost solitary among his farms, studying the great economic writers, discussing them from time to time with the only friend he had, occasionally making a short journey, and always practising what Rousseau calls that rarest kind of philosophy which consists in observing what we see every day. By chance he fell on an English newspaper. He was amazed to find that a body of practical men in England were at the moment actually engaged, and engaged with the reasonable prospect of success, in pressing for that Free Trade of which he had only dared to dream as a triumph of reason possible in some distant future. For two years he watched the progress of the agitation with eager interest. As was natural, what he saw rapidly stirred in him a lively desire for a similar illumination in his own country. He sat down to write an account of the English movement. In the summer of 1845 he went to Paris to see his book through the press. With his long hair and unfashionable hat, his rustic clothes and homely umbrella, he had the air of an honest countryman come to see the marvels of the town. But there was a look of thought on his square brow, a light in his full dark eye, and a keenness in his expression, which told people that they were dealing with an enthusiast and a man of ideas. Bastiat took the opportunity of being in Paris to push on to London, there to behold with his own eyes the men who had so long excited his wonder and his admiration. He hastened to the office of the League, with copies of his book in his hand. "They told me," he wrote to his friend, "that Cobden was on the point of starting for Manchester, and that he was most likely preparing for the journey at that moment. An Englishman's preparation consists of swallowing a beefsteak and thrusting two shirts into a carpet-bag. I hurried to Cobden's house, where I found him, and we had a conversation which lasted for two hours. He understands French very well, speaks it a little, and I understand his English. I explained the state of opinion in France, the results that I expect from my book, and so on." Cobden in short received him with his usual cordiality, told him that the League was a sort of freemasonry, that he ought to take up his quarters at the hotel of the League, and to spend his evenings there in listening to the fireside talk of Mr. Bright and the rest of the band. A day or two afterwards, at Cobden's solicitation, Bastiat went down to Manchester. His wonder at the ingenious methods and the prodigious scale of the League increased with all that he saw. His admiration for Cobden as a public leader grew into hearty affection for him as a private friend, and this friendship became one of the chief delights of the few busy years of life that remained to him.

There had never been any anxiety among the men of the League to stir foreign opinion. "We came to the conclusion," Cobden said, "that the less we attempted to persuade foreigners to adopt our trade principles, the better; for we discovered so much suspicion of the motives of England, that it was lending an argument to the Protectionists abroad to incite the popular feeling against the Free Traders, by enabling them to say—'See what these men are wanting to do: they are partisans of Englishmen, and they are seeking to prostrate our industries at the feet of that perfidious nation.' . . . To take away this pretence we avowed our total indifference whether other nations became Free Traders or not: but we should abolish Protection for our own sakes, and leave other countries to take whatever course they liked best."[1] When Bastiat came to the work of agitation in his own country, he found all the difficulties that his friends of the League had foreseen.

His book, *Cobden et la Ligue*, came gradually into greater vogue as the movement grew more important, and when the hour of triumph came in England, Bastiat shared its glory in France, as one who had foreseen its importance at a time when no French newspaper had been courageous or intelligent enough to give its readers any information on a subject which was necessarily so unwelcome in a country of monopolies. Bastiat felt that the title of his book had perhaps wounded some of Cobden's fellow-workers, and among men less strenuous and single-minded he might have been right. He defended himself by the reflection that in France, and perhaps

[1] *Cobden to Mr. Van der Maeren*, Oct. 5, 1856.

1845. Æt. 41.

we are not very different in England, it is necessary that a doctrine should be personified in an individual. A great movement, he said, must be summed up in a proper name. Without the imposing figure of O'Connell the agitation in Ireland would have passed without notice in the French journals. "The human mind," he wrote to Cobden, "has need of flags, banners, incarnations, proper names; and this is more true in France than anywhere else. Who knows that your career may not excite the emulation of some man of genius in this country?"[1]

Bastiat was always conscious of the difference between Cobden's gifts and his own, and nobody knew better than himself how much more fit he was for a life of speculation than for the career of an agitator. But there was no one else in France to begin the work of propagandism and the organization of opinion. Cobden told him that the movement which had been made from those below to those above in England, ought in France to proceed in the opposite course. There they would do best to begin at the top. In France in 1846 they had scarcely any railways, and they had no penny postage. They were not accustomed to subscriptions, and still less were they accustomed to great public meetings. Worse than all this, the popular interest was at that epoch turned away from the received doctrines of political economy in the direction of Communism and Fourierism. These systems spoke a language infinitely more attractive to the imagination of the common people. Bastiat, fired by Cobden's example, set bravely to work to make converts among men of mark. Besides being a serious thinker, he had the gifts, always so valuable in France, of irony, of apt and humorous illustration, of pungent dialectic.

[1] Dec. 1845, *Œuv.* i. 117.

1845.
ÆT. 41.

The style and finish of the *Economic Sophisms*, in which he refuted the fallacies of Monopoly, are even declared to be worthy of the author of the *Provincial Letters*. But the movement did not prosper. At Bordeaux, indeed, where the producers of wine were eager for fresh markets, a Free Trade association was formed, and it throve. Elsewhere the cause made little way. Political differences ran so high as to prevent hearty co-operation on a purely economical platform. The newspapers were written by lads of twenty, with the ignorance and the recklessness proper to their age. They were conducted by men who were in close connexion with the politicians, so that everything in their hands became a question between Ministry and Opposition. Worst of all they were venal. Prejudice, error, and calumny were paid for by the line. One was sold to the Russians, another to Protection, this to the university, that to the bank. "Our agitation," Bastiat wrote to Cobden, "agitates very little. We still need a man of action. When will he arise? I cannot tell. I ought to be that man; I am urged to the part by the unanimous confidence of my colleagues, but I cannot. The character is not there, and all the advice in the world cannot make an oak out of a reed."[1] We know not what encouragement Cobden gave to his friend, for by an evil chance his letters to Bastiat were all destroyed. Their correspondence was tolerably constant, and if Bastiat was indebted to Cobden for the energy of his views on Free Trade, Cobden may well have had his own views strengthened and diversified by Bastiat's keen and active logic. Bastiat always said that he valued the spirit of free exchange more than free exchange itself, and Cobden

[1] *Bastiat to Cobden*, March 20 and April 20, 1847, *Œuv.* i. 156-9.

had already been approaching this doctrine before Bastiat became his friend.

The League was now in the seventh year of its labours. In 1839 their subscriptions had only reached what afterwards seemed the modest amount of £5000. The following year they rose to nearly £8000. In 1843 the Council asked for £50,000 and got it. In 1844 they asked for twice as much, and by the end of the year between £80,000 and £90,000 had been paid in. They were now spending £1000 a week. In spite of the activity which was involved in these profuse supplies, the outlook of the cause was, perhaps, never less hopeful or encouraging. The terrible depression which had at first given so poignant an impulse to the agitation had vanished. Peel's great manipulation of the tariff had done something to bring about a revival of trade. Much more had been done by two magnificent harvests. Wheat which had been up at sixty-seven shillings when Cobden came into Parliament, and then at sixty-one shillings in 1843, was now down at forty-five. Trade and commerce were thriving. The revenue was flourishing. Pauperism had declined. The winter had lasted for five months and had been very rigorous, yet even the agricultural labourers had suffered less distress than in the winters before. This happy state of things was in fact a demonstration of the truth of what Cobden and his friends were struggling to impress upon the country, namely that a moderate price of food was a condition of good wages and brisk trade.[1] The plain inference

[1] At a meeting held in Oldham, a workman got up in the body of the hall. He had been thinking, he said, on the subject of the Corn Laws for twenty years; as there was no possibility that he should ever see Sir Robert Peel, as he never came down into that

1845.

ÆT. 41.

from what had been going on for two years before men's eyes, was that every impediment in the way of abundant food was an impediment in the way both of the comfort of the population and the prosperity of national industry. What good harvests had done for two years, repeal of the Corn Law would help to do in perpetuity. "The present state of our finances and manufactures," said Cobden, at the beginning of 1845, "is an illustration of the truth of the Free Trade doctrines." Yet oddly enough, the very circumstances which showed that the Leaguers were right, made people for the moment less in earnest for the success of their programme. So long as times were good, the Ministers were safe and the League was powerless. Meetings were still thronged, and a great bazaar was opened at Covent Garden in the spring, which was a nine-days' wonder. This notwithstanding, there was a certain pause out of doors in the actuality of the struggle.

The change did not escape the acute observation

neighbourhood, and as he, the speaker, could not bear the expense of a journey to London, he begged Mr. Cobden to convey to the Prime Minister the following train of thought:—"When provisions are high, the people have so much to pay for them that they have little or nothing left to buy clothes with; and when they have little to buy clothes with, few clothes are sold; and when there are few clothes sold, there are too many to sell; and when there are too many to sell they are very cheap; and when they are very cheap, there cannot be much paid for making them; and consequently the manufacturing working man's wages are reduced, the mills are shut up, business is ruined, and general distress is spread through the country. But when as now the working man has the said 25s. [the fall in the price of wheat] left in his pocket, he buys more clothing with it, ay, and other articles of comfort too, and that increases the demand for them, and the greater the demand, you know, makes them rise in price, and the rising in price enables the working man to get higher wages and the master better profits. This, therefore, is the way I prove that high provisions make lower wages, and cheap provisions make higher wages."—Quoted in Cobden's *Speeches*, i. 251.

of the League. They at once altered their tactics. The previous year had been devoted to agitation in the country. They now came round to the opinion that Parliament, after all, was the best place in which to agitate. "You speak with a loud voice," said Cobden, "when you are talking on the floor of the House; and if you have anything to say that hits hard, it is a very long whip and reaches all over the kingdom." It was in Parliament that they were best able to conduct an assault on the Monopolist citadel from a new side. They had tried in their short campaign to show the farmers themselves that Protection was no better for them than for other people. They now made a vigorous effort to bring the same thing home to the farmers' friends in Parliament. "It gives me increased hopes," Cobden wrote to his friend, George Combe, "to hear that you, who are a calm observer, think that we are making such rapid progress in our agitation. We who are in the whirl of it, can hardly form an opinion whether we are advancing or only revolving. But I think there are symptoms that the enemy is preparing for a retreat. The squires in the House are evidently without confidence in themselves, while the farmers are losing all faith in their old protectors, and Peel is doing his best to shake the confidence of both landlords and tenants in any Minister. Good will come out of this. People will be thrown back upon their own resources of judgment. In fact, the public will be taught to think for themselves. With respect to Mr. W., he and I are very friendly; I have had nothing but civility, and indeed kindness, at his hands ever since I came into the House. He is a man of very great kindliness of nature, full of *bonhomie* in fact. If he has a fault, it is in being too placable, possessing too much love of approbation, which makes him rather fond of praising people, especially his opponents. He is, however, upon the whole, a fine-hearted man."[1]

In the midst of the general prosperity, there was one great interest which did not thrive: this was the interest of the tenant-farmer. Deputations waited upon the Prime Minister to tell him that the farmers in Norfolk were paying rent out of capital; that half the small farmers in Devonshire were insolvent, and the others were rapidly sinking to the same condition; that the agriculturists of the whole of the south of England, from the Trent to the Land's End, were in a state of embarrassment and distress.[2] There was scarcely a week in which these topics did not find their way into the Parliamentary debates. Cobden brought forward a motion for a Select Committee to inquire into the causes of the alleged agricultural distress. A few nights afterwards one of the country gentlemen in the House moved a resolution for affording relief to the landed interests in the application of surplus revenue. Then came a proposal from a League member for a Committee to find out what was really the nature and amount of the peculiar burdens of which the landed interest had to complain. Mr. Bright moved for a Committee on the Game Laws. Mr. Villiers pressed his regular annual motion for total and immediate repeal. Lord John Russell introduced a string of nine resolutions, dealing with the Corn Laws, the law of parochial settlement, national education, and systematic colonisation, all with a view to the permanent improvement of the condition of the working class, and especially of the labourers in husbandry.

"Bright did his work admirably," says Cobden,

[1] *To George Combe*, London, Feb. 23, 1845.

[2] Cobden's *Speeches*, i. 261.

"and won golden opinions from all men. His speech took the squires quite aback. At the morning meeting of the county members at Peel's, to decide upon the course to be taken, the Prime Minister advised his pack not to be drawn into any discussion by the violent speech of the member for Durham, but to allow the Committee to be granted *sub silentio*! This affair will do us good in a variety of ways. It has put Bright in a right position—shown that he has power, and it will draw the sympathy of the farmers to the League. The latter conviction seemed to weigh heavily upon the spirits of the squires. They seemed to feel that we had put them in a false position towards their tenants, and the blockheads could not conceal their spite towards the League. I pleaded guilty for the League to all they charged us with on this score."[1]

The result of these incessant challenges to the landlords and to the Ministers was a thorough sifting of the arguments, and the establishment of a perfectly clear and intelligible position. No Committee was granted, except Mr. Bright's, but discussion brought out the main facts as clearly as any Committee could have done. It became stamped on men's minds, that while abundant food stimulated manufactures and promoted the comfort of the whole body of workmen and labourers, legislative protection was not saving, and could not save, the farmers. The contention, again, that the landlords were subjected to special burdens, and were therefore entitled to special exemptions, had completely broken down. The whole process went on under the closely attentive eyes of the Prime Minister. The year before, said Cobden, he had not penetrated the quality of his Protectionist friends. This year they set up for

[1] *To Mr. George Wilson*, London, Feb. 28, 1845.

themselves; they found out their weakness, and, what is more, they let Sir Robert find it out also.[1]

Cobden himself helped to the result by one of the most important speeches that he ever made. "We are certainly," he wrote to his wife, "taking more prominent ground this session than ever, and the tone of the farmers' friends is very subdued indeed. They never open their mouths if they can help it, and then they speak in a very humble strain. I am quite in a fidget about my speech on Thursday. You will think it very strange in an old hack demagogue like me, if I confess that I am as nervous as a maid the day before her wedding. The reason is, I suppose, that I know a good deal is expected from me, and I am afraid I shall disappoint others as well as myself. I have sent for Mr. Lattimore, who came up and spent an evening with me, on purpose to give me a lesson about the farmers' view of the question."[2]

"I was terribly out of sorts with the task," he said, after it was all over, "and when I got up to speak, I was all in a maze." In fact, an intimate friend who had stood on many a platform with him, found him in the lobby, pale, nervous, and confident that he should break down in the middle of his speech. "No, you will not," said his friend; "your nervousness convinces me that you will make a better speech than you ever made before in your life." And that is what actually happened. In sending his wife a copy of the *Times* containing a report of his speech, Cobden wrote to her that everybody in the House on both sides spoke highly of it, and declared it to be his best. "But I don't think," he adds, "that it

[1] *Speeches*, i. 290.

[2] *To Mrs. Cobden*, March 11, 1845.

was as good as it ought to have been."[1] The Prime Minister had followed every sentence with earnest attention; his face grew more and more solemn as the argument proceeded. At length he crumpled up the notes which he had been taking, and was heard by an onlooker, who was close by, to say to Mr. Sidney Herbert, who sat next him on the bench, "*You* must answer this, for *I* cannot." And in fact, Mr. Sidney Herbert did make the answer, while Peel listened in silence.[2]

This speech should be read in connexion with the companion speech made the year before, and already referred to (pp. 315-316). Much of Cobden's speaking, and especially at this time, though never deficient in point and matter, was loose in its form and slipshod in arrangement. That it should be so, was unavoidable under the circumstances in which his addresses were made. These two speeches, on the contrary, show him at his best. They are models of the way in which a great case should be presented to the House of Commons, as well as admirable examples of effective selection, luminous arrangement, and honest cogency of reasoning in intricate and difficult matter. Besides all this, they show how completely Cobden had worked out the whole con-

[1] *To Mrs. Cobden*, March 14, 1845.

[2] In the course of his speech Mr. Sidney Herbert said that it was very distasteful to him, as a member of the agricultural body, to be always coming to Parliament "whining for protection." The expression was unlucky, and gave Mr. Disraeli the hint for one of his most pungent sallies. The agriculturists, he said, referring to Peel's inconsistencies, must not contrast too nicely the hours of courtship with the moments of possession. "There was little said now about the gentlemen of England; when the beloved object has ceased to charm, it is vain to appeal to the feelings. Instead of listening to their complaints, he sends down his valet, a well-behaved person, to make it known that we are to have no 'whining' here. Such is the fate of the great agricultural interest; that beauty which everybody wooed, and one deluded."

ception of economic policy and the whole scheme of statesmanship, of which the repeal of the Corn Law was only a detail and a condition precedent. Many of the subscribers to the League were no doubt only thinking that Free Trade would bring them new armies of good customers. The Whigs, on the other hand, while sincerely concerned for the social state of the realm, picked up the notion of Free Trade vaguely, along with education and colonization, as one remedy among others. Cobden alone seemed to discern what Free Trade meant, how it was being forced upon us by increase of population and other causes, and how many changes it would bring with it in the whole social structure. It was this commanding grasp of the entire policy of his subject, which gradually gave Cobden such a hold over the receptive intelligence of Sir Robert Peel that at last it amounted to a fascination that was irresistible.

Why are the farmers distressed? Cobden asked. Why are English farmers less successful than English manufacturers? Because they are working their trade with insufficient capital. Throughout England, south of the Trènt and including Wales, the farmers' capital is not more than five pounds an acre, whereas for carrying on the business successfully it ought to be twice as much. How is it that in a country overflowing with capital, where every other pursuit is abounding with money, when money is going to France for railways and to Pennsylvania for bonds, when it is connecting the Atlantic with the Pacific by canals, and diving to the bottom of the Mexican mines for investments, it yet finds no employment in the most attractive of all spots, the soil of this country itself? The answer is plain. There is no security of tenure such as will warrant men of capital in investing their money in the soil. But what is the connexion between this insecurity of tenure and agricultural protection? The reply is that the Protectionist landowners are in a vicious circle. They think the Corn Laws are a great mine of wealth; they want voters to retain them, and therefore they will have dependent tenants on whom they may count at the elections. If they insist on having dependent tenants they will not get men of spirit and of capital. The policy reacts upon them. If they have not men of skill and capital they cannot have full provision and employment for the labourer. And then comes round the vicious close of the circle, pauperism, poor-rates, county-rates, and all the other "special burdens" of the landed interest—special burdens of their own express creation.[1] Their fundamental error lay in thinking that rents could only be kept up by Protection. Even if this had been true, Protection had become impossible, from the pressure of population. But it was not true.

To the farmers Cobden had never given a probable reduction of rents as one of the reasons for repealing the Corn Law. He told them something still more important. "Though I have not promised reduction of rent," he said, "I have, however, always maintained that with Free Trade in corn, and with moderate prices, if the present rents are to be maintained, it must be by means of a different system of managing property from that which you now pursue. You must have men of capital on your land; you must let your land on mercantile principles; you must not be afraid of an independent and energetic man who will vote as he pleases; you must give up inordinate game-preserving."[2]

This was the skeleton of Cobden's argument, and

[1] *Speeches*, i. 264-5.
[2] *Ibid.* i. 402-3, March 8, 1849.

each member of it was clothed with exactly the amount of graphic illustrations from sound authorities that was calculated to bring the case effectively home. The representatives of the farmers were surprised to be told of many things, which they immediately wondered that they had not thought of before. The farmers of Kent, Suffolk, and Surrey enjoyed a protection in their hops, but they had in return to pay for the protection on other articles which they did not produce. Those of Chester, Gloucester, and Wilts had an interest in protecting cheese, but they were heavily taxed for the oats and beans which they wanted for their beasts. The farmers in the Lothians had the benefit of a restrictive duty on wheat, but this was a trifle compared with the disadvantage of having to pay duty on linseed cake and other items of provender for cattle. Everybody, in short, was taxed for the benefit of everybody else. If the farmer derived so little good from Protection, the labourer derived still less. Members were startled to be told that more goods had been exported to Brazil in a year than had been consumed in the same time by the whole agricultural peasantry and their families in England; that no labourer in England spent more than thirty shillings a year in manufactures, if the article of shoes were excepted; that the same class did not pay fifteen shillings a head per annum to the revenue, and that the whole of their contributions to the revenue did not amount to three-quarters of a million a year. This, said Cobden triumphantly, is the pass to which thirty years of Protection have brought the agricultural interest. "There never was a more monstrous delusion than to suppose that that which goes to increase the trade of the country, and to extend its manufactures and commerce; that which increases

1845. — Æt. 41.

our population, enlarges the number of your customers, and diminishes your burdens by multiplying the shoulders that are to bear them, and giving them increased strength to bear them, can possibly tend to lessen the value of land."[1]

Mr. Disraeli once said that Free Trade was not a principle, it was an expedient. In Cobden's hands just the reverse is true: Free Trade is not an expedient; it is a principle, a doctrine, and a system. He is often charged with arguing his case too exclusively on the immediate exigencies of the situation. It was hardly possible for him to do otherwise. Neither the House of Commons nor the multitude at Covent Garden would have listened with patience to a lecture on international exchanges. But whenever he had a chance, Cobden took care to rest his argument on the importance of a free circulation in the currents of exchange. In his speech of the previous year, he had blamed Sir Robert Peel for promising cheap prices as the result of his tariff. The price of commodities, said Cobden, may spring from two causes:—a temporary, fleeting, and retributive high price, produced by scarcity; or a permanent and natural high price, produced by prosperity. The price of wool, for example, had been highest when the importation was greatest; it sprang from the prosperity of the consumers. Peel, therefore, took the "least comprehensive and statesmanlike view of his measures when he proposed to lower prices, instead of aiming to maintain them by *enlarging the circle of exchange.*" Prices would take care of themselves without detriment to the consumer, provided only

[1] *Speeches*, i. 382. Some extremely interesting supplementary criticisms on Cobden's view of the effects of Protection on agricultural interests are to be found in Mr. Fawcett's *Free Trade and Protection*, pp. 37-47.

that the stream of commodities were allowed to flow freely and without artificial interruption. (See below, vol. ii. pp. 334-335.)

This important idea was probably far beyond the reach of most of Cobden's hearers. I know there are many heads, he once said, who cannot comprehend and master a proposition in political economy, for I believe that that study is the highest exercise of the human mind, and that the exact sciences require by no means so hard an effort.[1] If, however, Cobden's economic language was a desperate jargon to the country gentlemen, it came with the power of revelation to their leader. "Sir Robert Peel," said Mr. Disraeli, in his subtle and striking portrait of his great enemy, "had a dangerous sympathy with the creations of others. He was ever on the look-out for new ideas, and when he did so he embraced them with eagerness and often with precipitancy. Although apparently wrapped up in himself and supposed to be egotistical, except in seasons of rare exaltedness, as in the year 1844-5, he was really deficient in self-confidence. There was always some person representing some theory or system exercising an influence over his mind. In his 'sallet days' it was Mr. Horner or Sir Samuel Romilly; in later and more important periods it was the Duke of Wellington, the King of the French, Mr. Jones Loyd, some others, and finally Mr. Cobden."[2]

It was in this session that Mr. Disraeli first opened his raking fire upon the Prime Minister. In 1842, as has been already seen (p. 258), he declared that Peel's policy was in exact, permanent, and perfect consistency with the principles of Free Trade

[1] *Speeches*, i. 383, Feb. 27, 1846.
[2] *Lord George Bentinck*, p. 221.

1845.

Æt. 41.

laid down by Mr. Pitt. But clouds had risen on the horizon since then. Things had happened which made the rising gladiator change his mind, not as to the national expediency of Free Trade, but as to the personal expediency of carrying his sword to the opposite camp. Sir Robert, soon after coming into power, observed to a friend that he knew too little of the young men of the party, and expressed a wish to know more. The friend invited him to dinner, and among the men of promise who were presented to their chief was Mr. Disraeli. Peel, one of the most formal and even pedantic of men, was repelled by the extravagant dress, the singular mannerism, the unbusinesslike air of the strange genius who sat at table with him. Nothing came of the interview, and the mortified aspirant had to bide his time. In 1845 Mr. Disraeli felt, as he afterwards said, that Protection was in the condition in which Protestantism had been in 1828. With a shrewder instinct than Peel, he scented the elements of a formidable and destructive mutiny. Success was not certain, but it was possible enough to be worth trying. With unparalleled daring he hastened to sound the attack. In the session of 1845 Peel seemed to be at the height of his power. Yet this was the session in which Mr. Disraeli mocked him as a fine actor of the part of the choleric gentleman; as the great parliamentary middleman, who bamboozled one party and plundered the other; as the political Petruchio, who had tamed the Liberal shrew by her own tactics; as the Tory who had found the Whigs bathing and stolen their clothes. "For my part," he said on one of these occasions, "if we are to have Free Trade, I, who honour genius, prefer that such measures should be proposed by the member for Stockport, rather than by one who by skilful parliamentary manœuvres has tampered with the generous confidence of a great people and a great party."

Yet Mr. Disraeli, whose sagacity was always of far too powerful a kind to allow him to blink facts, knew very well, as he afterwards said, that practically for the moment the Conservative Government was stronger at the end of the session of 1845 than even at the commencement of the session of 1842. "If they had forfeited the hearts of their adherents, they had not lost their votes; while both in Parliament and the country they had succeeded in appropriating a mass of loose, superficial opinion, not trammelled by party ties, and which complacently recognized in their measures the gradual and moderate fulfilment of a latitudinarian policy both in Church and State." The same keen observer goes on to remark of those with whom we are immediately concerned, that in spite of their powers of debate and their external organization, the close of the session found the members of the Manchester confederacy reduced to silence. The state of prices, of the harvests, of commerce had rendered appeals varied even by the persuasive ingenuity of Mr. Cobden a wearisome iteration.[1]

Cobden himself, however, knew exactly how things stood, and foresaw with precision how they would move. In the summer of 1845, when Parliament had found his appeal a wearisome iteration, he had before him one of those immense multitudes, such as could only be assembled, he said, in ancient Rome to witness the brutal conflicts of men, or as can now be found in Spain to witness the brutal conflicts of animals. What, he asked, if you could get into the innermost minds of the

[1] *Life of Bentinck*, p. 7.

Ministers, would you find them thinking as to the repeal of the Corn Laws? "I know it as well as though I were in their hearts. It is this: they are all afraid that this Corn Law cannot be maintained—no, not a rag of it, during a period of scarcity prices, of a famine season, such as we had in '39, '40, and '41. They know it. They are prepared when such a time comes, to abolish the Corn Laws, and they have made up their minds to it. There is no doubt in the world of it. They are going to repeal it," he went on, "as I told you—mark my words—at a season of distress. That distress may come; aye, three weeks of showery weather when the wheat is in bloom or ripening, would repeal these Corn Laws."[1] You cannot call statesmanship, he scornfully argued, a policy which leaves the industrial scheme of such a country as ours to stand or fall in such a way as this on the cast of a die. It was not long before events put Cobden startlingly in the right.

The great popular agitation of the year, as it happened, was caused by a measure which touched a very different kind of sensibility. This session Peel introduced the memorable proposal for the augmentation of the grant to the Catholic College at Maynooth. That laudable measure was a small detail in the policy of breaking up the old system of Ascendancy—a policy made necessary by the revolution of Catholic Emancipation, in which Peel had assisted in so remarkable a way. Unfortunately, Peel never saw, what clear-sighted men like Lord Clare saw at the time of the Union, that the tenure of land was the only real object of interest to the people to whom he had given political emancipation. His attitude in reference to the Encumbered Estates Act showed that he did not possess the key to the

[1] *Speeches*, i. 292, 299.

Irish question. But his views on the solution of the religious difficulty were thoroughly statesmanlike, so far as that particular difficulty went. Nothing that he ever did showed greater courage than the Maynooth grant; for though he carried his second reading by the enormous majority of 147, Mr. Gladstone was undoubtedly right when he reluctantly affirmed that the minority represented the prevailing sense of a great majority of the people of England and Scotland.[1] The principles on which Peel defended the increased grant to Maynooth, pointed very directly towards a scheme for the endowment of the Catholic clergy. It was for this reason, among others, that Lord John Russell supported the increased grant. "The arguments," he said, "which are so sound, and as I think so incontrovertible, for an endowment for the education of the Roman Catholic priesthood, would prove on another occasion equally sound and incontrovertible for an endowment to maintain that priesthood." It is doubtful whether any Liberal leader will ever again be able to take what was once so wise and just a position, but there is still room for the position which Cobden took. Mr. Bright opposed the grant altogether, on the ground that no purely ecclesiastical institution should be paid for out of the public taxes. Cobden, on the contrary, both spoke and voted for the Ministerial Bill. He was unable to find in it anything relating to the endowment of the Catholic clergy: what he

[1] Mr. Gladstone had resigned the office of President of the Board of Trade at the beginning of the session, on the rather singular ground that while he approved of the Maynooth grant and was going to support it, he had once written a book in which a different view of the proper relations between State and Church had been laid down. "As a general rule, those who have borne solemn testimony on great constitutional questions, ought not to be parties to proposing a material departure from them."

voted for was simply and purely an extended educational grant. What objection could there be to giving a good education, in any manner in which it can be most effectually given, to a body of men who are to be the instructors of many millions of people? You give large grants to elementary schools in Ireland; you vote money to the university, from which the Catholic clergy cannot benefit; but if you support instruction to Roman Catholics at all, it is wise and politic to give it to the clergy before every other order. On the merits he would support the proposal, and he would do so all the more cheerfully on the ground that it was acceptable to the Irish people.[1] This is as wise as political wisdom can be, but the present state of the Irish University question looks as if Mr. Bright's view, and not Cobden's, had won the day.

The following extracts from letters to his wife will show how Cobden passed the time from day to day, during this anxious and wearisome session:—

"*London, Feb.* 11, 1845.—I met Lord Howick [the present Earl Grey] at dinner, as was told you by Miss Bright. He did not convert me to Whiggery, nor did he make any attempt upon my virtue. He is in very good temper with the League, and quite disposed to help us, and to throw the fixed duty overboard. Bright made a very powerful but rasping speech the other night. The milk-and-water people will find fault with him, but he is a noble fellow, and ought to be backed up by every genuine Free Trader."

"*April* 11.—We are all being plagued to death

[1] April 18. In twenty-five years Cobden and Mr. Bright only went twice into different lobbies. This was one occasion. The other concerned the expenditure at South Kensington. Cobden as a Commissioner for the Great Exhibition supported Prince Albert's policy.

with the fanatics about the Maynooth grant. The dissenters and the Church people have joined together to put the screw upon the members. However, I expect that Peel will carry his measure by a large majority."

"*April* 14.—We are still being very much persecuted by the fanatics; all the bigots in the country seem to be using the privilege of writing their remonstrances to me."

"*April* 28.—I can't fix the day, I am sorry to say, when I shall positively see you. There is a notice of motion standing by Lord John Russell upon the state of the labouring population, which I am almost compelled to take a part in. If I were to be absent, it would be construed into a slight on the Whig party. It stands for Friday, but I am not without hope that he may put it off till after the Whitsun holidays. I will learn his views to-morrow if I can."

"*June* 19.—On Wednesday I was to speak at Covent Garden, and being confined all the day in the Committee-room, and having to prepare my speech after four o'clock, I knew I should be excused writing. I find it very difficult to get up my spirits to appear before a large audience like that at Covent Garden. Indeed I feel myself to be only acting a part, in appearing to speak with energy, hope, and confidence. I can't go through another period such as the present session, to be harassed and annoyed as I have been in every possible way; it would kill me. I have not the least idea when I shall be released from my attendance at the Committee. To-day we have been bored with a three hours' speech from a counsel, who would have nothing else to do if he released us from our confinement. I expect we shall have another week of it at least."

1845.
Æt. 41.

"*June* 20.—Now I will give you a specimen of my day's work. Our Committee meets at twelve and sits till four. Then the House commences, and lasts on an average till twelve. Twice last week I sat till two o'clock in the House, having been under the roof for fourteen hours. Next morning I can't be down till nine o'clock, and scarcely have I got breakfast, and glanced at the Votes and Proceedings for the day, when I must start again for the House. You will, I think, excuse me after this, if I am not a very good correspondent."

"*June* 24.—There never was such a case of petty persecution as I am enduring in this Railway Committee! We have been now nearly five weeks sitting, hearing witnesses, and listening to the tedious harangues of counsel about a lot of paltry lines among the little towns and villages in Norfolk and Suffolk. I thought we should have got to the end of our work in a fortnight or three weeks, but now we are threatened with another week or ten days. And the great misfortune is, that we have no power to put any restraint upon the tongues of the counsel, who are paid in proportion to the length of time they can waste. But I have made up my mind to go down to Manchester on Friday night at any rate, although I shall be obliged to come up again on Sunday night, to be here in the Committee at twelve o'clock."

"*June* 26.—The meeting at Covent Garden was as usual a bumper, but I did not think the speaking was quite up to the mark. I have had a successful motion for a Commission to inquire into the subject of the Railway gauges. I moved it again yesterday as a substantive motion, and it was agreed to by all parties. It is well to do something practical in the House occasionally, as it gives one the standing of a man of business."

Over all these busy interests hung a heavy cloud of the gloomiest thoughts. Throughout the session Cobden's mind had been harassed almost beyond endurance by a host of dark cares; and it is only by knowing what these amounted to, that we can measure the intensity of a devotion to public concerns which could sustain itself unabated under this galling pressure. The following extracts from letters to his brother will suffice to show us what was going on. At the end of the session of 1844, he had allowed a groan to escape him, extorted by the reports which his brother had sent him of the state of their business:—"I shall have a month or two for private business, and, Heaven knows, it is not before it is required. It is a dog's life I am leading, and I wish I could see my way out of the collar."[1] But in the recess of 1844, as in that of the previous year, he had been speedily dragged back from his own affairs to those of the League and the country. Throughout the spring of 1845, however, things were rapidly approaching a crisis from which there seemed to be no escape:—

"*April* 7.—I shall certainly be down a week before the Whitsuntide holidays, so as to have at least a fortnight. The fidgets have so got possession of me that I cannot master them. For the first time I feel fairly down and dead-beaten. It is of no use writing all one feels. Entreat J. S. to work down the stock of odds and ends of cloth, and keep down everything as low as possible. And remind Charles again of the critical importance of finding something for the machinery to do in the interval between the seasons. It is of no use your writing bad news to me. I can't help it while here."

"*April* 18.—I do not see any difficulty in giving

[1] *To F. W. Cobden*, Leamington, 8th August 1844.

adequate attention to the business, and still retaining, ostensibly at all events, the same public position as heretofore. But whether this can be done or not, I shall of course make everything else subservient to the one point in which honour is involved. There is no doubt that our pattern department, so far as the home trade is concerned, has been a failure this spring. This is now irremediable, and it is of no use dwelling on it. But it cannot be overlooked in any estimate of the management at the works and the warehouse, and of the cause of failure."

"*May* 26.—I am fixed in the Norfolk Committee to-day, and do not feel the least chance of being released for a week, and it may be a month; and for this there is no help, for if I were to leave for twenty-four hours, the Sergeant-at-Arms would be after me."

"*June* 6.—I am sorry to say it is impossible for me to come down even for a day. Our Committee have determined to sit on Saturdays, and the rule of the House precludes me from being absent even for an hour. God only knows when this odious Committee will come to a close. If you should wish to say anything about money-matters, write to me. If you want a little temporary assistance, pray see Mr. ——, and give him a message from me to the effect that I shall feel obliged if he will try to get a few thousand pounds in a similar manner to the former transaction.

"But when I come down after the session, we must put our business upon a different footing, so as to be able to avoid troubling anybody. I would have written to ——, but really, in my prominent position, it is a very delicate matter to write about. You had better, therefore, take an opportunity of seeing him privately, and pray beg him to treat the matter as very confidential. I have so many vigilant foes, that a whisper about my credit would be exaggerated a thousandfold."

"*June* 19.—Your letters keep me on the tenter-hooks, for I know not in what extremity you may be placed. I am in the same predicament as ever. The Committee will in all probability last a week more. To-day we have been treated to a three hours' speech by a counsel upon a mere fraction of the group. What makes it more difficult to escape is that the Committee does not give a decision on any part until we have heard the whole, and consequently nobody not acquainted with the evidence already taken could step in to fill my place. Sir Benjamin Hall, very luckily for him, was pitched from his horse on his head the second day of our meeting, and he was excused from further attendance, and as we have nobody else in his place and as four are the quorum, we can't proceed to business in the absence of one."

"*June* 24.—I will try to put off any meeting of the Committee on Saturday, so as to be able to come down on Friday night, but I shall be obliged to be in town again on Monday morning by twelve. I see no end to this tedious affair. We have an appointment for another branch to begin on Monday. The truth is, the rival schemes fight for time, in order to delay the passing of the Bills during the present session. But I will at all risks come down on Friday afternoon by the express train which will land me in Manchester at ten o'clock, and I should like to have a bed at your lodgings, and there I must see John Brooks privately on the Saturday morning. I have turned the subject over in every way, and I see no other solution of it than in absolutely withdrawing myself from public life, first having secured such a

1845.

Æt. 41.

promise of support from some of my friends as shall secure me from the effects of the shock. I have made up my mind to this, and shall not have a moment's peace of mind until I have fairly got out of my present false position. In fact, I would not go through another four months like the past for any earthly consideration whatever."

A friend of Cobden's, who was engaged in the same business, has told me how he received a message one afternoon in the winter before this, that Cobden wished to see him. He went over to the office in Mosley Street, and found him on the edge of dark sitting with his feet on the fender, looking gloomily into the languishing fire. He was evidently in great misery. Cobden had sent for him to seek his advice how to extricate himself from the difficulties in which his business had become involved. They summoned a second friend to their sombre councils. There was no doubt either of the seriousness of the position or of the causes to which it was due. His business, they told him, wanted a head. If he persisted in his present course, nothing on earth could keep him from ruin. He must retire from public life, and must retire from it without the loss of a day. Cobden struggled desperately against the sentence. The battle, he said, was so momentous, and perhaps so nearly won. One of his counsellors asked him how he could either work or rest with a black load like this upon his mind. "Oh," said Cobden, "when I am about public affairs I never think of it; it does not touch me; I am asleep the moment my head is on the pillow."

A few months later the difficulty could no longer be evaded. In September Cobden, at the cost of anguish which we may imagine, came to the terrible resolution to give up public affairs. He wrote a letter, describing his position and the resolve to which it had driven him, to the friend who had for four unresting years been his daily comrade and fellow-soldier, and whose mere presence at his side, he once said, was more to him than the active support of a hundred other men. Mr. Bright was then travelling in Scotland. The letter found him one evening at a hotel in Inverness. It was the wettest autumn in the memory of man, and the rain came over the hills in a downpour that never ceased by night or by day. It was the rain that rained away the Corn Laws. Cobden begged of Mr. Bright to burn what he had written, and the injunction was obeyed. It was a beautiful letter, Mr. Bright has said: surely we may say no less of the reply:—

"Inverness, *September 20th*, 1845.

"My dear Cobden—I received your letter of the 15th yesterday evening, on my arrival here. Its contents have made me more sad than I can express; it seems as if this untoward event contained within it an affliction personal for myself, great public loss, a heavy blow to one for whom I feel a sincere friendship, and not a little of danger to the great cause in which we have been fellow-labourers.

"I would return home without a day's delay, if I had a valid excuse for my sisters who are here with me. We have now been out nearly three weeks, and may possibly be as much longer before we reach home; our plan being pretty well chalked out beforehand, I don't see how I can greatly change it without giving a sufficient reason. But it does not appear needful that you should take any hasty step in the matter. Too much is at stake, both for you and for the public, to make any sudden decision advisable. I may therefore be home in time for us to have some conversation before anything comes before the public. Nothing of it shall pass my lips, and I would urge nothing to be done till the latest moment, in the hope that some way of escape may yet be found. I am of opinion that your retirement would be tantamount to a dissolution of the League; its mainspring would be gone. I can in no degree take your place. As a second I can fight; but there are incapacities about me, of which I am fully conscious, which prevent my being more than a second in such a work as we have laboured in. Do not think I wish to add to your trouble by writing thus; but I am most anxious that some delay should take place, and therefore I urge that which I fully believe, that the League's existence depends mostly upon you, and that if the shock cannot be avoided, it should be given only after the weightiest consideration, and in such way as to produce the least evil.

"Be assured that in all this disappointment you have my heartfelt sympathy. We have worked long and hard and cordially together; and I can say most truly that the more I have known of you, the more have I had reason to admire and esteem you, and now when a heavy cloud seems upon us, I must not wholly give up the hope that we may yet labour in the good cause until all is gained for which we have striven. You speak of the attempts which have been made to raise the passion which led to the death of Abel, and to weaken us by destroying the confidence which was needful to our successful co-operation. If such attempts have been made, they have wholly failed. To help on the cause, I am sure each of us would in any way have led or followed; we held our natural and just position, and hence our success. In myself I know nothing that at this moment would rejoice me more, except the absence of these difficulties, than that my retirement from the field could in any way maintain you in the front rank. The victory is now in reality gained, and our object will before very long be accomplished; but it is often as difficult to leave a victory as to gain it, and the sagacity of leaders cannot be dispensed with while anything remains to be done. Be assured I shall think of little else but this distressing turn of affairs till I meet you; and whilst I am sorry that such should be the position of things, I cannot but applaud the determination you show to look them full in the face, and to grapple with the difficulties whilst they are yet surmountable.

"I have written this letter under feelings to which I have not been able to give expression, but you will believe that

I am, with much sympathy and esteem,
Your sincere friend,
JOHN BRIGHT."

The writer, however, felt the bad tidings lying too heavily on him to be able to endure inaction. A day or two later Mr. Bright changed his plans and hastened southwards. Helpful projects revolved in his mind, as he watched the postboys before him pressing on through the steaming rain. When he reached Manchester, he and one or two friends procured the sum of money which sufficed to tide over the emergency. For the moment Cobden was free to return to the cause which was now on the eve of victory.

CHAPTER XV

THE AUTUMN OF 1845

1845.

Æt. 41.

The story of the autumn of 1845 has often been told, and it is not necessary that it should be told over again in any detail in these pages. It constitutes one of the most memorable episodes in the history of party. It was the turning-point in the career of one of the most remarkable of English Ministers. It marked the decisive step in the greatest of all revolutions in our commercial policy. And it remains the central incident in the public life of the statesman who is the subject of these memoirs.

In his powerful speech in 1844 Cobden had reminded the House of Commons, for men were apt to forget it, he said, that in Ireland there was a duty at that day of eighteen shillings a quarter upon the import of foreign wheat. Will it be believed in future ages, he cried, that in a country periodically on the point of actual famine—at a time when its inhabitants subsisted on the lowest food, the very roots of the earth—there was a law in existence which virtually prohibited the importation of bread?[1] The crisis had now arrived. The session was hardly at an end before disquieting rumours began to come over from Ireland. As the autumn advanced, it

[1] *Speeches*, i. 164.

became certain that the potato crop was a disastrous failure. The Prime Minister had, in his own words, devoted almost every hour of his time, after the severe labours of the session, to watching chances and reading evidence night and day, in anticipation of the heavy calamity which hung over the nation. By the middle of October the apprehension of actual scarcity had become very vivid, and he wrote to Sir James Graham that the only effectual remedy was the removal of impediments to import. On the last day of the month, the members of the Cabinet met in great haste. Three other meetings took place within the week. A marked divergence of opinion instantly became manifest. Sir Robert Peel wished to summon Parliament, and to advise the suspension for a limited period of the restrictions on importation. Lord Aberdeen, Mr. Sidney Herbert, and Sir James Graham supported this view. The other members of the Cabinet, following Lord Stanley and the Duke of Wellington, dissented. Peel did not disguise, and the dissidents were well aware, how difficult it might be to put the Corn Duties on again if they had once been taken off. It was felt on both sides that the great struggle which had been going on ever since the Whigs proposed their fixed duty, and in which Peel had shown so many ominous signs of change, was now coming to an issue. On both sides there was a natural reluctance to precipitate it. On the 6th of November Ministers separated without coming to a decision.

A skilful enemy was intently watching their proceedings from the northern metropolis. On the 22nd of November Lord John Russell launched from Edinburgh his famous letter to his constituents in the City of London. He had seen in the public prints that Ministers had met; that they had consulted together for many days; and that nothing had been done. Under these circumstances he thought that the Government were not performing their duty to their Sovereign and their country. The present state of the country could not be viewed without apprehension. Procrastination might produce a state of suffering that was frightful to contemplate, but bold precaution might avert serious evils. It was no longer worth while to contend for a fixed duty. Let them all then unite to put an end to a system which had been proved to be the blight of commerce, the bane of agriculture, the source of bitter division among classes, the cause of penury, fever, mortality, and crime among the people. If this end was to be achieved, it must be gained by the unequivocal expression of the public voice.

The Edinburgh Letter was the formal announcement that Lord John Russell had come round to Cobden's programme, the winning of Free Trade by agitation. Sir Robert Peel's conversion, as everybody knows, was very freely imputed both at the time and afterwards to interested and ambitious motives. It is hard to understand on what ground the same imputation might not have been sustained in the case of the corresponding conversion of Lord John. The obvious truth is that they were both of them too clear-sighted not to perceive that events had, at last, shown that Cobden and his friends were in the right, and that the time had come for admitting it. Lord John Russell's adhesion made the victory of the League certain. Mr. Bright happened to be on the platform at a railway station in Yorkshire, as Lord John Russell passed through on his way from the north to Osborne. He stepped into the carriage for a few moments. "Your letter," said Mr. Bright, "has now made the total and immediate repeal of the Corn Law inevitable; nothing can save it." The letter had in fact done no less than this.

Immediately on its publication Sir Robert Peel summoned his Cabinet. His view had been that Parliament ought to be called together, on the assumption that the measure of relief which he was prepared to introduce would virtually compel a reconsideration of the whole question of Protection. After the Edinburgh Letter he considered that this step would appear to be a servile acquiescence in the views of the leader of the Opposition. Still he was prepared to stand to his post, and to run the risk of this reproach, provided that his colleagues were unanimous. They were not so. Lord Stanley was intractable, and others in the Government were nearly as hostile. Thinking, therefore, that he should fail in the attempt to settle the question, and that after vehement contests and the new combinations that would be formed, probably worse terms would be made than if some one else were to undertake the settlement of the question, the Minister felt it his duty to resign. That event took place on the 5th of December. For a fortnight the country remained without a responsible Administration.

The share of the League in this startling catastrophe did not escape Cobden's eye. The prospect of famine in Ireland had no sooner become definite, than the League at once prepared for action. Before the end of October, and before the first of the Cabinet Councils, they held a great meeting of many thousands of persons at Manchester, and announced a series of meetings in the other great towns of the kingdom. The Ministers were quite aware what this meant, and that they could not face it. Sir James Graham warned Peel that the Anti-Corn-Law ferment was about to commence. It would, he said, be the most formidable movement in modern times. There was a pause for a few days during the deliberations of the Government, because everybody expected that each successive mail would carry to him the welcome decision of the Cabinet that the ports had been already opened. And why were they not opened? asked Cobden. Because the League was known to be strong enough to prevent them from being shut again. If there had been no Anti-Corn-Law League in the middle of November, the ports would have been opened a month ago. It was because they knew well in the Cabinet, and because the landlords knew well, that the question of total and immediate repeal of the Corn Law was at stake, that they were ready to risk, like desperate gamblers, all that might befall during the next six months, rather than part with that law.[1] When the Cabinets came to an end without any action being taken, then genuine alarm spread through the country, and the storm of agitation began in good earnest. People knew pretty well where the difficulty lay. They were told that it was the Duke of Wellington and Lord Stanley who had decided that the people of England and Ireland should not be allowed to feed themselves. Cobden went to a great gathering at Birmingham (November 13th). If I mistake not, he said, you have tried the metal of the noble warrior before in Birmingham. The Duke is a man whom all like to honour for his high courage, his firmness of resolve, his indomitable perseverance. "But let me remind him," cried Cobden, amid a storm of strenuous and persistent approval, "that notwithstanding all his victories in the field, he never yet entered into a contest with Englishmen in which he was not beaten." Even the

[1] *Speeches*, i. 328, Nov. 13, 1845.

Edinburgh Letter, in spite of Cobden's trust in the high integrity of the writer, did not disarm his vigilance. The letter had transformed Lord John "from the most obscure into the most popular and prominent man of the day." But the Whig party was nothing without the Free Traders. The Tory party was broken to atoms by the rupture among their leaders. The League alone stood erect and aloft amid the ruins of the factions.[1]

The activity of the League was incessant. Now that their question had become practically urgent, and an occasion for the fall of ministries and the strife of parties, public interest in their proceedings acquired a new keenness. "I had reckoned upon getting home on Saturday," Cobden writes to his wife from Stroud (Dec. 4), "but Lord Ducie has put the screw upon us. We have no alternative but to sleep at his house on Saturday night, in order to attend a meeting in the afternoon at his neighbouring town of Wooton-under-Edge. We could not resist his appeal. This throws me out in my plans, and I shall not see you till Wednesday. We shall go up to London on Sunday afternoon to sleep there, and meet Villiers and others for a talk, and on Monday we shall go to Notts, next day to Derby, and on Wednesday home. The *Times* newspaper of to-day, which has just come to hand here, reports that the Government has determined to call Parliament together the first week in January, and propose total repeal![2] If this be true, the day of my

[1] *Speeches*, i. 349, Dec. 17.

[2] The publication of the Cabinet secret made a wonderful stir at the time. The *Standard* and the *Herald* denounced it as an atrocious fabrication. But the *Times* stuck to its text, and laughed at the two "melancholy prints" who had been "hobbling about the Corn Laws to the very last," unconscious that the repeal of the Corn Laws was "a thing for statesmen to do, not for old women to maunder about."

emancipation is nearer than I expected. But we must be on our guard, and not expect too much from the Government. They will attempt to cheat us yet. Our meetings are everywhere gloriously attended. There is a perfect unanimity among all classes; not a syllable about Chartism or any other *ism*, and not a word of dissent. Bright and I are almost off our legs, five days this week in crowded meetings."

"*Bristol*, *Dec.* 5, 1845.—I slept last night at James Rhoades's, and had many kind inquiries and invitations. We had a very delightful meeting at Bath in a splendid Town Hall, the Mayor in the chair. We are having meetings every night, and I see no other prospect now but to run the gauntlet every night till the meeting of Parliament. But I hope we are getting to the death-struggle. Have you seen *Punch* with me on horseback and Lord John offering to hold the horse, and also as the shadow when Peel is opening the gate of monopoly."

"*London*, *Dec.* 15, 1845.—We have had a good meeting in the City to-day. The knowing people say that they have never seen so large and unanimous a gathering. There is no doubt that the City will return *four* Free Traders at the next election. By the way I don't hear anything decided about the decision of the Government question. People begin to doubt whether Lord John will form an Administration after all. Some knowing folks say Peel will be sent for again."

"*London*, *Dec.* 13. (*To George Combe.*)—Politics are like a magic-lantern just now, every day brings some new and unlooked-for change. What a righteous retribution has fallen upon the late Ministry! The men who passed the present Corn Law in the face of starving millions in the spring of

1842 have been driven from power and place by their own sliding scale! May their successors profit by the example! There is still a great struggle before us, but we will beat the unrighteous few who wish to profit by the sufferings of the many."

Two days after Cobden had been talking to the people of Birmingham in a triumphant strain about the League standing erect amid the ruins of the factions, he had an opportunity of measuring the estimate in which he was held by one at least of the factions. Sir Robert Peel resigned on the 5th of December. The Queen sent for Lord John Russell, and commissioned him to form an Administration. Lord John wrote two letters to Cobden on the same day. In the first, he gave the leader of the body which had shaken down a great Ministry and compelled an important revolution in policy, a provisional invitation to take one of the humblest posts in the ministerial hierarchy:—

"CHESHAM PLACE, *Dec.* 19, 1845.

"DEAR SIR—I do not expect that I shall be able to form an Administration. If I should, however, on this occasion or a future one, I shall ask you to assist me by accepting the office of Vice-President of the Board of Trade, Lord Clarendon being the President, and the Vice-President having to represent the department in the House of Commons.

I remain, yours faithfully,

J. RUSSELL."

The reader will smile at this proposal, when he thinks of the composition of Liberal Governments since the death of Lord Palmerston. The difference between then and now marks the decay of Whig predominance within the five-and-thirty years that

1845. — ÆT. 41.

have intervened. Cobden's reply to the unflattering offer might have been foreseen. There is little doubt that it would have been the same, even if the offer had been of a more serious kind.

"MANCHESTER, *Dec.* 20, 1845.

"DEAR LORD JOHN—I feel greatly honoured by the offer of the office of Vice-President of the Board of Trade, in the event of your being able to form an Administration. In preferring to remain at my post as the out-of-doors advocate of Free Trade, I am acting from the conviction that I can render you more efficient assistance in carrying out our principle by retaining my present position, than by entering your Government in an official capacity. Again assuring you how highly I esteem this expression of your confidence,

I remain, dear Lord John,
Most faithfully yours,
RICHARD COBDEN."

This reply crossed the second note which Lord John Russell had written to him on the previous day:—

"*Dec.* 19, 1845.

"DEAR SIR—In consequence of what I wrote this morning, I now write to inform you that I have not been able to form a Ministry.

"All those who were to be my colleagues had agreed to the total repeal of the Corn Laws. Other differences on another subject have caused our failure.

I remain, yours faithfully,
J. RUSSELL."

1845.

ÆT. 41.

The differences which were the cause of failure were with Lord Grey.[1] He objected to Lord Palmerston as Foreign Secretary. The intrigue, says one who was very competent to judge such matters, was neither contrived with dexterity nor conducted with temper, but it extricated the Whig leader from an embarrassing position.[2] Lord John Russell's plea was not only that in face of the risks to be encountered unity was indispensable, but that as Lord Grey was among the first of his party who declared for complete Free Trade in corn, it would be unjustifiable to attempt to carry it without him. Viewed from this distance of time, and in the light of the present decline of the Whig caste, the plea, it must be confessed, is one of singular tenuity. No one doubts the sincerity either of Lord John's attempt to form a Government, or of his honest acquiescence in its failure. It was obviously much easier for Sir Robert Peel to settle the Corn question, because he would have the votes of the Whigs and the Free Traders, as well as that of a large body, if not the majority, of his usual supporters. It was not certain that Lord John could have settled it, for the simple reason that many of the Conservatives, especially in the House of Lords, would have declined to follow him in a policy which they hardly persuaded themselves to accept from Wellington and Peel.

On the failure of his rival, Sir Robert Peel went to Windsor, withdrew his resignation, and returned to London, having already resumed the functions of

[1] The Lord Howick of the previous chapter. He had become a peer on the death of his father in July 1845. The seat which he then vacated at Sunderland was won by Mr. Hudson, the Railway King, against Colonel Perronet Thompson. Cobden spoke with sufficient pungency of the victorious candidate soon afterwards. See *Speeches*, i. 312-3.

[2] Mr. Disraeli's *Lord George Bentinck*, p. 23.

the First Minister of the Crown. He hoped by speaking to his colleagues from the point of a definitely accepted position, to secure the support of those who had dissented from him at the beginning of the month. One at least of the survivors, who was in a position to know Peel's mind at this moment, holds it for certain that the Minister returned to town in the afternoon of the 20th, in full confidence that he would carry his party with him in the tremendous step which he had resolved to take. Lord Stanley withdrew at once,[1] but Peel persisted in thinking that the schism would end there. It was not many weeks before he found out his mistake. Thirty years after these events, when Peel's bitterest assailant had by a singular destiny raised himself to the height of power from which Peel was now looking down upon him, he made an interesting remark on a criticism that had been published upon his career. "The writer," said Lord Beaconsfield, "fails to do justice to a striking distinction in my political history. The Duke of Wellington in passing Catholic Emancipation, and Sir Robert Peel in repealing the Corn Laws, conceded necessary measures of progress, but *they broke up the party*. I passed Household Suffrage, but I kept the party together and brought it into power." It has often been contended by contemporaries with good information as to the state of things, that Peel would have been as successful as Mr. Disraeli after-

[1] Lord Stanley's place at the Colonial Office was taken by Mr. Gladstone, who had left the Ministry under circumstances already described (p. 351). He had no seat in Parliament during the important session of 1846, having resigned Newark, for which he had been returned by the Duke of Newcastle. The Duke was one of the stoutest opponents of Free Trade, successfully using all his influence to secure the defeat in North Notts of his own son, whom Peel now promoted to the office of Irish Secretary and a seat in the Cabinet.

wards was, in getting his party through an awkward gap, if he had only consented to call them together and had candidly laid before them the political considerations on which his new policy was founded. Those who hold this opinion are possibly right. It is, however, easy to perceive that Peel's situation was distinguished by two fatal peculiarities. One was that he had gone through the same process before: he had already done by Protestantism as he was now doing by Protection; he had suddenly carried out a policy of which he had been the declared and conspicuous opponent. It was the champion of Protestantism and the Church, who had repealed the Test and Corporation Acts, who had carried Catholic Emancipation, who had increased the Maynooth Grant, and who was believed to be meditating the endowment of the Irish priests. Feats of this kind do not bear repetition. In the second place, it was comparatively easy to persuade the Conservatives to assent to a lower franchise, because few of them in their hearts believed that any manipulation of the suffrage would take away from them anything which they really valued. Very many of them, on the other hand, did believe firmly that the repeal of the Corn Laws would take away from them their rents, which they valued extremely. Political plausibilities will reconcile men to everything, save the deprivation of their property. It seems doubtful then whether Sir Robert Peel could under any circumstances have prevailed upon his party to follow him. It is not to their dishonour that it should have been so. The Minister was honestly convinced, but the party was not. Even Cobden, when looking at the battle from a distance, thought that it would be wrong "that the House which was elected to maintain Protection should

1845.
Æt. 41.

abandon its pledges and do the very reverse." Long afterwards, when Peel's *Memoirs* were given to the world, Cobden still held that there would be "much that is difficult to reconcile in his conduct in this question, after everything is said and confessed that he can urge in his defence."[1] The simplest explanation is the true one. It is a mistake to assume that because Peel was a great parliamentary commander, he had been mastered by the parliamentary vice of measuring national welfare by the conveniences of his party or the maintenance of a majority in a division. A colleague of Sir Robert Peel in this Administration, who has had unrivalled opportunities of seeing great public personages, speaks of him as the most "laboriously conscientious" man that he has ever known.[2] It was his conscience that had become involved in the change of commercial policy. He could, as he believed, and as he afterwards told Cobden himself, have parried the power of the League for three or four years. But he had come to the conviction that the maintenance of restriction was both unsound and dangerous, was not only impolitic but unjust. It was impossible for him to conceal his conviction, or to act as if it did not exist. Confidence in public men, he said, is shaken when they change their opinions, but confidence ought to be much more shaken when public men have not the courage to change their course when convinced of their error. But why did he not consult political decorum by allowing Lord John Russell to carry repeal, or at least by taking the opinion of the country?[3] Because Lord John

[1] *Letter to J. Parkes*, May 26, 1856.

[2] "Allowing for differences in grasp and experience," he went on, "the Prince Consort was in this respect of the same type."

[3] Mr. Disraeli dwelt much on a certain inconsistency on this

could not have carried repeal; and Peel could neither see any advantage in indecision or irrational delay, nor could he admit the incompetency of the present Parliament to deal with that, as with every other object of public concern.[1]

"I have reason to believe," said Cobden afterwards, "that some discussions which I raised in the House with a view to proving that the agriculturists themselves were, as a whole, injured by Protection, gave him some confidence in the practicability of a change of policy." This may well have been so. The speech in which Peel announced and vindicated the new policy is little more than an echo of Cobden's parliamentary speeches of 1844 and 1845, and this accounts for the extraordinary prominence which he afterwards gave in so remarkable a manner to Cobden's share in what was done. Peel has explained the course along which his mind was travelling. His confidence in the necessity of Protection was lessened by the experiment of 1842. He felt from the first the increasing difficulty of applying to articles of food the principles which had been applied to so many other articles. Later experiments pointed in the same way. Certain important articles of agricultural produce were now admitted at low rates. Among these were oxen, sheep, cows, salted and

point. Peel always said that he felt that he was not the person who ought to propose repeal; and he repudiated as a foul calumny the assertion that he wished to interfere in the settlement of the question by Lord John Russell. But, asked Mr. Disraeli, what was it but your wish to interfere in this manner which broke up your Cabinet at the beginning of December? As Peel expressly said that it was only the refusal of his colleagues to assent to repeal which prevented him from remaining in office on the platform of the Edinburgh Letter, Mr. Disraeli's charge, so far as it goes, cannot be satisfactorily met.

[1] Tamworth Letter, 1847. For other reasons see Peel's letter to Cobden, below, p. 426.

1845.
ÆT. 41.

fresh meat. A chorus of sinister prophecy rose from the injured interests. There was even a panic. Forced sales of stock took place. It would be impossible to compete with the foreign grazier. Meat would be reduced to threepence a pound. The falsification of these prophecies, as Peel reminded his constituents after his fall, was destined to have a great effect on the course of public opinion. People began to be less apprehensive of the probable consequences of a more liberal intercourse in other articles of agricultural produce.[1]

Then he perceived an increase of consumption of articles of first necessity, much more rapid than the increase in population, and this greatly augmented the responsibility of undertaking to regulate the supply of food by legislative restraints. It greatly aggravated, moreover, the peril of these restraints in the case of any sudden check to prosperity.[2]

Besides these considerations, Peel says that his faith in restrictions on the importation of corn had been weakened by general reasoning; by many concurring proofs that the wages of labour do not vary with the price of corn; by serious doubts whether, in the present condition of the country, the present plenty were not ensured for the future in a higher degree by free intercourse in corn, than by restrictions for the purpose of protecting domestic agriculture. Clear as all this is to a generation whose vision is not obscured by the passions of contemporaries, resentment and suspicion at the time were emotions that might have been expected. It speedily became certain that they were violent enough to endanger the new policy, to wreck the party, and to overthrow for ever the great Minister who had been its chief.

[1] *Memoirs*, ii. 103.
[2] Tamworth Letter of 1847, in *Memoirs*, ii. 105.

Meanwhile the League made ready to give him effective support. Whatever may have been the case with Sir Robert Peel himself, it is certain that other people were afraid of the operations of the League. It was this confederation which kept both the Whig advocates of a fixed duty and the Protectionist advocates of the existing law in order. In the last week in the year a meeting was held at Manchester, at which it was resolved to raise the enormous sum of a quarter of a million of money for the purposes of agitation. The scene has often been described, how one man after another called out in quick succession, "A thousand pounds for me!" "A thousand pounds for us!" and so forth, until, in less than a couple of hours, sixty thousand pounds had been subscribed on the spot. There were twenty-three persons or firms who put down one thousand pounds each, and twenty-five persons half as much. Cobden, who was always received at every public gathering during this stirring crisis with an indescribable vehemence of sympathy and applause, addressed a few words to the excited and resolute men before him. "This meeting," he said, "will afford to any Administration the best possible support in carrying out its principles. If Sir Robert Peel will go on in an intelligible and straightforward course, he will see that there is strength enough in the country to support him; and I should not be speaking the sentiments of the meeting, if I did not say that if he takes the straightforward, honest course, he will have the support of the League and the country as fully and as cordially as any other Prime Minister."[1]

At this time circumstances naturally began to work a complete change in Cobden's attitude towards

[1] See Prentice's *History of the League*, ii. 415.

1845. — ÆT. 41.

Sir Robert Peel. Three weeks before, when the Minister left office, Cobden had allowed the excitement of the hour to betray him into public expressions of exultation, which were almost ferocious in their severity. Miss Martineau has explained how this fierce outburst shocked some of his friends. They appear, as has already been mentioned in another connexion (p. 223), to have used the friends' privilege of dealing very faithfully with him. Cobden had speedily become conscious of his error. One of those who remonstrated with him was his old friend, George Combe, to whom he replied as follows:—

"It was wrong to exult in Peel's fall, and yet the scene of my indiscretion was calculated to throw me off my guard, and give my feelings for a moment the mastery of my judgment. I was speaking in the face of nearly the entire adult male population of Stockport, whose terrible sufferings in 1841, when Peel took the government from the Whigs to maintain the very system which was starving them, were fresh in my memory. The news of the retirement of the Peel Ministry reached Stockport a couple of hours before the meeting took place. When it was announced, the whole audience sprang up, and gave three times three cheers. I was quite taken aback, and out came that virulent attack upon Peel, for which I have been gently rapped on the knuckles by Miss Martineau, yourself, and many other esteemed correspondents. It was an unpremeditated ebullition. Tell your good brother I will keep a more watchful guard over the old serpent that is within me for the future. You must not judge me by what I say at these tumultuous public meetings." [1]

The rest of this letter, describing his feelings

[1] *To G. Combe*, Manchester, Dec. 29, 1845. See Miss Martineau's *Autobiography*, ii. 259-62.

about public life, has been given in a preceding chapter (p. 224). In a second letter, replying we may suppose to a request of Combe's that he might be allowed to show the first to some of their common friends, Cobden referred fiercely enough, as he had previously done in public, to the extremely painful incident of 1843: it has been already described in its place.[1]

"You are at liberty to make any use you please of that letter of mine, and I really feel gratified and proud that you take so much interest in preserving for me the good opinion of those whose esteem is worth having. Now let me add, that although, as between you and myself, I am eager to avow my regret at having been betrayed into a vindictive attack upon Peel, although I admit that Christian principle was violated in that speech, and that I should have better consulted what was due to myself if I had shown greater magnanimity on the occasion, still as between any other looker-on and myself, I must say that Peel's atrocious conduct towards me ought not to be lost sight of. I do not complain of his insinuating that I wished to incite to his assassination, and hounding on his party to destroy me in the eyes of the world. His conduct might have been excused on account of his state of mind, from the recent death of Drummond, and the distress and anxiety of his wife and daughter, who, I believe, unnerved him by their alarm for his safety. But although this excused him at the instant, it did not atone for his having failed to retract or explain his foul charge subsequently, which, in fact, made and now makes it a deliberate attempt at moral assassination, which I cannot and ought not to forget, and therefore I should feel justified in repeating what I

[1] Above, chap. xii. pp. 276-81.

1846.
ÆT. 42.

said at Covent Garden, that I should forfeit my own respect and that of my friends if I ever exchanged a word with that man in private."[1]

No nature was ever less disposed for the harbouring of long resentments, and it was not many weeks from this time before a curious incident had the effect of finally effacing the last trace of enmity between these two honoured men. A vulgar attack happened to be made in the course of debate on the Chairman of the League, which drew a rebuke from a member who was himself renowned for bitterness of speech and the unbridled licence of his imputations. Mr. Disraeli defended the original assailant by appealing to the example of the Prime Minister, who had, if he did not mistake, accused a member of the League of abetting assassination. Sir Robert Peel immediately rose to explain that his intention at the time was to relieve Mr. Cobden in the most distinct manner from the imputation which by misapprehension he had put upon him. If any one present had stated to him that his reparation was not so complete, and his avowal of error not so unequivocal, as it ought to have been, he should at once have repeated it more plainly and distinctly. Cobden followed, saying that he had felt, and the country had felt, that the Minister's disavowal had not been so distinct as was to have been expected. He was glad that it had now been explicitly made, because it gave him an opportunity of expressing his own regret at the terms in which he had more than once referred to Sir Robert Peel. And so with the expression of a hope that the subject might never be revived, the incident came to an end.

[1] *To George Combe*, Manchester, Feb. 1846.

CHAPTER XVI

REPEAL OF THE CORN LAWS AND FALL OF THE GOVERNMENT

1846.

ÆT. 42.

THE public excitement and private anxieties of the year which had just come to an end had seriously shaken Cobden's health. Before Parliament opened he was laid up with a complicated affection of head, ears, and throat, the result of laborious speaking to great audiences in the open air or in vast halls. He remained liable for the rest of his life to deafness and hoarseness. All through the session of 1846 he was out of health. Fortunately, circumstances had now taken a turn which no longer demanded much more from him than silent vigilance.

A few days after the session opened, the Prime Minister announced his proposals. The repeal of the Corn Laws was to be total. But it was not to be immediate. The ports were not to be entirely open for three years. During this interval there was to be a sliding scale, with a maximum duty of ten shillings when the price of wheat should be under forty-eight shillings, and a minimum duty of four shillings when the price reached fifty-four shillings a quarter. The views of the League therefore would not be fully realized until February 1849.

The opponents of the Minister began to talk of an appeal to the country, and Cobden addressed

1846.
Æt. 42.

himself to this critical point in the one speech of any importance which he felt called upon to make through the whole of these protracted debates. He plied the Protectionists with defiant tests of the national opinion. The petitions for Repeal had ten times as many signatures as petitions for Protection. But, they cried, the most numerously signed were fictitious. Then let them try public meetings. He challenged them to hold a single public and open meeting anywhere in the land. Then for parliamentary representation. "I ought to know," he said, "as much about the state of the representation and of the registration as any man in this House. Probably no one has given so much attention to that question as I have done, and I distinctly deny that you have the slightest probability of gaining a numerical majority, if a dissolution took place to-morrow. Now I would not have said this three months ago; but your party is broken up." Four-fifths of the Conservatives from the towns in the north of England were followers of Sir Robert Peel, and not of the Protectionist Dukes. They had been for Free Trade all along, but they had confidence in the Minister, that he would do what was necessary at the proper time. But let them suppose that the Protectionists might have a numerical majority. What would be the character of the minority? It would contain the whole twenty members for the metropolis and the metropolitan county. Edinburgh and Dublin would follow London. There was not in all Great Britain a town of five-and-twenty thousand inhabitants, not even Liverpool or Bristol, which would not send members pledged to Free Trade. What would a majority of twenty or thirty men in pocket-boroughs and nomination counties do in face of such a minority as this? They would shrink aghast from the position in which they found themselves. The members who came up under such circumstances to maintain the Corn Laws from their Ripons and Stamfords, Woodstocks and Marlboroughs, would not defend their views a day after they had found out so vast a moral preponderance of public opinion as this.[1]

The characteristic of all Cobden's best speeches was a just distribution of facts as the groundwork of his reasoning, and this for its particular purpose was one of his best speeches. No attempt was made at the time, nor has been made since, to weaken his striking statement of the condition of the public mind. Even the Prime Minister was not prepared for such an overwhelming force of opinion. Towards the close of the session, when all was over, Peel met Mr. Bright in the division lobby and had some talk with him. He had no conception, he said, of the intense feeling of hatred with which the Corn Law had been regarded, more especially in Scotland.

The first reading was carried by a majority of 337 to 240. But an acute observer gave Cobden what was perhaps the superfluous warning, not to allow the victory to throw him off his guard. The difficulties were still to come, and they were very serious. In spite of the extraordinary position in which they had been left by the desertion of Peel and all the rest of their leaders in both Houses of Parliament, excepting only Lord Stanley, the Protectionists were undeniably strong. The bold and patient politician, of whom they then thought so lightly, but who was in fact the sustaining genius of their group, has described the steps by which they found new leaders and a coherent organization. Lord George Bentinck was not a great man, but then the most dexterous and far-seeing of parliamentary

[1] *Speeches*, i. No. xxi., Feb. 27, 1846.

manœuvrers had his ear and was constantly by his side. Mr. Disraeli must be said to have sinned against light. His compliments to Peel and Free Trade in 1842 prove it. Lord George Bentinck formed some views on the merits of Protection by and by, but the first impulse which moved him was resentment at betrayal. It is easy to say that the key to his action was incensed party spleen, but the emotion was not wholly discreditable. One day he walked away from the House in company with a conspicuous member of the League. With that amicable freedom of remark which parliamentary habits permit and nourish even between the stoutest adversaries, the Leaguer expressed his wonder that Lord George Bentinck should fear any evil from the removal of the duty. "Well," Lord George answered, "I keep horses in three counties, and they tell me that I shall save fifteen hundred a year by Free Trade. I don't care for that. *What I cannot bear is being sold.*" This was not the language of magnanimity or of statesmanship, but it aptly expressed the dogged anger of "the Manners, the Somersets, the Lowthers, and the Lennoxes, the Mileses and the Henleys, the Duncombes and the Liddells and the Yorkes," and all the rest of that host of men of metal and large-acred squires whom the strange rhapsodist of the band has enumerated in a list as sonorous as Homer's catalogue of the ships.[1] These honest worthies did not know much about the Circle of the Exchanges, but they believed that Free Trade would destroy rent, and that the League was bent on overthrowing the Church and the Throne; while they saw for themselves that their leader had become an apostate. But this country, as Cobden said at the time, is governed by

[1] *Lord George Bentinck*, p. 216, ch. xv.

the ignorance of the country. Their want of intelligence did not prevent them from possessing a dangerous power for the moment.

The majority on the first reading was a hollow and not an honest majority, and the Protectionists were quite aware of it. The remarkable peculiarity of the parliamentary contest was that not a hundred members of the House of Commons were in favour of total repeal, and fewer still were in favour of immediate repeal. Lord Palmerston, as Cobden wrote to a friend long after these events, showed unmistakable signs that he was not unwilling to head or join a party to keep a fixed duty, but he was too shrewd to make such an attempt when success was impossible.[1] In the Upper House it was notorious that not one Peer in ten was in his heart inclined to pass the Corn Bill. If the Lords were to be coerced into giving their assent, it was indispensable that the entire Whig party in the Commons should keep together and vote in every division. It was undoubtedly the interest of the Whigs to help Peel to get the Corn Law out of the way, and then to turn him out. But there was a natural temptation to trip him up before the time.

The curious balance of factions filled the air with the spirit of intrigue, and until the very last there was good reason to apprehend that the Peers might orce Peel to accept the compromise of a fixed duty, or else to extend the term for the expiration of the existing duty. No episode in our history shows in a more distressing light the trickery and chicane which some thinkers believe to be inseparable from parliamentary institutions. In this case, however, as in so many others, the mischief had its root not in parliamentary institutions, but in that con-

[1] *To J. Parkes*, June 10, 1857.

stitutional paradox, as perplexing in theory as it is equivocal in practice, which gives a hereditary chamber the prerogative of revising and checking the work of the representative chamber.

The session had not advanced very far, before other dangers loomed on the horizon. The Ministry was doomed in any case. Whether Peel succeeded or failed with the Corn Bill, nobody at this time thought it possible that he could carry on a Conservative Government in a new Parliament, and he could hardly become the chief of a Liberal Government. The question was whether and how he should repeal the Corn Law. Difficulties arose from a quarter where they were not expected. The misery of the winter in Ireland had produced its natural fruits in disorder and violence. The Ministry resorted for the eighteenth time since the Union to the stale device of a Coercion Bill, that stereotyped avowal—and always made, strange to say, without shame or contrition—of the secular neglect and incompetency of the English Government of Ireland. Two perilous inconveniences followed. The first was that the Irish members, led by O'Connell, persistently opposed by all the means in their power every step of this violent and shallow policy. It would have been ignoble if they had done less. But their just and laudable obstruction of the Coercion Bill interposed dangerous delays in the way of the Corn Bill. This, however, was not the only peril. The Coercion Bill laid the train for a combination which could hardly have been foreseen, but which was eventually irresistible. Cobden and his friends were hostile to the measure on the policy and the merits, nor in any case could their votes have saved the Ministry. Lord John Russell and the Whigs had no objection to a Coercion Bill, of which for that matter they have been the steadiest patrons, but they could not resist the temptation to pay off old scores when the Minister declared Coercion to be urgent, and then actually let it slumber for five months.[1] Lord George Bentinck discerned very early the elements of an invincible dilemma and a promising plot. If the Minister pushed the Coercion Bill, that would keep back the Corn Bill. If he gave the priority to the Corn Bill, this would prove that the Coercion Bill was not urgent, and therefore ought not to be supported.

Thus by an extraordinary and unparalleled state of political parties, a measure for which the country was sincerely anxious, which was confessedly required by the circumstances of the moment, and which the leader of the Opposition was as desirous of passing as the Prime Minister, seemed to be in constant risk of miscarrying at every moment, and was attended by every circumstance of embarrassment alike to supporters and opponents. The great disadvantage that Cobden saw in the critical state of the Government throughout the session, was the encouragement that it held out to the House of Lords to delay Repeal. This made his own course and that of the League all the clearer. It was their policy loudly and pointedly to denounce all compromise on the part either of the Minister or of equivocal friends. Cobden did not fear that the Whigs would take means to reject the Bill, for this reason, and perhaps

[1] We have an excellent illustration of the practice of making Ireland the shuttlecock of English parties, in the fact that the Whigs who had turned out Peel on the principle of Non-Coercion, had not been in office a month before they introduced an Irish Arms Bill. The opposition, however, was so sharp that the Bill was withdrawn in a fortnight. This Whig levity was a match for the Tory levity which had declared Coercion urgent in January, and taken no steps to secure it until June.

for no loftier one, that its rejection would afford Peel an opportunity of dissolving on the question; and a dissolution, as Cobden whether rightly or wrongly believed, would snuff the Whigs out, obliterate all old party distinctions, "and give Peel a five years' lease at the head of a mixed progressive party."[1] He was equally puzzled to understand why Peel should press the Coercion Bill forward, and why the Whigs should show such eagerness to avail themselves of Monopolist support to throw Peel out. He could only explain the second of the two perplexities, by supposing that "the Whigs are hugging the delusion that the country wants them back in office. For my part, I cannot meet with anybody whose face does not drop like the funds at the bare prospect of the change."

We shall see presently what Peel himself had to say to this idea of a mixed progressive party. Meanwhile, Cobden's dislike and distrust of the Whigs was as intense as ever, and even drew upon him remonstrances from some of his own allies. "What are the old Whig party," he asked impatiently, "going to do for us in North Notts?[2] There is a division with under 4000 voters, and a strong Liberal party. It was considered Whig until the base selfishness of the landlords of that party led them to desert their colours there and in every other county upon the bread question. My old friend, Bean, of Nottingham, reckoned the Liberal party safe upon the last register, and it is improved upon the present one. But he, honest man, has been reckoning all Whigs as Free Traders. Now, however, Peel's plunge must have brought over some of the Tories to Free Trade, and if there were any disposition on the

[1] *To Mr. Sturge*, June 10, 1846.
[2] Seat vacated by Lord Lincoln. See above, p. 372 *n*.

part of the Whig proprietors to bring in a Repealer, they could do it with the aid or neutrality of the Peelites. I look to the conduct of the Whigs in the counties as the test of their honesty on our question. Hitherto they have done nothing except to revile and oppose us. Not a county has been gained to Free Trade but by League money, and at a terrible cost of labour to the Leaguers. I invaded the West Riding, in November 1844, and held public meetings in all the great towns to rouse them to qualify 2000 votes. Lord Fitzwilliam wrote me advising me not to come, as I should do more harm than good! Had I followed his advice, Lord Morpeth might still have been rusticating at Castle Howard.[1] You will perhaps tell me, that the leaders of the Whig party can't control their old friends in the counties upon the Corn question. True. But then, what a bold farce is it now to attempt to parade the Whig party as the Free Traders *par excellence*! I will be no party to such a fraud as the attempt to build up its ruined popularity upon a question in which the Whig aristocracy and proprietors in the counties either take no interest, or, if so, only to resist it. I see no advantage but much

[1] Lord Wharncliffe, who held the office of President of the Council, died suddenly in the midst of the ministerial crisis. Mr. Stuart Wortley's consequent elevation to the peerage vacated the seat for the West Riding. "You know"—so Cobden told the story three years later—"that the West Riding of Yorkshire is considered the great index of public opinion in this country. In that great division, at present containing 37,000 voters, Lord Morpeth was defeated on the question of Free Trade, and two Protectionists were returned. I went into the West Riding with this 40s. freehold plan. I stated in every borough and district that we must have 5000 qualifications made. They were made. . . . Men qualified themselves with a view of helping the repeal of the Corn Laws, and in consequence of that movement Lord Morpeth walked over the course at the next election."—*Speeches*, ii. 494, Nov. 26, 1849.

1846.
Æt. 42.

danger to our cause from the present efforts to set up the old party distinctions, and calm reflection tells me that isolation is more and more the true policy of the League."[1] This idea held strong possession of him until the day of Peel's final defeat and resignation.

Before coming to that, it will be convenient to state very briefly the course of proceedings in Parliament. The motion was made to go into Committee on the Resolutions on the 9th February. Eighteen days later, after twelve nights of debate, and after one hundred and three speeches had been delivered, the Government were successful by a majority of ninety-seven. On March 2, the House went into Committee on the Resolutions, and Mr. Villiers's amendment that Repeal should be immediate as well as total, was lost by an immense majority, barely short of two hundred. The Corn Bill was then read a second time on March 27, by a majority of eighty-eight in a House of five hundred and sixteen; and it was finally carried in the House of Commons at four o'clock in the morning of May 16, by a majority of ninety-eight in a House of five hundred and fifty-six. The Lords made a much less effective opposition than, as is shown by Cobden's letters, was commonly expected. The second reading was carried by two hundred and eleven against one hundred and sixty-four, or a majority of forty-seven. Amendments were moved in Committee, but none of them met with success, and Lord Stanley, who led the Protectionists, declined to divide the House on the third reading. The Conservatives acted on the policy laid down by Peel himself seven years before, as one of the working principles of the great party which he had formed—"a party which, existing in the House of Commons, and deriving its strength from the popular will, should

[1] *To Mr. J. Parkes*, Feb. 16, 1846.

diminish the risk and deaden the shock of collisions between the two deliberative branches of the legislature."[1] The battle had been fought in the House of Commons, and as it had been lost there, then by Peel's salutary rule, the defeat was accepted as decisive.

This is the proper place for Cobden's own story of his interests and occupations during that agitated session. We must not forget that his private affairs had only been provisionally arranged in the previous autumn, and that they were as gloomy as his public position was triumphant. Before giving the shorter correspondence, written from day to day to his wife and his brother, it will be convenient to give three longer letters, affording a more general view of what at this time was engaging his thoughts.

March 7, 1846. (*To G. Combe.*)—"I am pretty well recovered from my local attack; a little deafness is all that remains. But the way in which I was prostrated by an insignificant cold in my head has convinced me (even if my doctor had not told it) how much my constitution has been impaired by the excitement and wear and tear of the last few years. The mainspring has been overweighted, and I must resolve upon some change to wind up the machinery, before I shall be able to enter upon any renewed labours. My medical friend boldly tells me that I ought to disappear from political life for a year or two, and seek a different kind of excitement in other scenes abroad. He talks to me of the hot baths of the Pyrenees as desirable for such cases; of a low pulse, feeble circulation, and a disordered skin, and he speaks of a winter to be passed in a southern latitude. Heaven knows what I shall do! But one thing is certain, I neither feel in health nor spirits to take that prominent place in the political world

[1] Peel's Speech at Merchant Taylors' Hall in 1839.

which the public voice seems to be ready to demand. The truth is, I have gradually and unexpectedly been forced upwards, by the accident of my position in connexion with a great principle (which would have elevated anybody else who had only tenacity of will enough to cling to it), and I feel, in the present state of my health, and from other private and domestic considerations, letting alone my mental incapacity, unable to pursue the elevated career which many partial friends and supporters would expect from me. But I am resolved to give primary consideration to my health, and to the welfare of those whom nature has given the first claim to my attentions. This, I think, no one will deny me. For I assure you that during the last five years so much have I been involved in the vortex of public agitation, that I have almost forgotten my own identity and completely lost sight of the comforts and interests of my wife and children.

"Besides, to confess the truth, I am less and less in love with what is generally called political life, and am not sure that I could play a successful part as a general politician. Party trammels, unless in favour of some well-defined and useful principle, would be irksome to me, and I should be restive and intractable to those who might expect me to run in their harness. However, all this may stand over till we have really accomplished the work which drew me into my present position. I am afraid our friends in the country are a little too confident. The Government measure is by no means safe with the Lords yet. They will mutilate or reject it if they think the country will suffer it. Bear in mind, if you please, that there are not twenty men in that assembly who in their hearts earnestly desire total repeal. Nay, I am of opinion that not one hundred men in the

Commons would be more disposed for the measure, if they could obey their own secret inclinations, without the influence of outward considerations. Amongst all the converts and conformers, I class Sir Robert Peel as one of the most sincere and earnest. I have no doubt he is acting from strong conviction. His mind has a natural leaning towards politico-economical truths. The man who could make it his hobby so early to work out the dry problem of the currency question, and arrive at such sound conclusions, could not fail to be equally able and willing to put in practice the other theories of Adam Smith. It is from this that I rely upon his not compromising our principle beyond the three years. But I must confess I have not the same confidence in Lord John and the Whigs. Not that I think the latter inferior in moral sentiment, but the *reverse*. But Lord John and his party do not understand the subject so well as Peel. The Whig leader is great upon questions of a constitutional character, and has a hereditary leaning towards a popular and liberal interpretation of the Constitution. But his mind is less adapted for the mastery of economical questions, and he attaches an inferior importance to them. Nor does he weigh the forces of public opinion so accurately as Peel. He breathes the atmosphere of a privileged clique. His sympathies are aristocratic. He is sometimes thinking of the House of Russell, whilst Peel is occupied upon Manchester. They are in a false position; Peel ought to be the leader of the middle class, and I am not sure that he is not destined to be so before the end of his career."

London, March 12. (*To Mr. T. Hunter.*)—"Many thanks for your warm-hearted letter. I have often thought of you, and our good friends, Potter and Ashworth, and of the anomalous position in which I was left when our consultations ended last autumn. Had it not been for the potato panic, which dawned upon us within a few weeks after we came to the wise decision respecting my own course of action, I should then have been bound by the necessity of circumstances to have abandoned my public career. That providential dispensation opened out a prospect of a speedy termination of our agitation which has not been disappointed. I therefore made arrangements of a temporary kind for the management of my private concerns. This, I concluded, was understood by you and my other privy councillors. But the arrangement was only provisional; and now that I trust we are really drawing towards a virtual settlement of the Corn question, my private concerns again press upon my attention. I am in a false situation, and every day increases its difficulty. My prominent position before the world leads the public to expect that I shall take a leading part in future political affairs, for which I do not feel in health or spirits to be equal, and which private considerations render altogether impossible.

"The truth is, that accident, quite as much as any merit on my own part, has forced me gradually into a notoriety for which I have not naturally much taste; but which, under all circumstances, is a source of continued mental embarrassment to me. How to escape from the dilemma has been for months the subject of cogitation with me. My own judgment leads irresistibly to one solution of the difficulty, by retiring from Parliament as soon as the Corn question is safe. I observe your allusion to a public demonstration; and the idea of a testimonial has reached me through so many channels, that it would be affectation to conceal from myself that something of the kind is in contemplation. I am not, I confess, sanguine about the success of such an effort, pecuniarily speaking, on the part of my friends. Public ebullitions of the kind never realize the expectations of their promoters, and there are reasons against such success in my own case. Out of Manchester I am regarded as a rich man, thanks to the exaggerations of the Duke of Richmond and the Protectionists.

"But, besides, there are others who have as good claims as myself upon public consideration for the labours given to the good cause. I have been often pained to see that my fame, both in England and on the Continent, has eclipsed that of my worthy fellow-labourers. But it would be an injustice which neither I nor the public voice would sanction, if I were to reap all the substantial fruits of our joint exertions, to the exclusion of others whose sacrifices and devotion have hardly been second to my own.

"As respects my own feelings on the subject of a testimonial, although I see it in a different light after the work is done to that in which I viewed it before, still, I must confess, that it is not otherwise than a distasteful theme. Were I a rich man, or even in independent circumstances, I could not endure the thoughts of it. But when I think of my age, and the wear and tear of my constitution, and reflect upon the welfare of those to whom nature has given the first, and for them, the only claims upon my consideration, I do not feel in a position to give a chivalrous refusal to any voluntary public subsidy. Like the poor apothecary, my poverty and not my will consents. Still, consulting my own feelings, I should like to be out of Parliament before any demonstration were made. I could hardly explain why I should prefer this, it is so peculiarly a matter of feeling. It is not with a view to escape from public usefulness hereafter. I am aware that success in my Free Trade labours will invest me with some moral power, which, after my health was thoroughly wound up again for a renewed effort, I should feel anxious to bring to bear upon great questions for the benefit of society. But I have a strong and instinctive feeling that an interregnum in my public life would rather increase than diminish my power of usefulness. Besides and independent of considerations of health, I am not anxious to be a party in any more political arrangements during the next year or two. Assuming even that the public placed me in a new position, free from anxieties of a private kind, still I should shrink from undertaking the office of a party politician. I do not think I should make a useful partisan, unless in the advancement of a defined and simple principle. Now the next year will witness a destruction of old, and a combination of new parties, to which I should be called upon to give support, and probably invited to take office. Official life would not suit me. My only path to public usefulness is in pursuing the same independent course as respects parties which I have hitherto followed. I am aware that others might take a different view; but still no one can be so fair a judge as myself of that which involves a knowledge of my own aptitude, springing from private tastes and feelings.

"I might add as a motive for leaving Parliament, a growing dislike for House of Commons life, and a distaste for mere party political action. But this applies to my present views only in as far as it affects my health and temporary purposes. It is a repugnance which might and ought to be overcome for the sake of usefulness; and there are enough good men in Parliament who sacrifice private convenience for public good, to compensate for the society of the herd who are brought there for inferior objects.

"I have now poured out my inward thoughts to you in unreserved confidence—thoughts which have not been committed to paper before. And I do it with the fullest satisfaction, for I know that, whilst you sympathize with my feelings, you will bring a cool judgment to my assistance. I may add that it is premature yet to consider the struggle at an end. The Lords are not yet decided what to do with the Government measure. There are rumours still of an attempt to compromise. It is reported that Lord Fitzwilliam is returning from Italy to head a fixed-duty party, and there is still a strong body in the Commons anxious for such a course. In fact there are not a hundred men in the Commons, or twenty in the Lords, who at heart are anxious for total repeal. They are coerced by the out-of-doors opinion, and nothing but the dread of the League organization enables Peel to persevere. But for our forty-shilling freehold bludgeons, the aristocracy would have resisted the Government measure almost to a man. My strongest hopes centre in Peel. I have far more confidence in him than the Whig leaders. He is acting from strong convictions. He understands politico-economical questions better than Lord John, and attaches far more importance to sound principles in practical legislation. He and Sir James Graham make no secret of their determination to stand or fall by their measure. Such being their decision, the only delay that can take place is in the event of a dissolution; and I think the Lords will shrink from such a desperate and fruitless alternative when the critical moment arrives."

1846.

Æt. 42.

April 2. (*To Mr. T. Hunter.*)—"So far as I can control my future course of action, I am prepared to do so; and the first step which duty requires, is to place myself in a private position at the earliest moment when I can make the change, without sacrificing the public interest which is to some extent involved in my person. In fact I should have long ago retired into private life, but for this consideration. It is still a little uncertain when we shall escape from the tenter-hooks of delay. Even if the Lords pass the Government measure without attempts at mutilation, of which, by the way, I am still not so sanguine as many people, then it will be two months yet before the royal hand can reach the Act for the total repeal of the Corn Law. Should the Peers attempt a compromise, I have reason to feel satisfied that the Government will be firm ; and then we may possibly have a dissolution. A sharp struggle in the country would in all probability be followed by total and immediate repeal, carried with a high hand. But, assuming the most probable event, viz. that the Lords do pass the Bill, then my mind is made up to accept the Chiltern Hundreds the day after it receives the royal assent.

"Now, my dear sir, the rest must be left to the chapter of fate, and I shall be prepared to meet it, come what may. This decision is entirely the result of my own cogitations. I have consulted nobody. If the rumour got abroad amongst my friends, I should be persecuted with advice or remonstrance, to which I should be expected to give answers involving explanations painful to me. And it is quite marvellous how apt the newspapers are to get raw material enough for an *on dit* if a man suffers his plans to go beyond his own bosom. I could, of course, make my health honestly the plea for leaving Parliament, and can show, if need be, the advice of the first medical men in London and Edinburgh to justify me in seeking at least a twelvemonth's relaxa tion from public life.

"I have thus given you an earnest of my determination to do all that I can to acquit myself of my private as well as public duties. It has always been to me a spectacle worthy of reproach to see a man sacrificing the welfare of his own domestic circle to the cravings of a morbid desire for public notoriety. And God, who knows our hearts, will free me from any such unworthy motives. I was driven along a groove by accident, too fast and too far to retreat with honour or without the risk of some loss to the country, but the happiest moment of my life will be that which releases me from the conflicting sense of rival duties, by restoring me again to private life."

A few days later he wrote to Mr. Edmund Potter:—

"Many thanks for your friendly letter. Though I appreciate your kindness even where it restrains you from writing to me, let me assure you that your handwriting always gives me pleasure. You would not doubt it, if you could have a peep at the letters which pour in upon me. I have sometimes thought of giving William Chambers a hint for an amusing paper in his journal upon the miseries of a popular man. First, half the mad people in the country who are still at large, and they are legion, address their incoherent ravings to the most notorious man of the hour. Next, the kindred tribe who think themselves poets, who are more difficult than the mad people to deal with, send their doggerel and solicit subscriptions to their volumes, with occasional requests to be allowed to dedicate them. Then there are the Jeremy Diddlers who begin their epistles with high-flown compliments upon my services to the millions, and always wind up with a request that I will bestow a trifle upon the individual who ventures to lay his distressing case before me. To add to my miseries, people have now got an idea that I am influential with the Government, and the small place-hunters are at me. Yesterday a man wrote from Yorkshire, wanting the situation of a gauger, and to-day a person in Herts requests me to procure him a place in the post-office. Then there are all the benevolent enthusiasts who have their pet reforms, who think that because a man has sacrificed himself in mind, body, and estate in attempting to do one thing, he is the very person to do all the rest. These good people dog me with their projects. Nothing in their eyes is impossible in my hands. One worthy man calls to assure me that I can reform the Church, and unite the Wesleyans with the Establishment.

"That zealous and excellent educationalist, Stone, of Glasgow, seized upon me yesterday. 'I have often thought,' said he, 'that Lord Ashley or Mr. Colquhoun was the man to carry a system of National Education through Parliament. But they have not moral courage; if you will take it in hand, in less than four years you will get a vote of twenty millions, and reconcile all the religious parties to one uniform system of religious education.' I replied that I had tried my hand on a small scale in the attempt to unite the sects in Lancashire in 1836, but that I took to the repeal of the Corn Laws as light amusement compared with the difficult task of inducing the priests of all denominations to agree to suffer the people to be educated. The next time I meet Dickens or Jerrold, I shall assuredly give them a hint for a new hero of the stage or the novel, 'The Popular Man.'

"In answer to your kind inquiries after my health, I am happy to say I am pretty free from any physical ailment. It is only in my nervous system that I am out of sorts. The last two or three months have

1846.
Æt. 42.

kept me on the rack, and worried me more than the last seven years of agitation. But if I could get out of the treadmill, and with a mind at ease take a twelvemonth's relaxation and total change of scene and climate as far off as Thebes or Persepolis, where there are no post-offices, newspapers, or politicians, I see no reason why I should not live to seventy; for I have faith in my tough and wiry body and a temperament naturally cool and controllable, excepting when my mind is harassed as it has been by circumstances connected with my private concerns, which I could not grapple with and master, solely because I was chained to another oar."

The extracts that now follow are from letters to Mrs. Cobden, except in the few cases where a footnote gives the name of some other correspondent:—

"*London, Jan.* 23.—Peel's speech last night[1] would have done capitally for Covent Garden Theatre, and Lord Francis Egerton's would have been a capital address from the chair if he had filled George Wilson's place. The Tories are in a state of frantic excitement, and the Carlton Club is all in confusion. Nobody knows his party. I have no doubt Peel will do our work thoroughly, or fall in the attempt. He will be able to carry his measure easily through the Commons, with the aid of the Opposition, but I have my suspicions that the Lords will throw it out and force a dissolution. Whatever happens, I can see a prospect of my emancipation at no distant date. I am going to-morrow to Windsor, to spend the Sunday with Mr. Grote."

"*Jan.* 26.—I spent yesterday at Grote's, about four miles from Slough, and met Senior the political economist, Parkes, and Lumley the lessee of the Italian Opera. We had a long walk of nearly twelve

[1] Announcing the necessity of a new commercial system.

1846.
Æt. 42.

miles round the country, and for want of training I find myself like an old posting-horse to-day, stiff and footsore. . . . There are reports to-day of some resignations about the Court, but I don't hear of anybody of consequence who is abandoning Peel. Still there is no knowing what to-morrow may bring forth. We hear nothing as to the details of Peel's plan to-morrow, for which we are all looking with great anxiety. But the report is still that he intends to go the whole hog. A very handsome gold snuff-box has just been presented to me by Mr. Collett, the member for Athlone."

"*Jan.* 28.—Peel is at last delivered, but I hardly know whether to call it a boy or a girl. Something between the two, I believe. His Corn measure makes an end of all Corn Laws in 1849, and in the meantime it is virtually a fixed duty of 4s. He has done more than was expected from him, and all *but* the right thing. Whether it will satisfy our ardent friends in the north is the question. Let me know all the gossip you hear about it. I abstained from saying a word in the House because I did not wish to commit myself, and I dissuaded Villiers and the rest of the Leaguers from speaking. It was too good a measure to be denounced, and not quite good enough for unqualified approbation, and therefore I thought it best to be quiet. To-day I have attended a meeting at Lord John's of the leaders of the Whig party. They seemed disposed to co-operate with Peel. But Villiers will bring on his motion for total and immediate repeal, and when that is lost we must do the best we can. The measure will pass the Commons with a very large majority, some people say seventy to one hundred, but the question still is what will be done in the Lords? I asked Lord John to-day what he thought the Peers would do with the

Bill, and he says if Lord Stanley heads the Protectionists they will reject it, but that the Lords will not put themselves under the Dukes of Richmond and Buckingham. I hear that Lord Stanley is not for fighting the battle of Monopoly. So much for the great question."

"*Jan.* 29.[1]—My own opinion is that we should not be justified in the eyes of the country if we did anything in the House to obstruct the measure, and I doubt whether any such step out of doors would be successful. In the House, Villiers will bring on his motion for total and immediate repeal, and I shall not be surprised if it were successful simply on agricultural grounds by our being able to demonstrate unanswerably that it is better for farmers and landowners to have the change at once rather than gradually. But we should have no chance on any other than agricultural grounds. To make the appeal from the manufacturing districts simply on the plea of *justice to the consumers*, would not have much sympathy here or elsewhere, and would have no effect upon Parliament while the question is merely one of less than three years' time. Therefore, while I would advise you to petition for the whole measure, I can't say I think any great demonstration as against Peel's compromise would have much sympathy elsewhere. Understand, I would not shift a hair's-breadth from our ground, but what I mean strongly to impress on you is my belief that any attempt at a powerful agitation against Peel's compromise would be a failure. And I should not like the League Council to take a step which did not at once receive a national support. For myself in the House I will undertake to prove unanswerably that it would be just to all, and especially politic for the agri-

[1] *To Geo. Wilson.*

1846. — ÆT. 42.

culturists, to make the repeal immediate, but if we fail on Villiers's motion to carry the immediate, I shall give my unhesitating support to Peel, and I will not join Whigs or Protectionists in any factious plan for tripping up his heels. I can't hold any different language from this out of doors, and therefore can hardly see the use of a public meeting till the measure comes on in Parliament."

"*Feb.* 9.[1]—The Queen's doctor, Sir James Clark (a good Leaguer at heart), has written to offer to pay me a friendly visit, and talk over the state of my constitution, with a view to advise me how to unstring the bow. He wrote me a croaking warning letter more than a year ago. As it is possible there may be a paragraph in some newspaper alluding to my health, I thought it best to let you know in case of inquiry. But don't write me a long dismal letter in return, for I can't read them, and it does no good. If Charles could come up for a week with a determination to work and think, he might help me with my letters, but he will make my head worse if he requires me to look after him, and so you must say plainly."

"*London, Feb.* 19.[2]—Your letter has followed me here. Peel's declaration in the House that he will adopt immediate repeal if it is voted by the Commons, seems to me to remove all difficulty from Villiers's path; he can now propose his old motion without the risk of doing any harm even if he should not succeed. As respects the future course of the League, the less that is said now about it publicly the better. If Peel's measure should become law, then the Council will be compelled to face the question, 'What shall the League do during the three years?' It has struck me that under such circumstances we might absolve the large subscribers from all further calls,

[1] *To F. W. Cobden.* [2] *To H. Ashworth.*

put the staff of the League on a peace footing, and merely keep alive a nominal organization to prevent any attempt to undo the good work we have effected. Not that I fear any reaction. On the contrary, I believe the popularity of Free Trade principles is only in its infancy, and that it will every year take firmer hold of the head and heart of the community. But there is perhaps something due to our repeated pledges that we will not dissolve until the Corn Laws are entirely abolished. In any case the work will be effectually finished during this year, provided the League preserve its firm and united position; and it is to prevent the slightest appearance of disunion that I would avoid now talking in public about the future course of the League. It is the League, and it only, that frightens the Peers. It is the League alone which enables Peel to repeal the law. But for the League the aristocracy would have hunted Peel to a premature grave, or consigned him like Lord Melbourne to a private station at the bare mention of total repeal. We must hold the same rod over the Lords until the measure is safe; after that I agree with you in thinking that it matters little whether the League dies with honours, or lingers out a few years of inglorious existence."

"*March* 6.[1]—Nobody knows to this day what the Lords will do, and I believe all depends upon their fears of the country. If there was not something behind corn which they dread even still more, I doubt if they would ever give up the key of the bread basket. They would turn out Peel with as little ceremony as they would dismiss a groom or keeper, if he had not the League at his back. It is strange to see the obtuseness of such men as Hume, who voted against Villiers's motion to *help Peel*. I

[1] *To F. W. Cobden.*

have reason to know that the latter was well pleased at the motion, and would have been glad if we had had a larger division. It helps Peel to be able to point to something beyond, which he does not satisfy. I wish we were out of it."

"*March* 25.[1]—I have received the notes. Moffatt mentioned to me the report in the city to which you refer. There is no help for these things, and the only wonder is that we have escaped so well. If you can keep this affair in any way afloat till the present Corn measure reaches the Queen's hands, I will solve the difficulty, by cutting the Gordian knot, or rather the House; and the rest must take its chance. I don't think I shall speak in this debate. It does no earthly good, and only wastes time. People are not likely to say I am silent because I can't answer Bentinck and Co. The Bill would be out of the Commons, according to appearances, before Easter."

"*March* 30.—We are uncertain which course will be taken by the Government to-night, whether the Corn or Coercion Bill is to be proceeded with. If the latter, I fear we shall not make another step with the Corn question before Easter. I don't like these delays."

"*April* 4.—It is my present intention to come home next Thursday unless there is anything special coming on that evening, which I don't think very likely. It happens most unluckily that the Government has forced on the Coercion Bill to the exclusion of corn, for owing to the pertinacious delay thrown in the way of its passing by the Irish members, I don't expect it will be read the first time before Easter, and as for corn there is no chance of hearing of it again till after the holidays. I wish to God we were out of the mess."

"*April* 6.—We are still in the midst of our Irish

[1] *To F. W. Cobden.*

squabble, and there is no chance of getting upon corn again before Easter. It is most mortifying this delay, for it gives the chance of the chapter of accidents to the enemy."

"*April* 23.—We are still in as great suspense as ever about the next step in the Corn Bill. The Irishmen threaten to delay us till next Friday week at least. But I hear that the general opinion is that the postponement will be favourable to the success of the measure in the Lords."

"*April* 25.—You will receive a *Times* by the post containing an amusing account of a flare-up in the House between Disraeli and Peel respecting some remarks of mine. You will also see that one of the Irish patriots has been trying to play us false about corn. But I don't find that the bulk of the liberal Irish members are inclined to any overt act of treachery, although I fear that many are in their hearts averse to *our* repeal."

"*April* 27.—Last Saturday I dined at Lord Monteagle's, and took Lady —— in to dinner, and really I must say I have not for five years met with a new acquaintance so much to my taste. I met there young Gough, son of Lord Gough, the hero of the Sutlej, and had some interesting private talk with him about the doings of his father. We are going on again to-night with the Coercion Bill, and there seems to be a prospect of the Irish Repealers pursuing a little more conciliatory course towards us. I hear that my speech on Friday is considered to have been very judicious, inasmuch as I spoke soft words, calculated to turn aside the wrath of the Irishmen. They are a very odd and unmanageable set, and I fear many of the most liberal patriots amongst them would, if they could find an excuse, pick a quarrel with us and vote against Free Trade,

1846.
Æt. 42.

or stay away. They are landlords, and like the rest afraid of rent."

"*April* 29.—I have three letters from you, but must not attempt now to give you a long reply. We are meeting this morning as usual on a Wednesday, at twelve o'clock till six in the House, and I have therefore little time for my correspondence. The Factory Bill is coming on which I wish to attend to. . . . You may tell our League friends that I begin to see daylight through the fog in which we have been so long enveloped. O'Connell tells me that we shall certainly divide upon the first reading of the Coercion Bill on Friday. That being out of the way, we shall go on to Corn on Monday, and next week will, I trust, see the Bill fairly out of the House. The general opinion is that the delay has been favourable to our prospects in the Lords."

"*May* 2.—The Corn measure comes on next Monday, and will continue before the House till it passes. Some people seem to expect that it will get out of our hands on Friday next. I still hear more and more favourable reports of the probable doings in the Lords."

"*May* 8.—The fact is we are here in a dead state of suspense, not quite certain what will be our fate in the Lords, and yet every day trying to learn something new, and still left in the same doubt. It is now said that we shall pass the third and last reading of the Bill in the Commons on Tuesday next. Then it will go up to the Lords, where the debates will be much shorter, for the Peers have no constituents to talk to. Lord Ducie says he thinks there will be only two nights' debates upon the second reading. Still I am told the Queen's assent cannot be given to the measure before the middle of June, and very likely not till the 20th. I dined last Saturday at

Labouchere's, in Belgrave Square, and sat beside Lady ——, a very handsome, sprightly, and unaffected dame. There was some very good singing after dinner. I have been obliged to mount a white cravat at these dinner-parties much against my will, but I found a black stock was quite out of character. So you see I am getting on."

"*May* 11.—I have been running about sight-seeing the last day or two. On Saturday I went to the Horticultural Society's great flower-show at Chiswick. It was a glorious day, and a most charming scene. How different from the drenching weather you and I experienced there."

"*May* 13.—I am sorry to say I see no chance of a division on the Corn Bill till Saturday morning at one or two o'clock, and that has quite thrown me out in my calculations about coming down. I fear I shall not be able to see you for a week or two later. The Factory Bill, upon which I must speak and vote, is before the House, and it is impossible to say when the division will take place. I have two invitations for dinner on Saturday, one to Lord Fitzwilliam's, and the other to Lord and Lady John Russell, and if I remain over that day, I shall prefer the latter, as I have twice refused invitations from them. I assure you I would rather find myself taking tea with you, than dining with lords and ladies. Do not trouble yourself to write to me every day. I don't wish to make it a task. But tell me all the gossip."

"*May* 15.[1]—There is at last a prospect of reading the Bill a third time to-night. The Protectionists promise fairly enough, but I have seen too much of their tactics to feel certain that they will not have another adjournment. There is a revival of rumours

[1] *To F. W. Cobden.*

again that the Lords will alter the Bill in Committee, and attempt a fixed-duty compromise, or a perpetuation of the reduced scale. It is certain to pass the second reading by a majority of thirty or forty, but it is not safe in the Committee, where proxies don't count. I should not now be able to leave town till the end of the month, when I shall take a week or ten days for the Whitsuntide recess."

"*May* 16.—I last night had the glorious privilege of giving a vote in the majority for the third reading of the Bill for the total repeal of the Corn Law. The Bill is now out of the House, and will go up to the Lords on Monday. I trust we shall never hear the name of 'Corn' again in the Commons. There was a good deal of cheering and waving of hats when the Speaker had put the question, 'that this Bill do now pass.' Lord Morpeth, Macaulay, and others came and shook hands with me, and congratulated me on the triumph of our cause. I did not speak, simply for the reason that I was afraid that I should give more life to the debate, and afford an excuse for another adjournment; otherwise I could have made a telling and conciliatory appeal. Villiers tried to speak at three o'clock this morning, but I did not think he took the right tone. He was fierce against the Protectionists, and only irritated them, and they wouldn't hear him. The reports about the doings in the Lords are still not satisfactory or conclusive. Many people fear still that they will alter the measure with a view to a compromise. But I hope we shall escape any further trouble upon the question. . . . I feel little doubt that I shall be able to pay a visit to your father at Midsummer. At least nothing but the Lords throwing back the Bill upon the country could prevent my going into Wales at the time, for

I shall confidently expect them to decide one way or another by the 15th of June. I shall certainly vote and speak against the Factory Bill next Friday."

"*May* 18.—We are so beset by contradictory rumours, that I know not what to say about our prospects in the Lords. Our good, conceited friend —— told me on Wednesday that he knew the Peers would *not* pass the measure, and on Saturday he assured me that they *would*. And this is a fair specimen of the way in which rumours vary from day to day. This morning Lord Monteagle called on me, and was strongly of opinion that they would 'move on, and not stand in people's way.' A few weeks will now decide the matter one way or another. I think I told you that I dined at Moffat's last Wednesday. As usual he gave us a first-rate dinner. After leaving Moffat's at eleven o'clock, I went to a squeeze at Mrs. ——. It was as usual hardly possible to get inside the drawing-room doors. I only remained a quarter of an hour and then went home. On Saturday I dined at Lord and Lady John's, and met a select party, whose names I see in to-day's papers. . . . I am afraid if I associate much with the aristocracy, they will spoil me. I am already half seduced by the fascinating ease of their parties."

"*May* 19.[1]—I received your letters with the enclosures. We are still on the tenter-hooks respecting the conduct of the Lords. There is, however, one cheering point: the majority on the second reading is improving in the stock-books of the whippers-in. It is now expected that there will be a forty to fifty majority at the second reading. This will of course give us a better margin for the Committee. The Government and Lord John (who is very anxious to get the measure through) are

[1] *To F. W. Cobden.*

1846. — ÆT. 42.

doing all they can to insure success. The Ministers from Lisbon, Florence, and other Continental cities (where they are Peers) are coming home to vote in Committee. Last night was a propitious beginning in the Lords. The Duke of Richmond was in a passion, and his tone and manner did not look like a winner."

"*May* 20.—We are still worried incessantly with rumours of intrigues at headquarters. Every day yields a fresh report. But I will write fuller to-morrow. Villiers is at my elbow with a new piece of gossip."

"*May* 20.[1]—I have looked through your letter to Lord Stanley, and will tell you frankly that I felt surprise that you should have wasted your time and thrown away your talents upon so very hopeless an object. He will neither read nor listen to facts or arguments, and after his double refusal to see a deputation, I really think it would be too great a condescension if you were to solicit his attention to the question at issue. This is my opinion, and Bright and Wilson, to whom I have spoken, appear to agree. But if you would like the letter to be handed to him, I will do it. Your evidence before the Lords' Committee was again the topic of eulogy from Lord Monteagle yesterday, who called on me with a copy of his report. Everything is in uncertainty as to what the Lords will do in Committee. The Protectionists have had a great flare-up to-day at Willis's Rooms, and they appear to be in great spirits. I fear we shall yet be obliged to launch our bark again upon the troubled waters of agitation. But in the meantime the calm moderation of the League is our best title to public support if we should be driven to an appeal to the country."

"*May* 22.—Yesterday I dined with Lord and Lady Fortescue, and met Lords Normanby, Campbell,

[1] *To H. Ashworth.*

and Morpeth. I sat at dinner beside the Duchess of Inverness, the widow of the Duke of Sussex, a plain little woman, but clever, and a very decided Free Trader."

"*May* 23.—I have sent you a *Chronicle* containing a brief report of my few remarks in the House last night. Be good enough to cut it out, and send it to me that I may correct it for Hansard. It was two o'clock when I spoke, and it was impossible to do justice to the subject. Count on my being at home, saving accidents, on Thursday to tea."

"*May* 23.—A meeting of the Whig Peers has to-day been held at Lord Lansdowne's, and they have unanimously resolved to support the Government measure in all its details. There were several of these Whig Peers who up to yesterday were understood to be resolved to vote in Committee for a small fixed duty, and the danger was understood to be with them. They were beginning, however, to be afraid that Peel might dissolve, and thus annihilate the Whig party, and so they are as a party more inclined to let the measure pass now in order to get a chance of coming in after Peel's retirement. I am assured by Edward Ellice, one of the late Whig Cabinet, that the Bill is now safe and that it will be law in three weeks. Heaven send us such good luck!"

"*June* 10.[1]—There is another fit of apprehension about the Corn Bill owing to the uncertainty of Peel's position. I can't understand his motive for constantly poking his Coercive Bill in our faces at these critical moments. The Lords will take courage at anything that seems to weaken the Government morally. They are like a fellow going to be hanged who looks out for a reprieve, and is always hoping for a lucky escape until the drop falls."

[1] *To F. W. Cobden.*

"*June* 13.—I have scarcely a doubt that in less than ten days the Corn Bill will be law. But we cannot say it is as safe as if carried. . . . I breakfasted yesterday morning with Monckton Milnes, and met Suleiman Pasha, Prince Louis Napoleon, Count D'Orsay, D'Israeli, and a queer party of odds and ends. The Pasha is a strong-built energetic-looking man of sixty. After breakfast he got upon the subject of military tactics, and fought the battle of Nezib over again with forks, spoons, and tumblers upon the table in a very animated way. The young Napoleon is evidently a weak fellow, but mild and amiable. I was disappointed in the physique of Count D'Orsay, who is a fleshy animal-looking creature, instead of the *spirituel* person I expected to see. He certainly dresses *à merveille*, and is besides a clever fellow."

"*June* 16.—The Corn Bill is now safe beyond all risk, and we may act as if it had passed. . . . I met Sir James Clark and Doctor Combe at Kingston on Sunday, and we took tea together. Sir James was strong in his advice to me to go abroad, and the doctor was half disposed with his niece to go with us to Egypt. Combe and I went to Hampton Court Gardens in a carriage, and had a walk there. I am afraid Peel is going out immediately after the Corn Bill passes, which will be a very great damper to the country; and the excitement in the country consequent on a change of Government, will, I fear, interfere with a public project in which you and I are interested."

"*June* 18.—The Lords will not read the Corn Bill the third time before Tuesday next, and I shall be detained in town to vote on the Coercion Bill on Thursday, after which I shall leave for Manchester. I send you a *Spectator* paper, by which you will see that I am a 'likeable' person. I hope you will appreciate this."

"*June* 23.—I have been plagued for several days with sitting to Herbert for the picture of the Council of the League, and it completely upsets my afternoons. Besides my mind has been more than ever upon the worry about that affair which is to come off after the Corn Bill is settled, and about which I hear all sorts of reports. You must therefore excuse me if I could not sit down to write a letter of news. . . . I thought the Corn Bill would certainly be read the third time on Tuesday (to-morrow), but I now begin to think it will be put off till Thursday. There is literally no end to this suspense. But there are reports of Peel being out of office on Friday next, and the Peers may yet ride restive."

"*June* 26.—MY DEAREST KATE,—Hurrah! Hurrah! the Corn Bill is law, and now my work is done. I shall come down to-morrow morning by the six o'clock train in order to be present at a Council meeting at three, and shall hope to be home in time for a late tea."

By what has always been noticed as a striking coincidence, and has even been heroically described as Nemesis, the Corn Bill passed the House of Lords on the same night on which the Coercion Bill was rejected in the House of Commons. On this memorable night the last speech before the division was made by Cobden. He could not, he said, regard the vote which he was about to give against the Irish Bill as one of no confidence, for it was evident that the Prime Minister could not be maintained in power by a single vote. If he had a majority that night, Lord George Bentinck would soon put him to the test again on some other subject. In any case, Cobden refused to stultify

1846. — ÆT. 42.

himself as Lord George and his friends were doing, by voting black to be white merely to serve a particular purpose. But though he was bound to vote against the Coercion Bill, he rejoiced to think that Sir Robert Peel would carry with him the esteem and gratitude of a greater number of the population of this empire than had ever followed the retirement of any other Minister.

This closed the debate. The Government were beaten by the heavy majority of seventy-three. The fallen Minister announced his resignation of office to the House three days later (June 29) in a remarkable speech. As Mr. Disraeli thinks, it was considered one of glorification and of pique. But the candour of posterity will insist on recognizing in every period of it the exaltation of a patriotic and justifiable pride. In this speech Sir Robert Peel pronounced that eulogium which is well worn, it is true, but which cannot be omitted here. "In reference to our proposing these measures," he said, "I have no wish to rob any person of the credit which is justly due to him for them. But I may say that neither the gentlemen sitting on the benches opposite, nor myself, nor the gentlemen sitting round me—I say that neither of us are the parties who are strictly entitled to the merit. There has been a combination of parties, and that combination of parties together with the influence of the Government, has led to the ultimate success of the measures. But, Sir, there is a name which ought to be associated with the success of these measures: it is not the name of the noble Lord, the member for London, neither is it my name. Sir, the name which ought to be, and which will be associated with the success of these measures is the name of a man who, acting, I believe, from pure and disinterested motives, has advocated their cause with untiring energy, and by appeals to reason, expressed by an eloquence, the more to be admired because it was unaffected and unadorned—the name which ought to be and will be associated with the success of these measures is the name of Richard Cobden. Without scruple, Sir, I attribute the success of these measures to him."

Cumbrous as they are in expression, the words were received with loud approbation in the House and with fervent sympathy in the country, and they made a deep mark on men's minds, because they were felt to be not less truly than magnanimously spoken.

CHAPTER XVII

CORRESPONDENCE WITH SIR ROBERT PEEL—CESSATION OF THE WORK OF THE LEAGUE

1846.

Æt. 42.

THREE days before the vote which broke up the Administration, Cobden had taken a rather singular step. As he afterwards told a friend, it was the only thing that he ever did as a member of the League without the knowledge of Mr. Bright. He wrote a long and very earnest letter to the Prime Minister, urging him, in the tolerably certain event of defeat on the Coercion Bill, to dissolve Parliament.

"76 UPPER BERKELEY STREET, PORTMAN SQUARE,
"23 *June* 1846.

"SIR—I have tried to think of a plan by which I could have half an hour's conversation with you upon public matters, but I do not think it would be possible for us to have an interview with the guarantee of privacy. I therefore take a course which will be startling to you, by committing the thoughts which are passing in my mind freely to paper. Let me premise that no human being has or ever will have the slightest knowledge or suspicion that I am writing this letter. I keep no copy, and ask for no reply. I only stipulate that you will put it in the fire when you have perused it, without in any way alluding to its contents, or permitting it to meet the eye of any other person whatever.[1] I shall not waste a word in apologizing for the directness—nay, the abruptness—with which I state my views.

"It is said you are about to resign. I assume that it is so. On public grounds this will be a national misfortune. The trade of the country, which has languished through six months during the time that the Corn Bill has been in suspense, and which would now assume a more confident tone, will be again plunged into renewed unsettlement by your resignation. Again, the great principle of commercial freedom with which your name is associated abroad, will be to some extent jeopardized by your retirement. It will fill the whole civilized world with doubt and perplexity to see a Minister, whom they believed all-powerful, because he was able to carry the most difficult measure of our time, fall at the very moment of his triumph. Foreigners, who do not comprehend the machinery of our Government, or the springs of party movements, will doubt if the people of England are really favourable to Free Trade. They will have misgivings of the permanence of our new policy, and this doubt will retard their movements in the same direction. You have probably thought of all this.

"My object, however, in writing is more particularly to draw your attention from the state of

[1] Cobden did not know that Sir Robert Peel put nothing into the fire. He once said to one of his younger followers,—"My dear ——, no public man who values his character, ever destroys a letter or a paper." As a matter of fact, Peel put up every night all the letters and notes that had come to him in the day, and it is understood that considerably more than a hundred thousand papers are in the possession of his literary executors. Some who exercise themselves upon the minor moralities of private life, will be shocked that he did not respect his correspondent's stipulation.

1846. — Æт. 42.

parties in the House, as towards your Government, to the position you hold as Prime Minister in the opinion of the country. Are you aware of the strength of your position with the country? If so, why bow to a chance medley of factions in the Legislature, with a nation ready and waiting to be called to your rescue? Few persons have more opportunities forced upon them than myself of being acquainted with the relative forces of public opinion. I will not speak of the populace, which to a man is with you; but of the active and intelligent middle classes, with whom you have engrossed a sympathy and interest greater than was ever before possessed by a Minister. The period of the Reform Bill witnessed a greater enthusiasm, but it was less rational and less enduring. It was directed towards half a dozen popular objects —Grey, Russell, Brougham, etc. Now, the whole interest centres in yourself. You represent the IDEA of the age, and it has no other representative amongst statesmen. You could be returned to Parliament with acclamation by any one of the most numerous and wealthy constituencies of the kingdom. Fox once said that 'Middlesex and Yorkshire together make all England.' You may add Lancashire, and call them your own. Are you justified towards the Queen, the people, and the great question of our generation, in abandoning this grand and glorious position? Will you yourself stand the test of an impartial historian?

"You will perceive that I point to a dissolution as the solution of your difficulties in Parliament. I anticipate your objections. You will say,—'If I had had the grounds for a dissolution whilst the Corn Bill was pending, I should have secured a majority for that measure; but now I have no such exclusive call upon the country, by which to set aside old party distinctions.' There are no substantial lines of demarcation now in the country betwixt the Peelites and the so-called Whig or Liberal party. The chiefs are still keeping up a show of hostility in the House; but their troops out of doors have piled their arms, and are mingling and fraternizing together. This fusion must sooner or later take place in the House. The independent men, nearly all who do not look for office, are ready for the amalgamation. They are with difficulty kept apart by the instinct of party discipline. One dissolution, judiciously brought about, would release every one of them from those bonds which time and circumstances have so greatly loosened.

"I have said that a dissolution should be judiciously brought about. I assume, of course, that you would not deem it necessary to stand or fall by the present Coercion Bill. I assume, moreover, that you are alive to the all-pervading force of the arguments you have used in favour of Free Trade principles, that they are eternal truths, applicable to all articles of exchange, as well as corn; and that they must be carried out in every item of our tariff. I assume that you foresaw, when you propounded the Corn Bill, that it involved the necessity of applying the same principle to sugar, coffee, etc. This assumption is the basis of all I have said, or have to say. Any other hypothesis would imply that you had not grasped in its full comprehensiveness the greatness of your position, or the means by which you could alone achieve the greatest triumph of a century. For I need not tell you that the only way in which the soul of a great nation can be stirred, is by appealing to its sympathies with a true principle in its unalloyed simplicity. Nay, further, it is necessary for the concentration of a people's mind that an individual should become the incarnation of a principle. It is from this necessity that I have been identified, out of doors, beyond my poor deserts, as the exponent of Free Trade. You, and no other, are its embodiment amongst statesmen;—and it is for this reason alone that I venture to talk to you in a strain that would otherwise be grossly impertinent.

"To return to the practical question of a dissolution. Assuming that your Cabinet will concur, or that you will place yourself in a position independently of others to appeal to the country, this is the course I should pursue under your circumstances. I would contrive to make it so far a judgment of the electors upon my own conduct as a Minister, as to secure support to myself in the next Parliament to carry out my principles. I would say in my place in Parliament to Lord George Bentinck and his party,—'I have been grossly maligned in this House, and in the newspaper press. I have been charged with treachery to the electors of this empire. My motives have been questioned, my character vilified, my policy denounced as destructive of the national interests. I have borne all this, looking only to the success of what I deemed a pressing public measure. I will not, however, stand convicted of these charges in the eyes of the civilized world until, at least, the nation has had the opportunity of giving its verdict. I will appeal to the electors of this empire; they shall decide between you and me—between your policy and mine. By their judgment I am content to stand or fall. They shall decide, not only upon my past policy, but whether the principles I have advocated shall be applied in their completeness to every item of our tariff. I am prepared to complete the work I have begun. All I ask is time, and the support of an enlightened and generous people.'

"This tone is essential, because it will release the members of a new Parliament from their old party ties. The hustings cry will be, 'Peel and Free Trade,' and every important constituency will send its members up to support *you*. I would dissolve within the next two months. Some people might urge that the counties would be in a less excited state if it were deferred; but any disadvantage in that respect would be more than compensated by the gain in the town constituencies. I would go to the country with my Free Trade laurels fresh upon my brow, and whilst the grievance under which I was suffering from the outrages of Protectionist speakers and writers was still rankling in the minds of people, whose sympathies have been greatly aroused by the conduct of Lord George Bentinck and his organs of the press towards you. Besides, I believe there are many county members who would tell their constituents honestly that Protection was a hopeless battle-cry, and that they would not pledge themselves to a system of personal persecution against yourself. Some of your persecutors would not enter the next Parliament.[1] Now I will anticipate what is passing in your mind. Do you shrink from the post of governing through the *bona fide* representatives of the middle class? Look at the facts, and can the country be otherwise ruled at all? There must be an end of the juggle of parties, the mere representatives of traditions, and some man must of necessity rule the State through its governing class. The Reform Bill decreed it; the passing of the Corn Bill has realized it. Are you afraid of the middle class? You must know them better than to suppose

[1] "Among other things," Cobden wrote to Mr. Parkes, "I remember mentioning the fact that Disraeli could not be again returned for Shrewsbury."

that they are given to extreme or violent measures. They are not democratic.

"Again, to anticipate what is passing in your thoughts. Do you apprehend a difficulty in effacing the line which separates you from the men on the opposite side of the House? I answer that the leaders of the Opposition personate no idea. You embody in your own person the idea of the age. Do you fear that other questions, which are latent on the 'Liberal' side of the House, would embarrass you if you were at the head of a considerable section of its members? What are they? Questions of organic reform have no vitality in the country, nor are they likely to have any force in the House until your work is done. Are the Whig leaders more favourable than yourself to institutional changes of any kind? Practical reforms are the order of the day, and you are by common consent the practical reformer. The Condition of England Question—there is your mission!

"As respects Ireland. That has become essentially a practical question too. If you are prepared to deal with Irish landlords as you have done with English, there will be the means of satisfying the people. You are not personally unpopular, but the reverse, with Irish members.

"Lastly, as respects your health. God only knows how you have endured, without sinking, the weight of public duties and the harassings of private remonstrances and importunities during the last six months. But I am of opinion that a dissolution, judiciously brought on, would place you comparatively on velvet for five years. It would lay in the dust your tormentors. It would explode the phantom of a Whig Opposition, and render impossible such a combination as is now, I fear, covertly harassing you.

But it is on the subject of your health alone that I feel I may be altogether at fault, and urging you to what may be impossible. In my public views of your position and power, I am not mistaken. Whatever may be the difficulties in your Cabinet, whether one or half-a-score of your colleagues may secede, you have in your own individual will the power, backed by the country, to accomplish all that the loftiest ambition or the truest patriotism ever aspired to identify with the name and fame of one individual.

"I hardly know how to conclude without apologizing for this most extraordinary liberty. If you credit me, as I believe you will, when I say that I have no object on earth but a desire to advance the interests of the nation and of humanity in writing to you, any apology will be unnecessary. If past experience do not indicate my motives, time, I hope, will.

"It is my intention, on the passing of the Corn Bill, to make instant arrangements for going abroad for at least a year, and it is not likely after Friday next that I shall appear in the House. This is my reason for venturing upon so abrupt a communication of all that is passing in my mind. I reiterate the assurance that no person will know that I have addressed you, and repeating my request that this letter be exclusively for your own eyes,

I have the honour to be, Sir, respectfully,

Your obedient servant,

RICHARD COBDEN.

"RT. HON. SIR ROBERT PEEL, BART. M.P."

"*P.S.*—I am of opinion that a dissolution, in the way I suggested, with yourself still in power, would very much facilitate the easy return of those on your side who voted with you. And any members of your Government who had a difficulty with their

1846.

Æt. 42.

present seats would, if they adhered to you, be at a premium with any free constituency. Were I in your position, although as a principle I do not think Cabinet Ministers ought to encumber themselves with large constituencies, I would accept an invitation to stand for London, Middlesex, South Lancashire, or West Yorkshire, expressly to show to the world the estimation in which my principles were held, and declaring at the same time that that was my sole motive for one Parliament only."

To this the Prime Minister replied on the following day, writing at the green table, and listening to the course of the debate as he wrote:—

"House of Commons,
"*Wednesday, June 24th*, 1846.

"Sir—I should not write from this place if I intended to weigh expressions, or to write to you in any other spirit than that of frankness and unreserve, by which your letter is characterized. First let me say that I am very sorry to hear you are about to leave London immediately. I meant to take the earliest opportunity, after the passing of the Corn Bill, to ask for the satisfaction of making your personal acquaintance, and of expressing a hope that every recollection of past personal differences was obliterated for ever. If you were aware of the opinions I have been expressing during the last two years to my most intimate friends with regard to the purity of your motives, your intellectual power, and ability to give effect to it by real eloquence—you would share in my surprise that all this time I was supposed to harbour some hostile personal feeling towards you.

"I need not give you the assurance that I shall

regard your letter as a communication more purely confidential than if it had been written to me by some person united to me by the closest bonds of private friendship.

"I do not think I mistake my position.

"I would have given, as I said I would give, every proof of fidelity to the measures which I introduced at the beginning of this session. I would have instantly advised dissolution if dissolution had been necessary to ensure their passing. I should have thought such an exercise of the prerogative justifiable—if it had given me a majority on no other question. If my retention of office, under any circumstances however adverse, had been necessary or would have been probably conducive to the success of those measures, I would have retained it. They will, however, I confidently trust, be the law of the land on Friday next.

"I do not agree with you as to the effect of my retirement from office as a justifiable ground, *after* the passing of those measures.

"You probably know or will readily believe that which is the truth—that such a position as mine entails the severest sacrifices. The strain on the mental power is far too severe; I will say nothing of ceremony—of the extent of private correspondence about mere personal objects—of the odious power which patronage confers—but what must be my feelings when I retire from the House of Commons after eight or nine hours' attendance on frequently superfluous or frivolous debate, and feel conscious that all that time should have been devoted to such matters as our relations with the United States—the adjustment of the Oregon dispute—our Indian policy—our political or commercial relations with the great members of the community of powerful nations?

1846. — Æt. 42.

"You will believe, I say, if you reflect on these things, that office and power may be anything but an object of ambition, and that I must be insane if I could have been induced by anything but a sense of public duty to undertake what I have undertaken in this session.

"But the world, the great and small vulgar, is not of this opinion. I am sorry to say they do not and cannot comprehend the motives which influence the *best* actions of public men. They think that public men change their course from corrupt motives, and their feeling is so predominant, that the character of public men is injured, and their practical authority and influence impaired, if in such a position as mine at the present moment any defeat be submitted to, which ought under ordinary circumstances to determine the fate of a Government, or there be any clinging to office.

"I think I should do more homage to the principles on which the Corn and Customs Bills are founded, by retirement on a perfectly justifiable ground, than either by retaining office without its proper authority, without the ability *to carry through* that which I undertake, or by encountering the serious risk of defeat after dissolution.

"I do not think a Minister is justified in advising dissolution under such circumstances as the present, unless he has a strong conviction that he will have a majority based not on temporary personal sympathies, not on concurrence of sentiment on one branch of policy, however important that may be, but on general approval of his whole policy.

"I should not think myself entitled to exercise this great prerogative, for the sole or the main purpose of deciding a personal question between myself and inflamed Protectionists—namely, whether

I had recently given good advice and honest advice to the Crown. The verdict of the country might be in my favour on that issue; but I might fail in obtaining a majority which should enable me after the first excitement had passed away, to carry on the Government, that is *to do* what I think conducive to the public welfare. I do not consider the evasion of difficulties, and the postponement of troublesome questions, the carrying on of a Government.

"I could perhaps have parried *even your power*, and *carried on the Government* in one sense for three or four years longer, if I could have consented to halloo on a majority in both Houses to defend the (not yet defunct) Corn Law of 1842, 'in all its integrity.'

"If you say that I individually at this moment embody or personify an idea, be it so. Then I must be very careful that, being the organ and representative of a prevailing and magnificent conception of the public mind, I do not sully that which I represent by warranting the suspicion even, that I am using the power it confers for any personal object.

"You have said little, and I have said nothing, about Ireland. But if I am defeated on the Irish Bill, will it be possible to divest dissolution (following soon after that defeat) of the character of an appeal to Great Britain against Ireland on a question of Irish Coercion? I should deeply lament this.

"I will ask you also to consider this. After the passing of the Corn and Customs Bill, considering how much trade has suffered of late from delays, debates, and uncertainty as to the final result, does not this country stand in need of *repose*? Would not a desperate political conflict throughout the length and breadth of the land impair or defer the beneficial effect of the passing of those measures?

1846. — ÆT. 42.

If it would, we are just in that degree abating satisfaction with the past, and reconcilement to the continued application of the principles of Free Trade.

"Consider also the effect of dissolution in Ireland; the rejection of the Irish Bill immediately preceding it.

"I have written this during the progress of the debates, to which I have been obliged to give some degree of attention. I may, therefore, have very imperfectly explained my views and feelings, but imperfect as that explanation may be, it will, I hope, suffice to convince you that I receive your communication in the spirit in which it was conceived, and that I set a just value on your good opinion and esteem.

"I have the honour to be, Sir,
With equal respect for your character and abilities,
Your faithful Servant,
ROBERT PEEL."

It is easy to understand the attractiveness of the idea with which Cobden was now possessed. It was thoroughly worked out in his own mind. By means of the forty-shilling freehold, the middle and industrious classes were to acquire a preponderance of political power. It was not the workmen as such, in whom Cobden had confidence. "You never heard me," he said to the Protectionists in the House of Commons, "quote the superior judgment of the working classes in any deliberations in this assembly: you never heard me cant about the superior claims of the working classes to arbitrate on this great question."[1] Political power was to be in the hands of people who had public spirit enough to save the

[1] *Speeches*, i. 372, Feb. 27, 1846.

thirty pounds or so that would buy them a qualification, if they could not get it in any other way. These middle and industrious classes would insist on pacific and thrifty administration, as the political condition of popular development. Circumstances had brought forward a powerful representative of such a policy in Sir Robert Peel; and Peel at the head of a fusion of Whigs and Economic Liberals would carry the country along the ways of a new and happier civilization. The old Whig watchword of Civil and Religious Liberty belonged to another generation, and it had ceased to be the exclusive cry of the Whigs even now. The repeal of the Corn Laws had broken up all parties. "I felt," said Cobden, "that I as much belonged to Sir James Graham's party, as I did to Lord John Russell's party."[1] There must be a great reconstruction, and Sir Robert Peel was to preside over it.

Such a scheme was admirable in itself. In substance it was destined to be partially realized one day, not by Peel, but by the most powerful and brilliant of his lieutenants. The singular fate which had marked the Minister's past career was an invincible obstacle to Cobden's project. It was too late. All the accepted decencies of party would have been outraged if the statesman who had led an army of Tory country gentlemen in one Parliament, should have hurried to lead an army of Liberal manufacturers in the next. The transition was too violent, the prospect of success too much of an accident. Nobody, again, could expect with Lord John Russell's view, and it was a just view, of Peel's long and successful opposition to measures and principles which he immediately took for his own on coming into power, that they should have been

[1] *Speeches*, ii. 507.

able to unite their forces under the lead of either of them. It would have seemed to Lord John quite as equivocal a transaction as the too famous coalition between Charles Fox and Lord North. What he did was to offer posts in his Administration to three of Sir Robert Peel's late colleagues,[1] and this was as far as he could go. They declined, and the country was thrown back upon a Whig Administration of the old type. When that Administration came to an end, the fusion which Cobden had desired came to pass. But Sir Robert Peel was there no more. The power which he would have used in furtherance of the wise and beneficent policy cherished by Cobden, fell into the hands of Lord Palmerston, who represented every element in the national character and traditions which Cobden thought most retrograde and dangerous.

Happily for the peace of the moment, these mortifications of the future were unknown and unsuspected. Ten days after his letter to the fallen Minister, Cobden received a communication from his successor.

"CHESHAM PLACE, *July* 2, 1846.

"MY DEAR SIR—The Queen having been pleased to entrust me with the task of forming an Administration, I have been anxious to place in office those who have maintained in our recent struggle the principles of Free Trade against Monopoly.

"The letter I received from you in November last, declining office, and the assurances I have received that you are going abroad for your health, have in combination with other circumstances prevented my asking your aid, nor, had I proposed to

[1] Lord Dalhousie, Sir James Graham, and Mr. Sidney Herbert.

you to join the Government could I have placed you anywhere but in the Cabinet. I have not hitherto perceived that you were disposed to adopt political life, apart from Free Trade, as a pursuit. I hope, however, you will do so, and that on your return to this country you will join a Liberal Administration.

"I care little whether the present arrangement remains for any long period in the direction of affairs. But I am anxious to see a large Liberal majority in the House of Commons devoted to improvement, both in this country and in Ireland. Mr. Charles Villiers has declined to take any office. I am about to propose to Mr. Milner Gibson to become Vice-President of the Board of Trade.

"I remain, with sentiments of regard and respect,

Yours very faithfully,

J. RUSSELL."

What were the "other circumstances" which prevented Lord John Russell from inviting Cobden to join his Government, we can only guess. It is pretty certain that they related to a project of which a good deal had been heard during the last four or five months. There would undeniably have been some difficulty in giving high office in the State to a politician whose friends were at the time publicly collecting funds for a national testimonial of a pecuniary kind. Whether the Whig chief was glad or not to have this excuse for leaving Cobden out of his Cabinet, the ground of the omission was not unreasonable.

The final meeting of the League took place on the same day on which Lord John Russell wrote to explain that he intended to show his appreciation of what was due to those "who had maintained in our

1846.

ÆT. 42.

recent struggle the principles of Free Trade against Monopoly," by offering Mr. Gibson a post without either dignity or influence. The Leaguers were too honestly satisfied with the triumph of the cause for which they had banded themselves together eight years ago, to take any interest in so small a matter as the distribution of good things in Downing Street and Whitehall. That was no affair of theirs. It was enough for them that they had removed a great obstacle to the material prosperity of the country, that they had effectually vindicated what the best among them believed to be an exalted and civilizing social principle, and that in doing this they had failed to reverence no law, shaken no institution, and injured no class nor order. It is impossible not to envy the feelings of men who had done so excellent a piece of work for their country in so spirited and honourable a way. When the announcement was made from the Chair that the Anti-Corn-Law League stood conditionally dissolved, a deep silence fell upon them all, as they reflected that they were about finally to separate from friends with whom they had been long and closely connected, and that they had no longer in common the pursuit of an object which had been the most cherished of their lives.[1]

The share which the League had in procuring the consummation of the commercial policy that Huskisson had first opened four-and-twenty years before, is not always rightly understood. One practical effect of a mischievous kind has followed from this misunderstanding. It has led people into the delusion that organization, if it be only on a sufficiently gigantic scale and sufficiently unrelenting

[1] See Mr. Bright's speech, quoted in Mr. Ashworth's little book, p. 213.

in its importunity, is capable of winning any virtuous cause. The agitation against the Corn Laws had several pretty obvious peculiarities, which ought not to be overlooked. A large and wealthy class had the strongest material interest in repeal. What was important was that this class now happened to represent the great army of consumers. Protection as a principle had long ago begun to give way, but it might have remained for a long time to come, if it had not been found in intolerable antagonism with the growing giant of industrial interests. It is not a piece of cynicism, but an important truth, to say that what brings great changes of policy is the spontaneous shifting and readjustment of interests, not the discovery of new principles. What the League actually did was this. Its energetic propagandism succeeded in making people believe in a general way that Free Trade was right, when the time should come. When the Irish famine brought the crisis, public opinion was prepared for the solution, and when protection on corn had disappeared, there was nothing left to support protection on sugar and ships. Then, again, the perseverance of the agitation had a more direct effect, as has been already seen from Cobden's letters. It frightened the ruling class. First, it prevented Peel, in the autumn of 1845, from opening the ports by an order in Council. Second, it forced the Whigs out of their fixed duty. Third, it made the House of Lords afraid of throwing out the repealing Bill.

There is another important circumstance which ought not to be left out of sight. One secret of the power of the League both over the mind of Sir Robert Peel, and over Parliament, arose from the narrow character of the representation at that time. The House of Commons to-day is a sufficiently imperfect and distorting mirror of public judgment and feeling. But things were far worse then. The total number of voters in the country was not much more than three-quarters of a million; six-sevenths of the male population of the country was excluded from any direct share of popular power; and property itself was so unfairly represented that Manchester, with double the value of the property of Buckinghamshire, returned only two members, while Bucks returned eleven. It was on this account, as Cobden said, it was because Manchester could not have its fair representation in Parliament, that it was obliged to organize a League and raise an agitation through the length and breadth of the land, in order to make itself felt.[1] It was just because the sober portion of the House of Commons were aware from how limited and exclusive a source they drew their authority, that the League represented so formidable, because so unknown, a force.

The same thought was present to the reflective mind of Peel. Cobden tells a story in one of his speeches which illustrates this. One evening in 1848 they were sitting in the House of Commons, when the news came that the Government of Louis Philippe had been overthrown and a Republic proclaimed. When the buzz of conversation ran round the House, as the startling intelligence was passed from member to member, Cobden said to Joseph Hume, who sat beside him, "Go across and tell Sir Robert Peel." Hume went to the front bench opposite, where Sir Robert was sitting in his usual isolation. "This comes," said Peel, when Hume had whispered the catastrophe, "this comes of trying to govern the country through a narrow representation in Parliament, without regarding the wishes

[1] *Speeches*, ii. 482, July 6, 1848.

of those outside. It is what this party behind me wanted me to do in the matter of the Corn Laws, and I would not do it."[1]

1846. — ÆT. 42.

Now that the work was finally done, Cobden was free to set out on that journey over Europe, which the doctors had urged upon him as the best means of repose, and which he promised himself should be made an opportunity of diligently preaching the new gospel among the economic Gentiles. Before starting on this long pilgrimage, he went to stay for a month with his family in Wales. Two days after the final meeting of the League, he thus describes to one of the earliest of his fellow-workers the frame of mind in which it had left him.

"I am going into the wilderness to pray for a return of the taste I once possessed for nature and simple quiet life. Here I am, in one day from Manchester, to the loveliest valley out of paradise. Ten years ago, before I was an agitator, I spent a day or two in this house. Comparing my sensations now with those I then experienced, I feel how much I have lost in winning public fame. The rough tempest has spoilt me for the quiet haven. I fear I shall never be able to cast anchor again. It seems as if some mesmeric hand were on my brain, or I was possessed by an unquiet fiend urging me forward in spite of myself. On Thursday I thought as I went to the meeting, that I should next day be a quiet and happy man. Next day brings me a suggestion from a private friend of the Emperor of Russia, assuring me that if instead of going to Italy and Egypt, I would take a trip to St. Petersburg, I could exercise an important influence upon the mind of Nicholas. Here am I at Llangollen, blind

[1] *Speeches*, ii. 548, Aug. 18, 1859.

to the loveliness of nature, and only eager to be on the road to Russia, taking Madrid, Vienna, Berlin, and Paris by the way! Let me see my boy to-morrow, who waits my coming at Machynlleth, and if he do not wean me, I am quite gone past recovery."[1]

His mind did not rest long. To Mr. Ashworth he wrote at the same date:—

"Now I am going to tell you of fresh projects that have been brewing in my brain. I have given up all idea of burying myself in Egypt or Italy. I am going on a private agitating tour through the Continent of Europe. The other day I got an intimation from Sir Roderick Murchison, the geologist—a friend and confidant of the Emperor of Russia—that I should have great influence with him if I went to St. Petersburg. To-day I get a letter from the Mayor of Bordeaux, written at Paris after dining at Duchatel's, the French Minister, conveying a suggestion from the latter that I should cross to Dieppe and visit the King of the French at his Chateau of Eu, where he would be glad to receive me between the 4th and 14th August.

"I have had similar hints respecting Madrid, Vienna, and Berlin. Well, I will, with God's assistance, during the next twelvemonth visit all the large states of Europe, see their potentates or statesmen, and endeavour to enforce those truths which have been irresistible at home. Why should I rust in inactivity? If the public spirit of my countrymen affords me the means of travelling as their missionary, I will be the first ambassador from the People of this country to the nations of the Continent. I am impelled to this step by an instinctive emotion such as never deceived me. I feel that I could succeed in making out a stronger case for the prohibitive

[1] *To Mr. Paulton*, July 4, 1846.

nations of Europe to compel them to adopt a freer system, than I had here to overturn our protective policy. But it is necessary that my design should not be made public, for that would create suspicion abroad. With the exception of a friend or two, under confidence, I shall not mention my intentions to anybody."

1846.

ÆT. 42.

A few days later he wrote to George Combe, in a mood of more even balance:—

"Your affectionate letter of the 28th of June has never been absent from my mind, although so long unacknowledged. I came here last week, with my wife and children, on a visit to her father's, and for a quiet ramble amongst the Welsh mountains. I thought I should be allowed to be forgotten after my address to my constituents. But every post brings me twenty or thirty letters, and such letters! I am teased to death by place-hunters of every degree, who wish me to procure them Government appointments. Brothers of peers, ay, 'honourables' are amongst the number. I have but one answer for all, 'I would not ask a favour of the Ministry to serve my own brother.' Then I am still importuned worse than ever by beggars of every description. The enclosed is a specimen which reached me this morning; put it in the fire.[1] I often think, what

[1] The letter referred to purported to be from a lady, who having nothing but her own exertions to depend upon, begged Mr. Cobden to become her "generous and noble-minded benefactor," to enable her to "begin to do something for herself." She says, "I do not see to use my needle; to rear poultry for London and other large market-towns is what my wishes are bent upon." For this purpose she suggests that Mr. Cobden should procure a loan of £5000 to be advanced by himself and nine other friends in Manchester, where, she delicately insinuates, he is so much beloved that the process will be a very easy one for him. The loan, principal and interest, she promises shall be faithfully paid in ten years at the most. The writer mentions that she has her eye upon a small estate which will serve her purpose.

must be the fate of Lord John or Peel with half the needy aristocracy knocking at the Treasury doors. Here is my excuse for not having answered your letter before.

"The settlement of the Free Trade controversy leaves the path free for other reforms, and Education must come next, and when I say that Education has yet to come, I need not add that I do not look for very great advances in our social state during our generation. You ask me whether the public mind is prepared for acting upon the moral law in our national affairs. I am afraid the animal is yet too predominant in the nature of Englishmen, and of men generally, to allow us to hope that the higher sentiments will gain their desired ascendency in your lifetime or mine. I have always had one test of the tendency of the world: what is its estimate of war and warriors, and on what do nations rely for their mutual security? Brute force is, I fear, as much worshipped now, in the statues to Wellington and the peerage to Gough, as they were two thousand years ago in the colossal proportions of Hercules or Jupiter. Our international relations are an armed truce, each nation relying entirely on its power to defend itself by physical force. We may teach Christianity and morality in our families; but as a people, we are, I fear, still animals in our predominant propensities.

"Perhaps you will remember that in my little pamphlets, I dwelt a good deal, ten years ago, upon the influence of our foreign policy upon our home affairs. I am as strongly as ever impressed with this view. I don't think the nations of the earth will have a chance of advancing morally in their domestic concerns to the degree of excellence which we sigh for, until the international relations of the world are put upon a different footing. The present system corrupts society, exhausts its wealth, raises up false gods for hero-worship, and fixes before the eyes of the rising generation a spurious if glittering standard of glory. It is because I do believe that the principle of Free Trade is calculated to alter the relations of the world for the better, in a moral point of view, that I bless God I have been allowed to take a prominent part in its advocacy. Still, do not let us be too gloomy. If we can keep the world from actual war, and I trust railroads, steamboats, cheap postage and our own example in Free Trade will do that, a great impulse will from this time be given to social reforms. The public mind is in a practical mood, and it will now precipitate itself upon Education, Temperance, reform of Criminals, care of Physical Health, et cetera, with greater zeal than ever. . . .

"Now, my dear friend, for a word or two upon a very delicate personal matter. You have seen the account of an ebullition of a pecuniary kind which is taking place in the country, a demonstration in favour of me exclusively to the neglect of others who have laboured long and zealously with me in the cause of Free Trade. I feel deeply the injustice of passing over Bright and Villiers, to say nothing of others; and nothing but the conviction that I am guiltless of ever having arrogated to myself the merit of others consoles me in the painful position in which the public have placed me, of being the vehicle for diverting the reward from men who are as worthy of all honour as myself. But I wish to speak to you upon a still more delicate view of this unpalatable affair. I do not like to be recompensed for a public service at all, and I am sensible that my moral influence will be impaired by the fact of my receiving a tribute in money from the public. I should have preferred to have either refused it, or to have done a glorious service by endowing a college. But as an honest man, and as a father and a husband, I cannot refuse to accept the money. You will probably be surprised when I tell you that I have shared the fate of nearly all leaders in revolutions or great reforms, by the complete sacrifice of my private prospects in life. In a word I was a poor man at the close of my agitation. I shall not go into details, because it would involve painful reminiscences; but suffice it to say that whilst the Duke of Richmond was taunting me with the profits of my business, I was suffering the complete loss of my private fortune, and I am not now afraid to confess to you that my health of body and peace of mind have suffered more in consequence of private anxieties during the last two years, than from my public labours. With strong domestic feelings and with an orderly mind, which was peculiarly sensitive to the immorality of risking the happiness of those whom nature had given the first claim on me, for the sake of a public object, I experienced a conflict between the demands of my responsible public station, and the prior duties which I owed to my family, which altogether nearly paralysed me. I should have retired from public life last August, had not some of my wealthy coadjutors in Lancashire forced me to continue at my post, and had they not compelled me to leave to them the cares of my private business. It is owing to the knowledge which my neighbours in Lancashire have of the sacrifices which I have incurred, that the subscription has been entered into; and I wish you to be in possession of the facts, because you are the man of all others whom I should wish to possess the materials for forming a correct knowledge of the motives which compel me to take a course that jars at first sight on our notion of purity and disinterestedness."[1]

1846.
Æt. 42.

It is not necessary to enter into a discussion of the propriety of Cobden's acceptance of the large sum of money, between seventy-five and eighty thousand pounds, which were collected in commemoration of his services to what the subscribers counted a great public cause. The chief Leaguers anxiously discussed the project of a joint testimonial to Cobden, Mr. Bright, and Mr. Villiers, all three to be included in a common subscription.[2] But nobody could say how the fund was to be divided. It was then discussed whether as much money could be collected for the three as for Cobden individually, and it was agreed that it could not, for it was Cobden who united the sections of the Free Trade party. He had undoubtedly sacrificed good chances of private prosperity for the interest of the community, and it would have been a painful and discreditable satire on human nature if he had been left in ruin, while everybody around him was thriving on the results of his unselfish devotion. It is true that many others had made sacrifices both of time and money, but they had not sacrificed everything as Cobden had done. The munificence of the subscription was singularly honourable to those who contributed to it. No generous or reasonable man will think that it impairs by one jot the purity of the motives that prompted the exertions of the public benefactor whose great services it commemorated and rewarded.

[1] *To Geo. Combe*, July 14, 1846.
[2] The League had already voted a present of ten thousand pounds to Mr. George Wilson, their indefatigable chairman.

CHAPTER XVIII

TOUR OVER EUROPE

1846-7.

Æt. 42-43.

Accompanied by his wife, Cobden landed at Dieppe on the 5th of August 1846. He arrived in the Thames on his return on the 11th of October 1847. He was absent, therefore, from England for fourteen months, and in the interval he had travelled in France, Spain, Italy, Germany, and Russia. His reception was everywhere that of a great discoverer in a science which interests the bulk of mankind much more keenly than any other, the science of wealth. He had persuaded the richest country in the world to revolutionize its commercial policy. People looked on him as a man who had found out a momentous secret. In nearly every important town that he visited in every great country in Europe, they celebrated his visit by a banquet, toasts, and congratulatory speeches. He had interviews with the Pope, with three or four kings, with ambassadors, and with all the prominent statesmen. He never lost an opportunity of speaking a word in season. Even from the Pope he entreated that His Holiness's influence might be used against bull-fighting in Spain. They were not all converted, but they all listened to him, and they all taught him something, whether they chose to learn anything from him in return or not.

The travellers passed rather more than eleven

1846.

ÆT. 42.

weeks in Spain, and at the beginning of the New Year found themselves in Italy. Here they remained from January until the end of June. From Venice they went north to the Austrian capital, and thence to Berlin. In the first week in August Mrs. Cobden started for England, while her husband turned his face eastwards. In Russia he passed five weeks, and three weeks more were usefully spent in the journey home by way of Lubeck and Hamburg.

When he returned to England he had such a conspectus and cosmorama of Europe in his mind as was possessed by no statesman in the country; of the great economic currents, of the special commercial interests, of the conflicting political issues, of the leading personages. Unless knowledge of such things is a superfluity for statesmen whose strong point is asserted to be foreign policy, Cobden was more fit to discuss the foreign policy of this country than any man in it. In less than a year after his return, Europe was shaken by a tremendous convulsion. The kings whom he had seen were forced from their thrones, and the greatest of the statesmen of the old world fled out in haste from Vienna. Neither they nor Cobden foresaw the storm that was so close upon them; but Cobden at least was aware of those movements in Paris which were silently unchaining the revolutionary forces. The following passage is from a letter written ten years later, but this is a proper place for it:—

"When I was in Paris in 1846, I saw Guizot, and though I had weighed him accurately as a politician, I pronounced him an intellectual pedant and a moral prude, with no more knowledge of men and things than is possessed by professors who live among their pupils, and he seemed to me to have become completely absorbed in the hard and unscrupulous will of

1846. ÆT. 42.

Louis Philippe. At that time I was the hero of a successful agitation, and was taken into the confidence of all the leaders of the opposition who were getting up the movement which led first to the banquets, and next to the Revolution. I was at Odillon Barrot's, and at Girardin's, and met in private conclave Beaumont, Tocqueville, Duvergier de Hauranne, Léon Faucher, Bastiat, and others. I was of course a good deal consulted as to the way of managing such things, and am afraid I must plead guilty to having been an accessory before the fact to much that was afterwards done with so little immediate advantage to those concerned. I remember in particular telling Odillon Barrot, in all sincerity, that he would have made a very successful agitator on an English platform. His bluff figure and vehement style of oratory would have almost made him another Bright. But to the point. I naturally made inquiries as to what amount of parliamentary reform they were aiming at, and to my surprise found that all they wanted was a small addition to the electoral list (not exceeding 200,000 voters), comprising 'les capacités,' the professions, and a certain small increase from a slightly reduced tax-paying franchise. Upon my expressing my amazement that they should go for such a small measure (which, to be sure, appeared insignificant to me, just fresh from the total repeal of the Corn Laws), they answered that it would satisfy them for the present; it would recognize the principle of progress; and they frankly confessed that the bulk of the people were not fit for the suffrage, and that there was no security for constitutional government excepting in a restricted electoral class. Well, when these moderate men afterwards brought forward their harmless scheme, Guizot mounted the rostrum, and flourished his rod, and in true pedagogical style told them they

Febbroni, to Fossombroni; to all those statesmen, in a word, who had preserved down to our own days the great work which they had set on foot.

Mrs. Cobden said that it was fortunate that her husband had not too high an opinion of himself, or else the Italians would have turned his head, so many attentions, both public and private, were showered upon him. Even at a tranquil little town like Perugia a troop of musicians sallied out to serenade him at his hotel, the Agricultural Society sent a silver medal and a diploma, and in the evening at the Casino the concert was closed by the recitation of verses in honour of Richard Cobden.

On their arrival at Genoa, on their return from all these honours (May 20), they found that O'Connell had died there the previous day. They at once proceeded to pay a visit to his son, and from O'Connell's servant, who had been with him for thirteen years, they heard the circumstances of the great patriot's end."[1]

Cobden's diaries of this long and instructive tour are so copious that they would more than fill one of these volumes. They afford a complete economic panorama of the countries which he visited, and abound in acute observations, and judicious hints of all kinds from the Free Trader's point of view. Their facts, however, are now out of date, and their interest is mostly historic. The reader will probably be satisfied with a moderate number of extracts, recording Cobden's interviews with important people, and his impressions of historic scenes.

"*Dieppe*, *Aug. 6th*, 1846.—Called and left my card with the King's aide-de-camp, at the château.

[1] The common report that O'Connell intended to quit England and close his days at Rome was untrue: on the contrary, his own inclination was to stay at Derrynane, and the journey to Italy was only undertaken at the urgent solicitation of his friends. He was conscious up to the moment of his death.

The King was out in the forest for a drive; on his return received an invitation to call at the château at eight o'clock. We found thirty or forty persons in the saloon, the King, Queen, and Madame Adelaide, the King's sister, in the middle of the room. Louis Philippe was very civil and very communicative, talked much against war, and ridiculed the idea of an acquisition of more territory, saying, 'What would be the use of our taking Charleville, or Philippeville? Why, it would give us a dozen more bad deputies, that's all!' Said the people would not now tolerate war, and much in that strain. He alluded to the League and my labours, but I could not bring him to the subject of Free Trade as affecting his own country's interests. He spoke of the iron monopoly of France as being, if possible, worse than our corn monopoly. He and the Queen spoke in high terms of the kindness of the English people towards them. After this short interview I came away with the impression that the King did not like the close discussion of the Free Trade question, but that he preferred dwelling on generalities. I formed the opinion that he is a clever *actor*, and perhaps that is all we can say of the ablest sovereigns of this or any other country.

"He was not very complimentary to Lord Palmerston, applying to him a French maxim, which may be turned into the English version, 'If you bray a fool in a mortar, he will remain a fool still.' He repeated two or three times that he wished there were no custom-houses, but 'how is revenue to be raised?' He quoted a conversation with Washington, in which the latter had deplored the necessity of raising the whole of the American revenue from customs' duties. I had heard in England, before starting, that Louis Philippe was himself deeply interested in the preservation of monopoly; and that his large property in forests would be diminished in value by the free importation of coals and iron. But I will not hastily prejudge his Majesty so far as to believe, without better proofs, that he is actuated by a personal interest in secretly opposing the progress of Free Trade principles. It is difficult, however, to conceive that a man of his sagacity and knowledge can be blind to the importance of these principles in consolidating the peace of empires."

"*Paris, August 10th.*—Early in the morning a call from Domville, my old French master; engaged him to give me an hour's instruction every morning during my stay in Paris.[1] Afterwards Horace Say called, a noble-looking man—a rare phrenological and physiognomical development."

"*August 15th, Saturday.*—French lesson. Went with Léon Faucher to call upon M. Thiers; walked and gossiped in his garden, and talked without reserve upon Free Trade. I warned him not to pronounce an opinion against us, thus to fall into the same predicament as Peel did. He seems never to have thought upon the subject, but promises fairly. A lively little man without dignity, and with nothing to impress you with a sense of power."

"*Barcelona, December 8th.*—Reached Barcelona at half-past five o'clock; as it was half an hour after sunset, the health officers did not visit us, and we were shut up in our floating prison till the following morning. This system of requiring pratique at every port for vessels in the coasting-trade is most useless and vexatious, and would be submitted to by none but Spaniards. They shrug their shoulders

[1] By his diligent use of this opportunity Cobden succeeded in acquiring a really good command over the French language for colloquial and other purposes.

like Turks, and say, 'It was always so.' The waiter on the steamer told us that the best part of the profits of his situation came from smuggling, and that the smuggling was all done through the connivance of the Government employés; he stated that the contraband goods conveyed by him were generally carried on shore by the custom-house officers themselves. This agrees with all that I heard from the consuls and merchants on the Mediterranean coast. The French consul at Carthagena remarked whilst speaking of the universal corruption of the custom-house officers, 'With money you might pass the tower of Notre Dame through the custom-house without observation, but without money you could not pass *this*,' holding up his pocket-handkerchief."

"*Perpignan, December 14th and 15th.*—Luxuriated in the comforts of a French inn. I felt almost ready to hug the furniture, kiss the white table-cloth, and shake hands with the waiters, so attractive did they all look after my Spanish discomforts! Sat indoors and wrote letters. Walked once only into the town, an irregular, confined, and ugly fortified place. The only annoyance I experienced was from the military music and the parading and drilling of the troops."

"*Narbonne, December 16th.*—Left Perpignan this morning at eleven o'clock. The road to Narbonne passed along the marshy shores of the Mediterranean; very uninteresting scenery. But the sensation of passing along a French road in an English carriage was quite delightful after the Spanish travelling. The men wearing the blue blouse. What a contrast in the appearance of the two peoples! On one side the mountain, the grave, sombre, dignified, dark Spaniard; here the lively, supple, facetious, amiable Frenchman, who seems ready to adapt himself to any mood to please you."

"*Montpellier, December* 17*th.*—Separated from our travelling companions[1] this morning at Narbonne; they started at eight o'clock for Toulouse, and we at the same hour for Montpellier. Our road lay along a rich and populous but uninteresting country, through Beziers, and for some distance close to the Mediterranean. The people were busy in the fields, cutting off the long dry shoots of the vines with a pair of pruning shears, and leaving nothing but the stumps. When within ten miles of Montpellier, snow began to fall, and it continued during the rest of the journey."

"*Nice, Jan. 3rd*, 1847.—Sir George Napier called; lost his left arm at Ciudad Rodrigo; is younger brother of the conqueror of Scinde, brother of the historian of the Peninsular War, and of the commodore. Told me some anecdotes of the wars with the Caffirs at the Cape of Good Hope, where he was governor seven years. Says the Hottentots make good soldiers when officered by English; described a regiment of them (dragoons), commanded by his son; very small men, but superior to the Caffirs or Dutch Boers; that they required restraining, so daring their courage, etc. This confirms my opinion that all races of men are equal in valour when placed under like circumstances."

"*Nice, Jan. 4th.*—Saw a large number of men assembled in the open place; peasants chiefly, conscripts for the army; went amongst them, a sturdy-looking set, and apparently not dissatisfied with their fate; am told they are generally only liable to serve for fourteen months. Called on M. Lacroix, the Consul, who said the Government of Sardinia has a monopoly of salt, gunpowder, and tobacco; that the province or county of Nice is not included in the general

[1] Mr. and Mrs. Schwabe.

customs-law of the kingdom, but has its own privileges; that corn from foreign countries pays a duty, but that all other articles, excepting those monopolized by Government, are imported free. Called upon an old Frenchman, named Sergent, in his ninety-seventh year, who acted a prominent part in the scenes of the first revolution, and is one of the few men living who signed or voted for the execution of the king; was originally an engraver, and there were several of his productions on the walls of his room, but nothing commemorative of Napoleon's exploits."[1]

"*Nice, Jan. 5th.*—Dined with Mr. Davenport, and met M. Sergent. Took tea with Sir George Napier and Lady N.; met M. Gastand, a merchant of the town, who told me that woollens are imported from France into Nice, and again smuggled into that country, the drawback of twenty per cent allowed in France upon the exportation affording a profit on this singular traffic; says that the refined sugar exported from Marseilles receives a drawback of six per cent, and that this sugar is sold cheaper in Nice than in France."

"*Genoa, Jan. 13th.*—This morning the Marquis d'Azeglio called, with Mr. William Gibbs—the former a Piedmontese who has written poetry, romances, and political works, and is also an artist. He told me he had been expelled from Rome by the late Pope, and from Lombardy and Florence, in consequence of his writings. An amiable and intelligent man, evincing rational views upon the moral progress of his country, and deprecating revolutionary violence as inimical to the advance of liberal principles."

[1] Sergent is commonly credited with a leading share in the organization and direction of the September Massacres in 1792; on the other hand he is supposed to have saved several victims from the guillotine. Louis Philippe, who had been his colleague in the Jacobin Club, gave him a pension of 1800 francs.

"*Genoa, Jan.* 16*th.*—Called on Dr. —— and Mr. Brown (Consul); the latter showed me a copy of Junius, with numerous notes in pencil by Horne Tooke on the margin; described the demagogue, whom he knew personally, as a finished scoundrel. In the evening dined with a party of about fifty persons, Marquis d'Azeglio president. The consuls of France, Spain, Belgium, and Tuscany present, as well as several of the Genoese nobles, and merchants of different countries. French was universally spoken. My speech was intended for the Ministers at Turin rather than my hearers. In this country, where there is no representative system, public opinion has no direct mode of influencing the policy of the State, and therefore I used such arguments as were calculated to have weight with the Government, and induce them to favour Free Trade as a means of increasing the national revenue."

"*Genoa, Jan.* 17*th.*—In the evening M. Papa called and remained for a long talk about the affairs of the country. The law for the division of the landed property on the death of proprietors is nearly the same here as in France, it being shared equally by the children. An entail can be settled upon the eldest son only with the consent of the king, and it is not willingly granted. The nobles or patricians of Genoa are all Marquises, they having derived the title from Charles the Fifth of Spain. The present representatives of these old families have generally much degenerated from their energetic and public-spirited ancestors."

"*Genoa, Jan.* 18*th.*—In the evening I visited the governor (Marchese Paulucci) at his reception. A large party filled his rooms, some dancing; a large majority of the men, officers in the army. The governor thanked me for the tone in which I had spoken at the public dinner given to me on Saturday; said that he had naturally felt a little anxious to know how the proceedings had been conducted, and complimented me upon my tact, etc.[1] In speaking about the power of Russia to make an irruption into Europe, I expressed an opinion that she had not the money to march 40,000 soldiers out of her territory; he agreed with me, and mentioned an anecdote in confirmation. He said that when he was military governor of a district in the Caucasus, he was applied to for a plan of operations for the invasion of Persia; that, when he handed in to the Minister his estimate of the number of troops to be set in motion, the latter was so surprised at the smallness of the force that he declared it was not worthy of the occasion, and that he could not present it to the emperor. 'But how will you transport a greater number of men to the scene of operations if I add them to my estimate?' said the general. 'Oh! we must build boats and construct waggons,' was the reply. 'Where is the money to come from?' was the rejoinder. At last the plan was laid before the emperor, who saw the difficulty and confirmed the view of the general."

"*Rome, Jan. 22nd.*—In Tuscany no Corn Law of any kind has been allowed to exist by the present

[1] "Although disposed to be grateful for their public banquets, of which I have had upwards of a dozen in Italy, besides private parties without number, yet I can see other motives besides compliments to me in their meetings. In the first place the old spirit of rivalry has been at work amongst the different towns. But secondly, the Italian Liberals have seized upon my presence as an excuse for holding a meeting on a public question, to make speeches and offer toasts, *often for the first time.* They consider this a step gained, and so it is. And I have been sometimes surprised that the Government have allowed it. In Austrian Italy such demonstrations are quite unprecedented."—*Cobden to George Combe,* June 1847.

dynasty for many generations. Mr. Lloyd told me an anecdote of one of the leaders of the revolutionary party of 1831, who, when asked by him what practical reforms he wished to carry by a change in the Government, remarked that one of the grievances he wished to remedy was the want of adequate protection for the land. So that had this patriot been able to induce the people to upset the Grand Duke's authority, he would have rewarded them with a Corn Law! Was told that the grass of which the far-famed Leghorn bonnets are made can only be grown in perfection in Tuscany, that it has been sown elsewhere, but without success, and that the seed from which it is grown is the produce of a few fields only; inquire further on my return about this. Left Leghorn at six o'clock for Civita Vecchia, and arrived there at eight the following morning. . . . Left at half-past twelve for Rome, the road lying along the beach for several miles. Almost immediately on quitting the town the country assumed the character of a wild common, covered with shrubs and tufts of long grass, and this neglected appearance of the soil continued with slight interruptions of cultivated patches as long as daylight lasted. Noticed the fine bullocks of a light grey colour, with dark shoulders, and having very long branching horns, noble-looking animals. It was an indistinct moonlight as we came near Rome. . . . On turning a corner of the road we came suddenly upon a full and close view of the dome of St. Peter's which stood out boldly in the evening sky."

"*Rome, Jan. 23rd.*—The effect of the colonnade is much impaired by the high square buildings of the Vatican, which rise high above on the right, and detract even from the appearance of the great façade. On the first sight of the interior, I was not struck so much with its grandeur or sublimity, as with the beauty and richness of its details. I felt impressed with more solemnity in entering York Minster for the first time than in St. Peter's. The glare and glitter of so much gold and such varieties of marble distract the eye, and prevent it taking in the whole form of the building in one *coup-d'œil*, as we do in the simple stone of our unadorned Gothic Cathedrals. I was disappointed too in the statues, many of which are poor things."

"*Rome, Jan.* 25*th.*— . . . Then to the Vatican, and passed a couple of hours in walking leisurely through the numerous galleries of sculpture where the enthusiastic admirer of the art may revel to intoxication amidst the most perfect forms; here I was more than satisfied. I had not pictured to myself anything so extensive or varied. Not only is the human figure of both sexes and all ages in every possible graceful attitude transferred to marble, which all but breathes and moves, but there are perfect models of animals too, and all arranged with consummate taste and skill in rooms that are worthy of enshrining such treasures. The Laocoon to my eye is the masterpiece. The Apollo Belvidere is perfect in anatomy, but the features express no feeling. Saw Raphael's masterpiece; the drawing faultless, but the subjects were unhappily dictated by monkish patrons, and they confined the artist too much to the expression of a very limited range of sentiments, as veneration, etc."

"*Feb.* 8*th.*—In the evening to a ball at the French Embassy, in the Colonna Palace—a magnificent suite of rooms, filled with Italians, French, and English. Saw Count Rossi for the first time (the Ambassador), a sharp-faced, intellectual-looking man; I suspect he is more of the diplomatist than the political economist, and more of a politician than a Free Trader. Met the young Prince Broglie, an intelligent youth; was introduced to Antonelli, the Finance Minister; and had a long conversation with Grassellini, the Governor of Rome, urging him to signalize his reign over the city by lighting it with gas, and laying down foot pavements. Left at twelve o'clock."

"*Feb. 10th.*—I was entertained at a public dinner in the hall of the Chamber of Commerce; about thirty-five persons present, Marquis Potenziani in the chair; Prince Corsini, very aged, Prince Canino (Bonaparte), Duke of Bracciano (Torlonia), Marquis Dragonetti, etc., amongst the guests. The healths of the Pope and the Queen of England drank together as one toast! I spoke in English, about a dozen of the company appearing to understand me. Doctor Pantaleone then read an Italian translation of my speech, which was well received and elicited cheers for the translator from those who had understood the English. A Doctor Masi, a celebrated improvisatore, delivered an improvisation in the course of the evening upon myself; his look and gestures were strikingly eloquent, even to one who could not understand his language. There was a wild expression of inspiration in his countenance which realized the idea of a poet's fine frenzy, and the effect was heightened by his long black hair, which streamed from a high pale brow down upon his shoulders. His emotions imparted to the audience an electrical effect, which now roused them to immoderate excitement and next melted them to tears. One of his verses produced an unanimous call for an encore; he paused for a moment, drew his fingers through his hair, then tried to reproduce the verse, but there came forth another cast of rhymes. His last verse, which drew tears from those around, was translated to me, and conveyed this sentiment: 'When you go back to England, say you found Italy a corpse, but upon it was planted a green branch, which will one day flower again and bring forth fruit.' The dinner went off with great spirit, and, remembering that we were sitting so near the walls of the Vatican, I thought it the most cheering proof of the widespread sympathy for Free Trade principles that I had seen in the course of all my travels."

"*February 11th.*—Called on Prince Corsini, Colonel Caldwell, Lord Ossulston, then to the Corso again, to join in the fun of the Carnival, streets more crowded than ever with carriages and masquers, the English everywhere and always the most uproarious. If there be any excess of boisterousness visible, it is ten to one that it proceeds from the English or other foreigners. The Italians do little more than exchange bouquets or little bonbons in a very quiet, graceful way, throwing them to each other from their carriages or balconies, but the English shovel upon each other the chalk *confettis*, with all the zeal and energy of navigators. It is quite certain that a carnival in England would not pass over so peaceably as here; people would begin with sugar-plums, and go on to apples and oranges, then proceed to potatoes, and end probably with stones."

"*Rome, February 12th.*—Called on Mr. Hemans, son of the poetess, who is editing the *Roman Advertiser*, an English weekly paper, and gave him a copy of my speech. Then accompanied Prince Canino in an open carriage to see the foxhounds throw off in the Campagna, beyond the tomb of Cæcilia Metella; the hounds drew the ruins of aqueducts and tombs, under the direction of 'Dick' and 'George,' the whippers-in, in regular Melton style, but not finding, they proceeded across the Campagna to a wood at a distance. The prince followed the field in his drag, leaving the road, and going across the country, just as we should have done in an American prairie. We soon found ourselves upon a trackless waste, with no other habitations than here and there a wigwam, for the temporary accommodation of the shepherds during the winter months, the only part of the year when man or beast can exist in this region. The Marquis d'Azeglio called on me on his arrival from Genoa. We had a long chat upon the prospects of Italy; his political views appear to me sound and rational, and he is evidently under the influence of patriotic feelings. There is always hope for a country that produces such men.

"In the evening to the American Consul's, and found a number of his countrymen and women in masquerade dresses, everything about them lively excepting the spirits of the actors. Introduced to several of 'our most distinguished citizens'—a title for a bore."

"*February 13th.*—Dined with Mr. and Mrs. S. Gurney, met young Bunsens, and some other Germans, the Prussian Minister, etc. Speaking to the latter about his being almost the only Protestant representative at the court of the Pope, he said that Peel had applied to the Prussian Government to know whether it found it advantageous or otherwise to have a diplomatic connexion with the Holy See, and that the answer given was, that the disadvantages rather predominated, and that if that Government stood in the position of England, it would prefer to remain without diplomatic relations with Rome. Next to Prince Canino's soirée, very mixed, but very agreeable, and many intelligent men there.

Was introduced to the Count of Syracuse, brother of the King of Naples, with whom I had a long talk about Ireland, France, and other matters. Found him, for a king's brother, a very clear-headed, well-informed man. Talked with the Sardinian Minister about Turkey, where he had been ambassador for eight years. The Marquis Dragonetti, an able man. Was introduced to several others of note."

"*February* 14*th.*—They who argue that the working people are elevated in intellect and prompted to habits of cleanliness and self-respect by having free access to public buildings devoted to the arts, must not quote the ragged, dirty crowds who frequent St. Peter's to kiss the toe of the statue of the saint!"

"*Feb.* 16*th.*—The statue of Moses by Michael Angelo in the Church of San Pietro in Vincoli, did not impress me on looking at it as I expected. The execution may be all that the sculptor desires, but to my eye the face wants both dignity and honesty of expression, and the head fails to impress me with the idea of wisdom or capacity in the great law-giver."

"*Feb.* 19*th.*—To the Barberini Palace to see a very small collection of paintings, one of them the far-famed Beatrice Cenci by Guido. The touching pensiveness of the face produces such an impression that it will be present in one's recollection when perhaps every other picture in Rome is forgotten.

"In the evening took tea with Mrs. Jameson, authoress of works on early painters, an agreeable woman, whose good-nature and sense prevent her from displaying the unpleasant qualities of too many literary ladies. Met Mr. Gibson, the sculptor, who talked about robbers and assassins, with a graphic description of them and their victims, which was quite professional."

"*Feb. 22nd.*—Went with Mrs. Jameson to the Vatican, walked through the sculpture galleries. The Braccio Nuovo contains a statue of Demosthenes in an attitude most earnest; there is no appearance of effort or art in the figure, and yet it is endowed with the earnest and sincere expression which an actor would seek to imitate. The countenance expresses a total forgetfulness of self and everything but the subject on which the mind of the orator is intent. The sculptor has not only succeeded in making his marble convey the idea of sincerity, but it almost makes you think it *feels* sincere. The whole art of the work lies in this impress of earnestness, and it proves that the artist knew where the secret of oratory lies, and I can fancy that Demosthenes himself might have been the instructor of the sculptor on this point. The full-length statue of the Roman lady in the same gallery is dignified, chaste, and graceful.

"Walked with Mrs. Jameson into the Sistine Chapel, to see Michael Angelo's frescoes; the Last Judgment at one end, and the whole of the ceiling from his pencil. It is a deplorable misapplication of the time and talent of a man of genius to devote years to the painting of the ceiling of a chapel, at which one can only look by an effort that costs too much inconvenience to the neck to leave the mind at ease to enjoy the pleasure of the painting. . . . With all the enthusiasm of my fair companion, I could not feel much gratification at this celebrated work of art.

"At seven o'clock was presented to the Pope in his private cabinet, where I found him in a white flannel friar's dress, sitting at a small writing-desk surrounded with papers. The approach to this little room was through several lofty and spacious apart-

1847. —— ÆT. 43.

ments. The curtained doors and the long flowing robes of the attendants reminded me, oddly enough, of my interview with Mehemet Ali at Cairo. Pius IX. received me with a hearty and unaffected expression of pleasure at meeting one who had been concerned in a great and good work in England; commended my perseverance and the means by which the principle of Free Trade had been made to triumph; and he remarked that England was the only country where such triumphs were achieved by years of legal and moral exertion. He professed himself to be favourable to Free Trade, and said all he could do should be done to forward it, but modestly added that he could do but little. I pointed to Tuscany, his next neighbour, as a good example to follow, and said that England had not been ashamed to take a lesson from that country; and I added that Tuscany was an inconvenient neighbour, owing to the smuggling which would be carried on until his tariff was put upon the same moderate scale. He spoke of the wide frontier of his territories as being favourable to the contraband trade, and alluded to the desirableness of a custom-house union in Italy. In parting, I called his attention to the practice in Spain of having bull-fights in honour of the saints and virgins on the fête days, and gave him an extract from a Madrid paper, giving an account of a bull-fight there in honour of its patroness, the Virgin. After a little conversation upon the cruelty and demoralization of these spectacles, he thanked me for having drawn his attention to it, and promised to give instructions upon the subject to an envoy whom he was about to send to Spain. He concluded by another complimentary phrase or two, and we left. I was impressed with the notion that he is sincere, kind-hearted, and good, and that he is possessed of strong common sense and sound understanding. He did not strike me as a man of commanding genius."

1847.

ÆT. 43.

"*Feb. 23rd.*—Dined with Count Rossi, the French Ambassador. A splendid banquet, at which the foreign ambassadors in Rome, including the Turkish envoy going to Vienna, were present. Looking round the table I saw represented, Italy, France, Germany, Russia, England, Turkey, and Syria, the latter by a bishop of the Maronites."

"*Feb. 24th.*—We have been in Rome a month, have seen some of the wonders of the ancients, and have been overwhelmed with the kindness of friends, but I long for a quiet day or two in travelling over the Campagna, where the sheep will be the only living objects that will surround us. I came here expecting repose, and have found excitement, crowded evening parties, and late hours. At eleven o'clock at night Dr. Masi called again, bringing me sundry packets of his newspaper, the *Contemporaneo*, which he desires to transmit by me to Naples, thus making me a kind of moral smuggler."

"*Naples, Feb. 27th.*—Left Rome Thursday morning, 25th February, at half-past eight, for Naples, by the new Appian Way, which leaves the old road of that name a little to the right on quitting the city, but falls into it a few miles off. The course of this celebrated old road may be distinctly traced at a distance by the mounds and ruins of tombs and temples with which its sides are fringed. Snow fell as we passed out of Rome. The view of the Campagna, with the ruined aqueducts stretching across its desolate surface, presented a striking contrast to the luxurious and busy scene which we had but a few minutes before taken leave of within the city walls. These stately and graceful aqueducts are nearly the only ruins which excite feelings of regret, being perhaps the sole buildings which did not merit destruction by the crimes, the folly, and the injustice which attended their construction, or the purposes to which they were devoted.

"We are now in the territory of the King of the Two Sicilies, who can certainly boast of ruling over more beggars than any other sovereign. Mendicancy seems to be the profession of all the labouring people whenever they have an opportunity of practising it. No sooner is a traveller's carriage seen than young and old pounce upon it; the peasant woman throws down her load that she may keep up with the vehicle, bawling out incessantly for charity; the boy who is watching the sheep, a field or two off, hurries across hedge and ditch to intercept you as you go up the hill; and when the carriage stops to change horses, it is surrounded by lame, halt, and blind, scrambling and screaming for alms. The rags and misery remind me of Ireland. The only persons I see in the small towns and villages with clean, sleek skins and good clothes on their backs are priests and soldiers."

"*March 4th.*—Went with M. D'Azala to the Museum, first to see the room containing jewellery and ornaments, but did not think them generally in such good taste or so well executed as those I had seen in Campana's collection of Etruscan works of a similar kind in Rome. Next to the rooms containing the articles in bronze, brought principally from Pompeii. Here I found specimens of all the common household utensils—lamps, jugs, pans, moulds for pastry, some of them in the form of shells, others of animals; scales and steelyards, mirrors, bells, articles for the toilet, including rouge; bread in loaves, with the name of the maker stamped on them, surgical instruments, cupping cups in bronze, locks, keys, hinges, tickets for the theatre; in fact, I was introduced to the mode of domestic everyday life amongst the ancients. . . . After seeing this portion of the Museum I came away without proceeding farther, preferring to mix up no other objects with my enjoyment to-day of certainly the most novel and interesting collection of curiosities I ever beheld."

"*Naples, March 6th.*—At eleven o'clock went with Mr. Close to the palace to see the King by appointment; conversed for a short time with him upon Free Trade, about which he did not appear to be altogether ignorant or without some favourable sympathies. He questioned me about the future solution of the Irish difficulty, a question which seems to be uppermost in the minds of all statesmen and public men on the Continent. The King is a stout and tall man, heavy-looking, and of restricted capacity. I am told he is amiable and correct in his domestic life, excessively devout and entirely in the hands of his confessor, of whom report does not speak favourably."

"*March 16th.*—I went to the Museum to see the collection of bronzes again whilst the houses from which they were taken in Pompeii were fresh in my memory. I was introduced to the members of the Academy of Science, who were holding an ordinary meeting in their room in the same building. A complimentary address to me was delivered by Sig. Mancini, and responded to by other members, and I thanked them briefly in French."

"*Turin, May 26th*, 1847.—Had an interview with his Majesty Charles Albert, a very tall and dignified figure, with a sombre, but not unamiable expression of countenance; received me frankly; talked of railroads, machinery, agriculture, and similar practical questions. Said he hoped I was contented with what his Government had done in the application of my principles, and informed me that his Ministry had resolved upon a further reduction of duties on iron, cotton, etc. He is said to have good intentions, but to want firmness of character.

"In the evening, Count Revel, Minister of Finance, came in, with whom I had a long discussion upon Free Trade; a sensible man. Speaking to Signor Cibrario upon the subject of the commerce of the Middle Ages in Italy, he said that the principle of Protection or Colbertism was unknown; that, however, there were innumerable impediments to industry and internal commerce, owing to the corporations of trades and the custom-houses which surrounded every little state and almost every little city."

"*May 28th*, 1847.—Went at eight o'clock in the morning to hear a lecture by Signor Scialoja, Professor of Political Economy at the University, a Neapolitan of considerable talent, who delivered his address with much eloquence, extempore with the aid of notes. In the course of his lecture he alluded in flattering terms to my presence, which elicited applause from a crowded auditory, comprising, in addition to the students, numerous visitors, officers in the army, clergymen, advocates, etc. On my leaving the hall at the close I was cheered by a crowd of students in the court. Count Petitti and Count Cavour took breakfast with me."

"*Milan, June 3rd.*—Attended a meeting of La Società d'Incoraggiamento of Milan. About 200 persons were present, consisting of members and their friends. A paper was read by Signor G. Sacchi upon the doctrine of Romagnosi (a Milanese writer) on Free Trade, in which he alluded in complimentary terms to my presence. Then Signor A. Mauri (the secretary) read an eulogistic address to me. After which Chevalier Maffei read a paper upon Milton, with a long translation from the first book of 'Paradise Lost.' In conclusion I delivered a short address in French, thanking the Society, and recommending the study of political economy to the young men present. The meeting terminated with enthusiastic expressions of satisfaction. In the evening was entertained at a public dinner (the first ever held in Milan) by about eighty persons, including most of the leading literary men of the place, Signor G. Basevi, advocate, in the chair. This gentleman, who, I was told, is of the Jewish persuasion, had the moral courage to act as counsel in defence of Hofer, the Tyrolese leader, when he was tried by a military commission at Mantua and sentenced to be shot. Not having before taken part in a similar demonstration, he was unacquainted with the mode of conducting a meeting. He began the toasts in the midst of the dinner, by proposing my health in an eloquent speech. Then followed three or four others who all proposed my health. Before the dinner was concluded, other orators, who had become a little heated with wine, wished to speak. One of them broke through the rule laid down, and almost entered upon the forbidden ground of Austrian politics. However, by dint of management and entreaty the excited spirits were calmed, and the banquet went off pretty well. Received an anonymous letter entreating me not to propose the health of the Emperor of Austria."

"*Lake Como, June 7th.*—Lounged away the morning over Madame D'Arblay's *Memoirs*, and Lady C. Bury's *George IV*. Heard also some gossip about the residents on the shores of the lake, not the most favourable to their morality. After dinner made an excursion to the town of Como, and saw the Cathedral."

"*Desenzano, June 9th.*—Found Signor Salevi an intelligent and amiable man, his head and countenance striking; is writing a book upon prison reform, and a great promoter of infant schools, of which he says there are three well conducted in Brescia, and supported by voluntary contributions. Speaking about the proprietorship of land, which is in this neighbourhood very much divided, he expressed his surprise that England, so greatly in advance of Europe in other respects, should still preserve so much of the feudal system in respect to the law of real property. He thinks the law of succession, as established in the Code Napoleon, highly favourable to the mass of the people; that nothing gives dignity to a man, and develops his self-respect so effectually, as the ownership of property, however small. In Lombardy, as in Piedmont, one-half the property is at the disposal of a father on his decease; the remainder is by law given equally amongst his children. I find everywhere on the Continent, amongst all classes, the same unfavourable opinion of our law of primogeniture in England."

"*Venice, June 21st.*—In the evening dined at a public entertainment at the island of Giudecca, under an alcove of vines; the party consisted of about seventy persons, Count Priuli in the chair, the podesta or mayor by his side, the French and American consuls being present. At the close of the sumptuous repast, the chairman called upon Dr. Locatelli to propose my health in behalf of the meeting, and he read a short and eloquent speech, to which I replied in French. It had been arranged that no other speeches should be made. M. Chalaye, a French gentleman who was in China representing the French Government during our late war there, and who is now appointed Consul to Peru, made a strong appeal privately to the chairman, to be allowed to make a speech, but without success. We left the table, and after taking coffee, the party entered their gondolas, which were waiting, and accompanied by the excellent band of music belonging to an Austrian regiment, which had played during the dinner, we proceeded in procession down the Grand Canal to the Rialto bridge. The music and the gay liveries of some of our boatmen soon attracted a great number of gondolas; the sound and sight also brought everybody into their balconies; as we returned, the moon, which had risen, gave a fresh charm to the picturesque scene, which was sufficiently romantic to excite poetical emotions even in the mind of a political economist."

"*Trieste*, *June* 26*th*.—Left Venice this morning at six o'clock in the Austrian Lloyd's steamboat, a handsome, large, and clean vessel. It was low water, and as we came out of the port, through the tortuous channel which winds amongst the islands, it afforded a good view of the advantages which the Queen of the Adriatic possessed behind these intricate barriers. The view of the city at a few miles' distance, with its palaces, towers, and domes, rising from the level of the water, and its low country at the back shut in by high mountains, is very magnificent. Reached Trieste at two o'clock. The coast hilly, and the town stands upon a confined spot shut in by the high land, which rises immediately at the back. The ships lie in an open roadstead, and are exposed to certain winds. The number of square-rigged vessels and the activity in the port offer a contrast to the scene at Venice."

"*Trieste, July 1st.*—Dined at a public dinner given to me by about ninety of the principal merchants in the saloon of the theatre. M. Schläpfer, president of the Exchange Committee, in the chair. The speeches were delivered in the midst of the dinner. M. De Bruck, the projector and chief director of Austrian Lloyd's spoke well. Signor Dell' Ongaro, who is an Italian and a poet, read a speech, in which he made allusion to Italian nationality, which drew forth some hasty remarks from M. De Bruck, and led to a scene of some excitement. After dinner I persuaded them to shake hands. In speaking to the chairman during the dinner, he described the iron-masters in Styria as not having in a series of years realized much money, notwithstanding their being protected by heavy duties. Many of the nobility are interested in these furnaces; their businesses badly managed. He gives a still worse description of the cotton-spinners and manufacturers, who cling to the ways of their fathers, and do not improve their machinery, being very inferior to the Swiss; does not know of an instance of one of them retiring from business with a fortune, and few of them are rich in floating capital. A good band of an Austrian regiment performed during the dinner."

"*Vienna, July 7th.*—Looked in to see the famous monumental tomb by Canova, an original and successful design. I think, however, this sculptor lived to enjoy the best of his fame, and that posterity will hardly preserve the warmth of enthusiasm for his genius that was felt by the generation in which he lived."

"*Vienna, July 10th.*—Paid a visit in company with M. de H. to Prince Metternich, whose appearance hardly denotes the veteran of seventy-five. His head and countenance convey the impression of high polish rather than native force of character, and his conversation is more subtle than profound. He talks incessantly, perhaps in order to choose his own topics; the state of Italy was his principal theme, and he professed to be apprehensive of violent disorders in that country. He entered into a long essay upon differences of race, and the antagonisms of nationality in Europe. 'Why did Italy still have favourable feelings towards France, notwithstanding the injuries she had received from the latter country? Because the two nations were of the same race. Why were England and France so inveterately opposed? Because upon their opposite coasts the Teutonic and Latin races came into close contact.' Again and again he returned to the state of Italy, spoke of their jealousies and hatreds, one town of another; said that a man in Milan would not lend his money upon mortgage in Cremona or Padua, because 'he could not see the church steeple.' It struck me that his hatred of the Italians partook of the feeling described by Rochefoucault when he says that we never forgive those whom we have injured. Speaking of Austria, he dilated upon the great diversity of the character and condition of the people, and seemed to be vindicating his conservative policy. 'How could they have a representative system, when men from different parts of the empire, if assembled as representatives in the capital, could not understand each other? The Emperor was King of Hungary, of Lombardy, and of Bohemia, Count of Tyrol, and Archduke of Austria.' He alluded to the generally comfortable state of the people, and wished me to examine into their condition. He seemed to speak on the defensive, like a man conscious that public opinion in Europe was not favourable to his policy; he threw in parenthetically, and with a delicate finesse, some compliments, such as 'I wish I was an Englishman.' 'I speak like yourself, as a practical man, and not in the language of romance.' 'You and I are of the same race,' etc. He alluded to Ireland, and said he could not discover a key for the solution of the difficulty: in other countries reforms were wanted, but there a social system must be created out of chaos. He is probably the last of those State physicians who, looking only to the symptoms of a nation, content themselves with superficial remedies from day to day, and never attempt to probe beneath the surface, to discover the source of the evils which afflict the social system. This order of statesmen will pass away with him, because too much light has been shed upon the laboratory of Governments, to allow them to impose upon mankind with the old formulas.

"After leaving Prince Metternich, I called upon Baron Kübeck, Minister of Finance, a man of a totally different character from his chief. He is a simple, sincere, and straightforward man; expressed himself favourably to a relaxation of the protective system, but spoke of the difficulties which powerful interests put in his way; said that Dr. List had succeeded in misleading the public mind on the question of Protection. A visit from Prince Esterhazy, who was upwards of twenty years ambassador in England; he remarked that diplomacy upon the old system was now mere humbug, for that the world was much too well informed upon all that was going on in every country to allow ambassadors to mystify matters."

"*Dresden*, *July* 21*st*.—Called on M. Zeschau, the Saxon Finance Minister, an able, hard-working man, who also fills the office of Minister for Foreign Affairs; tells me the land is much divided in Saxony, that the owner of an estate worth £60,000 is deemed a large proprietor; the majority of the farmers cultivate their own land; in some of the hilly districts the weavers rent a small patch of ground for garden or potatoes; the feudal service, or corvée, has been abolished in Saxony since 1833, having been commuted into fixed payments, which will be redeemed gradually in a few years. He spoke of Ireland, and said he would dispose of the uncultivated land in the same way as they do in Saxony of the mines of coal, etc. If after a certain fixed period the proprietor of the land will not work them, they are let by the Government to other parties, subject to the payment of a rent to the owner, according to the produce raised."

"*Dresden, July 22nd.*—Went with M. Krug to see the collection of jewels, and articles of carving, sculpture, etc., in the green vaults. Then to the royal library, and made the acquaintance of M. Falkenstein, the chief librarian, a learned and interesting man, who showed us a manuscript work by Luther, and some other curiosities. M. Falkenstein is acquainted with Hebrew, Greek, and Latin critically, is also learned in the Arabic, Persian, and Sclavonic languages, speaks French, German, English, Italian, etc.; his salary, as head librarian, having no one over him, is £150, and he has a wife and six children! Speaking of Luther's coarseness, he said that there are some of his letters in the library so grossly violent and abusive that they are unfit to be read in the presence of women. M. Falkenstein is the author of a life of Kosciusko, the Polish patriot, whom he knew when he was a boy at Soleure, in Switzerland, where the old warrior died. He described him as

1847. ÆT. 43.

very amiable and charitable; he was accustomed to ride an old horse who was so used to the habit of his master of giving alms to beggars, that he would stop instinctively when he came near to a man in rags. . . . Saw in a shop-window to-day a silk handkerchief for sale, with my portrait engraved and my name attached."

"*Berlin, July 28th.*—Went to Babelsberg, near Potsdam, at five in the afternoon, to visit the Prince of Prussia, the King's brother and heir presumptive to the throne.[1] A little before seven I found the Prince and Princess and their attendants in the garden. He is a straight-forward, soldier-like man, she a clever woman, speaking English well. A school for the officers' sons had been invited to visit the grounds; the youths, dressed in a military costume, were inspected by the Prince, and afterwards the Princess walked along the lines and accosted some of the boys in the front rank. Then some large balls were produced, and the Princess began the fun by throwing them amongst the lads, who scrambled for them; the Prince joined in the amusement, and they pelted each other with great glee. The King soon afterwards arrived from his palace at Sans Souci, and went familiarly amongst the scholars, who were afterwards entertained at a long table with cakes, chocolate, etc. The rest of us then sat down to tea at a couple of tables under the trees, the Princess presiding and pouring out the tea, the King and the rest partaking unostentatiously, everybody seated, and with hats and caps on. The King speaks English well, is highly educated, said to be clever, but impulsive, and not practical. He is fifty-two, with a portly figure, and a thoroughly good-natured, unaffected German face.

[1] The present Emperor of Germany.

"Met Baron Von Humboldt, a still sturdy little man, with a clear grey eye, born in 1769, and in his seventy-eighth year; tells me he allows himself only four to five hours' sleep. He has a fine massive forehead, his manners are courtier-like, he lives in the palace of Sans Souci, near the King. He spoke highly of Jefferson, whom he knew intimately; remarked of Lord Brougham that, like Raphael, he had three manners, and that he had known him in his earliest and best manner. At dusk we entered the château, sat down at a large round table, and were served with a plain supper; were afterwards conveyed to the railway station in a carriage, and reached Berlin at eleven o'clock."

"*Berlin, July 29th.*—Went with Mr. Howard to call upon Dr. Eichhorn, at present Minister of Public Instruction, but formerly in the Department of Trade, and who took an active part in the formation of the Zollverein, an able and enthusiastic man; he stated that the originators of the customs-union did not contemplate the establishment of a protective system; on the contrary, it was distinctly laid down that the duties on foreign goods should not as a rule exceed ten per cent. To the opera in the evening, and was introduced to M. Nothomb, the Belgian Minister, a clever, ready man. M. Nothomb thinks the Corn Laws of Belgium will soon be abolished, and says, after the late calamities, arising from the scarcity of food, all Europe ought to unite in abolishing for ever every restriction on the corn trade; he thinks the next Ministry in Belgium, although its head will probably be an ardent Free Trader, will be obliged to advance still further in the path of restriction; that the majority of the chambers is monopolist. '*An absolute Government may represent an idea, but elective legislatures represent interests.*' The enlightened Ministers of Prussia are overruled by the clamours of the chambers of Würtemberg, Bavaria, and Baden, the majorities of which are protectionist. He remarked that France stood in the way of European progress, for, so long as she maintained her prohibitive system, the other nations of the Continent would be slow to adopt the principles of Free Trade."

"*Berlin, July 30th.*—Went with Mr. Howard to call on M. Kuhne, one of the originators of the Zollverein. When Saxony joined it, she objected to the high duties which were payable upon foreign goods. Now the manufacturers of that country are wanting still higher protection; he is not of opinion that Hamburgh will join the Zollverein; is not sanguine about effecting any reduction of the protective duties; only hopes to prevent their augmentation. M. Kuhne has the character of being an able and honest man. To the museum; the collection of statues and busts but a poor affair after seeing the galleries of Italy, and the pictures very inferior to those at Dresden or Vienna. Called on M. Dieterici, Director of the Bureau of Statistics, an earnest Free Trader, says all the leading statesmen of Prussia are opposed to the protective system, which is forced upon the Zollverein by the states of the south, particularly Bavaria, Baden, and Würtemberg, and by the manufacturers of the Rhenish provinces. Professor Tellkampf called; he says the real object which the Prussian Government has in view, talking of differential duties on navigation to England, is to coerce Holland into a more liberal system, and probably to induce her to join the Zollverein. . . . In the conversation with M. Kuhne he touched upon the state of Ireland, and remarked that society has to be reconstructed in that country; that we have the work of Cromwell and William to do over again in a better manner."

"*Berlin, July 31st.*—Several persons called in the morning. Went by railway to Potsdam to dine with the King at three o'clock at Sans Souci. About twenty-five to thirty persons sat down, nearly all in court costume, and most of them in military dresses. The King good-humoured and affable, very little ceremony, the dinner over at half-past four, when the company walked in the garden. On coming away the King shook hands. In the evening attended a public dinner given to me by about 180 Free Traders of Berlin, the mayor of the city in the chair; he commenced the speaking at the second course, and it was kept up throughout the dinner, which was prolonged for nearly three hours. Two-thirds of the meeting appeared to understand my English speech, which was afterwards translated into German by Dr. Asher. The speeches were rather long, and the auditory phlegmatic when compared with an Italian dinner-party. Mr. Warren, the United States Consul at Trieste, made the best speech, in German. Alluding to my tour in France, Spain, Italy, and Germany, he said that no English politician of former times, no Chatham, Burke, or Fox could have obtained those proofs of public sympathy in foreign countries which had been offered to me; in their days the politics of one state were considered hostile to others; not only each nation was opposed to its neighbour, but city was against city, town against country, class was arranged against class, and corporations were in hostility to individual rights: he adduced the fact of my favourable reception in foreign countries as a proof of the existence of a broader and more generous view of the interests of mankind."

1847. ÆT. 43.

"*Berlin, August 1st.*—Baron Von Humboldt called, expressed in strong and courteous terms his disapproval of Lord Palmerston's foreign policy in Portugal and Greece, especially of his demanding from the latter a peremptory payment of a paltry sum of money. I expressed my doubts if the Greeks were at present fitted for constitutional self-government, upon which he remarked that it was much easier for a nation to preserve its independence than its freedom. . . . Wrote a note to Dr. Asher declining his invitation to address a party of Free Traders, and expressing my determination not to interfere in the domestic concerns of Prussia."

"*Berlin, August 5th.*—The Prussian law of 1818, and the tariff which followed it, form the foundation of the German Zollverein. The former system of Frederick the Great, and which had lasted for upwards of half a century, was one of the most prohibitive in respect to the importation of foreign goods ever enforced. The prohibition of the entrance of foreign manufactures, even of those of Saxony, was the rule. Yet the manufactures of Eastern Prussia continued to decline; whilst in Saxony, Westphalia, and the Rhenish provinces industry grew up, and flourished without protection. At the end of fifty years of the trial of Frederick's system, such was the result. . . . The law of 26th of May 1818 sets forth freedom of commerce as the fundamental principle of the new system of customs; it enacted that as a rule the duty on foreign manufactures shall not exceed ten per cent *ad valorem* according to the average prices."

"*Stettin, August 7th.*—Took leave of Kate this morning at the Hamburgh railway, and then started for Stettin at seven, in company with Mr. Swaine. The railway passes through a poor sandy country thinly peopled, and with light crops of grain. The exportation of corn was prohibited this year from Prussia, also of potatoes in May; one of the Ministers stated in the Diet publicly that the latter measure could be of no use, inasmuch as at that time, no potatoes could be sent out of the country with advantage, but advocating the law on the plea that it was necessary to tranquillize the people; the use of potatoes was also interdicted in distilleries for three months, by which the food for cattle (the residue of the potatoes) was curtailed, and caused great embarrassment to the proprietors. . . . In the evening dined with about eighty or ninety persons, who assembled at a day's notice to meet me; the company sat at dinner for nearly four hours; speeches between each course; the orators launched freely into politics."

"*Stettin, August 8th.*—The Baltic ports are in no way benefited by the manufacturing interests of the south and the Rhenish provinces, and they are directly sacrificed by the protective system. The few furnaces for making iron in Silesia, and those on the Rhine, have imposed a tax upon the whole community, by laying a duty of 20s. a ton upon pig-iron. Silesia is a wheat-growing country for export. The protective duties of the Zollverein are particularly injurious to the Baltic provinces of Prussia, which export wheat, timber, and other raw produce. The manufacturing districts of Rhenish Prussia are entirely cut off and detached from this part of the kingdom; they receive their imports, and send out their exports by the Rhine, not through a Prussian port; thus the protective system stands in the way of the increase of the foreign trade in the Prussian ports, and stops the growth of the mercantile marine, without even offering the compensation of an artificial trade in manufactures. In fact, owing to her peculiar geographical position, the maritime prosperity of Prussia is more completely sacrificed than in any other State by the protective system."

"*Dantzic*, *August* 10*th*, 1847.— . . . Dined with about fifty of the merchants. Nearly all appeared to understand English, several speakers, all in English, excepting one. There are about five or six British merchants only here—mostly Scotch. Dantzic is thoroughly English in its sympathies."

"*Tauroggen*, *Russia*, *August* 13*th*.—Left Königsberg at seven o'clock this morning in an extra post courier in company with one of Mr. Adelson's clerks, whom he kindly sent with me across the Russian frontier.

"My companion, who is a Pole and a Russian subject, and, as he terms himself, an Israelite, gives me a poor picture of the character of the Polish nobility. Making a comparison between them and the Russians, he remarked that the latter are barbarians, but the former are civilized scamps; there is some respect for truth in the Russian, but none in the Pole. Crossed the Niemen at Tilsit; were detained upon the bridge of boats for half an hour whilst several long rafts of timber passed; the men who were upon them, and who live for months upon the voyage down from Volhynia to Memel on these floats, had a wild, savage appearance, reminding me of the Irish. Soon after, reached the Russian frontier. I rallied my companion on his rather thoughtful aspect on approaching his native country. 'It is not exactly fear that I feel,' he replied, 'but I do find a disagreeable sensation here,' striking his breast; 'perhaps it is something in the air which always affects me at this spot.' Arrived at Tauroggen at eight o'clock, the distance from Königsberg being about a hundred English miles. The chief of the Custom House was very civil, and declined to search my luggage."

"*Riga*, *Aug.* 16*th.*—The distance from Tauroggen to Riga is about 220 versts, or about 160 miles, which are accomplished in eighteen hours exactly, at an expense of 42s. The country generally a plain as far as the eye can reach, with here and there only some slight undulations; mostly a light soil and sandy, but everywhere capable of cultivation. Large tracts covered with forests of fir, interspersed with oak, birch, etc., with patches here and there of cultivated land. The country very thinly peopled; the villages consist of a few wooden houses thatched; scarcely saw a stone or brick house. The villages through which we passed on the high road on the beginning of our journey were generally peopled with Jews, a dirty, idle-looking people, the men wearing long robes with a girdle, and the women often with turbans, the men also wearing the long beard. These wretched beings creep about their wretched villages, or glance suspiciously out of their doors, as if they had a suspicion of some danger at every step. They never work with their hands in the fields or on the roads excepting to avert actual starvation."

"*St. Petersburgh*, *Aug.* 20*th.*—Called on Count Nesselrode, the Foreign Minister, a polite little man of sixty-five, with a profusion of smiles. Like Metternich, he strikes me more as an adept at finesse and diplomacy, than as a man of genius or of powerful talent. He was very, very civil, spoke of my Free Trade labours, which he said would be beneficial to Russia, offered me letters to facilitate my journey to Moscow, and invited me to dine. Called on Lord Bloomfield, our Minister, an agreeable man."

1847. — ÆT. 43.

"*St. Petersburgh, Aug.* 21*st.*—Went at six o'clock, in company with Colonel Townsend, Captain Little, and another, to see the grand parade, about twenty-five versts from St. Petersburgh. The Emperor, the finest man in the field; the Empress, a very emaciated, care-worn person, resembling in her melancholy expression the Queen of the French. It is remarkable that two of the most unhappy and suffering countenances, and the most attenuated frames I have seen on the Continent, are those of these two royal personages, the wives of the greatest sovereigns of the Continent, who have accidentally ascended thrones to which they were not claimants by the right of succession; yet these victims of anxiety are envied as the favourites of fortune."

"*Moscow, Aug.* 25*th.*—Started from St. Petersburgh on Sunday morning, at seven, and reached this place at six this morning. During the first day, passed through several villages built entirely of wood, generally of logs laid horizontally upon each other; some of these are not without efforts at refinement, being ornamented with rude carved work, and the fronts sometimes gaudily painted. Many of the houses appeared quite new, and others were in the course of erection; it being Sunday, the inhabitants were in their best clothes; work seemed everywhere suspended. There appears a great traffic between the old and new metropolis, both in merchandise and passengers; mail-coaches, diligences, and private carriages very numerous. The face of the country flat and monotonous; a strip of cultivated land, growing rye, oats, etc., runs generally along the roadside, and beyond, the eye rests upon the eternal pine forests. The inns at the post stations excellent; in two of them the walls of the rooms were covered with English engravings of Morland's village scenes; tea everywhere good, and served promptly, in the English fashion. On alighting I saw about thirty men, lying in two rows upon the pavement, in the open air, wrapped in their coats or sheepskins, some of their heads resting on a pillow of hay, and others upon the rough stones. I was told, on inquiry, that they were postillions waiting to be called up, as their services might be required—a hard life."

"*Moscow*, *August 25th.*—After a couple of hours' sleep in a clean and comfortable bed at Howard's English lodging-house, I sallied out alone for a stroll of an hour or two. This city surprises me; I was not prepared for so interesting and unique a spectacle. One might fancy himself in Bagdad or Grenada a thousand years ago. The people are more Asiatic in their appearance and dress than at St. Petersburgh, and also more superstitious, I should say, judging from the ceremonials of bowing and crossing which I see going on at every church door, and opposite to every little picture of the Virgin. Everywhere struck with astonishment at the novel and beautiful features of this picturesque city of the Czars."

"*Nishni Novogorod*, *August 27th.*—Left Moscow at half-past seven on Wednesday evening in the same carriage by which I had come from St. Petersburgh. It was dusk when I passed beyond the suburbs of the widely extended city of upwards of 300,000 souls. The next morning's light revealed the same scenery as that through which I had passed previously; the country so flat and the view so constantly bounded with straight lines of fir forests, that I was frequently under the illusion that the ocean was visible in the distant horizon. . . . Reached Nishni Novogorod at six o'clock this evening, and passed through a long avenue of wooden booths full of merchandise, and amidst crowds of people to the hotel, where I found

1847.
Æt. 43.

comfortable quarters. Baron Alexander Meyendorff called, chief of a kind of Board of Trade at Moscow, an active-minded and intelligent German, possessing much statistical knowledge about Russian trade and manufactures. . . . He thinks the geographical and climatical features of Russia will always prevent its being anything but a great village, as he termed it, it being such a vast, unbroken plain; there are no varieties of climate or occupations, and as the weather is intensely cold for half the year, every person wants double the quantity of land which would suffice to maintain him in more genial climates; as there is no coal, the pine forests are as necessary as his rye field. Wherever the winter endures for upwards of half the year, the population must as a general rule be thin."

"*Nishni Novogorod*, *August 28th.*—The Bokhara caravan arrived yesterday, bringing about a thousand hundredweight of cotton from Asia, of a short staple like our Surats, with skins, common prints, dressing-gowns of silk, and other articles. I visited three merchants, some of them handsome swarthy men; their goods were brought upon camels as far as Orenberg; the journey from Bokhara to Nishni occupies about three months. This caravan had been stopped by a tribe of the Kirghese. One of these men, a knowing, talkative fellow, had been in London and picked up a few words of English. In the evening dined and took tea with Baron A. de Meyendorff, and met Baronoff, the great printer and manufacturer, an energetic and sensible man. . . . He has taken some land on lease in the territory of the Khan of Khiva for growing madder for his print works; he says that the madder he gets from Asia is cheaper than that which he formerly got from France and Holland, in the proportion of two and a half to one."

"*Moscow*, *Aug.* 31*st*.—Found my companion a man of great good-nature, and full of information upon the commerce and manufactures of Russia.

1847.
ÆT. 43.

". . . The Emperor and the higher functionaries of the Government are anxious for good administration, and they are all enlightened and able men, but the subordinates or bureaucracy are generally a corrupt or ignorant body. There are three or four grave difficulties for the future—the emancipation of the serfs—the religious tone, which is one of mere unmeaning formalities, and which, if not adapted to the progress of ideas, will become a cause of infidelity on the one hand, and blind bigotry on the other—the *tiers-état*, comprising the freed serfs, the manufacturers, and the bureaucracy: all these are elements tending to dangerous collisions of opinion for the future, unless gradually provided against by the Government.

". . . At Bogorodsk we paid a visit to the halting-station of prisoners who are on their way from Moscow to Siberia; upwards of twenty were lying upon wooden benches, their heads resting upon bundles of clothes. Baron Meyendorff questioned them as to the cause of their banishment; three confessed that theirs was murder, and another coining: several were for smaller offences; the latter were not ironed like the greater criminals. One man said he was exiled because he had no passport, which meant that he was a vagabond. One man was recognised by the Baron as having been a servant in a nobleman's family which he was acquainted with, and he stated, in answer to the inquiry, that he was sent to Siberia because he was ill-tempered to his owner and master; this man, like all the rest, seemed to be in a state of mental resignation quite oriental. 'If God has allowed me to be banished, I suppose I deserve it,' was his remark. In another room was a prisoner, a nobleman, as he was called, who confessed to the Baron that poverty had led him to commit an act of forgery; he was not ironed, nor was his head shaved like the rest. In a third room were two women; one of them said her offence was being without a passport; the other was a woman who stated herself to be a widow, and whose little daughter, a child about seven years of age, was sleeping upon a bundle of old clothes at her side. She said she was banished at the request of her mistress, she being her serf, because she was ill-tempered. I gave these poor women some silver.

"... On leaving the mill, a few steps brought me into the midst of the agricultural operations in the neighbourhood, and what a contrast did the implements of husbandry present to the master-pieces of machinery which I had just been inspecting! The ploughs were constructed upon the model of those in use a thousand years ago; the scythes and reaping-hooks might have been the implements of the ancient Scythians; the spades in the hands of the peasants were either entirely of wood or merely tipped with iron; the fields were yielding scarcely a third of the crop of grain which an English farmer would derive from similar land; there was no science traceable in the manuring or cropping of the land, no intelligence in the improving of the breed of the cattle, and I could not help asking myself by what perversity of judgment an agricultural people could be led to borrow from England its newest discoveries in machinery for spinning cotton, and to reject the lessons which it offered for the improvement of that industry upon which the wealth and strength of the Russian empire so pre-eminently depend.

". . . Baron Meyendorff tells me that an association of merchants proposes to export a cargo of Russian manufactures to the Pacific as an experiment, and amongst the articles which they think of sending are boots and shoes, sail-cloth, cordage, low-priced woollens, linen towels, coarse linens, such as ravenduck; articles made of wood, such as boxes, etc.; and nails, etc. Here are many manufactured products which are natural to Russia, and who can say how much the development of such indigenous industries may be interfered with by the protection of cotton goods, etc.? Baron Meyendorff considers Russia more favoured than any other country in the production of wools. In Russia there are public granaries in every commune, in which, according to law, there ought always to be a store of grain kept for the safety of the people against scarcity; this, like all their laws in this great empire, is little more than waste paper. Instead of ordering the erection of public granaries, the Government would have done more wisely to have devoted its attention to the construction of roads by which grain could have circulated more freely in the country, and thus have prevented the occasional famine in one part of the empire whilst there is a glut in another. If roads were made in Russia, the merchants and dealers in grain would supply the wants of any particular district by equalising the supply of all."

"*St. Petersburgh, Sept. 7th.*—Some time ago a Yankee adventurer asked permission to establish a hunting-station on the North American territory belonging to Russia, but it was refused. A year or two after this occurred, Baron Meyendorff happened to be calling upon his friend, the Home Minister, who, putting a letter into his hand, remarked, 'Here is something to amuse you; it has occasioned me half an hour's incessant laughter.' It was a despatch from the governor of Irkutsk, describing in pompous language an 'invasion,' which had taken place in the North American territory of the Russian empire by an armed force, consisting of from eighty to one hundred men, commanded by an American, and having three pieces of artillery. It was the Yankee fur-trader, who had taken French leave and squatted himself upon the most favourable situation in the Czar's dominions for carrying on his hunting operations. The question arose how he was to be ejected. There was no Russian armed force or authority of any kind within many hundreds, perhaps thousand miles of the invading army. The expense of fitting out an armament for the purpose was then calculated, but the distance and the difficulty of approaching the Yankee headquarters were such formidable obstacles, that it was thought better to leave the enemy in possession of his conquered territory, and there he remains now, carrying on his operations against the bears and the beavers of the Czar without molestation. This gives an idea of the weakness of a Government whose dominions extend to upwards of a twelvemonth's journey from its capital."

"*St. Petersburgh, Sept.* 11*th.*— . . . Dined at the English club, and met a party of Russians; they rise from table as soon as they have swallowed their dinner, and proceed to the card-table, billiards, or skittles. There is no intellectual society, no topic of general interest is discussed—an un-idea'd party. My table companions, the English merchants, were of opinion that extensive smuggling is carried on, particularly in sugar; they spoke freely of the corruption of the employés, and the general propensity to live beyond their means. One of them mentioned an anecdote of the corruption of the Government employés. He had a contract with one of the departments for a quantity of *lignum vitæ* at eight roubles a pood; upon its being delivered it was pronounced inferior, and rejected after being stamped at the end of each log; he called at the bureau to complain and remonstrate, but without success; and on leaving was followed by a person who asked his address and said he would call upon him. He was as good as his word, and the following conversation occurred: 'You have charged your wood too low; it is not possible to furnish a good quality at eight roubles; you must send in another delivery at twelve roubles.' 'But I have no other quality,' was the reply. 'Leave that to me,' said the person. 'You must address a petition to the department, saying that you are prepared to send in another delivery; I will draw up the petition, you must sign it; I will manage the rest, and you will pay me 1000 roubles, which will be half the difference of the extra price you will receive.' He consulted with his friends, who advised him to comply, and he accordingly signed the petition. The person then had the rejected *lignum vitæ* conveyed to a warehouse, where the ends were sawed off the logs to remove the stamp, and the identical wood was delivered, and passed for full weight and good quality."

"*St. Petersburgh, Sept.* 12*th.*—Went in the morning to the Kasan Cathedral, where I found a full congregation, two-thirds at least being men. Went with Mr. Edwards by railway to see the horse-races at Tsarskoe Selo; a large proportion of the persons who went by the train were English. The Emperor and his family and a good muster of fashionables were present on the course, but the amusements wanted life and animation, which nothing but a mass of people capable of feeling and expressing an interest

1847. Æt. 43.

in the sports of the day can present. Afterwards went to the Vauxhall of Petersburgh to dine. An Englishman accosted me in a broad Devonshire accent, and said he was a freeman of Tavistock, and would give me a plumper if I came there as a candidate. Met another man from Stockport who is in a cotton-mill here; he says it works from six A.M. to eight P.M., stopping for an hour; that the engine runs thirteen hours a day; says double the number of hands, as compared with the English mills, are employed to produce a given result; the English labourer is the cheapest in Europe."

"*St. Petersburgh, Sept.* 13*th.*—Mr. Edwards, attaché to the English Ministry, mentioned an anecdote illustrative of the inordinate self-complacency of my countrymen. They complained to him that at the Commercial Association, a kind of club consisting of natives and English, the air of 'Rule Britannia' had been hissed by the Russians; they were discomposed at the idea of foreigners being averse to the naval domination of England!"

"*St. Petersburgh, Sept.* 15*th.*—Paid a visit to the Minister of Finance; he invited me to speak to him frankly as to my opinions on the manufactures of Russia, and I profited by the opportunity of making a Free Trade speech to him of half an hour's length. He was reported to me as an incompetent, ignorant man, but he has at least the merit of being willing to learn; he listened like a man of good common sense, and his observations were very much to the point. M. de Boutowsky called, who has written a work upon political economy and in favour of Free Trade, in the Russian language. In the course of the conversation he remarked that Peter the Great commenced the system of regulating and interfering with trade and manufactures in Russia. Another instance added to those of Cromwell, Frederick the Great, Louis XIV., Napoleon, and Mehemet Ali, showing that warriors and despots are generally bad economists, and that they instinctively carry their ideas of force and violence into the civil policy of their Governments. Free Trade is a principle which recognises the paramount advantage of individual action. Military conquerors, on the contrary, trust only to the organized efforts of bodies of men directed by their own personal will.

"Dined with Count Nesselrode, and sat beside Count Kisseleff, one of the ablest of the Ministers, having the direction of the public domains. After dinner, other persons of rank joined us in the drawing-room, and we had a lively discussion upon Free Trade. Count Kisseleff talked freely and without much knowledge of the question, whilst Nesselrode sat quietly with the rest of the company listening to the controversy. My opponents were moderate in their pretensions, and made a stand only for the protection of industries in their infancy. All parties threw overboard cotton-spinning as an exotic which ought not to be encouraged in Russia. A Free Trade debate in Nesselrode's drawing-room must at least have been a novelty."

"*St. Petersburgh, Sept. 23rd.*—Called by invitation upon Prince Oldenburgh, cousin of the Emperor, a man of amiable and intelligent mind, a patron of schools and charities. He spoke with affection and admiration of England, of its people, their religious and moral character, their public spirit, and domestic virtues. Speaking of Russia, he said that its two greatest evils were corruption and drunkenness. Was entertained at a public dinner by about two hundred merchants and others at the establishment of mineral waters in one of the islands ; a fine hall, prettily decorated, and with a band of music in an adjoining room. After I had spoken, an Englishman named Hodgson, manager of Loader's spinning-mill, who was formerly a Radical orator in England, addressed the meeting, pretty much in the style of some of my old Chartist opponents in England, which afforded me an opportunity of replying to him, greatly to the satisfaction of the meeting. I was struck with the freedom of speech and absence of restraint which pervaded the meeting, and which contrasted with the timidity I had sometimes seen in Italy and Austria. The meeting went off well, and everybody seemed well satisfied. Such a numerous party had never assembled at a public dinner in St. Petersburgh."

"*Lubeck, Sept. 29th.*—Left Cronstadt at two o'clock on Sunday morning, 26th, by the *Nicolai* steamer, and after a favourable passage without adventures of any kind reached Travenmunde at eight o'clock this morning. My head was too much disturbed by the sea voyage to be fit for numerous introductions, so after breakfasting and resting a few hours, I proceeded in company with our Consul, who had been so good as to come down to meet me, to Lubeck, a pleasant drive of nine miles."

"*Lubeck, Sept. 30th.*—Captain Stanley Carr called; he has a large estate about four miles distant, which he has occupied for twenty years, and cultivates with great success upon the English system. He has a thousand acres under the plough, a small steam-engine for thrashing, and all the best implements. He says he employs three times as many people as were at work upon the land before he bought it; he raises four times as much produce; has drained and subsoiled the farm; sells his butter and cattle at twenty-five per cent higher prices than his neighbours. Speaking of his visit to Bohemia, where he spent three months of last year, he said the agriculture was in a very wretched state. The peasants were without capital, and the *corvée* system prevailed, by which the landlord's land was cultivated so badly by the peasantry that he would not accept an estate at a gift, to be obliged to work it upon that system. He told me an anecdote of a man engaged in the manufactory of iron in that country, who complained of the competition of the English, who 'paid the freight to Hamburgh, and then the expense of carrying it up the Elbe to Bohemia, and then,' he added, 'they undersell me twenty-five per cent at my own door, and be d—d to them!' In consequence of which he went off to Vienna to call for higher protection to the iron manufacture, by way of supporting 'native industry'! . . . In the evening was entertained by a party of about seventy merchants and others of Lubeck at a public dinner. After dinner went to 'the cellar' under the Town Hall, a famous resort for the people, where they drink beer, sing, and listen to music. On descending into these vaults, I was enveloped in clouds of smoke. At one end was a band of music; in another recess was a festive meeting of the German *savans*, some of whom, with their wives, were seated at tables; others were crowded round a speaker, who was addressing them, whilst almost invisible in a cloud of smoke. It resembled a midnight scene in a 'coal-hole' or 'finis' in London—yet in this odd place was to be found a hundred of the first professors and literary men of Germany. I was introduced to Grimm, the famous critic and linguist."

"*Hamburgh, Oct. 5th*, 1847.—In the evening dined with about seven hundred persons at a Free Trade banquet; Mr. Ruperti in the chair. Sat down at half-past five, and the dinner and speeches lasted till ten. The speakers were free in the range of their topics, advocated the freedom of the press, quizzed the regulations of the city of Hamburgh, and turned into ridicule the Congress of Vienna and the Germanic diet."

"*Manchester*, *Oct.* 12*th.*—Left the Elbe on Saturday morning, 9th, and reached London on Monday at eleven o'clock. Was told on board that the steamers carry cattle from Hamburgh to London for thirty shillings a head, and sheep for three shillings. Slept at the Victoria Hotel, Euston Square, on Monday, and left for Manchester by the six o'clock train on Tuesday, reaching home at three o'clock."

CHAPTER XIX

ELECTION FOR THE WEST RIDING—PURCHASE OF DUNFORD—CORRESPONDENCE

1847.
Æt. 43.

During Cobden's absence in the autumn of 1847, a general election had taken place. While he was at St. Petersburg he learned that he had been returned not only for his former borough of Stockport, but for the great constituency of the West Riding of Yorkshire. He wrote to thank Mr. Bright for his powerful and friendly services at the election. "But I cannot conceal from you," he went on to say, "that my return for the West Riding has very much embarrassed and annoyed me. Personally and publicly speaking, I should have preferred Stockport. It is the greatest compliment ever offered to a public man; but had I been consulted, I should have respectfully declined."[1] After the compliment had actually been conferred, it was too late to refuse it, and Cobden represented the West Riding in two Parliaments, until the political crash came in 1857. The triumph of Cobden's election for the great Yorkshire constituency was matched by the election of Mr. Bright for Manchester, in spite of the active and unscrupulous efforts of some old-fashioned Liberals. They pretended to find him violent and reckless, he wanted social position, and so forth. For the time

[1] Sept. 18, 1847.

1847. Æt. 43.

they were swept away by the overwhelming wave of Mr. Bright's popularity, but they nursed their wrath and had their revenge ten years afterwards.

Another important step had been taken while Cobden was abroad. His business was brought to an end, and the affairs relating to it wound up by one or two of his friends. A considerable portion of the sum which had been subscribed for the national testimonial to him, had been absorbed in settling outstanding claims. With a part of what remained Cobden, immediately after his return from his travels, purchased the small property at Dunford on which he was born. He gave up his house in Manchester, and when in London lived for some years to come at Westbourne Terrace. Afterwards he lived in lodgings during the session, or more frequently accepted quarters at the house of one of his more intimate friends, Mr. Hargreaves, Mr. Schwabe, or Mr. Paulton. His home was henceforth at Dunford. His brother Frederick, who had shared the failure of their fortunes at Manchester, took up his abode with him and remained until his death in 1858. Five or six years after the acquisition of his little estate, Cobden pulled down the ancestral farm-house, and built a modest residence upon the site. In this for the rest of his life he passed all the time that he could spare from public labours. Once in these days, Cobden was addressing a meeting at Aylesbury. He talked of the relations of landlord and tenant, and referred by way of illustration to his own small property. Great is the baseness of men. Somebody in the crowd called out to ask him how he had got his property. "I am indebted for it," said Cobden with honest readiness, "to the bounty of my countrymen. It was the scene of my birth and my infancy; it was the property of my ancestors; and it is by the munificence of my countrymen that this small estate, which had been alienated from my father by necessity, has again come into my hands, and enabled me to light up afresh the hearth of my father where I spent my own childhood. I say that no warrior duke who owns a vast domain by the vote of the Imperial Parliament, holds his property by a more honourable title than I possess mine."[1] If the baseness of men is great, so too is their generosity of response to a magnanimous appeal, and the boisterous cheering of the crowd showed that they felt Cobden's answer to be good and sufficient.

The following is Cobden's own account, at the time, of the country in which he had once more struck a little root. He is writing to Mr. Ashworth:—

"*Midhurst*, *Oct.* 7, 1850.—I have been for some weeks in one of the most secluded corners of England. Although my letter is dated from the quiet little close borough of Midhurst, the house in which I am living is about one and a half miles distant, in the neighbouring rural parish of Heyshott. The roof which now shelters me is that under which I was born, and the room where I now sleep is the one in which I first drew breath. It is an old farm-house, which had for many years been turned into labourers' cottages. With the aid of the whitewasher and carpenter, we have made a comfortable weather-proof retreat for summer; and we are surrounded with pleasant woods, and within a couple of miles of the summit of the South Down hills, where we have the finest air and some of the prettiest views in England. At some future day I shall be delighted to initiate you into rural life. A Sussex hill-side village will be an interesting field for an exploring excursion for you. We have

[1] *Speeches*, i. 440, Jan. 9, 1850. In the same place will be found his account of the way in which he dealt with his land.

a population under three hundred in our parish. The acreage is about 2000, of which one proprietor, Colonel Wyndham, owns 1200 acres. He is a non-resident, as indeed are all the other proprietors. The clergyman is also non-resident. He lives at the village of Stedham, about three miles distant, where he has another living and a parsonage-house. He comes over to our parish to perform service once on Sundays, alternately in the morning and afternoon. The church is in a ruinous state, the tower having fallen down many years ago. The parson draws about £300 a year in tithes, besides the produce of a few acres of glebe land. He is a decent man, with a large family, spoken well of by everybody, and himself admits the evils of clerical absenteeism. We have no school and no schoolmaster, unless I give that title to a couple of cottages where illiterate old women collect a score or two of infants whilst their parents are in the fields. Thus 'our village' is without resident proprietors or clergyman or schoolmaster. Add to these disadvantages, that the farmers are generally deficient of capital, and do not employ so many labourers as they might. The rates have been up to this time about six shillings in the pound. We are not under the new Poor Law, but in a Gilbert's Union, and almost all our expense is for outdoor relief.

"Here is a picture which will lead you to expect when you visit us a very ignorant and very poor population. There is no post-office in the village. Every morning an old man, aged about seventy, goes into Midhurst for the letters. He charges a penny for every despatch he carries, including such miscellaneous articles as horse collars, legs of mutton, empty sacks, and wheelbarrows. His letter-bag for the whole village contains on an average from two to three letters daily, including newspapers. The only newspapers which enter the parish are two copies of *Bell's Weekly Messenger*, a sound old Tory Protectionist much patronized by drowsy farmers. The wages paid by the farmers are very low, not exceeding eight shillings a week. I am employing an old man nearly seventy, and his son about twenty-two, and his nephew about nineteen, at digging and removing some fences. I pay the two former nine shillings a week and the last eight shillings, and I am giving a shilling a week more than anybody else is paying. What surprises me is to observe how well the poor fellows work, and how long they last. The South Down air, in the absence of South Down mutton, has something to do with the healthiness of these people, I daresay. The labourers have generally a garden, and an allotment of a quarter of an acre; for the latter they pay three and ninepence a year rent. We are in the midst of woods, and on the borders of common land, so that fuel is cheap. All the poor have a right to cut turf on the common for their firing, which costs two shillings and threepence per thousand. The labourers who live in my cottages have pigs in their sties, but I believe it is not so universally. I have satisfied myself that, however badly off the labourers may be at present, their condition was worse in the time of high-priced corn. In 1847, when bread was double its present price, the wages of the farm labourers were not raised more than two to three shillings a week. At that time a man with a family spent all he earned for bread, and still had not enough to sustain his household. I have it both from the labourers themselves and the millers from whom they buy their flour, that they ran so deeply in debt for food during the high prices of 1847, that they have scarcely been able in some cases up to the present to pay off their score. The *class feeling* amongst the agricultural labourers is in favour of a cheap loaf. They dare not say much about it openly, but their instincts are serving them in the absence of economical knowledge, and they are unanimously against Chowler and the Protectionists.

I can hardly pretend that in this world's-end spot we can say that any impulse has been given to the demand for agricultural labourers by the Free Trade policy. Ours is about the last place which will feel its good effects. But there is one good sign which augurs well for the future. Skilled labourers, such as masons, joiners, blacksmiths, painters, and so on, are in very great request, and it is difficult to get work of that kind done in moderate time. I am inclined to think that in more favourable situations an impulse has likewise been imparted to unskilled labour. It is certain that during the late harvest-time there was a great difficulty in obtaining hands on the south side of the Downs towards the sea-coast, where labour is in more demand than here under the north side of the hills. I long to live to see an agricultural labourer strike for wages!"

Before he had been many weeks in England, Cobden was drawn into the eager discussion of other parts of his policy, which were fully as important as Free Trade itself. The substitution of Lord Palmerston for Lord Aberdeen at the Foreign Office was instantly followed by the active intervention of the British Government in the affairs of other countries. There was an immediate demand for increased expenditure on armaments. Augmented expenditure meant augmented taxation. Each of the three items of the programme was the direct contradictory of the system which Cobden believed to be not only expedient but even indispensable. His political history from this time down to the year when they both died, is one long antagonism to the ideas which were concentrated in Lord Palmerston. Yet Cobden was too reasonable to believe that there could be a material reduction in armaments, until a great change had taken place in the public opinion of the country with respect to its foreign policy. He always said that no Minister could reduce armaments or expenditure, until the English people abandoned the notion that they were to regulate the affairs of the world. "In all my travels," he wrote to Mr. Bright, "three reflections constantly occur to me: how much unnecessary solicitude and alarm England devotes to the affairs of foreign countries; with how little knowledge we enter upon the task of regulating the concerns of other people; and how much better we might employ our energies in improving matters at home."[1] He knew that the influential opinion of the country was still against him, and that it would be long before it turned. "Until that time," he said, in words which may be usefully remembered by politicians who are fain to reap before they have sown, "I am content to be on this question as I have been on others in a minority, and in a minority to remain, until I get a majority."

While he was away that famous intrigue known as the Spanish Marriages took place. The King of the French, guided by the austere and devout Guizot, so contrived the marriages of the Queen of Spain and her sister, that in the calculated default of issue from the Queen, the crown of Spain would go to the issue of her sister and the Duke of Montpensier, Louis Philippe's son. Cobden, as we shall see, did not believe that the King was looking so far as this. It was in any case a disgraceful and odious transaction, but events very speedily proved how little reason

[1] *To Mr. Bright*, Sept. 18, 1847.

1847. — ÆT. 43

there was why it should throw the English Foreign Office into a paroxysm. Cobden was moved to write to Mr. Bright upon it:—

"My object in writing again is to speak upon the Marriage question. I have seen with humiliation that the daily newspaper press of England has been lashing the public mind into an excitement (or at least trying to do so) upon the alliance of the Duke of Montpensier with the Infanta. I saw this boy and girl married, and as I looked at them, I could not help exclaiming to myself, 'What a couple to excite the animosity of the people of England and France!' Have we not outgrown the days when sixty millions of people could be set at loggerheads by a family intrigue? Yes, we have probably grown wiser than to repeat the War of Succession, but I see almost as great an evil as actual hostilities in the tone of the press and the intrigues of the diplomatists of England and France. They keep the two nations in a state of distrust and alienation, they familiarize us with the notion that war is still a possible event, and worse still, they furnish the pretext for continually augmenting our standing armaments, and thus oppressing and degrading the people with taxation, interrupting the progress of fiscal reforms, and keeping us in a hostile attitude ready for war.

"I began my political life by writing against this system of foreign interference, and every year's experience confirms me in my early impression that it lies at the bottom of much of our misgovernment at home. My visit to Spain has strengthened, if possible, a hundredfold my conviction that all attempts of England to control or influence the destinies, political and social, of that country are worse than useless. They are mischievous alike to Spaniards and Englishmen. They are a peculiar people not understood by us. They have one characteristic, however, which their whole history might have revealed to us, *i.e.* their inveterate repugnance to all foreign influences and alliances, and their unconquerable resistance to foreign control. No country in Europe besides is so isolated in its prejudices of race and caste. It has ever been so, whether in the times of the Romans, of the Saracens, of Louis XIV., or of Napoleon. No people are more willing to call in the aid of foreign arms or diplomacy to fight their battles, but they despise and suspect the motives of all who come to help them, and they turn against them the moment their temporary purpose is gained. As for any other nation permanently swaying the destinies of Spain, or finding in it an ally to be depended on against other Powers, it would be as easy to gain such an object with the Bedouins of the desert, with whom, by the way, the Spaniards have no slight affinity of character. No one who knows the people, nobody who has read their history, can doubt this; and yet our diplomatists and newspaper-writers are pretending alarm at the marriage of the youngest son of Louis Philippe with the Infanta, on the ground of the possible future union of the two countries under one head, or at least under one influence. Nobody knows the absurdity of any such contingency better than Louis Philippe. He feels, no doubt, that it is difficult enough to secure *one* throne permanently for his dynasty, and unless his sagacity be greatly overrated, he would shrink from the possibility of one of his descendants ever attempting to wear at the same time the crowns of Spain and France. I believe the French king to have had but one object,—to secure a rich wife for his younger son. He is perhaps a little avaricious in his old age, like most other men. But I care nothing for his motives or policy. Looking to the facts, I ask why should the French and English people allow themselves to be embroiled by such family manœuvres? He may have been treacherous to our Queen, but why should kings and queens be allowed to enter into any marriage compacts in the name of their people? You will perhaps tell me when you write that the bulk of the middle class, the reflecting portion of the people of England, do not sympathize with the London daily press on the subject of the Marriage question; and I know that there is a considerable portion of the more intelligent French people who do not approve of all that is written in the Paris papers. But, unhappily, the bulk of mankind do not think for themselves. The newspapers write in the name of the two countries, and to a great extent they form public opinion. Governments and diplomatists act upon the views expressed in the influential journals.

". . . There is one way in which this system of interfering in the politics of Spain is especially mischievous. It prevents Spanish parties from being formed upon a purely domestic basis, and thus puts off the day when the politicians shall devote themselves to their own reforms. At present, all the intrigues of Madrid revolve round the diplomatic manœuvres of France and England. There is another evil arising out of it. It gives the bulk of the Spaniards a false notion of their own position. They are a proud people, they think all Europe is busy with their affairs, they hear of France and England being on the point of going to war about the marriage of one of their princesses, they imagine that Spain is the most important country in the world, and thus they forget their own ignorance, poverty, and political degradation, and of course do not occupy themselves in domestic reforms. If left to themselves, they would soon find out their inferiority, for they are not without a certain kind of common sense.

"I have always had an instinctive monomania against this system of foreign interference, protocolling, diplomatizing, etc., and I should be glad if you and our other Free Trade friends, who have beaten the daily broad-sheets into common sense upon another question, would oppose yourselves to the Palmerston system, and try to prevent the Foreign Office from undoing the good which the Board of Trade has done to the people. But you must not disguise from yourself that the evil has its roots in the pugnacious, energetic, self-sufficient, foreigner-despising and pitying character of that noble insular creature, John Bull. Read Washington Irving's description of him fumbling for his cudgel always the moment he hears of any row taking place anywhere on the face of the earth, and bristling up with anger at the very idea of any other people daring to have a quarrel without first asking his consent or inviting him to take a part in it.

". . . And the worst fact is, that however often we increase our establishments, we never reduce them. Thus in 1834 and 1835, Mr. Urquhart and the daily press did their utmost to frighten the people of England into the notion that Russia was going to swallow Turkey, and then would land some fine morning at Yarmouth to make a breakfast of England. Our armaments were accordingly increased. In 1840 the Whigs called for 5000 additional soldiers to put down Chartism. In 1846 still further armaments were voted to meet the Oregon dispute. These pretences have all vanished, but the ships and soldiers remain, and taxes are paid to support them. Keep your eye upon our good friend

1847. Æt. 43.

Ward, or depend on it he will be wanting more ships on the plea of our unsettled relations with Spain and France. Probably that is the reason why you read of Admiral Parker being sent to this coast, and his fleet placed at the orders of Mr. Bulwer, of steamers passing between Gibraltar and the Fleet, etc. All this may be intended to prepare John Bull for a haul upon his purse for more ships next session; at least it may be an argument to pass the navy estimates with acclamation. As for any other rational object being gained, it is not in my power here on the spot to comprehend it. The English merchants laugh at the pretence set up by our Admiral to the Spanish authorities on the coast to excuse his appearance in such force 'that he comes to protect British interests.' The British residents have no fear of any injuries. I have seen Englishmen who have lived here during about a score of revolutions, and witnessed a hundred changes of Ministries, and who laugh at the idea of any danger. To sum up in a word, our meddling with this country is purely mischievous to all parties, and can do no good to Spaniards or Englishmen. And I hope you will do your best to stem the spirit with which it is encouraged in the daily press. I was glad to see the good sense in your paper, the *Manchester Examiner*, upon the subject, and equally sorry to observe that our good friend, James Wilson, had been carried away by the current. I wrote to him from Madrid. I fear it is too much to expect any man to live in London in the atmosphere of the clubs and political cliques, and preserve the independent national tone in his paper, which we had hoped for in the *Economist*."[1]

Lord Palmerston's intervention in the affairs of

[1] *To Mr. Bright*, Oct. 24, 1846.

Portugal was more active, and even more wantonly preposterous. All that Cobden said on this subject was literally true. The British fleet was kept in the Tagus for many months in order to protect the Queen of Portugal against her own subjects. What had England to gain? Portugal was one of the smallest, poorest, most decayed and abject of European countries. As for her commerce, said Cobden, if that is what you seek, you are sure of that, for the simple reason that you take four-fifths of all her port wine, and if you did not, no one else would drink it. Our statesmen, he went on, actually undertook to say who should govern Portugal, and they stipulated that the Cortes should be governed on constitutional principles. The Cortes was elected, and what happened? The people returned almost every man favourable to the very statesman who, as Lord Palmerston insisted, was to have no influence in Portugal.[1]

What Cobden heard from Bastiat made him all the more anxious to bring England round to a more sedate policy. The chief obstacles to the propagandism of Free Trade in France, said Bastiat, come from your side of the Channel. He was confronted by the fact that at the very time when Peel consummated the policy of Free Trade, he asked for an extra credit for the army, as if to proclaim, said Bastiat, that he had no faith in his own work, and as if to thrust back our best arguments down our own throats. Thirteen years

[1] *Speeches*, i. 466, Jan. 27, 1848. See for the other side of the matter, Mr. Ashley's *Life of Lord Palmerston*, ii. 14-30. Lord Palmerston's reference (p. 16) to the anxiety and uneasiness of the Queen and the Prince Consort at Windsor shows, among many other proofs, how well-founded were Cobden's notions of the particular forces that were at work behind the policy of Intervention.

1848.
Æт. 44.

afterwards, when Cobden was himself engaged in converting France to Free Trade, while Lord Palmerston was at the same moment increasing the fleet, raising new fortifications, and making incendiary speeches, Bastiat's words of 1847 may have come back to his mind: "Besides the extra credit, the policy of your Government is still marked by a spirit of *taquinerie*, which irritates the French people, and makes it lose whatever impartiality it may have had left."[1]

"I must speak to you in all frankness," Bastiat proceeded, in his urgent way. "In adopting Free Trade England has not adopted the policy that flows logically from Free Trade. Will she do so? I cannot doubt it, but when? The position taken by you and your friends in Parliament will have an immense influence on the course of our undertaking. If you energetically disarm your diplomacy, if you succeed in reducing your naval forces, we shall be strong. If not, what kind of figure shall we cut before our public? When we predict that Free Trade will draw English policy into the way of justice, peace, economy, colonial emancipation, France is not bound to take our word for it. There exists an inveterate mistrust of England, I will even say a sentiment of hostility, as old as the two names of *French* and *English*. Well, there are excuses for this sentiment. What is wrong is that it envelops all your parties and all your fellow-citizens in the same reprobation. But ought not nations to judge one another by external acts? They often say that we ought not to confound nations with their Governments. There is some truth and some falsehood in this maxim; and I venture to say that it is false as regards nations that possess constitutional means of

[1] *Bastiat*, i. 152.

making *opinion* prevail. England ought to bring her political system into harmony with her new economic system."[1]

Cobden in reply seems to have treated this apprehension of English naval force, and the hostile use to which it might be put, as a device of the French Protectionists to draw attention from the true issue. No, answered Bastiat manfully; "I know my country; it sees that England is capable of crushing all the navies in the world; it knows that it is led by an oligarchy which has no scruples. That is what disturbs its sight, and hinders it from understanding Free Trade. I say more, that even if it did understand Free Trade, it would not care for it on account of its purely economic advantages. What you have to show it above all else is that freedom of exchange will cause the disappearance of those military perils which France apprehends. England ought seriously to disarm; spontaneously to drop her underground opposition to the unlucky Algerian conquest; and spontaneously to put an end to the dangers that grow out of the Right of Search."[2] When the Revolution of 1848 came, Bastiat was more pressing than ever. France could not be the first to disarm; and if she did disarm, she would be drawn into war. England, by her favoured position, was alone able to set the example. If she could only understand all this and act upon it, "she would save the future of Europe." Bastiat, however, was not long in awakening to the fact that not Protection but Socialism was now the foe that menaced France. He turned round with admirable versatility, and brought to bear on the new monster the same keen and patient scrutiny, the same skilful

[1] *Bastiat to Cobden*, Oct. 15, 1847.

[2] *Œuv.* i. 167-170.

dexterity in reasoning and illustration, which had done such good service against the more venerable heresy. The pamphlets which he wrote between 1848 and 1850 contain by much the most penetrating and effective examination that the great Socialist writers in France have ever received.

This memorable year was an unfavourable moment for Cobden's projects, but the happy circumstance that Great Britain alone passed through the political cyclone without anything more formidable than Mr. Smith O'Brien's insurrection in Ireland, and the harmless explosion of Chartism on Kennington Common, was too remarkable for men not to seek to explain it. The explanation that commended itself to most observers was that Free Trade had both mitigated the pressure of those economic evils which had provoked violent risings in other countries, and that, besides this, it had removed from the minds of the English workmen the sense that the Government was oppressive, unjust, or indifferent to their well-being. "My belief is," said Sir Robert Peel, in a powerful speech which he made the following year, vindicating his commercial policy, "that you have gained the confidence and goodwill of a powerful class in this country by parting with that which was thought to be directly for the benefit of the landed interest. I think it was that confidence in the generosity and justice of Parliament, which in no small degree enabled you to pass triumphantly through the storm that convulsed other countries during the year 1848."[1]

The Protectionist party had not yet accepted defeat, nor did they finally accept it until they came

[1] July 6, 1849. This comprehensive defence of Free Trade is well worth reading at the present day, when the same fallacies which Peel then exposed have come to life again.

into power in 1852. All through the year that intervened they turned nearly every debate into a Protectionist debate. After Lord George Bentinck's death in the autumn of 1848, they were led in the House of Commons by Mr. Disraeli, whose persistent and audacious patience was inspired by the seeming confidence that a Protectionist reaction was inevitable. The reaction never came. The Navigation Laws, and protection on West Indian Sugar, followed the Corn Law. Free trade in corn was only the prelude to free trade in sugar and free trade in ships. But the interests died hard.[1] Even the landlords made tenacious efforts to get back, in the shape of specious readjustments of rates and taxes, something of what they believed that they were going to lose on their rents. Cobden remained in the forefront of this long controversy, though he was no longer one of the leaders of a forlorn hope.

The Irish famine and the Irish insurrection forced the minds of politicians of every colour to the tormenting problem to which Cobden had paid such profound attention on his first entry into public life. National Education, another of the sincerest interests of his earlier days, once more engaged him, and he found himself, as he had already done by his vote on the Maynooth grant, in antagonism to a large section of Nonconformist politicians for whom in every other matter he had the warmest admiration. The following extracts from his correspondence show how he viewed these and other less important topics, as they came before him.

"*London*, *Feb.* 22, 1848. (*To Mrs. Cobden.*)—There seems to be a terrible storm brewing against the Whig Budget. Unfortunately the outcry is rather

[1] The Sugar Duties Bill became law in 1848, but the Navigation Act was not passed until the summer of 1849.

against the mode of raising the money than the mode of expending it, and I do not sympathize with those who advocate armaments and then grumble at the cost. For my part I would make the influential classes pay the money, and then they will be more careful in the expenditure. I get a good many letters of support from all parts of the country, and some poetry, as you will see."

"*Feb.* 24.—Nothing is being talked about to-day but the *émeutes* in Paris. From the last accounts it seems that Louis Philippe has been obliged to give way and change his Ministry owing to the troops and the national guards having shown signs of fraternizing with the people. By and by Governments will discover that it is no use to keep large standing armies, as they cannot depend on them at a pinch. You are right in saying that the Income Tax has brought people to their senses. It is disgusting to see the same men who clamoured for armaments, now refusing to pay for them."

"*London, Feb.* 29. (*To George Combe.*)—These are stirring events in France. I am most anxious about our neutrality in the squabbles which will ensue on the Continent. I dread the revival of the Treaty of Vienna by our red-tapists, should France reach to the Rhine or come in collision with Austria or Russia. Besides, there is a great horror at the present changes in the minds of our Court and aristocracy. There will be a natural repugnance on the part of our Government, composed as it is entirely of the aristocracy, to go on cordially with a Republic, and it will be easy to find points of disagreement, when the will is ready for a quarrel. I know that the tone of the clubs and coteries of London is decidedly hostile, and there is an expectation in the same quarters that we shall have a war.

1848.

Æt. 44.

It is striking to observe how little the views and feelings of the dominant class are in unison with those of the people at large. I agree with you that the republican form of Government will put France to a too severe test. Yet it is difficult to see what other form will suit it. The people are too clever and active to submit to a despotism. All the props of a Monarchy, such as an aristocracy and State Church, are gone. After all a Republic is more in harmony than any other form with the manners of the people, for there is a strong passion for social equality in France. However, the duty of every man in England is to raise the cry for neutrality."[1]

"*March* 8. (*To Mrs. Cobden.*)—We are a little anxious up here lest there should be riots in the north. We hear bad accounts from Glasgow, but I suppose they are exaggerated. I hope we shall have no imitations of the French fashions in this respect."

"*March* 10. (*To Mrs. Cobden.*)—We were very late in the House again last night. Disraeli was very amusing for two hours, talking about everything but the question.[2] He made poor McGregor a most ridiculous figure. The Whigs are getting hold of our friends.

"*London, March* 14. (*To Mrs. Cobden.*)—On

[1] After the Revolution became Socialistic, Peel said the same:—"I believe it to be essential to the peace of the world and to the stability of government, that the experiment now making in France shall have a fair trial without being embarrassed or obstructed by extrinsic intervention. Let us wait for the results of this experiment. Let us calmly contemplate whether it is possible that executive Governments can be great manufacturers, whether it can be possible for them to force capital to employ industry," etc.—Sir Robert Peel, April 18.

[2] Among other points he laughed at Cobden and Mr. Bright as representatives of Peace and Plenty in the face of a starving people and a world in arms. He also declared himself a "Free Trader, not a freebooter of the Manchester school."

1848.
Æt. 44.

getting back yesterday I found such a mass of letters that, what with them and the Committee I had to attend, and callers, and my speech last evening, I thought you would excuse my writing to you. I am more harassed than ever. The Committees are very important (I mean upon army, navy, and ordnance expenditure,[1] and upon the Bank of England), and occupy my time more than the House. I gave them some home truths last evening, but we were in a poor minority.[2] The Ministers frightened our friends about a resignation. Nobody did more to canvass for help for them than ——. He is far more to be blamed than Gibson, who is thoroughly with us in heart, and only votes with the Government because he is one of them. The electors ought to make allowance for him. He is a very good fellow, and it is a great pity that he ever joined the Whigs. There are many men on our side upon whom I relied, who went over to the Government, very much to my disgust. There are uncommonly few to be trusted in this atmosphere. Don't be alarmed. I am not going to set up any new League. It is a mistake of the newspapers."

"*March* 18. (*To Mrs. Cobden.*)—We have had incessant rain here for several days, and I have been thinking with some apprehension of its effects upon the grain in the ground, and upon the operations of the farmers in getting in their seed. To-day, however,

[1] As a means of conciliating public opinion, which was at this time in one of its cold and thrifty fits, Sir Charles Wood, the Chancellor of the Exchequer, moved for a Select and Secret Committee to inquire into the expenditure on army, navy, and ordnance. Cobden was an assiduous attendant, with his usual anxiety to hear all the facts of the case.

[2] On Mr. Hume's motion for altering the period of renewed Income Tax from three years to one. The "poor minority" was 138 against 363.

it is a fine clear day, and I am going with Porter[1] at four o'clock down to Wimbledon to stay till Monday. This week's work has nearly knocked me up. They talk of a Ten Hours Bill in Paris. I wish we had a Twelve Hours Bill, for I am at it from nine in the morning till midnight. We had a debate last evening upon the question of applying the Income Tax to Ireland, but I was shut out of the division, the door being closed in my face just as I was entering, otherwise I should have voted for the measure.[2] The news from Paris is more and more exciting. There seems to be a sort of reaction of the moderate party against the violent men. The Bank of France has suspended specie payments, which will lead to much mischief and confusion. I fear we have not seen the worst."

"*London, March* 21. (*To Mrs. Cobden.*)—I have sent you a *Times* containing a report of my speech last night. Be good enough to return it to me after you have read it, as I shall want to correct it for Hansard, and have not another copy. We were in a miserable minority.[3] The blue-jackets and red-coats were down upon me fiercely, as if I had been attacking them sword in hand. It reminded me of the old times when we were just beginning the Anti-Corn-Law battle in the House. We get astounding news from the Continent; a fresh revolution or a dethronement by every post."

"*March* 27. (*To Mrs. Cobden.*)—You need not be alarmed about my turning up right in the end, but at the present time I am not very fashionable in aristocratic circles. However, I have caught Admiral Dundas

[1] The author of Porter's *Progress of the Nation*.

[2] Moved by Sir B. Hall, opposed by the Government, and rejected by 218 to 138.

[3] Debate on Navy estimates; amendment for reduction of the force defeated by 347 to 38.

1848.
Æt. 44.

in a trap. You may remember that he contradicted me about my fact of a large ship lying at anchor so long at Malta. Well, a person has called upon me, and given me the minute particulars and dates of the times which all the admirals have been lying in Malta harbour during the last twelve years, extracted by him from the ship logs which are lying at Somerset House. Having got the particulars, I have given notice to Admiral Dundas that I shall move in the House for the official return of them to be extracted from the ships' logs. He says I shan't have the returns, but he can't deny that I *have* got them. I shall make a stir in the House, and turn the tables upon him. Whilst I was talking to the Admiral about it to-day in the Committee-room, Molesworth entered into the altercation with so much warmth that I thought there would have been an affair between them. The best of it all is, that I find the present Admiral in the Mediterranean (Sir William Parker), who sent such an insolent message to me about my speech at Manchester, which was read by Dundas in the House, has been lying himself for seven months and two days in Malta harbour with nearly 1000 hands, without ever stirring out of port."

"*London, April* 10. (*To Mrs. Cobden.*)—We have been all in excitement here with the Chartist meeting at Kennington Common, which after all has gone off very quietly, and does not appear to have been so numerously attended as was expected. In my opinion the Government and the newspapers have made far too much fuss about it. From all that I can learn there were not so many as 40,000 persons present, and they dispersed quietly. I do not think I shall be able to go north with you before next Monday week."

"*April* 15. (*To Mrs. Cobden.*)—You will have seen by the paper what a mess Feargus O'Connor has made of the Chartist petition. The poor dupes who have followed him are quite disheartened and disgusted, and ought to be so. They are now much more disposed to go along with the middle class."

"*May* 13. (*To Mrs. Cobden.*)—You will hear that all the papers are down upon me again. In making a few remarks about the Alien Bill, I said that the 'best way to repel Republicanism was to curtail some of the barbarous splendour of the Monarchy which went to the aggrandizement of the aristocracy.' My few words drew up Lord John as usual, and he was followed by Bright with a capital speech."

"*Manchester, April* 24. (*To G. Combe.*)—You know how cordially I agree with you upon the subject of Education. But I confess I see no chance of incorporating it in any new movement for an extension of the suffrage. The main strength of any such movement must be in the Liberal ranks of the middle class, and they are almost exclusively filled by Dissenters. To attempt to raise the question of National Education amongst them at the present moment, would be to throw a bombshell into their ranks to disperse them. In my opinion every extension of popular rights will bring us nearer to a plan of National Education, because it will give the poor a stronger motive to educate their children, and at the same time a greater power to carry the motive into practice. The real obstacle to a system of National Education has been in my opinion the State Church, and although the Dissenters are for the moment in a false position, they will, I hope, with time come right."

"*May* 15. (*To G. Combe.*)—There is no active feeling at present in favour of National Education.

The Dissenters, at least Baines's section, who have been the only movement party since the League was dissolved, have rather turned popular opinion against it.[1] I need not say how completely I agree with you that education alone can ensure good self-government. Don't suppose that I am changed, or that I intend to shirk the question. Above all, don't suspect that sitting for Yorkshire would shut my mouth. I made up my mind, on returning from the Continent, that the best chance I could give to our dissenting friends was to give them time to cool after the excitement of the late opposition to the Government measure, and therefore I have avoided throwing the topic in their faces. But I do not intend to preserve my silence much longer. If I take a part in a new Reform movement, I shall do my best to connect the Education question with it, not as a part of the new Reform Act, but by proclaiming my own convictions that it is by a national system of education alone that people can acquire or retain knowledge enough for self-government. In our Reform movement, sectarianism will not be predominant."

"*London, July* 23. (*To G. Combe.*)—What a wretched session has this been! It ought to be expunged from the minutes of Parliament. Three Coercion Bills for Ireland and the rest talk, talk, talk. There never was a Parliament in which so much power for good or evil was in the hands of the Minister as in this. Lord John could have commanded a majority for any judicious Liberal measures by the aid of Peel,

[1] See above, vol. i. pp. 322-323. "I confess," said Cobden, in 1851, "that for fifteen years my hopes of success in establishing a system of National Education, have always been associated with the idea of coupling the education of the country with the religious communities which exist." But he found religious discordances too violent, and he took refuge, as we shall presently see, in the secular system.

who was bound to support him, and the Liberals, who were eager to be led forward. But he has allowed himself to be baffled, bullied, and obstructed by Lord George Bentinck and the Protectionists, who have been so far encouraged by their success in Sugar and the Navigation Laws that I expect they will be quite ready to begin their reaction on Corn next session, and we may have to fight the Free Trade battle over again. The feebleness and incapacity of the Whigs are hardly sufficient to account for their failures as administrators. The fact is, they are the allies of the aristocracy rather than of the people, and they fight their opponents with gloves, not meaning to hurt them. They are buffers placed between the people and the privileged classes, to deaden the shock when they are brought into collision."

"*May* 15. (*To Mr. W. R. Greg.*)—No apology is, I assure you, necessary for your frank and friendly letter. There is not much difference in our views as to what is most wanted for the country. The only great point upon which we do not agree is as to the means. What we want before all things is a bold retrenchment of expenditure. I may take a too one-sided view of the matter, but I consider nine-tenths of all our future dangers to be *financial*, and when I came home from the Continent, it was with a determination to go on with Fiscal reform and economy as a sequence to Free Trade. I urged this line upon our friend James Wilson (who, by the way, has committed political suicide), and others, and I did not hesitate to say up to within the last three months that I would take no active part in agitating for organic questions. But when the series of political revolutions broke out on the Continent, all men's minds in England were suddenly turned

1848.

Æt. 44.

to similar topics; and the political atmosphere became so charged with the electric current, that it was no longer possible to avoid discussing organic questions. But I had no share in forcing forward the subject. I abstained from assisting in forming a party in the House for organic reforms, though I was much urged by a great number of members to head such a party."

"*July* 21. (*To H. Ashworth.*)—No man can defend or palliate such conduct as that of Smith O'Brien and his confederates. It would be a mercy to shut them up in a lunatic asylum. They are not seeking a repeal of the legislative union, but the establishment of a Republic, or probably the restoration of the Kings of Munster and Connaught! But the sad side of the picture is in the fact that we are doing nothing to satisfy the moderate party in Ireland, nothing which strengthens the hands even of John O'Connell and the priest party, who are opposed to the 'red republicans' of the Dublin clubs. There seems to be a strong impression here that this time there is to be a rebellion in Ireland. But I confess I have ceased to fear or hope anything from that country. Its utter helplessness to do anything for itself is our great difficulty. You can't find three Irishmen who will co-operate together for any rational object."

"*London, August* 28. (*To George Combe.*)—I would have answered your first letter from Ireland, but did not know how soon you were going back again to Edinburgh. With respect to the plan for holding sectional meetings of the House of Commons in Dublin, Edinburgh, and London for local purposes, it is too fanciful for my practical taste. I do not think that such a scheme will ever seriously engage the public attention. If local business be ever got rid of by the House of Commons, it should be transferred as much as possible to county courts. There is very little advantage, for instance, in carrying a Road Bill from Ross-shire to Edinburgh instead of to London, or from Galway to Dublin instead of to London. The private or local business occupies much less of the time of the House of Commons than many people suppose. An hour on an average at the opening of the sittings daily suffices; the rest is all done in select Committees, and a great deal of it by Mr. Green and Mr. Bernal, Chairmen of Committees, who, I suspect, would find it no advantage in Irish matters to be in Dublin. Bad as the system is of bringing to the House of Commons all the local business of the kingdom, I am sure it would not mend the matter to split us into three sections, as your friends propose, for two or three months, and then to reunite in London for imperial purposes. We should be in perpetual session.

1848.

ÆT. 44.

"Whilst we are constitution-tinkering, let me give you my plan. Each county to have its assembly elected by the people, to do the work which the unpaid magistrates and lords-lieutenant now do, and also much of the local business which now comes before Parliament. The head of this body, or rather the head of each county, to be the executive chief, partaking of the character of prefect, or governor of a state in the United States. By and by when you require to change the constitution of the House of Lords, these county legislators may each elect two senators to an upper chamber or senate.

"But the question is about Ireland. Why do your friends amuse one another with such bubble-blowing? The real difficulty in Ireland is the character and condition socially and morally of the people, from the peer to the Connaught peasant. It is not by forms of legislation or the locality of Parliaments, but by a change and improvement of the population, that Ireland is to have a start in the career of civilization and self-government. Now instead of phantom-hunting, why don't your friends (if they are worthy of being your friends) tell the truth to their countrymen, and teach them their duties as well as their rights? And let them begin by showing that they understand their own duties and act up to them. The most discouraging thing to an English Member of Parliament who wishes to do well to Ireland, is the quality of the men sent to represent it in the House of Commons. Hardly a man of business amongst them; and not three who are prepared cordially to co-operate together for any one common object. How would it mend matters if such men were sitting in Dublin instead of London? But the subject is boundless and hopeless, and I must not attempt to discuss it in a note."

"*Hayling Island*, *Hants*, *Oct.* 4. (*To George Combe.*)—Many thanks for your valuable letters upon Ireland and Germany. I really feel much indebted for your taking all these pains for my instruction.

"Leaving Germany—upon which I do not presume to offer an opinion beside yours—I do claim for myself the justice of having foreseen the danger in Ireland, or rather seen it—for its condition has little altered since I first began to reason. When about fourteen years ago I first found leisure from my private affairs to think about public business, I summed up my views of English politics in a pamphlet which contained many crude details (which I should not now print), but upon whose three broad propositions I have never changed my opinion. They were—First, that the great curse of our policy has been our love of intervention in foreign politics; secondly, that our greatest home difficulty is Ireland; and thirdly, that the United States is the great *economical* rival which will rule the destiny of England.

"It may appear strange that a man who had thought much about Ireland, and who had frequently been in that country (I had a cousin, a rector of the Church of England in Tipperary), should have been seven years in Parliament and not have spoken upon Irish questions. I will tell you the reason. I found the populace of Ireland represented in the House by a body of men, with O'Connell at their head, with whom I could feel no more sympathy or identity than with people whose language I did not understand. In fact, *morally* I felt a complete antagonism and repulsion towards them. O'Connell always treated me with friendly attention, but I never shook hands with him or faced his smile without a feeling of insecurity; and as for trusting him on any public question where his vanity or passions might interpose, I should have as soon thought of an alliance with an Ashantee chief.[1] I found that that which I regarded as the great Irish grievance—the Protestant Church Establishment—was never mentioned by the Irish Liberal members. Their Repeal cry was evidently an empty sound.

"The great obstacle to all progress both in Ireland and in England is the landlord spirit, which is dominant in political and social life. It is this spirit which prevents our dealing with the question of the tenure of land. The feudal system, as now maintained in Ireland, is totally unsuited to the state of the country. In fact, the feudal policy is

[1] Cobden is here unjust to O'Connell. He opposed the Corn Bill of 1815, and was true to the League in the fight from 1838 to 1846.

not carried out, for that would imply a responsibility on the part of the proprietor to keep and employ the people, whereas he is possibly living in Paris, whilst his agent is driving the peasantry from his estate and perhaps burning their cabins. What is wanting is a tribunal or legislature before which the case of Ireland may be pleaded, where the landlord spirit (excuse the repetition of the word) is not supreme. This is not to be found in our House of Commons. You would be astonished if behind the scenes in the Committees, and in the confidence of those men who frame Bills for Parliament, to observe how vigilant the spirit of landlordism is in guarding its privileges, and how much the legislator who would hope to carry a measure through both Houses, is obliged to consult its sovereign will and pleasure. Hence the difficulty of dealing with game laws, copy-holds, and such small matters, which grow into things of mighty import in the House of Commons, whilst the law of primogeniture is a sort of eleventh commandment in the eyes of our legislators.

"I think I know what is wanted in Ireland: a redistribution of land, as the only means of multiplying men of property. If I had absolute power I would instantly issue an edict applying the law of succession as it exists in France to the land of Ireland. There should be no more absentee proprietors drawing large rentals from Ireland, if I could prevent it. I would so divide the property as to render it necessary to live upon the spot to look after it. But you can do nothing effectual in that direction with our Houses, and therefore I am an advocate for letting in the householders as voters, so as to take away the domination of the squires. But I will do all in my power in the meantime to give a chance to Ireland, and I cordially agree with your views upon the policy that ought to be pursued towards it."

"*London*, *Oct.* 28. (*To George Combe.*)—I have to thank you for the *Scotsman* containing the whole of your observations upon the state of Ireland, in every syllable of which I agree with you. But excuse me if I say I miss in your articles, as in all other dissertations upon Ireland, a specific *plan*—I mean such a remedial scheme as might be embodied in an Act of Parliament. And it must be so from the very nature of the case, for the ills of Ireland are so complex, and its diseases so decidedly chronic, that no single remedy could possibly cure them. Indeed, if we were to apply a thousand remedies, the existing generation could hardly hope to live to see any great change in the condition of the Irish people; and this is probably one reason why politicians and Ministers of the day do not commit their fortunes to the cause of justice to Ireland.

"I have but one plan, but I don't know how to enforce it. Cut up the land into small properties. Let there be no estates so large as to favour absenteeism, even from the parish. How is this to be done, with feudalism still in the ascendant in Parliament and in the Cabinet? Pim is quite right when he draws the distinction between the case of Ireland, where the conquerors have not amalgamated with the conquered, and that of other countries, where the victors and vanquished have been invariably blended. For we are all conquered nations—some of us have been so repeatedly—but all, with the exception of Ireland, have absorbed their conquerors.

"Almost every crime and outrage in Ireland is connected with the occupation or ownership of land; and yet the Irish are not naturally an agricultural people, for they alone, of all the European emigrants who arrive in the United States, linger about the towns, and hesitate to avail themselves of the tempting advantages of the rural districts in the interior. But in Ireland, at least the south and west, there is no property but the soil, and no labour but upon the land, and you cannot reach the population in their material or moral condition but through the proprietorship of the land. Therefore, if I had the power, I would always make the proprietors of the soil resident, by breaking up the large properties. In other words, I would give Ireland to the Irish.

"I used to think that the Protestant Church was the crying evil in Ireland; and so it would be, if the Catholics of that country were Englishmen or Scots. But as an economical evil, it can hardly be said to affect the material condition of the people, seeing that the tithe-owners live in the parish, and are in many cases almost the only proprietors who do spend their income creditably at home; and as it is not felt apparently as a moral grievance, I do not think that the agitation against the Church Establishment would be likely to contribute to the contentment of the people. I confess that the apathy of the Irish Catholics upon the subject of the Protestant Church Establishment in that country excites my surprise, if not my contempt."

"*Dec.* 28. (*To Mr. Edward Baines.*)—I doubt the utility of your recurring to the Education question. My views have undergone no change for twenty years on the subject, excepting that they are infinitely strengthened, and I am convinced that I am as little likely to convert you as you me. Practically no good could come out of the controversy; for we must both admit that the *principle* of State Education is virtually settled, both here and in all civilized countries. It is not an infallible test I admit, but I don't think there are two men in the House of Commons who are opposed to the principle of National Education.

"I did not intend to touch upon a matter so delicate; but yet, upon second thoughts, it is best to be candid. My experience in public matters has long ago convinced me that to form a party, or act with a party, it is absolutely necessary to avoid seeking for points of collision, and on the contrary, to endeavour to be silent, as far as one can be so conscientiously, upon the differences one may see between his own opinions and those of his political allies. Applying this to your observations[1] upon my Budget, I would have laid on heavily in favour of such parts as I could agree with, and would have deferred pointing out any errors until I had given the common enemy time to do that (I say errors, but I do not admit them in this case). The same remark applies to the course the *Mercury* took upon the redistribution of electoral power, on which occasion it was to my mind demonstratively wrong in abandoning and turning against the strongest position of the Reformers. I do not press the Education question, because I presume your religious feelings were excited by the course the Government took whilst I was on the Continent. But I suppose all parties agree that education is the main cause of the split amongst the middle-class Liberals. Now, what I say to you I have always preached to others. For instance, I have been trying to persuade everybody about the *Daily News*, as to the impolicy, to say nothing of the injustice, of their gross attacks upon yourself and friends, and I have used precisely the same argument which I now use to you."

[1] In the *Leeds Mercury*.

"*Manchester, Nov.* 30. (*To Mrs. Cobden.*)—I find our League friends here very lukewarm about the West Riding election.[1] Many of them declare they will not vote. They seem quite out of humour with the religious intolerance of the Eardley party. I am very much inclined to think the Tories will win. Have you seen the news from Paris? Lamoriciere, the French Minister of War, has proposed to the Assembly to reduce the army nearly one half, and to save 170 millions of francs. This, if really carried out, will make our work safe in this country."

"*Manchester, Dec.* 8. (*To Mrs. Cobden.*)—I went down to Liverpool on Wednesday afternoon, and dined at Mellor's with a large party of the leading men, including Brown and Lawrence Heyworth, and slept there. Yesterday I met the Financial Reformers at their Council Board, Mr. Robertson Gladstone in the chair. They seem to be earnest men, but I did not exactly see the man capable of directing so great an undertaking. They approved of my plan of a Budget, and I agreed to address a letter with it to their chairman for publication. Last evening I met another party of the more earnest men of the Reform Association, at Mellor's."

The last extract refers to the subject which Cobden had now taken earnestly in hand. As he was always repeating, extravagant and ill-adjusted finance seemed to him the great mischief of our policy. Apart from its place in his general scheme, retrenchment was Cobden's device for meeting the cry of the Protectionists. It was an episode in the long battle against the enemies of Free Trade. The landed interest, they cried out, was ruined by rates and taxes. The

[1] Lord Morpeth, Cobden's colleague in the representation, now succeeded to the earldom of Carlisle. A contest took place, and Mr. Denison, the Conservative, defeated Sir Culling Eardley.

implication was that they could not exist without Protection. That was Mr. Disraeli's cue until he became Chancellor of the Exchequer. He made speech after speech and motion after motion to this effect. Cobden with equal persistency retorted that the proper relief for agriculture was not the imposition of a burden upon the consumers of bread, but a reduction of the common burdens of them all. He had begun his campaign in the session of 1848. The Government came forward with a proposal, which was afterwards ignominiously withdrawn, for an increase in the Income Tax. Cobden broke new ground by insisting on the superior expediency of direct over indirect taxation, provided that a just distinction were recognized between permanent and precarious incomes. His chief point was that the Government must either increase direct taxation, or else reduce expenditure; and he pressed the inference that expenditure must be decreased, and it must be decreased by reduction in armaments.

Cobden's contention cannot be said to have prospered; but the debates show how seriously his attack on expenditure was taken by those who opposed him. Mr. Disraeli laughed at him as the successor of the Abbé St. Pierre, Rousseau, and Robespierre in the dreams of perpetual peace, but he recognized the possibility of public opinion being brought round to Cobden's side. Even Peel thought it necessary formally to express his dissent from Cobden's views on national defence. Fresh from his victorious onslaught upon the Corn Law, he was dreaded by the House of Commons and the old political factions, as speaking the voice of an irresistible, if not an infallible, oracle. The Government had no root. The Opposition was nullified by the internecine quarrel between the Protectionists and the Peelites. The two parties in fact were so distracted, so uncertain in principle, and so unstable in composition, that they were profoundly afraid of the one party which knew its own mind and stood aloof from the conventional game. The Conservatives constantly felt, or pretended to feel, an irrational apprehension that the object of the Manchester school was, in the exaggerated language of one of them, to organize a force that should override the legislature and dictate to the House of Commons. The Financial Reform Association at Liverpool, with which Cobden had entered into relations, was expected to imitate the redoubtable achievements of the League. Similar associations sprang up both in the English and the Scotch capitals, and there was on many sides a stir and movement on the subject which for a time promised substantial results.

In a letter to Mr. Bright, Cobden sketched an outline of what was called a People's Budget, already referred to in his letter to Mr. Baines:—

"*London*, *Nov.* 16, 1848.—I have been thinking and talking about concocting a 'national budget,' to serve for an object for financial reformers to work up to, and to prevent their losing their time upon vague generalities. The plan must be one to unite all classes and interests, and to bring into one agitation the counties and the towns. I propose to reduce the army, navy, and ordnance from £18,500,000 to £10,000,000, and thus save £8,500,000. Upon the civil expenditure in all its branches, including the cost of collecting revenue, and the management of crown lands, I propose to save £1,500,000. I propose to lay a probate and legacy duty upon real property, to affect both entailed and unentailed estates, by which would be got £1,500,000. Here is £11,500,000, to be used in reducing and abolishing duties, which I propose to dispose of as follows:—

"*Customs:*

"Tea, reduce duty to 1s. per lb.

"Wood and timber, abolish duties.

"Butter and cheese, do.

"Upwards of 100 smaller articles of the tariff to be abolished. (I would only leave about fifteen articles in the tariff paying customs duties.)

"*Excise:*

"Malt, all duty abolished.

"Paper, do. do.

"Soap, do. do.

"Hops, do. do.

"Window tax, all off.

"Advertisement duty, do.

"All these changes could be effected with £11,500,000.

"There are other duties which I should prefer to remove, instead of one or two of them, but I have been guided materially by a desire to bring all interests to sympathize with the scheme. Thus the tea is to catch the merchants and all the old women in the country—the wood and timber, the ship-builders—the malt and hops, the farmers—paper and soap, the Scotch anti-excise people—the window-tax, the shopocracy of London, Bath, etc.—the advertisements, the press."

The scheme which Cobden here propounds to Mr. Bright, was elaborated in a speech made at Liverpool and afterwards set forth in a letter to the Financial Reform Association of that town, which led to much discussion, but which for reasons that we shall see in the next chapter did not become the starting-point of such an agitation as Cobden promised himself.

APPENDIX

NOTE A. (See p. 125)

COBDEN TO W. C. HUNT ON THE HOURS OF LABOUR

FALMOUTH, *October* 21, 1836.

" . . . . When upon the point of embarking on board the *Liverpool* steamer for Lisbon, a thought has occurred to me relative to the address which I left with you for the Stockport electors, and which induces me to trouble you with this letter. I have altogether omitted to advert to the Ten Hours Bill; and as it is a question that interests deeply the non-electors, whose influence, I am aware, is very considerable in your borough, I might be considered to have wilfully and designedly suppressed all allusion to the subject, if I did not explain my opinions unreservedly upon it. As respects the right and justice by which young persons ought to be protected from excessive labour, my mind has ever been decided, and I will not argue the matter for a moment with political economy; it is a question for the medical and not the economical profession; I will appeal to —— or Astley Cooper, and not to MacCulloch or Martineau. Nor does it require the aid of science to inform us that the tender germ of childhood is unfitted for that period of labour which even persons of mature age shrink from as excessive. In my opinion, and I hope to see the day when such a feeling is universal, *no child ought to be put to work in a cotton-mill at all so early as the age of thirteen years*; and after that the hours should be moderate, and the labour light, until such time as the human frame is rendered by nature capable of enduring the fatigues of adult labour. With such feelings as these strongly pervading my mind, I need not perhaps add that, had I been in the House of Commons during the last session of Parliament, I should have opposed with all my might Mr. Poulett Thomson's measure for postponing the operation of the clause for restricting the hours of infant labour. I am aware that many of the advocates of the cause of the factory children are in favour of a Ten Hours Bill for restricting the working of the engines, which in fact would be to limit the use of steam in all cotton establishments (for young persons are, I believe, at present employed in every branch of our staple manufacture, more or less) to ten hours a day. It has always, however, appeared to me that those who are in favour of this policy lose sight of the very important consequences which are involved in the principle. Have they considered that it would be the first example of a legislature of a free country interfering with the freedom of adult labour? Have they reflected that if we surrender into the hands of Government the power to make laws to fix the hours of labour at all, it has as good a right, upon the same principle, to make twenty hours the standard as ten? Have they taken into account that if the spinners and weavers are to be protected by Act of Parliament, then the thousand other mechanical and laborious trades must in justice have their claims attended to by the same tribunal? I believe it is now nearly three hundred years ago since laws were last enforced which regulated or interfered with the labour of the working classes. They were the relics of the feudal ages, and to escape from the operation of such a species of legislation was considered as a transition from a state of slavery to that of freedom. Now it appears to me, however unconscious the advocates of such a policy may be of such consequences, that if we admit the right of the Government to settle the hours of labour, we are in principle going back again to that point from which our ancestors escaped three centuries ago. Let not the people—I mean the masses—think lightly of those great principles upon which their strength wholly rests. The privileged and usurping few may advocate expediency in lieu of principles, but depend upon it we, reformers, must cling to first principles, and be prepared to carry them out, fearless of consequences. Am I told that the industrious classes in Lancashire are incapable of protecting themselves from oppression unless by the shield of the legislature? I am loath to believe it. Nay, as I am opposed to the plan of legislating upon such a subject, I am bound to suggest another remedy. *I would, then, advise the working classes to make themselves free of the labour market of the world, and this they can do by accumulating twenty pounds each*, which will give them the command of the only market in which labour is at a higher rate than in England—I mean that of the UNITED STATES. If every working man would save this sum, he might be as independent of his employer as the latter, with his great capital, is of his workmen. Were this universal, we should hear no more of the tyranny of the employers. If I am told that my scheme is chimerical because the working classes cannot depend upon each other, I answer that I have better hopes of them, and I look forward to many other improvements of a similar kind. All that is required, in my opinion, is that the operatives understand their own interests, and be not put upon a false scent; let them trust only to themselves, and not depend upon the legislature, which will never avail them. I yield to no man in the world (be he ever so stout an advocate of the Ten Hours Bill) in a hearty goodwill towards the great body of the working classes; but my sympathy is not of that morbid kind which would lead me to despond over their future prospects. Nor do I partake of that spurious humanity, which would indulge in an unreasoning kind of philanthropy at the expense of the independence of the great bulk of the community. Mine is that masculine species of charity which would lead me to inculcate in the minds of the labouring classes, the love of independence, the privilege of self-respect, the disdain of being patronized or petted, the desire to accumulate, and the ambition to rise. I know it has been found easier to please the people by holding out flattering and delusive prospects of cheap benefits to be derived from Parliament, rather than by urging them to a course of self-reliance; but while I will not be the sycophant of the great, I cannot become the parasite of the poor; and I have sufficient confidence in the growing intelligence of the working classes to be induced to believe that they will now be found to contain a great proportion of minds, sufficiently enlightened by experience to concur with me in opinion that it is to themselves alone individually, that they, as well as every other great section of the community, must trust for working out their own regeneration and happiness. Again I say to them, '*Look not to Parliament*, *look only to yourselves*.'

"It would be easy for me to state reasons of a different description why the legislature ought not to be suffered to interfere with the freedom of the labour of the people. How very obvious, however, must it be that any law restricting the hours of labour would be inoperative so soon as it became the interest of masters and workmen to violate it! Where, then, would be the utility or wisdom of an enactment which owed its power entirely to the free will of the parties whom it professed to coerce? Surely they might act as effectually without the necessity of infringing and merely bringing into disrepute the law of the land! But it is impossible to pursue the question to the extent of its merits within the limits of a sheet of letter-paper. If I am told by the advocates of a Ten Hours Bill that the plan of putting a restriction upon the moving power is the only way of saving the infants from destruction, to what a sad point does this argument conduct us! It is, in fact, an avowal that the parents cannot be trusted to obey a law which forbids them to sacrifice their offspring. Against this lamentable aspersion upon the natural affection of the working classes I enter my solemn protest. I believe, on the contrary, that public opinion amongst them is sufficiently patent to prevent an unnatural connivance of the kind on the part of any considerable number of parents; and I am convinced that the morality of the people is rapidly advancing to that elevated standard which will very soon preclude the apprehension that any individual of this body will be found sufficiently depraved to be suspected of the guilt of infanticide."

END OF VOL. I.

Printed by R. & R. CLARK, LIMITED, *Edinburgh*.